HOPES AND SHADOWS

HOPES AND SHADOWS

EASTERN EUROPE AFTER COMMUNISM

J. F. BROWN

Duke University Press

Durham 1994

Printed in the United States of America on acid-free paper ∞
Typeset in Times Roman and Franklin Gothic
by Keystone Typesetting, Inc.
Second printing, 1996

Library of Congress Cataloging-in-Publication Data

Brown, J. F. (James F.), 1928–
Hopes and shadows : Eastern Europe after
Communism / J.F. Brown.
p. cm. Includes bibliographical references and index.
ISBN 0-8223-1446-0 (cloth). —
ISBN 0-8223-1464-9 (paper)
1. Europe, Eastern — Politics and government — 1989-
I. Title.
DJK51.B75 1994 947—dc20 93-47347 CIP

Parts of, or ideas in, chapters 6, 7, and 8 appeared in *Nationalism, Democracy, and Security in the Balkans,* a Rand Research study published by Dartmouth (Aldershot, UK, 1992), and in my chapter, "Turkey: Back to the Balkans?" in Graham Fuller, Ian O. Lesser, with Paul B. Henze and J. F. Brown, *Turkey's New Geopolitics: From the Balkans to Western China* (Boulder, Colo.: Westview Press, 1993). Parts of the introduction are taken from my chapter, "The East European Agenda," in Ivo John Lederer (ed.), *Western Approaches to Eastern Europe* (New York: Council on Foreign Relations Press, 1992). Reprinted by permission of Dartmouth, Westview Press, and the Council on Foreign Relations Press. In parts of the book, particularly the conclusion, ideas and passages are taken from various pieces I wrote during 1992 and 1993 for the *RFE/RL Research Report.*

To Holly, Sam, Josh, and any more who might show up

CONTENTS

PREFACE

"If a book cannot speak for itself, it is idle to speak for it." Edith Durham was right. But perhaps a few words are needed to explain this book. It is the third that I have written for Duke University Press on Eastern Europe in six years. It also has been the most difficult, requiring a degree of foolhardiness that could become all too evident as its analyses and predictions strive to weather the scrutiny of Eastern Europe's uncertain future.

Still, accepting the hazards involved, the perspective of four years since the revolutions of 1989 *is* long enough and safe enough to give both some idea of the complexities of the situation (some of them previously unsuspected) and of the problems that each country will be facing for well into the future. All of the East European countries are in the process of stumbling away from communism; that much is certain. But stumbling *toward* what? This question cannot yet be firmly answered. Some political entities, such as parts of the former Yugoslavia, already have lapsed into an atavism that few would have thought possible during the closing years of the twentieth century. In others, something similar may occur. But the declared aim of virtually all of the East European countries involves a *revolution* that is breathtaking in its ambition: the simultaneous construction of liberal democracy and a market economy. Coupled with this ambition, however, is the reassertion of national independence that has involved the breakup of some previously existing states—violently in the case of Yugoslavia—and that could threaten the success of political and economic reconstruction. The third leg of the revolution, therefore, endangers the other two. "Revolution" is a more apt word than the clinical, overused "transition," since it at least conveys the magnitude of the changes, the risks involved, and the turbulence that has gripped the region since 1989. Eastern Europe's revolution is also one that will never be fully completed. Even where, in the perspective of history, it will appear to have been successful, it will remain unfinished and imperfect, with most problems at best contained rather than solved.

Obviously, some countries will be more successful than others, largely because their history, mainly precommunist, made them better-equipped to withstand the rigors of the ongoing revolution. The patchwork quilt of Eastern Europe is again displaying its bewildering diversity, and this growing diversity raises questions about the continued usefulness itself of both the concept and the term "Eastern Europe." For more than forty years it was a convenient Cold War term, accurately conveying the strategic, geopolitical, and ideological situation, and a handy way of distinguishing the subject countries from the Soviet Union. Now, however, its usefulness is eroding fast. Even more, it is becoming more misleading every day as different countries recover or refurbish their distinct identities. Still, until the communist legacy is finally overcome, and as long as the ongoing revolution retains features common to the region as a whole, "Eastern Europe" will remain a term whose utility is not totally offset by its inaccuracy. As for the subregions of Eastern Europe, I have designated Poland, Hungary, and Czechoslovakia (now the Czech Republic and Slovakia) as East Central Europe, although, as I emphasize in the course of the book, more countries soon will have to be considered East Central European. Bulgaria, Romania, and Albania I have designated South-Eastern European, or, more loosely, the Balkans. The once and former Yugoslavia is designated and largely treated separately, although, for purposes of organization, parts of it are sometimes treated as South-East European.

This book was written while I was a guest at the RFE/RL Research Institute in Munich. Its director, Ross Johnson, is an old friend to whom I have had occasion to be grateful more than once in my life. Melvin Croan, of the University of Wisconsin, another old friend, read the manuscript and gave it the benefit of his intellectual authority, rigor, and wit. In Munich I took advantage of the Institute's inestimable archives and found the collegiality of many of its members of real value. They included Louisa Vinton, Vera Tolz, Anna Swidlicka, Sharon Fisher, Edith Oltay, Rada Nikolaeva, Eli Campbell, Jiri Pehe, Duncan Perry, Bohdan Nahaylo, Patrick Moore, Ben Slay, Louis Zanga, Milan Andrejevich, Michael Shafir, Dan Ionescu, Kjell Engelbrekt, and Bill Robinson. I also must thank librarians and archivists too numerous to mention. Especially, though, I must thank Iwanka Rebet, the head librarian, whose ready, quiet efficiency helped me so often. I also am grateful to John Richmond of the Institute's Publications Department for preparing the map. Valerie Millholland and Pam Morrison, of Duke University Press, have been anchors throughout, and Bob Mirandon, editing my third Duke book, has again blended flexibility with rigor. It was a mighty stroke of luck getting Maria Rerrich to type the manuscript. But she did much more than just make up for my hoary technological backwardness. She assiduously combed the text and saved me from many solecisms, inconsistencies, and other improprieties. My analyses and views are, of course, my own and not those of the Research Institute's management and staff or those of the RFE/RL management and its broadcast services. Any mistakes also are solely mine.

My wife, Margaret, as always, provided the kind of special help that lightens burdens and softens landings.

Oxford, January 1994

Map of Eastern Europe in 1991

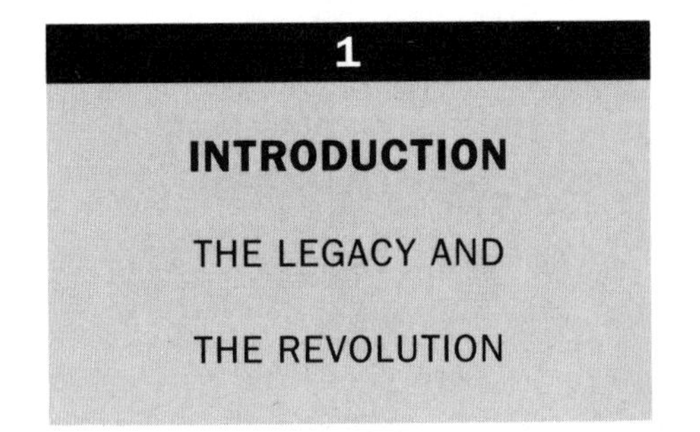

1

INTRODUCTION

THE LEGACY AND THE REVOLUTION

Eastern Europe is engaged in a revolution as it copes with a legacy. Both are intimidating. The revolution involves simultaneously building liberal democracy and a market economy. As such it is unprecedented. The legacy is bequeathed not only by communism but by elements in the precommunist history of the region. The legacy interacts with the revolution, influencing and hampering it, directly and indirectly. Indeed, probably the most constraining part of the legacy is *pre*-communist: the national reassertiveness that was repressed by communism but never submerged by it. For the second time in just a half-century Eastern Europe must build a new system. The old one was imposed by force; this new one must come through persuasion. This book seeks to describe and analyze the results so far. And the prospects.

In the last chapter of my book, *Surge to Freedom,* I gingerly submitted a checklist of the problems that would face the postcommunist East European countries.[1] Their fate would be decided by the way in which these interrelating problems were tackled. The problems varied from country to country, in both type and degree of tractability. But they existed everywhere, forming both the legacy of communist rule and the work for its successors. Very briefly, these problems were:

The development of a liberal, democratic political culture.

Clearing away of the "pollution of the mind" (Václav Havel's expression) that had gathered under communism—the moral, intellectual, and political deformation that the contrast between communist fiction and actual fact had inflicted on individuals and society as a whole. This is an educational, moral, and psychological problem.

Problems of power and politics—the activation of democratic institutions and procedures; the future of the former communist bureaucracies and the issue of collaboration with the old regime, particularly with the security apparatus.

> Problems of the economy — the transition from socialism to the market, and the theoretical, social, political, financial, cultural, and psychological questions involved.
>
> The environment — not just a question of the quality of life but often of life itself.
>
> The emigration urge, especially of "the best and the brightest," men and women equipped to help cope with the postcommunist problems. To this must now be added the waves of *immigration*, a more immediate and dangerous problem.

Finally, there were the three problems concerning foreign relations:

> Relations first with the Soviet Union and then with the successor states of the Soviet Union, especially Russia.
>
> Relations with the West — mainly Western Europe, the United States, and, if mainly in the economic sense, Japan.
>
> Relations with each other — intra-East European relations — and the huge and burgeoning issue of nationalism, as it affects state and ethnic relations.

These problems in themselves subsume both the revolution and the legacy, future tasks and past encumbrances. They constitute the East European agenda. Agendas often can impart pessimism but, especially after forty spiritually and morally enervating years of communist rule, this agenda is a particularly daunting one. But it is the only possible one. There is no going back. Some of the reassuring basics of "real, existing socialism" may be missed; Czech and Polish workers may moan; some Hungarians may get a bit wistful about Kádár; and in Romania even minicults of Ceauşescu may sprout from the disillusion. But, putting George Orwell's *Animal Farm* into the new political context — updating it, so to speak — nobody in Eastern Europe wants Farmer Jones back. At least, not in the way he used to behave. And if he were to begin behaving differently, he would not be Farmer Jones. Leninism in Eastern Europe is gone for good; wherever Eastern Europe might be going, however successful the "postcommunist" parties might be at the polls, it is not going back to that. No matter how much political capital some circles in every country are trying to gain from spreading the fear of a communist return to power — and no matter how much echo they have made in paranoid and/or disappointed sections of the population — there is no danger of "recommunization," in the old sense.

Overcoming the Past

The problem, indeed, is not so much with recommunization as decommunization. This in turn is part of Eastern Europe's *Vergangenheitsbewältigung* pattern, the problem of "overcoming the past," which is dealt with at some length in chapter 2. It is a problem to which the West Germans (although not East Germans) gave the name after World War II. It is more difficult and poignant in postcommunist Eastern Europe than it was in post-Nazi Germany. There, after all, the vast majority of Germans had supported the Nazis. The vast majority of East Europeans did not support their communist rulers. But the people were brought together with those rulers in many direct and indirect ways. The relationship was much longer and more complex than that in Nazi Germany. After six years of Hitler, Germany was at war; another six and he was gone. The communist system in Eastern Europe lasted more than forty years and looked as if it might go on indefinitely, perhaps forever. Pressures for compromise and accommodation multiplied. And then, sometimes in effortless sequence, followed cooperation, collaboration, and co-opting. Even in Poland, where communist rule was thinnest and most contested, there were more than 3 million communist party members in 1980, one in ten of the adult population. Hardly a single Polish family was without some association with the regime. Decommunization is a multifaceted problem involving matters of law, moral and political justice, excess or moderation, governmental efficiency and expediency, mass psychology, social cohesion, and political demagogy. Some see it as the rigorous pursuit of justice, others as the perpetuation of injustice; some maintain it is essential for a new beginning, others that it vitiates democracy right from the start; some see it as a breakthrough, others as a massive diversion. It is likely to remain the most divisive and dominant domestic issue in Eastern Europe for many years.

Toward the Rule of Law

Decommunization also will be a crucial test for the rule of law in Eastern Europe. For decades, laws were framed, interpreted, and implemented in the service of communist ideology. Even good laws often lost their value because of the ends to which they were put. Now the postcommunist East European states are genuinely trying to replace this perversion of law by the rule of law—law that protects rather than controls citizens, that regulates their relations with each other and with their freely elected governments, that preserves individual rights while guaranteeing social order.

Institutionalizing and guarding the rule of law is a mammoth task, especially at a time of uncertainty and of a hankering after retribution. Generally speaking, the postcommunist courts have done well in preserving legal principles in this complicated and impassioned environment and often have had the courage to make themselves unpopular in doing so. The big task for the courts, currently and for some time to come, will be to set precedents and guidelines, to establish principles on which the rule of law is based. As for decommunization, it is encouraging that many judges realize that the new order in Eastern Europe will, in good measure, be judged by the legal principles governing it, and that if they confront the old order with anything less than the highest principles, they will not be exorcising it but imitating it.

New constitutions are indispensable—written, exemplary, and clear. Every country in Eastern Europe started off by patching over communist originals. Some constitutions became more patched over than others, but even the most amended ones still offered no coherent definition and reflection of the revolutions that had taken place, or of the freedoms and responsibilities that should emanate from them. Romania and Bulgaria were the first to have new constitutions. Their enactment was both ironical and controversial since it was the work of governments composed of mutated, mutating, or downright unmutable communists. Hence, the legitimacy and authority of these constitutions were questioned. But, whatever their flaws (and their provenance), they still provided the framework for liberal and lawful government. Elsewhere, the enacting, even the drafting, of new constitutions have been delayed by inertia, political or national fractiousness, or the distraction of crisis situations. But the longer a country delays, the longer the interim, postcommunist phase in its history will be, and the longer before a new start can be made. A new constitution is not *in itself* a passport to the *Rechtsstaat,* but it is certainly part of the required documentation.

The lack of new constitutions also delayed the advent of efficient government. Everywhere a need existed for the separation of powers, including those within the executive itself, to be constitutionally affirmed, clearly defined, and reflecting of the new political realities.

The absence of such a separation not only subverts efficient government, but it tends to bring the democratic process into early disrepute. Poland early on became a case where lack of a constitution almost led to political anarchy. The succession of crises there were not only due to the incurable individualism of Poles, the irresponsibility of some ministers, advisers, and representatives, or the hubris of President Wałęsa, but to the fact that those parts of the constitution that should have restrained excesses in public life were drafted in the communist era, when totally different philosophies, institutions, and practices obtained. Even in Hungary where government began by working relatively well, there were disputes over presidential and governmental powers, again reflecting the need for constitutional provisions that regulate the new order rather than mirror the old.

Constitutions, of course, however felicitously phrased, need interpreting; hence Constitutional Courts. It is different to exaggerate the importance and the potential of this institution in the postcommunist lands. In Hungary the Constitutional Court has become a key player in public life. Some of its decisions were controversial, going against the popular grain. In Bulgaria, too, the Constitutional Court held out against discriminatory measures against the Turkish minority and against the decommunization mania. The more the Constitutional Courts realized that their job was to be proper, not popular, the better the chance of a lasting constitutional democracy.

"Them" and "Us": The Alienation Syndrome

Borrowing again from Orwell and *Animal Farm,* while few East Europeans want Farmer Jones back, many of them have become disappointed, even disillusioned, with the performance of his successors. Hence the revival of the Left in most countries. Materially, many East Europeans were better off under Jones. Whatever the gradations of popular opinion are they all point to one thing: the "them" and "us" syndrome in Eastern Europe is still alive and kicking. After flourishing for centuries, whatever the form of rule, it dropped out of sight for a few months after 1989 but is now discouragingly back, this profound mistrust of, and cleavage between, the rulers and the ruled.

Economic dissatisfaction and apprehensiveness have given it new impetus, and many East Europeans are likely to become even more distrustful of "them" as their standard of living continues to fall, unemployment rises, and inflation continues to hurt. In the meantime the nouveaux riches flaunt their sometimes dubious gains. Attitudes are exacerbated here by the social jealousy that has always existed—not just an East European but a pan-European phenomenon. (Communist principles of egalitarianism reinforced this attitude but did not originate it.) Add to this the endemic corruption, the spectacular scandals, plus the capitalist flair shown by many former communist luminaries, and it is not surprising to see East European shoulders shrugging or to hear their various regional equivalents of *plus ça change, plus c'est la même chose.*

The "them" and "us" syndrome in Eastern Europe will persist. Nor will it begin to disappear until democratic institutions and practices—which are already in place—become more representative of society as a whole. There is a particularly desperate need of adequate worker representation, not at the factory level, where it has tended to impede economic change, but in the political mainstream, at the parliamentary and local government level. This is not just morally right but also politically sound as a means of allaying the social consequences of the painful transitions caused by economic reform, and creating a balanced polity generally.

It is, though, easier said than done. Economic reform, particularly of the "shock therapy" variety (see chapter 5), effectively means the social disfranchisement of hundreds of thousands of workers throughout the region, the proles of the heavy industrial monsters that must become extinct if the new Eastern Europe is to have a future. The prospects of many of these men and women ever retraining, redeploying, or being reincarnated as entrepreneurs are practically nil. They represent not just a serious moral and social problem: they are also a pointer to political development in the region. For several years to come there is going to be a big pool of unemployable people in Eastern Europe, representing a danger to democratic development. All the more reason, therefore, to mitigate the danger by as benevolent a social policy as can be afforded, with meaningful representation of these groups in the political mainstream. It can most effectively and safely be done through Social Democracy. If this is not strong enough to attract sufficient worker confidence and support, to soften discontent and channel it peacefully and constructively, then proletarian discontent will be exploited by the unreconstructed extreme left and the new extreme right. Fortunately, the "postcommunist" parties successfully emerging in countries like Poland and Hungary are more

Social Democrat than Leninist and could play this crucial representational role.

Authoritarianism, "Diluted and Temporary"?

Amid all the problems of postcommunist Europe, the tasks of reconstruction in all their complexity, the dangers of social upheavals, of right- or left-nationalism, it is not surprising that suggestions have been made by public figures in Eastern Europe as well as in the West, that liberal democracy, at least for the short term future, would be a premature luxury, anarchic, self-indulgent and self-defeating. It is particularly endangering, so the argument goes, to market economic reforms, particularly of the "shock therapy" variety, which, because of their inevitably adverse social consequences, immediately become a political football endangering their eventual success. And since a minimum economic sufficiency is crucial to securing liberal democracy, a bit less democracy now could be the best means of guaranteeing more of it later on. In addition to this, too much democracy too soon allows nationalists of whatever ilk, racists, criminals, and a huge assortment of other undesirables, to go about their nefarious business without let or hindrance. Why not, therefore, a salutary dose of authoritarianism, "to get things done" and "till the worst is over?" It must, of course, be mild, enlightened, and definitely pro tem. Preferably, too, it should function through the democratic forms already in place.

The case is plausible and could well become clamoring. But it is unconvincing. The dose of authoritarianism being prescribed may sound harmless enough, but it is insidiously dangerous. It would mean braking, not just liberal political democracy, but also progress toward the rule of law, whose legal niceties and constitutional complexities are uniquely calculated to quicken authoritarian impulses. Indeed, braking is the wrong word. It conveys the idea that liberal political democracy and the rule of law can be put on hold, starting again where they left off once the coast is clear. The truth is that, especially in the East European conditions prevailing, once their progress were halted, democracy and the rule of law would not stay put, but retreat—and the retreat could well become a rout. And certainly the liberal tradition in Eastern Europe has never been so bright and sturdy for it to be put on the shelf for an indeterminate period, then taken down, polished up, and put back into service. In short, what might be good and inevitable for Yeltsin's Russia is neither for the East European countries.

It must, therefore, be either forward—however slowly—toward liberal democracy or backward—very quickly backward—to something that can best be termed fascism. Fascism always took some defining, but perhaps Ralf Dahrendorf best describes the type that could threaten the new Eastern Europe:

> I mean the combination of a nostalgic ideology of community which draws harsh boundaries between those who belong and those who do not, with a new political monopoly of a man or a "movement" and a strong emphasis on organisation and mobilisation rather than freedom of choice. The rule of law would be suspended; dissidents and deviants would be incarcerated; minorities would be singled out for popular wrath and official discrimination. Fascism in this sense need not be as horrific as German National Socialism; systematic genocide is not a necessary consequence of its rule, though it is always likely. It is in any case a tyranny which has its origin on what we have got used to calling the right, because it is allied with the military, the other forces of "law and order," it appeals to reactionary sentiments and it dreams of the purity of a bygone age rather than Utopian visions of a better future. Such fascism can have many names, Mussolini and Franco, Peron and Pinochet.[2]

Some of these symptoms are already depressingly familiar in post-communist Eastern Europe.

One of the attractions of authoritarianism, especially in a crisis situation, is that it is simple, precise, easily definable and recognizable—all things which liberal democracy, a slippery entity, is not. Liberal democracy today does have certain basic characteristics—representative government, universal suffrage, majority rule, minority rights, the rule of law, a social policy. But the sum of liberal democracy is greater than its parts. In an essay I wrote in the middle of 1991 I tried, not to define it, but to convey some of it in an East European context:

> There is also much confusion about what liberal democracy really is. Many just identify it with anticommunism, the difference between good and evil. Others, a little less Manichean, confuse it with the political pluralism already prevailing . . . . Only a few realize that liberal democracy is an end, a state of grace never

> actually reached (not even in the West), but eminently worth grasping for. These same few know that liberal economics is simply a means (perhaps not the only one) to try to reach that end. The means and the end may eventually coexist, even be complementary, but they can never be comparable because one is secondary to the other.[3]

The point is that liberal democracy, if it is to mean anything, must *always* be an aspiration. The quest for the Grail is never-ending, though never unavailing. If it is halted, slowed, or abandoned, it can never be resumed except, as in the case of Germany and Italy in the twentieth century, after catastrophe.

Open Society and Its Dangers

The 1989 revolution in Eastern Europe was essentially one of rejection. All revolutions are this, of course, but the great revolutions of modern times—the English in the 1640s, the American and French toward the end of the eighteenth century, and the Russian early in the twentieth—were all brimming with new ideologies and the numerous variations on them. In Eastern Europe it was a matter of throwing out "real existing socialism" and its leaders. What Eastern Europe's revolutionaries were "for" (and it should be remembered that, as in all revolutions, the revolutionaries constituted a relatively small percentage of the population), was nothing particularly original, certainly nothing specific. It was, again quoting Dahrendorf, an "open society":

> The countries of East Central Europe . . . have shed a closed system in order to create an open society, *the* open society to be exact, for while there can be many systems, there is only one open society. If any creed has won in the events of last year, it is the idea that we are all embarked on a journey into an uncertain future and have to work by trial and error within institutions which make it possible to bring about change without bloodshed.[4]

But inseparable from their notion of an open society was also the notion of "the West," both Western Europe and the United States. A porous but permissible generalization would be that, for most young people, as well as for the millions who had family ties there, the United States was the main attraction; for the older and perhaps better educated it was Western Europe. The West represented for them the "open society." It was, therefore, admired and exemplary, especially where it seemed to be the furthest distant from the "real existing socialism" they had endured. Western figures, like Ronald Reagan and Margaret Thatcher, who had been considered the most antipathetic to the socialist state of grace, were put on unassailable pedestals.

But what many East Europeans at first failed to realize was that an open society alone could be a dangerous place. It needs experience, institutions, procedures, the rule of law, civil society, and civic vigilance to transform it into something that makes for a fulfilling, inclusive, and stable public life. In spite of their manifold, and manifest, imperfections most Western countries do have these safeguards. They enable them to enjoy the benefits of the open society while holding off (sometimes only just) its dangers. None of the East European states have these safeguards to anywhere near enough degree to feel safe in an open society. With the exception of the now independent Slovakia, the East Central European states, including Slovenia, have some. But states like Romania and Bulgaria, not to mention Albania, and some of the Yugoslav successor states are only at the beginning of the road.

Without these safeguards an open society easily becomes a void, an open sewer into which pours the historical and human detritus that has once again become so depressingly familiar: nationalist hatreds; anti-Semitism; dictatorship; populism; sham parliamentary life or none at all; lawlessness, intolerance, Orwellian newspeak, and porno culture. Those are the dangers, and what we have been seeing in Eastern Europe since the beginning of 1990 is the race to fill the open society with genuine substance before it is filled with such detritus. In many ways it seems an uneven contest—mainly in South-Eastern Europe, but not only there. Many East Europeans are temporarily worn down and demoralized after more than forty years of communism, and many have no notion of what constitutes safeguards or dangers in the open society. This is one area where the West might help through education opportunities for East Europeans and through its own media—not preaching, but putting its own open society in perspective, and pointing out the serious dangers that threaten it, too.

The race for the true open society is certainly not a sprint, more a long-distance race, most likely a never-ending one. Certainly the dangers mentioned earlier will be constantly obtruding. Economic progress—again the minimum sufficiency—is of crucial importance. Failure to make real progress could condemn nations to a permanent state of sub-civilization. Similarly, a frail, precarious economy would always be at the mercy of an economic disaster that could sweep away the safeguards already in place in the open society. The Great Depression did this to parts of Eastern Europe in the early 1930s—and to Germany as well.

The Return of History

The open society with safeguards; a fulfilling, inclusive, and stable public life: a tall enough order at the best of times. How is it reached? Do precedents exist?

There is an abundance of "transition" literature, mostly based on Latin American and South European models. These models are suggestive and instructive up to a point, but could mislead if applied too literally to Eastern Europe. In the South European case, the differences of economic system and level were such as practically to disqualify any relevancy and, in the case of both Southern Europe and Latin America, the authoritarian type governments that formerly ruled there left many sectors of the public and private domains relatively untouched. They were neither totalitarian, nor did they aspire to be. The East European governments may not have been totalitarian, either, but they aspired to be—at least when they felt confident enough. The difference lay in the aspiration, and it was a basic one.

This is what makes history so important—in this context the historical differences not simply between Eastern Europe and, say, Latin America but also between the East European countries themselves. As in the case of the communist system in Eastern Europe which imposed broad similarities on the region but which also could never overcome crucial national differences, so in postcommunist Eastern Europe it is these national differences that will essentially modify any broader transitional process. History helps not only to understand and illuminate developments in Eastern Europe today; it may also help to anticipate them and ward off dangers inherent in them. As a guide to Eastern Europe today, better, then, turn not to Latin America but to historians like Joseph Rothschild, the late Hugh Seton-Watson, and others, to their histories of Eastern Europe between the two world wars, and to earlier histories of the empires to which the East European lands belonged. (They should never have been neglected, anyway.) Political scientists, some of them still smarting or posturing from their intellectual debacle after the collapse of communism, might best rethink and regroup till things settle down — if they ever do.

Nationalism into the Breach

In its spectacular way, it is nationalism that has brought back history and the historians, moving into the vacuum left by communist rule and threatening the new open societies. It has brought catastrophe to parts of former Yugoslavia and threatens more. It is potentially disruptive in other parts of South-Eastern Europe and eventually even in East-Central Europe, although there the danger of serious violence *appears* to be considerably less. Nationalism was manipulated by communist leaders to an extent that is not often realized. But its violent manifestations were suppressed and its very existence was ideologically submerged. Now it has bounced back like *Stehaufmännchen,* those "magic" dolls, once beloved of German infants, which, despite whatever pressing and pummeling, always revert back to their upright position. But as communism collapsed, the dolls of nationalism not only bounced back but also began to attack each other. The war of the *Stehaufmännchen* followed on naturally from the false peace of communist repression.

What today's intense national resentment and strife also shows is that the peace settlements after both World War I and World War II have become unraveled. As chapter 6 shows, three states emerging from World War I, or created as a result of it — the Soviet Union, Yugoslavia, and Czechoslovakia — have fallen apart. The security of the entire region has become precarious as the errors of the century's peacemakers — or the sheer impossibility of their task — have become increasingly evident.

Ideally, what would be needed now is a third comprehensive international arrangement aimed at giving the 21st century in Eastern Europe some chance of a promising debut. Practically, though, this is impossible. Versailles, then Yalta, and finally Paris in 1947, coming after the two most exhausting wars in history, could be dictated by the victors to the vanquished. But a third such major war is unthinkable. The pattern now, though, could be a series of bloody minor ones, such as have been occurring in Yugoslavia and the old Soviet Union in which each side seeks to impose its own justice and redress the perceived wrongs of its history. But "settlements" emerging from such collisions are obviously the least satisfactory of all, and the most temporary, leading to an even greater sense of injustice on the part of those defeated. International organizations, of course, exist to deter these minor wars or to end them through force and arbitration. But their ineffectiveness so far in the postcommunist period has tended to stimulate aggression rather than deter it, to reward rather than punish it. Unless an international system of arbitration and restraint is devised quickly, then the prospects for regional stability into the next century look dim indeed. If the forty-year "Pax Sovietica," despite all its injustices, becomes wistfully considered as an era of peace and stability, then that will in itself become the judgment on the new postcommunist order.

Pax Sovietica at least prevented violence, immanent in all issues of nationalism, from seriously erupting. But Pax Sovietica in retrospect was only a long interruption of Eastern Europe's historical "disimperialization" process and its corollary of national identification or rediscovery. The latter had begun in the nineteenth century and continued well into the twentieth. Nazi German, Fascist Italian, and Communist Russian conquests between the end of the first and second world wars were massive and violent reactions against this process: and then Pax Sovietica froze the process. Now after 1989 it is resuming in both Eastern Europe and the former Russian Empire and looks like going on till it exhausts itself. Yugoslavia and Czechoslovakia eventually failed precisely because they barred the progress toward the national identification of some of their constituent nations. The final emergence of Croatia, Slovenia, Bosnia-Hercegovina, and Slovakia means that the last of the subject nations of the Habsburg Empire are now free. By the same token, Macedonian independence rounds off the reaction against the Ottomans. The disimperialization is complete. The danger now is that, in its wake, new, "little imperialisms" will proliferate in the former Soviet Union and, as they did between the world wars, in Eastern Europe too.

The collapse of Yugoslavia and Czechoslovakia during this historical process is particularly poignant. It dramatizes the failure of the nineteenth-century Romantic idea that ethnic and linguistic similarity is enough to justify incorporating different nations into one state and expecting them to live happily ever after. Indeed, it showed that when such similar nations — as the Serbs and the Croats, the Czechs and the Slovaks — are drawn together, the relatively small differences that distinguish them tend to become so magnified, especially in situations of crisis and stress, that they assume a fatally divisive potency. The Soviet case is also partly an example of this, although there it was largely a question of unabashed imperialism covered over with red ideological paint. Ethnic togetherness, therefore, has not been a characteristic of the twentieth century, as many optimists and idealists, liberals and socialists, hoped. Quite the opposite: as the century comes to an end the bills of history need to be paid, and the grievances redressed.

Nationalism, therefore, in the East European context is the expression of nations identifying and asserting themselves after long periods of submergence, subjection, or constraint. For most of the men and women involved it is not just a priority aim but an all-consuming impulse, or passion. Many may sincerely believe in the virtues of democracy and the market, others may simply be paying them lip service, deferring to what is now de rigueur. But they all see them as secondary to the assertion of identity — something to come later. The worst result has been what has happened in Yugoslavia: the all-consuming impulse begets violence which then begets more. In the meantime political and economic reforms are lost, or harmfully delayed, in the triumph or the tragedy of the struggle. No one put it better than the beleaguered Bosnian president, Alija Izetbegović in 1990, well before his own nation was caught up in the misery of national conflict: "When you call for a public discussion about democracy, a couple of hundred intellectuals come. When it's about nationalism, you get tens of thousands of all sorts."[5]

An Ineffectual West?

This is something the world must live with well into the twenty-first century. It is as if the lessons the West has learned through bitter experience have been lost on parts of Eastern Europe. Some are acting like "Balkan" states at the beginning of this century rather than "European" states at the end of it. Perhaps the nationalist virus must work itself through their systems, spend itself, as it has largely done in Western Europe. If this is so, then parts of the region face a desperate future — that is, unless "the West," having at last cleaned out its own charnel house, has the resolution and skill to induce and help its Eastern neighbor to do the same.

This had been the great hope: that "the West" — the European Community and the United States, singly or through NATO — would indeed become the agent of order. The benevolent, burgeoning European Community would be ready and able both to succor and to stabilize, a community led by the most benevolent Germany the Continent has ever seen. And behind the Community was the might of NATO and America. That was the Eastern European hope that quickly became an illusion. Soon there arose serious doubts about Western unity and resolution. At the end of the 1980s a confident European Community was looking toward further unity, political as well as economic, seeing itself, and being seen, as guide and patron for an emancipated Eastern Europe. But much of this had changed by the early 1990s. The closer the Community got to uniting, the more it began to dither. Germany, the Community's natural leader, having bitten off more than it could quickly chew in the old GDR, was becoming particularly uncertain. The Maastricht treaty became not a symbol of progress but of nervousness. Eastern Europe, instead of being an opportunity, was becoming a nuisance. "A friend in need is a pest," seemed to have become the Community's unofficial motto. Nothing dramatized Western impotence more than the Yugoslav crisis. In its first test of international maturity the West was foundering. Europe was continuing to depend on the United States for a leadership the latter was no longer providing. Could Clinton's America ever provide this, with its domestic preoccupations, and the understandable American insistence that Uncle Sam cannot indefinitely go on pulling Europe's chestnuts out of the fire? And, in the end, this is, indeed, a *European* responsibility to be discharged (or shirked) by Europeans.

But the Yugoslav crisis and the possible extension of conflict throughout the Balkans have at least dispelled the previously commonly held notion that this region is *peripheral.* Its significance as a generator and a radiator of conflict is now largely realized. And the "Muslim" factor now adds almost a global dimension to the crisis in the region. It is this that could make Sarajevo today as consequential as it became in 1914. And it is this that makes an effective Western response so essential. Time is short and the consequences of neglect could be long standing.

Religion: Reassurances and Problems

Nationalism is not the only traditional factor returning to the East European scene: religion is also back in impressive strength. Renewed interest in religion is by no means a postcommunist phenomenon. It began to be evident at least ten years before 1989. Except in Poland, where nationalism and Catholicism were so closely intertwined, religion under communism had at first mainly been the preserve of older people; for many of the young the socialist "materialist worldview" or just plain skepticism superseded it. But as the new god revealed himself as palpably failing, so more and more young people rediscovered the old one.

The election of the Cracow archbishop, Karol Cardinal Wojtyła, to the papacy as John Paul II was the main turning point in this process, indeed one of the turning points in twentieth-century Eastern European history. Its impact was not simply, or even mainly, religious. It was also nationalistic and political, one of the causes and one of the symptoms of communism's approaching demise. In Poland itself, John Paul's election and his subsequent visits electrified his compatriots, strengthening even further the identification of Polish Catholicism with the nation's survival. But, though obviously less intense, his election had a similar impact elsewhere, most notably in Czechoslovakia. Throughout the region it strengthened anticommunist resistance simply because the election of a pope from the People's Republic of Poland made further mockery of the system's totalitarian pretensions.

Since 1989, religion's anticommunist dimension is no longer so strong or necessary. But in many instances its relationship to nationalism has remained, or become even closer. Poland has already been mentioned. But the link is also there in Croatia and Slovakia, though apparently to nowhere near the same extent in either as during or before World War II. In the Balkans, as well as Russia and Ukraine, the state Orthodox Churches strongly support their country's national causes. Serbia is the obvious case in point, but Bulgaria and Romania—not to mention Greece—are also examples. The churches, though, are not just adjuncts of nationalism's present revival; they are also a powerful means to recover a nation's past, which the communists first tried to blot out and then to exploit in their own interest. Here ritual and symbolism play an important part, as does the sense of community and mutual help that churchgoing fosters, and which communist rule did much to weaken.

But religion today also has a very private aspect, which need not exclude the national and symbolic aspects: the individual's search for something more profound, demanding, and rewarding than the communist ideology. Nor does this search stem only from the past: it is also a response to the helter-skelter of postcommunism, to the bewilderment of life since 1989.

This reawakened interest in religion is likely to persist. The churches, therefore, have occasion for rejoicing, and those of their members whose behavior under communism was exemplary have particular cause for satisfaction. But none of the churches—least of all, it would appear, the Roman Catholic Church—can afford to be complacent. Postcommunist religiosity looks like being tempered with a fair dose of anticlericalism. Criticism of the Catholic Church's wealth in Poland is mounting as is the resentment of what is considered the arrogance, narrow-mindedness, and conservatism of its leadership. This anticlerical resentment was the main reason for the Catholic parties' debacle in the September 1993 parliamentary elections (see chapter 3). It is the same, to some extent, in Hungary, the Czech Republic, and even Slovakia. The Vatican also comes in for much open and muted criticism on account of moral teachings seen by many as being totally divorced from reality and sometimes enunciated in a manner suggesting little difference between commissars and cardinals. The throne of Saint Peter is inviolable as long as a Pole sits on it—at least to Poles. But Polish obedience is highly selective, too, ending, as the popular saying goes, at the bedroom door. In the mainly Orthodox countries, an increase in religious feeling has been accompanied by a mounting criticism of the Church hierarchy. This is because of the active collaboration of the Church leaderships and many of the clergy with the communist regime. One way of recovering a following of sorts would be to beat the nationalist drum even more loudly. This might work for a time—but only as long as your side is winning. The nationalism of the Orthodox Churches makes some of their clergy as vulnerable as politicians.

In the end, though, the biggest danger to established religion in Eastern Europe will be the encroachment of liberalism, with all its comprehensive, chaotic mix. One aspect of it is already seen within the Churches themselves, many of the new, younger, members of the flock preferring do-it-yourself to rules and rituals and not getting much sympathy from the hierarchy in return. Liberalism and current clericalism are also on a collision course over much of the churches' moral and social teaching. The abortion issue has already divided many Poles; this indeed is a gigantic struggle that is only just beginning, with the Church steadily being put on the defense. The tactical victories the Polish Church has gained since 1989 on issues like abortion (largely), and religion in schools should be seen in the perspective of a larger struggle that it will eventually probably lose. And in the purely material sphere, the restitution of church property has become a controversial issue everywhere.

But while losing on many of its moral teachings, the Roman Catholic Church could regain some ground on the strength of its social message, especially if the socioeconomic situation deteriorates sharply under the rigors of the transition from socialism to capitalism. Catholic social teaching, although hardly anticapitalist, has never hidden its distrust of what it considers the "excesses" of capitalism. Pope John Paul II certainly sees nothing immaculate about capitalism. In a situation of massive hardship, therefore, the Catholic Church could recover some of the *political* influence it historically has had (but which it always went to pains to deny). It could find itself, though, in strange company. Its socioeconomic program would resemble that of the forces of the left, even the reformed communists. A leftist-Catholic reconciliation—the red and the black? Some may dismiss the idea as blasphemously absurd. It certainly would call for rather more flexibility than either side has usually been inclined to show. But the new Left is nothing if not malleable and, if led well, the Catholic Church has the stature, experience, and resource to handle situations like this with due finesse. And a Catholic/left-wing coalition would be less of a worry than a nationalist/left-wing (brown-red) one, of which there were signs in Slovakia and Romania—and Russia. It is probably less of a worry, too, than a Catholic/right-wing one.

Illusions and Scapegoats

In the early 1970s all the East European communist regimes—even Ceauşescu made halfhearted gestures—initiated programs of "consumerism." This was after, first, the Prague Spring in 1968 and then the Polish workers' revolt in December 1970 that toppled Gomułka. Consumerism was to be the dynamic that would take people's minds off restless politics and finally convince them that communism could deliver the goods. The new policy was seen at its most spectacular in Poland, under Gomułka's successor, Edward Gierek. There was unquestionably some public response to this new policy. It was popular, but this did not imply any more support for the regimes or faith in the system they were trying to build. East Europeans were glad for what they could get but were far from grateful. In any case most East Europeans knew that, in Western terms, their consumerism was like a nineteenth-century workhouse compared with a twentieth-century luxury hotel. And, as soon as consumerism began to fail, as it did toward the end of the 1970s, the public's alienation only increased. Even on its own level communism simply could not deliver.

But now, with the revolutions of 1989, many East Europeans began to indulge their long suppressed materialist fantasies. The time was *now,* and they were anxious to listen to anybody who told them their dreams could become reality—*now.*

Stan Tymiński! The name of this Polish-Peruvian-Canadian "mystery man" will take some forgetting, though many Poles must be anxious to. In the first round of the Polish presidential voting in November 1990 he knocked Premier Tadeusz Mazowiecki, a giant among anticommunists, out of the race, and in the final round of voting two weeks later got 25 percent of the vote against none other than Lech Wałęsa. Tymiński ran a lunatic campaign but for many Poles he was their boy from the Golden West and he offered the quickest of fixes for Poland's economic troubles. Tymiński told them they could have it now, and enough of them fell for it to put him in the history books and apparently confirm the Polish reputation for erratic politics.

But the Poles were not alone in jamming the postcommunist escape tunnel. The Bulgarians, often considered the most phlegmatic of the Slavs, had their own version of Stan Tymiński. He was Georges (spelled and pronounced *à la française*) Ganchev, an erstwhile athlete of some note, who spent a quarter of a century in exile, in London and then appropriately in Hollywood, before going home to the new opportunities presented by the fledgling Bulgarian democracy. His message was the same as Tymiński's although delivered more attractively by a more personable type of adventurer. He got 17 percent of the vote in the presidential election in January 1992. He was never in danger of winning but he lost by much less than almost anybody expected.

Tymiński and Ganchev told us something about the East European postcommunist psyche. But this psyche was revealed not just through impressive votes for exotic personalities and promises. The massive Czech and Slovak response to the voucher privatization scheme in 1991 and 1992 (see chapter 5) is a case in point. The voucher scheme was, in its way, the Czechoslovak counterpart to Poland's Stan Tymiński—the quick escape from the dank ordinariness left by communism to a travel-poster world of capitalism. The fact that the voucher scheme, after languishing for several weeks, picked up dramatically when an American-type mutual fund called Harvard Investment and Consulting began offering at least a tenfold profit on each book of vouchers sold to it, served to add a new, fabulous, dimension to it. Other mutual funds sprouted and within a short time 8 million people had bought books of vouchers and were on their way to market. Premier Václav Klaus would argue that dreams or escapism had nothing to do with the public's response: it was hard-headed realization of the benefits of finance capitalism. But it was much simpler and more human than that. The vouchers were an escape ticket, like the lottery tickets in some countries and the football pools in Britain. The pickings might be slimmer but the impulse was the same.

Tymiński, Ganchev, and the vouchers were also, therefore, a symptom of malaise, a contrast between hopes and disappointment, of bewilderment and divorce from reality. They reflected not just hopes but also the bitterness of many who, after 1989, felt that they were not climbing out of the pit dug by the communists but falling deeper into it. And, just as disappointment and confusion lead to gullibility, they lead also to scapegoating—looking for somebody to blame, as long as it was not themselves, and mixing up substance with symptoms.

In October 1991 Václav Havel diagnosed the distemper of his own countrymen with his usual insight and flair. What he said applies everywhere:

> At the same time, they feel frustration that nothing is as good as they wish or as they thought it would be after the revolution; and they are searching for a culprit—preferably a simple, comprehensible, and easily defined one, and that means a collective one. Thus one can read in the papers that some say it is the Freemasons who are to blame for all our troubles; others say that it is the Jews; others that it is the Slovaks; still others that it is the Romanies; and everybody says that it is the Communists.[6]

In other words, scapegoating! Much of the material in this book derives from scapegoating in one form or another. The danger is that it will not simply be a temporary disorder but will become a way of life, both private and public. The need is to create a political and economic environment in which East Europeans would begin to feel responsible for themselves, their own successes and failures, in which they would be citizens, not subjects. Creating this environment will not in itself mean that their revolution has been successfully completed. Far from it. But it will mean that the first indispensable, and very difficult, step has been taken. From then on it may not be any easier, but they will at least know that, however necessary outside help may be, the revolution is theirs and nobody else's.

The revolution in Eastern Europe after 1989 is the third revolution the East Europeans have been through in their modern history. The first was their achievement of independence in the nineteenth and early twentieth centuries; the second involved their resubjugation, this time by the Soviet Union after 1945 and their absorption into its imperial communist system. Now, since 1989, this new revolution is already in its second phase. First came the replacement of communist *rule,* its institutions and procedures; that was the easy part. The second phase involves progress away from the communist *system* and toward democracy, the market, and "Europe"; this is the immensely difficult part. The goals are clear. Can all of the East European countries reach them? Can some of them? Can any? For those who cannot, what are the alternatives, the second or third bests into which they may be forced by a combination of force majeure and their own fault?

Generalizations alone, however brilliant and insightful, cannot begin to answer these questions. They can be suggestive and stimulating, but overindulgence leads to oversimplification in unavailing efforts to encompass the unencompassable. In moderation, though, defining rather than distracting, generalizations not only are helpful but necessary. Certain patterns are apparent. Communist rule left common problems, calling, not so much for common responses, as for responses that have something in common. Hence, the need for this book to cover politics as well as economics on a region wide as well as on a country-by-country basis. The interaction should be evident.

Communist rule accounted for a large part of the modern history of all of the East European states: well above half of the histories of Poland, Czechoslovakia, Yugoslavia, and of Hungary as a totally separate state; about a third in the case of Romania and Bulgaria, if one ignores the nineteenth-century periods of formal Turkish suzerainty.

How big a break with the past did the imposition of communist rule involve in Eastern Europe? It may not have been the total break some have claimed. Certain attitudes — like "them" and "us," for example — continued or even were reinforced under communism. Generally, however, there was practically no continuity between the two eras — at least not at first. Stalinist communism — not just the prevailing, but the only, model at the time — was new, alien, and (except for Yugoslavia and Albania) foreign-imposed.[1] World War II and the ensuing tabula rasa in many parts of the region also widened the historical divide. The result was the biggest overall break in development since the Ottoman conquest of South-Eastern Europe beginning at the end of the fourteenth century. It was when the Stalinist era was over, in the mid-1950s, that continuity caught up with communism, almost by accident rather than by design — first, through the partial dismantling of Stalinism by Khrushchev, and then in the long period of hands-off stagnation under Brezhnev. In all of the East European states, although in some much more than in others, systemic modifications along national lines proceeded apace, aimed at adapting the system, making the best of it rather than making it better. Indeed, communist history in Eastern Europe between 1955 and 1989 was a case of socialist internationalism besieged by national specifications. But in the end these national specifications were unacceptable to East Europeans because, however much they modified the original system, the system remained recognizably communist.[2]

In the beginning this original system had its supporters, even where it was forcibly transplanted and not homegrown. Many people realized that it was time for a change — a big one — and some, especially young people, saw communism, however brutal its means, as a shortcut to a better future. But despite the claims, promises, and rationalizations, the prospects for a better future were drowned in the squalid realities of a present that never squared with what was being claimed for it. The brave new socialist world was anchored in the nineteenth century, its ideology, its concept of progress; the party elite, billed as Leninist blood-red incorruptibles, were exposed as Mafia-style capos, sometimes even less intelligent. Some genuine gains there were — in social mobility, literacy, health, and living standards, for example. But even these advances, by and large, could not be compared with those of previously comparable countries like Greece, Austria, and Finland.

The result was popular rejection, as was seen in 1989. But *total* rejection was not now possible. There was no tabula rasa as in 1945; no war had destroyed the old inheritance. The legacy was intact, comprehensive not partial, rejected but not easily removable. Not only that: parts of that legacy were indispensable — at least for now.

Doubts About the Destination

The East European countries had all passed from communism to postcommunism by the end of 1989. (In Albania the upheaval came a year later.) Except in the Romanian case, this transition had occurred with practically no bloodshed. The changeover was easy because (a) the communist system, even where it never had been overtly opposed, never had taken root; (b) the ruling elites massively lost confidence in themselves; (c) the Brezhnev Doctrine first fell into disuse and then into mortal limbo. (This was the transitional part of the revolution, for which Latin American and Southern European parallels may exist and could give instructive pointers.)[3]

Many East Europeans, though, in 1994 and probably for years to come would dispute the notion that the transition from communism to postcommunism, let alone to democracy, had irreversibly been made. Almost any cabbie in any city, with little encouragement or sometimes none at all, would aver that nothing basically had changed, that the communists were still everywhere — in the administration, the economy, the military, the police — and still running things behind a facade of democratic forms and behind the backs of democratic politicians. Such talk was not just ordinary street paranoia. There was a lot in what the cabbies said, part of the unwanted legacy, a spirit that could not be exorcised.

Another part of the legacy was a conspiratorial view of everything. And the conspiracies suspected were mostly not separate but linked, forming in the minds of many East Europeans a seamless web, the communist spider at the center of it. Thus, the persisting presence in public life of so many from the old order became proof to many that their own revolutions in 1989 were bogus, essentially the work of the KGB and/or its local counterparts in collusion with reform communists. It was not just the Romanians who suspected this duplicity about their new government (or were sure about it); the suspicion about the genuineness of their own historic changes was also widespread among Poles, Czechs and Slovaks, Bulgarians, Albanians, and Hungarians. As for the free elections that subsequently occurred throughout Eastern Europe, these were considered just massive distractions. So the webs were spun. The suspiciousness often was morbid. And it did not begin with communist rule; it just burgeoned under it, and after it.

The old nomenklatura did present a real and galling problem. But it was in a new environment now, which made it residual rather than ruling. Well-entrenched groups at the center and the periphery themselves could delay but not dictate, evade but not enforce, extend but not perpetuate. *Pace* the cabbies, the divide *had* been crossed. For one thing, there was nothing left anymore on the other side to go back to; nor, after the collapsed putsch in the Soviet Union in August 1991, was there anything that could conceivably restore it; the Brezhnev Doctrine never could be exhumed. Moreover, representative democratic institutions and procedures were in place in every country. Some might be working only creakily, but they insured against red restoration. Competitive elections under universal suffrage were held, mostly during 1990, and, although the Polish vote (held in 1989) was partially "closed" and the Romanian and Bulgarian manipulated, the results of all of them expressed the majority will. There was much more to democracy than elections, of course, but elections created another barricade against any communist counterrevolution. And the "communists" that were coming to power, or challenging for it, in Eastern Europe in 1994 were (a) mostly different from before, not just regretting the errors of Leninism but rejecting its essence; (b) functioning under democratic conditions that they would have to observe; (c) without external sustenance; and (d) in that position of power because their opponents had failed so egregiously.

The most important early task in postcommunist Eastern Europe was not to root out all the reds but to infuse the fledgling institutions with substance and lubricate the shaky procedures with the liberal spirit. As already conceded, a vague notion—the liberal spirit—impossible to define. Its presence is sometimes barely recognizable, but its absence is always palpable. Its absence was palpable enough in many parts of Eastern Europe in the early 1990s. The liberal spirit was engaged in an uphill struggle with the totalitarian mind-set, of which not only communists, current or erstwhile, but also many vociferous anticommunists were still the victims. The totalitarian mind-set, not residual totalitarians, was the real danger.

What was needed, therefore, went beyond democratic and judicial institutions, democratic procedures and legislation. But it could be fostered by them—partially and eventually. As mentioned in the introduction, an independent judiciary was imperative. Just as democratic institutions represented the "general will," so judicial institutions were needed to curb, guide, educate, and oppose it when necessary.[4]

The temptations of populism, where they involved circumventing the law and the elected representative institutions, had to be avoided at all costs. The protection of national minorities is absolutely essential, an issue addressed at some length in chapter 6. In the legal context the need was for laws that within the framework of majority rule treat minorities as collective legal entities, enjoying specific rights and assuming general responsibilities. Such laws are essential for the honor, reputation, stability, and dignity of the East European countries. Minority rights also demand international regulations and observation. But it was the *domestic* legislation that would show whether the issue was being addressed, burked, or manipulated.[5]

The Enlargement of Civil Society

Few concepts about Eastern Europe, first in the communist twilight and now in postcommunism, have been more belabored than that of civil society. In its fullest definition, civil society refers to a "third realm of pluralistic political, social, and cultural collectives" existing between the level of the individual and the level of the state.[6] Civil society, therefore, involves more than free elections, civil liberties, representative institutions, and an independent judiciary; it also involves the growth and development of civil, religious, and professional associations and trade unions—self-sufficient both organizationally and economically—that lie beyond the control of the state and are safeguarded by the rule of law. Civil society implies the existence of an active part of the population able and willing to assume responsibility for some aspects of public life. It is essential for the development of East European democracy. But just as essential is *civic vigilance,* the commitment to defend the emerging civil society from the danger that it faces.

Despite their failings, all of the East European states had a degree of civil society between the two world wars. As George Schöpflin has written:

> The pre-war politics of Central and Eastern Europe were ruled by authoritarian rather than by totalizing, legitimating, ideologies.

> The old elites relied on a mixture of traditional and charismatic legitimation, and they never sought to encompass all the spheres of social activity. Nor did they profess any over-arching ideology, except nationalism, and nationalism left some space for social initiatives. This made it possible for a range of activities—oppositional newspapers, non-state education, nascent trade unions and oppositional political parties—to exist, albeit often under pressure from an expanding state.[7]

These activities had been effectively submerged under communism by the end of the 1940s, and, generally speaking, societal activity remained submerged until the 1980s. Institutions under communism such as parliaments, trade unions, and cultural associations were transmission belts, directing society rather than fostering its development. Apart from the Prague Spring of 1968, the big exception to this rule was Poland. Not only the Polish uprisings of 1956, 1970, 1976, and 1980–81, but a situation after 1956 in which the reemergence of the Catholic Church and the almost full reemergence of the private peasantry put an effective end to any regime aspirations toward totalitarianism. Periodically, there also was considerable vigor among Polish cultural institutions, student bodies, and even political groupings. The emergence of KOR (the Workers' Defense Committee) in 1976 helped remake the alliance between intellectuals and workers. Most important of all, the election of the "Polish pope," Karol Wojtyła, in 1978 galvanized society and helped lead to the foundation of Solidarity in 1980 that changed the face of Poland and of Europe during the next decade. Even after the suppression of Solidarity as an organization in December 1981, its survival and example resulted in a burgeoning of independent and semi-independent activity in Poland.[8]

No other East European country could compare with Poland in the development of an active civil society. Hungary eventually passed more liberal laws on the right of association, but the Poles were the masters in self-organization.[9] In Hungary, no matter how relaxed the political, social, and cultural atmosphere, there were few "publics" carving out spheres of activity for themselves. But a very large private space grew in the shape of a secondary, often family, economy into which many Hungarians were sucked during the 1980s, eager, first, to make ends meet, and then to enjoy the wide range of goods and travel opportunities available. The regime encouraged an activity that simultaneously spurred the economy and—it hoped—dulled the political senses.

In communist Czechoslovakia the rudiments of civil society began to develop in the early 1960s. These cohered and multiplied during the Prague Spring, only to be virtually crushed by the Soviet-led invasion. Some of the fragments that remained of the Spring evolved into organized dissent in the Czech Lands after 1977 (Charter 77), which, following spasmodic persecutions, further evolved into open rebellion at the end of the 1980s. In Slovakia individual Catholic priests also suffered severe persecution. But state and society under Husák fashioned an arrangement that gave citizens a large measure of private freedom in relatively good economic conditions. In Bulgaria there was nothing, till ecological and other societies sprouted during the very last years of the Zhivkov regime.[10] In Albania and Romania there was nothing at all. Yugoslavia was a special case. To a Leninist like Tito the very notion of civil society was incomprehensible, but it thrived periodically in every republic, eventually mixing with nationalism in a heady brew.[11]

In postcommunist Eastern Europe an explosion of civil society took place. But what counts for the future is whether it all can cohere and be focused on the development of liberal democracy. For democracy to develop, in the face of many severe, inevitable, and healthy competitions of interest, the paramount prerequisite is a mutuality of purpose, a shared frame of reference among all social classes — intellectuals, the rising entrepreneurial class, workers, and peasants. The best available model to be reached for — even if never actually grasped — would be the social alliance that came into being after World War II in West Germany.

But so far few signs of such mutuality have developed anywhere. Where mutuality had existed, particularly between intellectuals and workers during the heat of the fray in 1989, it largely had dissolved. At times, Poland, Bulgaria, and Romania have been beset by serious labor unrest. In Czechoslovakia a relatively good social climate had been preserved because of good economic management and generous social welfare benefits. But would the same be the case in an independent Slovakia? Would it be, in the longer run, even in the Czech Republic? Most Hungarians were worse off economically than they had been before 1989, but a precarious social peace was being maintained in Hungary. Again, though, for how long? In Romania the Jiu Valley miners in their periodic descents on Bucharest had on two such occasions brought the country perilously close to civil war. In every country, part of the worker resentment seemed to be directed as much against the new entrepreneurial class as against the government. This general lack of social consensus appeared likely to persist until those improvements being registered in parts of the economy (at least in some countries, see chapter 5) became reflected in wage packets with better buying power. Despite the widespread resentment of successful entrepreneurs, many people in all of the Eastern European countries were prepared to put up with deteriorating social conditions as long as they had some hope of buying the plentiful consumer goods that were now available largely through the doings of these entrepreneurs. If the point was ever reached where they could not attain such purchasing ability, if these goods soared beyond the reach of large sections of the community, then, not just spasms but long periods of serious social trouble were more than likely to occur.

The Escape Urge

After forty years of grimness and grayness, after 1989 as well as before it, escapism has assumed various forms throughout the region. Get-rich-quick dreams have been mentioned in chapter 1, but emigration was a still more actual means of escape. In 1989 and 1990 an estimated 1.2 million East Europeans left their homes for the West;[12] estimates in 1992 were that some 2 million more would leave.[13] Many did not *intend* to emigrate permanently: a few years away, material and mental enrichment, and then return, better-equipped to serve self and country. That was the idea—or the excuse—for going. How many actually would return was open to question; many of the more enterprising, those who could "make it," would not. The contrast with seventy years earlier could not have been greater. After World War I many emigrants returned to their new or newly created countries—a higher percentage than are doing so now. And after 1989 the number of leavers would have been much greater than it was but for Western immigration restrictions. To take the best-known and saddest example: if the shiploads of Albanians had not been returned from Bari in Italy in the summer of 1991 (see chapter 8), within several months few young people would have been left in Albania.[14]

If anything, the general urge to emigrate was becoming stronger. A survey conducted by the Demoscop Public Opinion Research Institute in Warsaw in early 1992 found that 62 percent of those questioned between the ages of eighteen and twenty-four wanted to leave Poland permanently: in the age group from fifteen to seventeen years 50 percent wanted to.[15] Economic conditions undoubtedly were a key reason; a sense of anticlimax and frustrated ambition also played roles. Youthful restlessness was bound to surge, anyway, after communism's stunting blight (although both Poland and Hungary had been liberal in allowing Western travel). Television, too, played its unsettling part. The West now came into most East Europeans' living rooms. The same television that played such an important role in hastening the end of communism was now making the postcommunism revolution all the more difficult.[16]

Apathy and Its Consequences

Societal apathy, especially toward the political process, was, like emigration, a form of dissociation or alienation. But by the end of 1993 it was, at least as reflected in voter turnout, confined to Poland and Hungary. In Poland it had been a worrying symptom right from the beginning. Voter turnout was only about 60 percent in the first parliamentary elections in June 1989.[17] Some abstentions probably resulted from disgust over the "arranged" nature of the poll: the built-in 65 percent procommunist majority. But in the second presidential election round in December 1990 the vote was just above 53 percent;[18] in the parliamentary elections in October 1991 it was just under 42 percent.[19] In the September 1993 elections, however, it rose to just over 52 percent. In Hungary about two-thirds of the electorate voted in the first round of the March–April parliamentary elections in 1990, but only 45.5 percent cast ballots in the second, a disappointing proportion for the first free Hungarian elections since 1946.[20] In subsequent by-elections, moreover, the numbers got as low as 10 percent and rarely reached 25 percent.[21]

Elsewhere in Eastern Europe voter participation was much higher. It touched 96 percent in the Czechoslovak parliamentary elections in June 1990. But in the second parliamentary elections exactly two years later it dropped to about 85 percent.[22] In Romania the turnout dropped from about 86 percent in June 1990 to about 76 percent in the parliamentary elections of September 1992.[23] In Bulgaria more than 90 percent of the electorate voted in the first round of the parliamentary elections in June 1990,[24] and a respectable 80 percent voted in October 1991.[25] In Albania a record 98.92 percent voted in December 1990, while the figure was just above 90.35 percent in March 1992.[26]

Why, then, Hungary and Poland and not (yet?) the others? Part of the reason was because in both these countries the destruction of the communist regimes was a drawn-out process. Hence, by the time free elections came, much political excitement had been expended. Later, the continuing drop in voter turnout resulted from increasing skepticism about the potency of the ballot box, a variation on the "them" and "us" syndrome. In Hungary, too, a feeling grew on the part of the electorate that the parliament represented the political/intellectual establishment in Budapest more than it did the country as a whole.[27] Czechoslovakia's 96 percent turnout in June 1990 was a referendum against a communist regime that had been upended only a few months before. In effect, the democratic fever was still raging. The drop two years later was universally expected. The fever had abated; disappointment had caused skepticism. Czechoslovakia, too, as a state, was literally winding down. After the split at the beginning of 1993, it would be intriguing to see how many Czechs and Slovaks vote in their now different republics. (General elections were legally due in both countries only in 1996, but communal elections were due in 1994.) The Czechs always have been political animals, and voting there might continue high. But politics mean much less to Slovaks, and in Slovakia, for a number of reasons, the poll could be disappointingly low.

In the Balkans the huge turnouts in the first elections were not, as they were in Czechoslovakia, referendums against the communist system. On the contrary, they were partly to be explained by old communist habits lingering on, like mass voting and conformity, especially in the rural areas. There was a large procommunist, as well as anticommunist, vote. The results in Romania, Bulgaria, and Albania also reflected the tenacity of the conservative psyche, regardless of the issues or contestants. In the second set of elections, though—Bulgaria: October 1991, Albania: March 1992, Romania: September 1992—voting was still at a high level. This was mainly because, with the opposition parties now more coherent, a wider choice was offered. Bulgaria and Albania opted for a change, and the communists (now socialists) lost. In Romania, with its simultaneous presidential elections, the situation was more complicated. There was no real change, but, at least, competitive politics had made their debut.

In future there seemed the real danger of voter apathy spreading to most East European countries, reflecting an increasing dissociation from public life. Politics could, therefore, be left by default in the hands of a relatively small new ruling class, atop a narrowly based pyramid of public support, as had often been the case in pre-World War II Eastern Europe, and in the communist era, too, when the massive obligatory turnouts at elections were but the cover for oligarchic rule.

During several conversations I had with intellectuals in Eastern Europe in 1991 and 1992, this possibility was discussed. Some explicitly or implicitly welcomed the prospect. Power, they claimed, was rightly theirs by tradition and by right of superior knowledge and broader, balanced perspective. Others regretted such a prospect, but many of them viewed it as an inescapable fact of life. Popular apathy would necessitate it. Power, therefore, which ideally should be shared, would, willy-nilly, become concentrated.

If concentration occurred, it would be disappointing after the enthusiasm of 1989. But some "realists" already were looking on the bright side. Concentration would, they argued, help stabilize a volatile, potentially disorderly situation. And, if the form and substance of representative democracy were to be preserved, a market economy secured, ethnic and international tensions reduced, then rule by the few was preferable to misrule by the mob. Such concentration would achieve what many Americans see as the blessing of their own 50–55 percent turnouts: keeping power in the hands of those who know, care, and own. Anything much higher than a 50 percent turnout would open the gates to the great unwashed.

The argument was plausible, but great dangers were involved. The "them" and "us" gulf would be deepened and perpetuated. Sooner or later, the self-disenfranchised also could resort to extra-systemic, violent methods to achieve their ends, or simply to vent their anger. They also could become prey to antidemocratic or nationalistic demagogy from the right or the left. Again, the pre-World War II situation. The humiliations and privations of forty years of communism would have availed little.

Movements Decompose, Parties Take Shape

Soon after the fall of communism, two apparently contradictory developments occurred in political organization within East European countries. As repression gave way to self-expression, scores, even hundreds, of political parties, groups, or grouplets sprouted overnight. In Romania in 1991, for example, more than two hundred organizations emerged, of which 141 were officially registered to contest elections.[28]

This shardlike profusion was accompanied by the presence, or the emergence, of large, mostly ramshackle political conglomerates, or "unity" organizations. They were Solidarity in Poland; the Hungarian Democratic Forum (HDF) in Hungary; the Civic Forum in Czechoslovakia (called Public Against Violence in Slovakia); the Union of Democratic Forces (UDF) in Bulgaria; and the National Salvation Front (NSF) in Romania. The first four were democratic movements, while the NSF in Romania contained a bewildering mixture of political currents, dominated by former communists and supported by many adherents of the old Ceauşescu regime as the best means of saving their skins and their jobs. All except the UDF in Bulgaria came to power immediately, with UDF having to wait till Bulgaria's second parliamentary election in October 1991 before being able to do so.

Even by early 1991 the situation among political organizations throughout Eastern Europe was beginning to change. The proliferation of pigmy parties began to be checked, and their numbers now would decrease. Electoral laws (except at first in Poland) required a minimum percentage of support at the polls before parliamentary representation was possible. This requirement introduced an element of sobering pragmatism into political life. At the same time, the big political conglomerates themselves began to crack. Solidarity did so with spectacular acrimony; Civic Forum did so with rather more (Czech) restraint, but still with much malevolence. The Romanian National Salvation Front split in two, also acrimoniously, well before the parliamentary elections in September 1992. The Hungarian Democratic Forum preserved its apparent unity till the summer of 1992, when its nationalist wing openly challenged its more moderate center.

The first trend was good—the reduction or concentration of the splinters; and Poland, too, adopted an election law that brought some sense into its electoral procedures. The second—the breakup of the unwieldy conglomerates—was inevitable. In the long run, it also would be good, injecting some realism into the political scene. Most of the East European states, though, seemed headed for a protracted period of *coalition governments.* These could have their advantages; at least they often reflected the popular will better than single-party governments. Nor, in themselves, need coalition governments be weak and unstable. But they do need a degree of calm and consensus in public life that was hardly present in postcommunist Eastern Europe. Indeed, the bitterness and, often, irresponsibility was such as to raise the question whether any consensual framework could *ever* be fashioned. In fact, by early 1993 political responsibility throughout much of the region seemed to be deteriorating. In Poland Wałęsa and his enemies were locked in an enervating and demeaning battle. In Hungary there was the Csurka phenomenon; in Slovakia the political primitivism as represented by Vladimír Mečiár. There was a coarsening of political conduct in the Czech Republic; often venomous disarray in Romania; petty antagonisms and vindictiveness in Bulgaria; plain backwardness in Albania. In no country was there much to suggest the evolution of a constructive political culture. What was developing was combative, not competitive, politics. It was often a form of political barbarity, of skinhead public conduct, giving consolation only to those already resigned to the authoritarian recourse.

Governmental attitudes toward the media were also a depressing reminder of how much still needed to be done. The media existed primarily to serve the government and report its views. Despite all of the protestations about press freedoms, this conviction was deeply held. Manipulation, therefore, was what governmental policy amounted to — skillfully applied in, say, the Czech Republic, fairly skillfully in Poland, crudely in Slovakia, hypocritically in Hungary, blatantly in Croatia and Serbia. Television was mainly in state hands, anyway, and the governments were doing their best to keep it that way.[29] The need for a vigorously independent, and responsible, press was, therefore, all the greater. There were good newspapers in all of the East European states, playing a constructive role. But even these often let their standards of responsibility and restraint slip. There also were some excellent, independent-minded journalists, although their work often betrayed a didactic, opinionated approach — the unholy combination of communist journalistic practice and the European continental tradition.

Right, Left, and Center

As previous political figurations were fading and new ones were emerging, the old concepts of "left" and "right" in politics needed reexamining, particularly as they applied to economic and social questions. It is a complex subject worthy of closer and more exhaustive study. The following three points indicate the complexity of the issue:

(1) Left of center did not necessarily imply a policy of greater state intervention in *economic* affairs. In the Czech Lands it still continued to do so, but in Hungary, for example, the Hungarian Democratic Forum, generally a center-right to far-right formation, was more interventionist than were the Alliance of Free Democrats and the Federation of Democratic Youth, whose economic policy was more Thatcherite or Reaganite—or, at least, more liberal in the classical sense. In Poland, too, some "conservative" forces, that is, those represented in the Olszewski government in 1992, were, by inclination, much less devoted to "the market" than were some of the groupings that they constantly were denouncing as "leftist." ("Leftist," of course, was a useful polemical adjective because to many it smacked of communism.) In Poland the Church, adhering to a traditional Catholic doctrine and especially to Pope John Paul II's strong views on the subject, was markedly interventionist.[30] Generally, too, the center-right to far-right parties throughout Eastern Europe were, on national grounds, more leery of Western ownership in the economy.

(2) On social issues—divorce, women's emancipation, particularly abortion—"left" did mean liberal and "right" conservative. (Still, liberal thinking on some of these issues could be found among conservative groupings.) In general, the liberal "left" in Poland and Hungary stood for more social and individual freedom. The left also tended to be anticlerical in the historic sense.

(3) On nationalism there was a meeting of the minds between some members of burgeoning far-right, avowedly nationalist parties and the far-left, "socialist" parties. This conjunction had been evident so far in Slovakia, Bulgaria, Romania, Serbia, and possibly Albania (see chapter 6). In Poland and Hungary the erstwhile communists, however, still shunned the nationalist right.

Some of the old political labels, therefore, were now anachronistic and misleading. The whole pattern was in flux. It would take time before it settled. When it did, new political definitions would be needed.

Personalities, Parliaments, and Power

Thus, the void left after communist rule was proving difficult to fill. Representative democratic institutions were quickly erected and procedures adopted. But in some important respects they were symbols for the future rather than reflections of the present. They were "ahead" of the popular political consciousness, or maturity—aspirations, sometimes, rather than realizations. Many East Europeans had thought of postcommunism in terms of a quick fix, whereas democratic procedures promise anything but.

Personalities can play an important role in such situations. Political leaders are a means by which citizens can interact with authority, identify with it, support or oppose it. Personalities also can provide much-needed reassurance to societies that have lost their moorings. Wałęsa in Poland and Havel in Czechoslovakia at first admirably filled that need.[31] They had proved themselves in the struggle against communism and had presided over the immediate transition with sureness of touch. Elsewhere, there were no personalities of such immediately recognized stature. In Hungary, where representative government had been ushered in gently and soon was working well, there was no real need for charisma at the helm. And Premier József Antall certainly provided none. But he had character, a capacity to conciliate, and real political skills.[32] In Romania President Ion Iliescu was clearly the ablest political figure after 1989.[33] But in the polarized, paranoid atmosphere of postcommunist Romania, he often was divisive rather than cohesive. His former association with Ceauşescu meant that he never could hope for public legitimacy in the eyes of many Romanians. He had his back to the wall from his first day in office, and though he comfortably won two presidential elections, he remained a bitterly contested figure. The president of Bulgaria, by contrast, though once a communist, had actively opposed and been victimized by the regime. Zhelyu Zhelev was as dull as Antall, but he was more amenable, with a quiet dignity that won respect abroad as well as at home.[34] On the other hand, Sali Berisha, "Salu," as he was universally known, elected president of Albania in March 1992, exuded charisma. How much consistency existed behind the flamboyance remained to be seen.[35]

This, then, was Eastern Europe's first postcommunist leadership lineup—a mixture of effulgence and dullness, of world figures and provincial unknowns. But all of them, except Berisha, were by early 1993 becoming eclipsed or controversial figures. Both Wałęsa and Havel were suffering from their own leadership deficiencies, combined with political and institutional frustrations. Wałęsa was a fingertip politician, a tribune of the plebs, a folk hero, and more intelligent than some Polish intellectuals would give him credit for—more politically intelligent, in fact, than many of them were. Nor was he ever afraid of making the big decision. But he often lacked both vision and plain managerial competence. His primitive egoism and arrogance also offended many followers (see chapter 3). Havel's problem was different. He was no politician at all, cerebral or fingertip, floundering when firmness was needed, impetuous when caution was required. He was always a beacon of moral wisdom and sincerity—admired, respected, liked. But the dissolution of Czechoslovakia was a devastating defeat for him, and already by the end of 1992 he was coming to be regarded as one of yesterday's men, along with his other fellow dissidents. In the provincial rough and tumble of Czech politics he was often resented for the very qualities for which he had once been admired, especially his courage in the face of communist oppression. Most Czechs had shown little such courage, and Havel was an awkward reminder for them. He also represented a fairness and a conciliatory attitude that many Czechs either could not understand or found intimidating. In Hungary, Antall, weakened by a serious illness from which he soon died, his government deeply divided and slipping dangerously in the opinion polls, was nowhere near the preeminently respected figure he had been only two years before. Zhelev was caught up in a battle with the opposition United Democratic Front which regarded him as power-hungry, on the one side, and far too lenient toward former communists, on the other. Iliescu, with his background, would always be suspect, even if his services to postcommunist Romania eventually might be recognized.

Institutions and Procedures

But political leaders are often only as good as their institutions let them be. It was not just his own personality and the vindictiveness of others that were hampering Wałęsa. He was practically immobilized by a fractious parliament and a constitution that, until its partial reform late in 1992, caused incessant haggling about the division of governmental powers. Poland was now reaping the *dis*advantages of its jump start against the communist system in 1989, when discretion seemed the better part of valor. The *Proporz* Sejm, communist-dominated by agreement, "elected" in 1989 over the voters' overwhelming democratic preference, proceeded to obstruct practically every move toward effective democratic government, several moves suggested by Wałęsa himself. Later, the fully democratic parliamentary elections in October 1991 returned a fragmented parliament, and not until the second half of 1992, with the formation of the coalition government of Hanna Suchocka, was there any real cooperation between president and government. The powers of the government also were strengthened by some constitutional and procedural changes. But then the Suchocka government was defeated in the spring of 1993 by a capricious and irresponsible vote, and new elections were called. It was still too early to say for sure whether the nightmare scenario for Poland—a return to the anarchy of pre-1926 politics, before Piłsudski took matters into his own hands—had been totally banished.

The Czechoslovak case, until the state's collapse at the end of 1992, was complicated by the federal state structure, the existence of three parliaments—Federal, Czech, and Slovak (see chapter 3). The last two would have been jealous of their prerogatives at the best of times, but the Slovak Question from the beginning of 1991 to the end of 1992 virtually paralyzed Czechoslovak politics. Havel eventually became fully aware of the danger and of the need for a more equal status for Slovakia within the federation. But the Slovak Question was proving intractable. Whether it ever could have been solved through workable institutional and procedural changes that still maintained a constitutional link was questionable. In the event, that approach never was tried.

Antall was made to look effective for so long partly because representative parliamentary government was working better in Hungary. Antall's own party (or grouping), the Hungarian Democratic Forum, won an impressive plurality in the 1990 elections, and its mandate was scheduled to last till 1994. But as early as the middle of 1992, as mentioned, the centrifugal tendencies within the Forum became obvious to the general public—as well as to the world. The Alliance of Free Democrats, the strongest opposition party, also was plagued by leadership problems. There were serious constitutional difficulties as well. From the beginning Antall was the only leading East European national figure who was premier, not president, and the constitution blurred parts of the dividing line between his powers and those of the president, Árpád Göncz, a Free Democrat.[36] The two men were personally and politically incompatible—and Hungarian public life suffered.

In Bulgaria, in a political culture lower than Hungary's, the parliamentary system always seemed less stable. After the victory of the Union of Democratic Forces (UDF) in October 1991, the new ruling coalition was uneasy and divided, and many, though by no means all, opposition socialists, still prisoners of their old communist instincts, could not adapt to competitive politics. Moreover, the large Turkish minority, whose parliamentary representation was becoming a key factor in Bulgarian parliamentary life, injected an ethnic factor into Bulgarian politics that did not exist in Hungary. One Bulgarian privately described his country's politics to me as a "mine field." A year later his description was vindicated when the UDF government fell apart, and political life was thrown into disarray. The mine field had exploded (see chapter 4). Still, taking the Balkans as a yardstick, Bulgarian politics were faring better than many had expected, and Bulgaria was still being called the Balkan "oasis."

Figures of Transition

In historical perspective, all of the immediate postcommunist leaders in Eastern Europe will be seen as transitional. But some have been more constructively transitional than others, in the sense that they helped complete, or further, a process, which, without them, might not have occurred — at least not as peacefully as it did. Initially, some may have seen themselves, not as men of transition, but of destiny. But, even in the former, more mundane capacity, their place in history will have been secured.

The most recognizable cases have been those former communist leaders, holdovers from the previous era, who presided over the transfer of power and helped bring their countries into the postcommunist era. And they did this, not in any sense of embracing the new order, but by accepting the inevitable and by knowingly using their authority to make the transition smoother. The most obvious cases were Milan Kučan in Slovenia, and in Albania, Ramiz Alia, Enver Hoxha's successor from 1985 as both head of state and party leader. Judging by the relatively smooth way in which Slovenia evolved into parliamentary democracy and then into independence, Kučan, former communist party leader and then democratically elected president, probably will be judged by history as the most successful transitional figure in the entire region. Alia was the first president of postcommunist Albania, elected in its first free election in March 1991 and then defeated in the second vote one year afterward.[37] It could, of course, be argued that what Alia presided over was not so much transition as chaos. But chaos was better than civil war, which well might have broken out but for his perceptiveness and restraint.

Ion Iliescu unquestionably will go down in history as the key transitional figure in Romania. Stability in postcommunist Romania has been more precarious than anywhere else in Eastern Europe (outside Yugoslavia and Albania), and at times Iliescu's actions appeared to make it still more precarious. But without him, Romania might have slipped into civil war. The question now is whether Iliescu can become something more than a transitional figure—a constructive statesman leading Romania toward a prosperous democracy. (His presidential term lasts till 1996.) Such an optimistic prognosis is more than doubtful; but Romania's problem is that no one else in public life looks equal to the task. In Bulgaria, Andrei Lukanov, though not as clearly as in the cases of Kučan, Ramiz Alia, and Iliescu, was also a key transitional figure. His communist mind-set was unmistakable, but he was not inflexible, and, during his short but crucial tenure as socialist premier during 1991, he came to realize that the old order was irretrievable and the new one irreversible. He also, with some success, tried to persuade some of his followers to think—and act—likewise.

These communist holdovers are obvious cases. But Wałęsa and Havel are figures of transition, too. Their permanent place in history is assured—more, though, for what they did before, during, and immediately after 1989, than for what they tried to do afterward. Their true greatness lay in the communist, not in the postcommunist, era. Essentially, their own limitations weakened their role in postcommunist Eastern Europe. Had Wałęsa been content from then on to play the role of elder statesman, counseling rather than domineering, his crucial services to his country might have continued indefinitely. But he would not have been Wałęsa if he had. The limelight had to be his; the twilight was for others. His hero was Piłsudski—a great man but the wrong sort of model for postcommunist Poland. Wałęsa's humiliation at the September 1993 elections in Poland should have been the signal to him that Poland had outgrown him (see chapter 3). Havel's case is more poignant. His hero was Tomáš Masaryk—a much better example in the circumstances than Piłsudski. But, as just mentioned, Havel was overcome by a combination of his own political deficiencies and the character and developing mood of the Czech and Slovak publics.

The prestige that he restored to the Czech reputation, and his own personal nobility, however, were indispensable in the first year of Czechoslovakia's freedom.

Figures of Disruption

There remains to discuss another type of political figure shooting up from the East European soil that is currently so fertile for him: the demagogue. He had been present from day one of Eastern Europe's postcommunist history. Tymiński and Ganchev were prime examples. But they were ephemeral figures. Wałęsa himself, at his worst, has been the demagogue par excellence, but most of the time there obviously was more to him than that.

Like all demagogues, the postcommunist type not only appealed to the passions but tapped a core of legitimate desire and justified grievance. In the early 1990s Eastern Europe presented a broad choice of demagogue—ranging from bigger to smaller. In Poland several of the smaller variety were sprouting up with the decommunization issue. Vladimír Mečiár, the "father" of Slovak independence, always had been one of the bigger.[38] For the sake of his new country he would have to undo the reputation he had built. Petre Roman, prime minister of Romania till October 1991, was a mixture of statesman and demagogue, apparently driven by ambition and a pathetic determination to suppress his partly Jewish background.[39] But the most dangerous demagogue by far in Romania, and probably the whole of Eastern Europe, was Gheorghe Funar, mayor of Cluj in Transylvania, leader of the Party of Romanian National Unity (see chapter 6). At the same time Hungary was offering two prime examples of the species, one major, one minor. István Csurka gained worldwide notoriety for a neofascist racist tract published in August 1992. He became one of Hungary's most prominent politicians, a once and perhaps future threat to the developing democracy there (see chapter 3). József Torgyán, leader of the re-created Independent Smallholders, a party he proceeded to split, was of less consequence and caliber. But he combined a raucous nationalism with a genuine concern for his constituency, Hungary's resurrected private farming class. As such, he was never to be underestimated.[40] The possibility of his forming an alliance with Csurka represented a real danger. They might be personally incompatible—but politically?

The climate in Eastern Europe would continue to be propitious for demagogues. Nationalism, racism, decommunization, insecurity, confusion, economic misery, social envy, political passion and hatred—all of these existed in plenty. So, by and large, did a lack of developed political culture and an abundance of societal and private mistrust. Again, it was a race against time to achieve the minimum sufficiency in economics and the degree of political and civic coherence that would make demagogy irrelevant.

The Military: In or Out of Politics?

Historically, there is no consistent pattern of military involvement in East European politics. Poland after 1926 was subject to varying gradations of military rule; in Serbia and after 1918 in Yugoslavia the role of the military often was decisive; in Bulgaria and Romania, it occasionally was so. In Hungary and Czechoslovakia the military played virtually no role. Under communism, the military's task throughout the region was minimal, except in Hungary in 1956 and in Poland during and after December 1981. In 1965 a minor military conspiracy took place in Bulgaria, and in Romania the military, discontent with him for more than a decade, played an important role in defeating Ceauşescu in December 1989. The East European countries, therefore, did not generally have the tradition of active military intervention that existed in Latin America or even in Southern Europe. Political power sometimes may have depended more on the barracks than the ballot box, but the military remained mostly out of sight, if not out of mind.

Still, in the instability characterizing several East European countries after 1989, speculation about the role of the military was bound to increase. In Yugoslavia it became not so much speculation as a terrible reality (see chapter 7). In the rest of Eastern Europe it centered mainly on Romania, on whether the army would not just present its bill for its role in December 1989, but decide that it—and it alone—could cope with the ensuing instability. Would Romania suffer a military coup, would a strong military component move into government, or would an ostensibly civil government need the military crutch? General Victor Stănculescu, defense minister and then a key economics minister, was the object of much conjecture in 1990, an experience on which he appeared to thrive.[41] But he subsequently left the government and slid into obscurity. After the elections in September–October 1992, however, when Iliescu was voted president by a clear majority, parliament became even more fragmented. And with political life so polarized and precarious, and the sense of public responsibility so undeveloped, the danger of Romania finally becoming ungovernable was considerable. So was the danger of ethnic strife in Transylvania. These two possibilities, probably interacting, might invite a "military solution."

In neighboring Bulgaria such danger seemed considerably weaker. Serious discontent arose in the military itself at the abrupt decommunization campaign within the senior officer corps.[42] Indeed, the swiftness with which this campaign began may have suggested some civilian nervousness. A new professional officer lobby, the Rakovski Legion, also was founded toward the end of 1990. It was ostensibly a trade union, but some of its officers held strong nationalist views and were ideologically and temperamentally impatient with "democracy." It would have to be watched; some nervous Bulgarians feared it could possibly evolve into another Military League, the military grouping that backed the overthrow of the Agrarian leader, Stamboliski, in 1923 and took part in the *Zveno* officers' coup of 1934. But short of political or economic collapse in Bulgaria, military intervention, or even influential involvement, appeared remote. In the case, though, of weakness in the face of a threat to Bulgarian national interests relating, say, to the power of the Turkish minority, to Turkey itself, or perhaps—if international circumstances changed drastically—to Macedonia, then the military's influence in politics could grow rapidly.

In Albania the danger seemed greater. The new government in Tirana needed the armed forces, as well as the police, first to restore and then to preserve order. If it could not count on them, it would lose power. Similarly, if the government could not feed its population, it would be the loser. As in Romania—but probably more immediately—the last option might be the military. The civil disorder with which Albania would be threatened would make any civilian government beholden to the military. Moreover, the entire relationship with Kosovo, the increased Serbian repression there that could cause an uprising, the pressure for closer association, eventually for reunion, with Albania—any of these factors could bring the Albanian military to the fore. True, the military was in a state of considerable disarray after the fall of communism, but, largely thanks to American help, it was reviving. Relations with the newly independent state of Macedonia also were likely to be strained by the situation of the large Albanian minority there. Relations with Greece already were severely tested (see chapter 6). In short, both domestic and foreign affairs could combine to give the military a real influence in the affairs of postcommunist Albania.

In East Central Europe the possibilities of military intervention or involvement have appeared to be much less of a threat. In Poland in the spring of 1992 speculation flurried over a struggle between Wałęsa, as president, and the government, specifically the defense ministry, for control over the military. Undoubtedly, in a manner less than propitiate, Wałęsa had been trying to whip up support for himself among senior officers, some of whom were alleged to be impatient with democratic government. (This rumored discontent, indeed, was hardly surprising since almost all of them were carryovers from communist rule.) The state of affairs that developed led to suspicions that Wałęsa might not just admire Marshal Piłsudski but might seek to emulate him. Jan Parys, the civilian minister of defense, made some thinly veiled insinuations and was then briefly rusticated. On his return he repeated and amplified the charges and was promptly dismissed.[43] The whole episode revealed more about the level of Polish public life than of the true state of civil-military relations.

In Hungary and Czechoslovakia the armed forces, such as they were, worried more about their very existence than about having any political influence. In Czechoslovakia, though, after the communist minister of defense's threat, shortly before the "velvet revolution," that the army would do its *socialist* duty, there was a hurry to remove him and his kind once the revolution was over. In the Czech lands the army would now do its "*democratic*" duty.[44] Newly independent, struggling Slovakia could not be so sure about its military. The civil order looked precarious, the economic situation perilous, and relations with Hungary still could worsen. It would be a disastrous confession of defeat for such a brand-new state to have recourse to the military. But Slovaks would see it as better than anarchy or oblivion.

To sum up. Four factors were likely to determine the role of the military in Eastern Europe and civil-military relations, generally: (1) the degree of political stability, a factor that could become increasingly relevant as economic reform bites into the social fabric; (2) the perceived threat to the national interest; (3) the scale and manner of the decommunization process in the officer corps, upward of 90 percent of whose members had been communist party members; (4)

officers' pay, perquisites, conditions, and prestige. Large-scale military discontent on any combination of these factors could undermine relations with the civil authority. Still, there seemed little danger, in the foreseeable future, of any East European government becoming as dependent on the military as the Russian government was after October 1993.

Decommunization: The Needs and the Dangers

Vergangenheitsbewältigung, introduced in chapter 1, needs amplification and closer examination — an all-pervasive factor that will not go away.

The past weighs heavily on Eastern Europe — the precommunist past as well as the communist. The latter needs to be overcome; so do some aspects of the former; others need coming to terms with; practically none ever can be recaptured. But the precommunist past is vague and impressionistic. The communist past is concentrated, focused, and immediately relevant to the issues of today. It overshadows public life. East Europeans may recover from this past more quickly than we think, but its influence will continue for at least a generation.

The communist past is a tangled web that hardly lends itself to dissection and categorization. Once the connection to that past is cut, its separate strands give no idea of the complexity of the whole. But with this disclaimer, one can identify several aspects of the past that are central to the issue of overcoming it.

First, there are those relating to individual behavior. Transcending all of them was the "moral pollution" stressed by Havel: the duplicity, deceit, hypocrisy, pretense, evasiveness, and betrayal that became widespread human characteristics under communism. These were partly due to the cultural impact of communism itself, a factor that Ken Jowitt has graphically described.[45] But they also partly resulted from resisting this impact and from the sheer necessity of surviving under communism. The insulation of the real self, to which many resorted, also induced a multisided apathy.

But that was in the private realm. Decommunization and its extension, the process of lustration, is very much a public issue and is one of extraordinary complexity.[46] First of all, decommunization of a certain type and to a certain extent was necessary. Communist criminals obviously had to be punished by means of a fair trial. For far too long former security officers were living undisturbed, on good pensions, while some of their victims were getting little compensation or none at all. But these were the most blatant cases. Within the economy, especially, numerous former communist officials retained posts of influence and profit. Two types needed to be distinguished in this nomenklatura "privatization" (although public opinion in Eastern Europe usually did not). There was the growing number of communist officials who genuinely became entrepreneurs and who, therefore, were aiding the efforts to reach a market economy and becoming part of the new middle class. No matter how galling their success might be, it eventually was beneficial to the new East European order. But in every East European country—as well as in every part of the former Soviet Union—a sinister communist "mafia" was at work in the economy, too. It spread its net far and wide throughout the embryonic economic system.

This mafia worked in several ways. First, communist managers often blocked the promotion of supporters of democratic change or even dismissed them when criticized. Second, they tended to fill vacant managerial positions with their friends from the party nomenklatura or with relatives of these friends. Third, former communist bureaucrats in local administration frequently relied on various means to make it difficult, if not impossible, for private entrepreneurs to set up private businesses. Fourth, local government officials appointed by the previous regime often collaborated with managers in enterprises to sabotage attempts to introduce reforms in a particular enterprise or region. Fifth, officials at various ministries often intentionally hindered the implementation of decisions taken by ministers.[47] This mafia obviously needed breaking up without delay, and there was considerable justice in the many complaints that it was proceeding far too slowly.

Some decommunization, therefore, was essential on moral and practical grounds. But, again on both moral and practical grounds, the process needed careful treatment, which it was not getting. In no country in Eastern Europe was the political culture developed enough for decommunization to be handled with the right blend of perspective, firmness, and fairness. Moreover, the inquisitorial mind-set, a variation on the communist mind-set, was turning out to be a characteristic not only of communists but of some of their most vociferous enemies. Demagogues galore swarmed over this issue. Those who were urging restraint often themselves fell under suspicion of collaboration. It was the McCarthy era in the United States, magnified beyond comprehension and distorted beyond recognition. Perhaps it was no coincidence that in Czechoslovakia where anticommunist activity had been minimal, the lustration pressure was very strong. (Czechoslovakia, though, especially the Czech lands, has a long history of lustration. Even before independence, in the nineteenth century, Czechs could be "dismissed from the nation" for lack of patriotism. And after 1918, 1945, 1968, and now after 1989, lustration has taken place—much of it necessary, some of it not.)

Indiscriminate decommunization carried four big dangers: (1) it jeopardized the establishment of the rule of law, enshrining the notion of collective guilt and rejecting the canon of due process; (2) it was further dividing rather than healing society; (3) it was a massive diversion from reconstruction; (4) it could deprive the new societies of much badly needed expertise.[48] In other words, it could derail the whole reconstruction process and lead to the negation of liberal democracy.

Dealing with the former communist *leaders* was a vexed question that was not being answered with any kind of consistency or dignity. A strong feeling emerged among many East Europeans that proceedings should be brought against their former leaders as both a symbol of moral justice and a signal of deterrence for the future. The problem was that nothing on the statute books referred to the crimes of repression with which the leaders had at least been associated. As a result, the few who were being put in the dock were charged only with much lesser crimes, the validity of which could be questioned and the triviality of which seemed absurd. In Romania several of Ceauşescu's underlings were sentenced for crimes during the brief, bloody rebellion against the old order. But in the rest of Eastern Europe things were not so clear-cut. Nothing as ludicrous as the Honecker fiasco in Berlin in early 1993 surfaced elsewhere. But in Bulgaria the trial and sentencing of Todor Zhivkov, and other former leaders, and in Albania of Nexhmije Hoxha, Enver's widow, brought justice not so much into disrepute as into ridicule. Generally, it was felt that these people were being tried for small crimes of which they were not guilty and not being tried for the huge crimes of which they were.

During the course of 1991, however, another aspect of overcoming the past began to dominate public life. This involved the old security apparatuses. The issue was not so much what they themselves had done during communist rule, but who had done it with them—their collaborators, stooges, and informants. The opening of the old GDR Stasi files created a sensation. Something similar threatened in Czechoslovakia when its police files were opened. In Romania it had been a public issue ever since Ceaușescu's death.[49]

In Poland the issue was used blatantly for political ends by the Olszewski government in the summer of 1992, and then it was used again several months later by Olszewski adherents, now out of office, in a concerted effort to destroy Wałęsa's reputation and drive him from office (see chapter 3).[50] It was constantly on the verge of exploding in Bulgaria and Hungary. Everywhere, these files were threatening to poison the well of public life in Eastern Europe. They were the biggest single factor in the surge of paranoia sweeping the entire region. It now was impossible to destroy them. Some already *had* been destroyed, mainly by the security police themselves; some apparently had been deliberately doctored. But any official attempts to destroy the remaining bulk of them would only generate more suspicion. The ideal solution would be for special commissions of inquiry to examine the files and pass judgment. But, assuming suitable people could be found for such tasks, would they be believed?

Backing into the Future?

Overcoming the past, then, was necessary. But the effort was fraught with danger that could prejudice the future. And some East Europeans were asking how long the process would take. Some political careers were being made on the premise that it would indeed be practically neverending. Most countries already had had two elections that had been fought mainly on the anticommunist issue, and it looked as if several more elections throughout the region would be run, at least in good measure, on decommunization issues. The past, therefore, could continue to dominate for years to come.

At some point, though, facing the future would have to take precedence and would have to involve the assumption of responsibility rather than shifting it. If real progress toward democracy and the market were to be sustained, citizens, not just political leaders, would have to assume the task. Communism left a deplorable legacy, and the vast majority of East Europeans are paying heavily for it. But blaming communists is not the quickest way to rid themselves of that legacy. It was becoming high time that they started blaming themselves for at least some present shortcomings. This crucial psychological obstacle had to be surmounted. Eastern Europe could not go into the twenty-first century still attacking the ghosts of the twentieth. Its more responsible leaders knew this to be the case. It was a painful message to deliver; but none was more necessary.

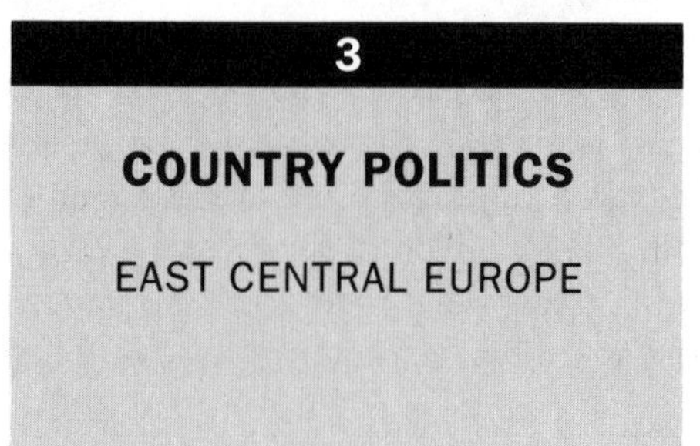

3

COUNTRY POLITICS

EAST CENTRAL EUROPE

"A triad of hope" was how the three East Central European countries — Czechoslovakia, Poland, and Hungary — were being described soon after the revolutionary changes of 1989. The expression was both descriptive and comparative, conveying a sense of optimism about the region itself and an unstated contrast with the countries of South Eastern Europe, which soon began to be associated, not so much with hope as with despair.

The hope was that the political and economic revolutions would be completed in these three countries, say, by the end of the century. This tacit timetable was based on the political culture and the civic traditions of the states concerned, however spotty, and the expected political and economic progress in the postcommunist era. Generally, the hope has remained realistic, but by the middle of 1993, in terms of both its fulfillment and the time it would take, the optimism had become considerably more sober. Economic progress might now be more confidently predicted, but political progress remained problematic, patchy at best. And Czechoslovakia, the country from which probably the most had been expected, had disappeared from the map of Europe. Slovakia, from the moment of its birth, became one of Eastern Europe's new problem children, and, as the following discussion shows, the new Czech Republic could have more basic problems than most observers (and most Czechs) first realized. Politics in Poland were plagued from the beginning by egoism, perversity, and irresponsibility, while in Hungary a provincial atavism returned after its submergence for nearly a half-century.

If unchecked, these dangers could divert and reverse the undoubted progress already made. Economic forecasters are fond of "phases" — phases of depression, stabilization, recovery, and so on. Specific years, too, are described as crucial, turning points, etc. Except when revolutions occur, this game is less useful when applied to political development, because politics are less tangible than economics. But with these reservations in mind, the years 1993 and 1994 could indeed be crucial, turning point years. They will show whether the Czech nation can begin to form a self-confident polity, whether Slovakia's birth pangs become symptoms of mortality, whether Polish politics can survive the death wish of many of its practitioners, and whether Hungary can finally come to terms, in a democratic way, with the adversities and injustices of the early part of the twentieth century.

CZECHOSLOVAKIA
From Deliverance to Dissolution

November 1989, the velvet revolution; January 1993 the not so velvet divorce, after seventy-four years of uneasy, once interrupted, marriage. What the world had watched with admiration, it now observed with sadness and a certain disbelief. The only consolation was that Czechoslovakia was not like Yugoslavia. But that was setting the sights rather low. What happened?

It really was a question of what never happened. Slovakia never could fulfill its own sense of identity coupled with the Czech Lands, as some politically articulate Slovaks had hoped it could after World War I. An integral part of Hungary for a thousand years and subject, especially during the nineteenth century, to a ruthless campaign of Magyarization, Slovaks were considered unripe for independence in 1918. Indeed, a slow national reawakening during the nineteenth century had occurred, but it was still confined to a tiny elite. The great mass of Slovaks, politically, economically, and culturally primitive, with little national self-consciousness, in the shadow of a large Hungarian community that saw itself a *Herrenvolk* and often behaved like one, were manifestly *not* in a position to avail themselves of the principle of national self-determination that the victors of World War I so inconsistently imposed. The safest course — the only course — therefore, was association with the Czechs in a single state, and this necessary outcome was understood by the tiny Slovak elite. Ethnically and linguistically, the two nations were strikingly similar, like the Serbs and the Croats who also were about to be joined in a multinational state.

But like the Serbs and the Croats, the Czechs and the Slovaks had strikingly dissimilar histories. Although the Czechs had lost their political, religious, and cultural independence to the Habsburgs in the early seventeenth century, their fate under the Austrians was infinitely less unfortunate than that of the Slovaks under the Hungarians. Besides enjoying a considerable degree of political autonomy, which facilitated their great national reawakening in the nineteenth century, the Czechs experienced an economic expansion that made Bohemia and Moravia the workshop of the Habsburg empire and one of the most advanced industrial regions in Europe.

The Czechs were advanced and the Slovaks backward by any European yardstick. The Czechs tended to be materialistic, freethinking, or they took their Roman Catholicism rather lightly, whereas most Slovaks were deeply Catholic and much less tolerant than Czechs. It was a relationship that was bound to see the dominance of one nation over the other. This occurred despite the fact that Tomáš Masaryk had promised Slovakia autonomy in the Pittsburgh Agreement of 1918 that paved the way for the establishment of Czechoslovakia.[1] Masaryk's failure to keep his promise was to become the first big Slovak grievance against the Czechs and against Czechoslovakia. Masaryk, however, may have had good reasons for ignoring his previous commitment. Granting the Slovaks autonomy would have led to demands from the Germans in the new Czechoslovakia, as well as by the Hungarians in Slovakia, for autonomy of their own. The new state, therefore, would have been fragmented almost from its inception. There was, too, in those first heady years of independence an undoubted Czech aggressiveness toward Germans and a sense of superiority toward Slovaks—a provincial chauvinism hardly conducive to far-seeing generosity. Whatever the reason, it was played on by the gathering forces of Slovak nationalism as proof that the Czechs could not be trusted. Masaryk and most Czech politicians became, in fact, strong "*Czechoslovakists,*" playing down to the point of oblivion the differences between the two nations. But "Czechoslovakism" meant, in effect, Czech domination, a reality seen not only in a Czech preponderance in the central government institutions and procedures but of the economic and educational systems within Slovakia itself. The Czechs could argue—correctly—that very few Slovaks were qualified; but they often behaved as if there were even fewer than there were.

Mutual Recrimination

But the growing Slovak resentment in the 1920s and 1930s against Czech dominance and domineering was to be matched by the Czech sense of disillusion over Slovak behavior in 1938 and 1939, when Czechoslovakia was being dismembered by Nazi Germany and others, and then, throughout World War II. The Slovak republic from 1939 until 1945 under German patronage and under the presidency of Father Josef Tiso left a sense of treachery and betrayal among Czechs that soured relations for the future. But even for the considerable number of Slovaks who had strong reservations about it, the Tiso republic was the first modern expression of Slovakia's statehood, and this fact alone made it an important step in the historical progress of their nation.

After World War II, therefore, the feelings between Czechs and Slovaks were bitter and recriminatory. And after the communist seizure of power in February 1948, the bitterness continued, barely covered by the cloak of fraternalism. The Prague "centralists" hunted down alleged Slovak "bourgeois nationalists" in the early 1950s. The most prominent of them, Vladimír Clementis, former foreign minister, was executed, and Gustáv Husák, later party leader and president, together with his friend and famous communist poet and politician, Laço Novomeský, were sentenced initially to life imprisonment in 1954. Subsequently, the trappings of Slovak party and state autonomy were whittled away until, after the promulgation of the new Czechoslovak "socialist" constitution of 1960, that autonomy became little more than an outer shell.

In the course of the 1960s it was increased Slovak communist agitation against this intensification of Prague "centralism" that seriously weakened the hard-line regime of the Czechoslovak leader, Antonín Novotný, which eventually fell at the beginning of 1968.[2] Slovak agitation, therefore, helped prepare the ground for the Prague Spring, an interaction that seemed to be reflected in the election of the Slovak Alexander Dubček as Novotný's successor. But it was precisely at this moment of apparent mutuality that the basic differences between the Czech and the Slovak attitudes to reform emerged. For Czech reformers the Prague Spring meant political and economic reform; for Slovaks it meant national emancipation. For the Czechs it meant, in effect, moving away from Soviet ideological tutelage; for the Slovaks it meant moving away primarily from Czech domination. That was the logic of the historical situation. It was not that the Slovaks detested the Czechs more than the Soviets—rather that the given situation gave them the opportunity to achieve certain goals but not others. Distancing themselves from the Czechs seemed possible, emancipating themselves from the Soviets did not.

Had the great Czechoslovak reform not been aborted in August 1968, these basic differences of approach might have been eased. Federal status for Slovakia, one of the big reforms of the Prague Spring and the only one surviving (however limply) the post-August "normalization," could have been contained within the broader, state-wide, political and economic reforms that were being enacted or planned. But the Soviet-led invasion shattered this hope. The crushing of reform induced a mood of bitter despondency among Czechs of all classes, especially the intelligentsia, and the urge to find scapegoats. After the reform-communist leaders, who were rounded on for raising hopes "bound" to be shattered, the Slovaks seemed the obvious culprits to be blamed by the Czechs for "letting them down" yet again. The Slovaks had seen the Prague Spring as a national rather than a democratic opportunity—one with anti-Czech overtones. And what they gained was not totally lost. Slovakia kept its federal status and, during the whole normalization process, enjoyed a much easier regime than did the Czechs.[3] Many Czechs, therefore, again felt betrayed by the "ingrate" Slovaks.

The Distancing

After 1968, though, a new element steadily entered into the Czech-Slovak relationship. Since 1918 the Czechs, whatever else they were to the Slovaks, had always been relevant to them. Slovakia as the weaker partner needed Czech help and, although many Slovaks would contest this judgment, the Czechs had not been ungenerous in giving it. The help proffered, however, and the manner with which it was often disbursed, made many Slovaks not only less than grateful: it deepened their inferiority complex toward Czechs. Many observers during the interwar republic and during the 1950s and 1960s noticed the chip on the shoulder attitude of Slovaks toward Czechs, and it remained obvious in the post-World War II emigration. But after 1968

Slovakia became much more self-contained, more distant from the Czech Lands. After World War II there had been far fewer Czechs in the proliferating Slovak bureaucracy than before it, but now there were virtually none.[4] The senior jobs they used to fill were now taken by younger Slovak cadres. Politically, economically, culturally, and, above all, psychologically, Czechs and the Czech Lands simply became less relevant—and because less relevant, they also were deemed less superior. (Indeed, many Slovaks, anticommunist as well as communist, derived a snide satisfaction from the post-1968 Slovak power and influence in the Czechoslovak federation as a whole. The Slovak Husák was Czechoslovak party leader and, after 1975, president as well. Continuing a trend that had slowly begun in 1945, more and more Slovaks with their families moved to Prague in federal positions, causing complaint among Czechs historically used to all the traffic going the other way.) And as Czechs became less relevant, so Slovaks, particularly the younger generation, dropped the chips off their shoulders. Psychologically, Slovaks were moving into a preindependence phase. The Czechs were off their backs; now it should be the Soviets' turn.

In fact, getting other nations off their backs has been the main preoccupation of Slovaks throughout the twentieth century. In their search for identity, they historically had to contend with the Hungarians; then after 1918 with the Czechs; then after 1948 with the Czechs and the Soviets. Soviet domination seemed a constant, but Czech domination was melting before their eyes and, as it did so, it tempered Slovak dissatisfaction with the communist system as a whole.

This tempering of the Slovaks' dissatisfaction partly explains why their participation in Czechoslovak dissident movements during the late 1970s and throughout the 1980s was so strikingly small. Not that there were many Czech dissidents, either, but what political dissidence in Czechoslovakia there was, was almost entirely Czech. In February 1977, when the Charter 77 movement was established, some Slovaks apparently even saw it as a Czech move against the Slovak Husák[5]—the national again taking precedence over the democratic.

It was Slovak reluctance to support dissidence that gave another twist to the Czech sense of betrayal by Slovaks. The vast majority of Czechs did not participate in dissidence, but, to some degree, they supported it, however inactively or sometimes even grudgingly. The fact that the vast majority of Slovaks did neither became another cause for resentment—as well as a chance to transfer guilt. The triumphant culmination of dissidence in Czechoslovakia, the velvet revolution of November 1989 was, again, more or less a wholly Czech affair. Most Slovaks supported it—after all, the communist system had become a house of cards that was collapsing—but its origins and its overwhelming thrust were unquestionably Czech.

Where, then, was Slovakia to fit in the new, independent Czechoslovakia? What was to be the new Czech-Slovak relationship? The Czechs were the victors of November 1989, and the initiative lay with them. Moreover, the dissident group around Václav Havel enjoyed worldwide fame and appreciation. The initiative for framing the future of Czech-Slovak relations would lay with them. And it was precisely they who were to make the first great error that led to the split and the end of Czechoslovakia's existence.

The Lost Opportunity

At first, it seemed that at no time in the seventy-four-year history of Czechoslovakia was the situation more propitious for a viable arrangement between Czechs and Slovaks than after the velvet revolution. True, the mutual grudges had not evaporated, and the scars could not disappear, but such was the euphoria over the collapse of the Soviet system in Eastern Europe and the high international reputation which the country was enjoying that it seemed a new start might be made. In Slovakia a noisy nationalist party demanding full independence did immediately emerge, but it was having relatively little impact on an electorate that apparently favored the continuing association of the two nations in a single constitutional framework.[6]

The great error of the new Czech ruling elite in Prague was its failure to put Slovakia on top of its agenda. And some blame must go to Václav Havel himself. Havel strongly believed in the Czech-Slovak relationship and regretted the status of poor relation that the Slovaks had suffered. But even he was not prepared to give the Slovak question the importance and immediacy it deserved, both for itself and for the survival of Czechoslovakia. No one can fairly accuse Havel of typical Czech arrogance toward Slovaks—and the arrogance continued to be evident among many Czechs after November 1989—but he can be accused of what many Slovaks considered even worse than Czech arrogance: Czech neglect. Opinion grew among Slovaks that

the Czechs were making them wait, that they had more ir
things to do.[7] And the Slovaks were partly right. There was, i
mass of important things that the new Czechoslovak governn
to do, and all of those things were urgent. But nothing was more important or urgent than Slovakia. Had Havel been able to bring himself to realize this fact, he then could have used his overpowering authority to get priority for Slovakia and probably to prevail on both Czechs and Slovaks to exercise the degree of moderation necessary for compromise.

When he did begin to exert himself sufficiently on the issue, it was almost too late. More and more Slovaks were forming an opinion, not necessarily favoring independence as much as some form of sovereignty, and this shared opinion was becoming a coherent force. The surge of nationalism and separatism in Yugoslavia and soon in the Soviet Union also was beginning to affect some Slovaks. Still, if even by the middle of 1991 the Czech leaders had made proposals that met Slovak demands halfway, it is possible that some agreement to save the union could have been reached.

What was needed was a certain vision and generosity on the part of the Czechs. But all they—even Havel—offered was a matter-of-fact provincialism that progressively reduced any chance of success. The Czech argument was that federation (with its central government retaining basic powers and its two parts remaining ultimately subordinated to it) was the only basis on which Czechoslovakia could survive. The federation could be looser than before, but it still must exist. This remained the Czech argument up to the moment of dissolution. Right after November 1989, many Slovaks seemed prepared to accept this alternative, perhaps causing a certain complacency in Prague. But the quarrel about the name of the new democratic republic in the spring of 1990 reflected something of the growing incompatibility between the two sides. To most outsiders it all seemed a bit ridiculous; yet its symbolism was in deadly earnest for most Slovaks. Eventually, the compromise title "Czech and Slovak Federative Republic" was agreed on (Czecho-Slovakia, for short).[8] The country remained a federation, but only just and not for long.

There would have been no new title without pressure from the Slovaks, and the initial Czech reluctance reflected Prague's lack of both imagination and sensitivity. Any concessions made were always the result of Slovak demands rather than Czech initiatives. This was clear from the series of talks during 1990 on the competences of the federal, Czech, and Slovak governments. The atmosphere for these talks became progressively worse as polemical exchanges between prominent Czechs and Slovaks increased[9] and, especially, as some of the uglier aspects of extreme Slovak nationalism became apparent, most notably the marks of admiration, even reverence, for Father Tiso, head of the clerical-fascist Slovak republic in World War II.[10] (There were remarkable similarities between Slovakia and Croatia at this time—indeed, there continue to be—in the partial revival of a past that brought infamy to both nations.) But it was when the talks began in February 1991 on a new constitution for the federative republic that negotiations really became a dialogue of the deaf. By now the Slovaks' position had become virtually unacceptable to the Czechs. They were seeking confederation rather than any form of federation. Both republics should become sovereign states, legally independent of each other. They should then come together through a treaty or articles of confederation with joint defense, monetary union, and the coordination of some aspects of foreign policy.

Slovak demands, sometimes raised in a provocative way, were often inconsistent.[11] In Bratislava, much politicking and demagogy took place. But the notion among Slovaks of confederation as the only practical means of getting recognition for their sense of identity was something that gradually became accepted. The polls continued to show that relatively few Slovaks wanted outright independence and separation.[12] But they did want something essentially different from the *old* federal system. For them, this system meant Prague still being the capital, the Czechs ultimately still in charge, with the Slovaks second best at home and ignored abroad. The Czechs had always seen Czechoslovakia in this way, too, and few of them felt things needed to be different. At the popular level this was the basic difference between the two nations in their attitudes to a common state. (Again a comparison—or contrast—with the former Yugoslavia can be made here. The "confederation" that Slovenia and Croatia were demanding in 1991 [see chapter 7] was essentially a sham that would have left them totally independent. The Slovak proposal, however, whatever its inconsistencies, probably did carry some meaning, substance, and sincerity.)

At the political level it would not have seemed impossible for a compromise as proposed by the Slovaks to have been reached within the framework of a confederation. Some concept beyond federation was needed, but the Czech side refused either to entertain such an idea or, apparently, even imagine it. Many of them—even sophisticated and internationally minded Czechs—were insensitive, not so much to the Slovak desire for identity, but to Slovaks' insistence that, if this identity were to be achieved inside Czechoslovakia, then the structure of the state would have to be changed. It was the foundation of Czechoslovakia after 1918 that had fulfilled the Czechs' sense of identity, but now something new was needed to give the Slovaks theirs.

There were indications that Havel was coming to this realization, but by the beginning of 1992 his authority already had begun to wane, part of the general dissident ebb throughout Eastern Europe (see chapter 2). His popularity in the Czech Lands (and even in Slovakia) continued at a high rate. But the political authority in the Czech Lands was passing to Václav Klaus, federal minister of finance and leader of the Civic Democratic Party, the right-of-center offshoot of the Civic Forum. Though Klaus was ostensibly ready to concede some changes, he insisted that federation must be the basis of any Czech-Slovak state. Any notion of confederation he rejected entirely; better total separation than any compromise on this issue. Slovakia's search for its national identity must not be allowed to stand in the way of the free market economic reform within a federal Czechoslovakia. This reform, he hoped, would be a Czechoslovak one; but it could be solely a Czech reform, if need be, with the Slovaks going their own way in search of their identity. As the negotiations progressed Klaus also suspected, probably correctly, that the Slovaks wanted it both ways: a status that would give them what they wanted and, at the same time, a situation where the Czechs would continue mainly to bankroll certain aspects of their economy, plus the welfare state in Slovakia.[13] Not only Klaus, but many Czechs, considered this example as only the latest example of Slovaks seeing Czechoslovakia as a charitable organization existing mainly for their benefit.

The Maneuvering

In the end, therefore, the emerging Czech political leadership had no desire to save Czechoslovakia on any basis that would have been satisfactory to the Slovaks. That was the real reason they opposed the referendum which Havel and many others in both republics at first favored. Strictly speaking, such a referendum was the only constitutional way that the existing federal state could have been dissolved, and it seemed to many people, in Czechoslovakia and abroad, the only sensible and democratic procedure. Klaus and his supporters argued that a referendum actually would settle nothing since it would be difficult to agree on the wording of the questions and just as difficult to agree on interpretations of the answers. In short, a referendum would confuse rather than clarify. Obviously, these objections had some substance. But the real, unstated objection was that, despite all of the incidental confusion that a referendum would generate, it would clearly indicate, in some form or other, that Czechs and Slovaks should continue living together, if not in one state—using the term as historically understood—but in some form of coherent international, political, and economic association.[14] And the immediate effect of the referendum would be to force Klaus to negotiate and compromise.

A referendum also would have been embarrassing to the Slovak leadership. By the middle of 1992 this leadership rested firmly in the hands of Vladimír Mečiár. Formerly a leading member of Public Against Violence and a proponent of a Czech-Slovak federal relationship, Mečiár had formed a breakaway group called Movement for a Democratic Slovakia (HZDS), which, on the strength of an increasingly nationalist platform, quickly became the most powerful party in Slovakia. He, too, became the most popular political figure in Slovakia. He could relate to most ordinary Slovaks through both his personality and his politics, appealing not only to their sense of Slovak identity and to their national prejudices, but to their fear of the post-communist unknown.

This fear was mainly economic. Slovakia was much more economically vulnerable than the Czech Lands. Although parts of Slovakia had become relatively industrialized during Hungarian rule, large-scale industrialization had occurred only under the communists, with much of the new Slovak industry geared to demands of the Soviets, most notably the needs of their military-industrial complex. Parts of the Slovak landscape became dotted with huge heavy-industrial plants on which practically the entire working force for miles around became dependent. With the end of Soviet domination, the breakup of Comecon and the Warsaw Pact, the scrapping of the planned economic system, and the introduction of the market, many of these industrial plants were heading for extinction, the towns in which they were located for inexorable decay, and many in their work forces for permanent unemployment. And this process was likely to be all the faster with the "shock therapy" type of reform that was now part of Czechoslovak policy, with its impetus coming from the Czechs side and its direction in the unsolicitous hands of Václav Klaus. Mečiár became the champion of this doomed species of socialist heavy-industrial worker, and it was a doggedly loyal constituency. But it was a constituency that was, in the main, economically rather nationalistically motivated.[15] Many of its members might not be happy with the Czech association, but they would be even less happy without it. They knew on which side their bread was ultimately buttered. Mečiár, therefore, had to be careful. A referendum could produce the kind of result that also would tie his hands, or at least reduce his bargaining leverage, in negotiations with the Czechs.

No referendum, therefore, took place. The people's will on the survival of their country had to give way to the aims and the maneuverings of their elected politicians. And all the while the situation was drifting toward an impasse that must inevitably end in separation. The Czech and Slovak republic elections in June 1992 marked the decisive break. Although neither of their parties achieved a majority of votes, Klaus and Mečiár won handsomely enough with the plurality that each achieved. The backing Klaus got from the Czech electorate was all he needed to harden him in an uncompromising attitude that now became total. He never had made any secret of his view that negotiations, except in the framework of the federation, were useless. Now, as the new Czech prime minister, with his more flexible opponents routed, and with himself, not Havel, as clearly the most powerful political leader in the Czech Lands, his attitude to any future negotiations was clear: Slovak retreat or separation. And by now he evidently thought that separation was preferable, despite his protestations to the contrary.[16] Slovakia had become the querulous, sponging Eastern liability his instincts always told him it was.

Ironically, much of the Czech support for the preservation of the Slovak connection came from the older generations who had experienced the cases of Slovak betrayal in the previous half-century. Still, Czechoslovakia had meant for them a historic fulfillment (or compensation) and a certain status in the world. "Having Slovakia" enhanced the Czechs' view of themselves. It was, of course, a one-sided, superior view of what Czechoslovakia meant that was anathema to most Slovaks and was one of the principal reasons for the approaching breakup of the association. But the attitude was firmly held by Czechs, often not without some affection for individual Slovaks. Many Czechs also opposed total separation on more down-to-earth grounds. During an association that had lasted—with one short break—for most of this century, the multifaceted links binding the two parts of Czechoslovakia had become so dense as to be extremely hard to tear asunder. Many Slovaks balked at the independence option for the same reason, even including some of those who would be affected drastically by Klaus's economic reform. In the Czech Lands, however, many young people had lost whatever patience they might have had with Slovakia. They backed both Klaus's economics and his politics and looked forward to a Czech role in Europe—Western Europe. Mečiár's election victory in June 1992 only confirmed their image of Slovakia as a dim backwater.

Soon after the June 1992 elections, pro forma, futile negotiations resumed between the Czech and Slovak sides. Mečiár, strengthened electorally, continued to demand his confederation with safeguards, and Klaus continued to reject the idea, both of them with equal predictability. Mečiár's motives can be explained in two different ways: (1) He always believed in independence, and hence his confederation proposal was just a gambit to put the onus of the break on the Czechs. (2) He was sincere about his kind of confederation and thought that, as the break approached, Klaus would at least partly back down and hence give him a major political victory.

Both explanations are plausible. The key, though, may lie in a combination of the two. Mečiár believed in independence—but not yet. Highly aware of Slovakia's economic vulnerability, he therefore wanted as much Czech underpinning, and for as long a period as he could gain. A confederation would both delay and dull the sharpness of separation, putting Slovakia in a better position to cope with independence when it came. Perhaps, though, he sincerely believed that his notion of confederation would work indefinitely and that this kind of Czech connection would be viable and beneficial for Slovakia. It may, though, be wrong even to try to detect a long-term strategy in Mečiár's actions. He was (and remains) an impulsive, provincial, primitive politician—no matter how intelligent and successful—and though some of his advisers were more sophisticated, they, too, may have been guilty of totally misjudging the Czech reaction to the Slovak proposals.

But no hope ever existed that the Slovak proposals would be accepted by a Czech side that was becoming daily more determined to make the break. Perhaps if the Slovak proposals had not been so clearly self-serving, perhaps if the Czechs had been ready for compromise, some intermediate stage between federation and confederation could have been worked out, with both sides making history by pioneering a new form of statehood. But the necessary ingenuity or resourcefulness simply may not have existed. By the second half of 1992 the will certainly was not there. In October of that year, following a hitch in the Czechoslovak federal assembly over getting the federation formally abrogated, a vague, eleventh-hour Slovak proposal for a form of Czech-Slovak union was put forward. Ironically, the proposal was backed solidly by the former communist deputies. Whatever the political machinations that may have lurked behind this proposal, it seemed to reflect a last genuflection to Czechoslovakia. But the momentum, the logic, and the commitment to separation had become irresistible.

Alone in the World

On January 1, 1993, the Czech and Slovak Federative Republic ceased to be, and the Czech Republic and Slovakia came into being. Slovakia's beginning was particularly inauspicious and its outlook far from reassuring. Mečiár's political grouping immediately began to show serious signs of disunity, and Mečiár himself betrayed dictatorial tendencies—toward the media, university independence, and virtually anybody who stood in his way.[17] Almost immediately his personal popularity started to shrink. The difficulties and delays in electing a new president of the republic at the beginning of 1993 somehow symbolized an immaturity and lack of sophistication threatening Slovakia's international reputation and undermining its right to be taken seriously. The large Hungarian minority also had reason to be nervous about its status. Mečiár and others on the eve of Slovak independence had indicated that they favored a harder attitude toward questions of the minority's status.[18] With Hungary pressing for more rights and improved status for Hungarian minorities throughout Eastern Europe, and the Slovaks, aggressive in their newly achieved independence (and sometimes hypersensitive about it), the Hungarian minority, caught between the two, might suffer as a consequence, with Slovakia's international reputation becoming further undermined. Overshadowing everything was the new republic's precarious economic situation. Early economic collapse, predicted by some, did not occur and there were signs of considerable resilience in some sectors. But the worst tests were to come and there was little optimism about how Slovakia would cope.

These signs could be the reflection of a basic lack of statehood viability, a harbinger of Slovakia's collapse as a democratic polity, and its lapse into an authoritarianism that had nothing temporary, moderate, or pro tem about it. Some degree of preventive action by the Czech Republic could be needed because it would be the first to suffer by extension if Slovak democracy and the Slovak economy collapsed. (For one thing, however hard it tried to block them, the republic would be invaded by migrant waves of Slovak citizens; Gypsies already were pouring in.) But the Czech Republic could not cope alone. Western help was needed. Slovakia's geopolitical and strategic location is such that disaster there can never be insulated. It could seriously damage the stability that had existed so far in East-Central Europe. And, with doubts growing about the viability of Belarus, Ukraine, and Russia itself, that stability was in serious jeopardy. All in all, there was much to worry about. The "Slovak Question" had indeed ceased to exist. But it had now become the "Slovakia Question."

The Czech Republic apparently was facing none of the problems threatening Slovakia. Economically, it was potentially sounder than any East European country, and in the longer run it could expect the greatest level of Western investment. It also had a relatively homogeneous, Western-oriented population. Its economic and political institutions and procedures also were Western in grounding and inspiration. Now that it was without what many had considered the Slovak "incubus," it could, in the minds of many Czechs, concentrate on improving itself and securing its place in West European company.

This picture was plausible and the prospect appealing. But it was not the whole story. The Czech Republic *could* suffer from profound weaknesses, as serious in their own way as those of Slovakia. These weaknesses stemmed from the questions of Czech identity and Czech self-confidence. For the first time in modern history the Czechs were on their own, with both power over themselves alone and responsibility for themselves alone. (And, with a population of more than 10 million, they made up a small but far from minuscule state.) But there were doubts precisely about their capacity to sustain their power and responsibility and to firmly anchor their independence. Several observers noted the lack of Czech patriotic determination or independence of spirit. (The contrast with, say, the Poles was, as always, quite staggering.) What also was noted was a marked reappearance of provincialism in the Czech Lands between 1990 and 1992, as well as a petty-mindedness in public life that stood in sharp contrast to the open-minded magnanimity that radiated from the presidential palace and would continue doing so for as long as Havel remained there.

Doubts were rising, too, about the Czech Republic's international standing. The new Czech Republic came into being in an extraordinary way. It was not the result of any popular, patriotic drive for independence. In fact, it was essentially a by-product of the original Slovak demand for identity. It backed into the world rather than charging into it. Moreover, in terms of the existing situation, the Czech Republic is located in Central Europe, but its leaders reject the geopolitical consequences of this fact by insisting that it is part of *Western* Europe and wanting to have as little as possible to do with its problematic *Eastern* hinterland. Indeed, the fears about this hinterland—the potential instability for Czechoslovakia as a whole because its Slovak part was at the heart of what could become a hotbed of international instability—were probably another factor in prompting the Czechs to shed Slovakia. Asia begins at the Morava! Now, leaning westward, the Czechs see their future as part of the West European culture and comity of nations. They are aware of the German "danger"; their entire history could not allow them to forget it. But they are reassuring themselves with two considerations. First, the present Germany is the best united Germany in history; therefore, no military danger exists as it did in the recent past. Second, the danger of economic and cultural absorption by Germans can be mitigated or contained by membership in the European Community and NATO.

The Czechs are right on the first point, but they could be wrong on the second. Germany is indeed no security threat. Still, the European Community probably will be no preventive against German economic and, eventually, cultural expansion. For the Czechs, Germany *is* the European Community, and the Czech Republic is on its way to becoming essentially an economic protectorate of the reunited Federal Republic of Germany—obviously a greatly different protectorate from the one it suffered a half-century ago, but one implying some loss of real sovereignty just the same. The economic benefits might be considerable, but all-round losses could be severe. Again, the contrast here with Poland is worth drawing. However much German economic penetration of Poland there might be, it would present no threat whatsoever to the integrity of the Polish nation. With the Czechs one cannot be so sure. It was sadly symptomatic that the new state came into being without either its leaders or its people having decided on a proper name for it.

POLAND
Resilience Against Perversity

The Polish nation began the postcommunist era with self-confidence and hope. During forty years of communist rule it had maintained a continual opposition, not so much of active resistance as of consistent dissociation from it, punctuated by upheavals of violence. In 1980 Solidarity was established as a trade union movement. But within weeks it had become a national movement—workers, peasants, intellectuals—the first such political force of any permanence in East European history. The truly historic achievement, however, was to follow. After the disaster of December 1981 when Solidarity's organization was destroyed, it went underground and, in the Polish tradition of resistance, continued its struggle. That, and the Polish people's refusal to come to terms with the communist authorities, helped bring about the victories of 1988 and 1989. Communism as a whole was facing its terminal crisis, in the Soviet Union and Eastern Europe. But Solidarity had helped push it to the brink, and, more than anything else, its creation and survival had symbolized the Polish courage to fight and the character to endure.

Throughout the world, too, Poland stood as an emblem for freedom and hope. Its extraordinary prestige was personified by the fame of two men—Pope John Paul II and Lech Wałęsa. Both had played an extraordinary part in the preservation of Poland's pride and in its eventual triumph, and both of them symbolized the Polish nation's strength and appeal. Seldom has a nation enjoyed as much goodwill as Poland did in 1989.

Already by the middle of 1992 Poland's jubilation had become subdued and the world's goodwill tempered by a certain exasperation. The Polish political scene had become one of disorder and disintegration. What in previous contexts such as war, occupation, or repression had been prized as independence of spirit now appeared as anarchic, self-destructive indiscipline. Leadership had been replaced by squabbling incompetence, the sense of unity and purpose by uncertainty and drift. Spectacular cases of corruption were further eroding public trust.

There was a brief respite to this disorder in 1993 under the government of Hanna Suchocka, signs that Poland might be proceeding to a political and economic reconstruction worthy of a great nation and of one of Europe's larger states. But the signs were deceptive. The compulsive irresponsibility returned in the way the Suchocka government lost its confidence vote in the Sejm in May 1993. And in the parliamentary elections the following September, left-wing, "postcommunist" parties won a clear victory. It was the public's verdict on four years of not only economic hardship, but political squalor as well.

Background to Malaise

The sharp deterioration after 1989 is not easy to explain. Many, including some Poles in their more self-critical moments, would put it down to "national character": the alleged congenital inability of Poles to work together, not even until disaster was staring them in the face, but rather until disaster had actually struck. Fighting the enemy was much simpler than working with friends or with one another. No cause was worth the effort except survival, deliverance, honor. The stereotype is familiar enough. Nobody who knows Poles can be unaware of it. Balzac's quip, "Show a Pole a precipice and he will jump off it," seemed to be regaining its topicality.

To the extent that these generalizations are true, the post-1989 situation would now call for a massive change of national psychology, a task that could be the biggest challenge now faced by the Polish nation. For more than three centuries the Poles have suffered unprecedented tribulations. Now, at the end of the twentieth century, their national and territorial integrity seemed more assured than at any time for four centuries. Poland still lay between Germans and Russians, but this was a geopolitical unavoidability carrying less danger than ever before. A new psychology was sorely needed, therefore, because if the new security only served to reinforce the old psychology, then the prospects for Poland's national reconstruction were dismal indeed.

But though deeper historical reasons may partly explain the Polish malaise, more recent developments also have played their part. Most notably the communist experience. Thanks to their spirit, however, the Poles were able to make this experience less damaging in many respects than in other countries. A remarkable national spirit was maintained, to which, after 1956, even the communist leaderships, in their way, also contributed. Still, the communist legacy is difficult enough. Even more recently, the bloodless, gradual, "civilized" manner in which communist rule was eventually removed, itself created a situation of uncertainty ripe for demagogy, confusion, and irresponsibility. Although the final cracks in the facade of communist power began to appear in 1988, it was not until October 1991 that the communist hold on the Sejm (the lower house of parliament) finally was broken. In retrospect, it was clear that the democratic leaders could, almost from the beginning, have pressed for quicker and more comprehensive change, that they could have got the communists out much earlier than they did.[19] Yet even with Wałęsa replacing General Jaruzelski as president in December 1990 and a strong anticommunist majority finally in parliament the following year, there was still strong popular resentment over the large number of communists still entrenched in the administration and the economy, resisting change or manipulating it to their advantage. Here Poland was no different from any other East European country.

There were, indeed, ample grounds for resentment. But resentment now bred suspicion bordering on paranoia. Conspiracy theories—never far below the surface in Polish history—multiplied with a morbid inventiveness. Permanent or semipermanent arrangements were rumored to have been made among the participants at the roundtable sessions leading to the final agreements on power-sharing. The communists' agreement to form a government with the opposition allegedly had been made on the assurance, not just that there would be no judicial retribution, but that jobs, perks, privileges of all kinds would be kept as long as possible. Thus, what had been a historic democratic victory ensuring the *peaceful* transfer of power became, in the eyes of many, nothing more than a shady deal. In the eyes of many more it was (a new variation on the old theme) a conspiracy hatched by "them" (now including communist rulers and anticommunist would-be rulers) against "us."[20] And, further strengthening the link with the past, anti-Semitism enhanced the obsession with conspiracy and gave some Poles a graspable explanation of what was afoot.[21] The great victory, therefore, turned sour.

It did not do so immediately. At first there was support for the new democratic government and an apparent readiness to pay the economic and social costs of building a new life. This mood did not last long. The costs were becoming too great, the time for recovery seemed too long. Besides, the distribution of the hardships seemed increasingly unfair. Thus, the mood began to change, suspicions were awakened, and simple explanations sought. A less than encouraging backdrop was formed to the difficult tasks of transition and reconstruction. Not only was there voter apathy (referred to in chapter 2), but confusion and cynicism about Poland's future among both educated and uneducated Poles. Poles did not want to go back to the communist system—they were in no doubt about that; but they were unhappy about the present and the future it could bring. They were usually very unhappy about their present crop of leaders.

Too Many Leaders—Or None?

In my earlier book, *Surge to Freedom,* I waxed, if not lyrical, then enthusiastic about Poland's new democratic leaders. I referred to the Mazowiecki government, formed in August 1989, as follows: "It was not only a popular government; it was a good one."[22] It soon turned out to be neither. The growing seriousness of Poland's domestic situation (which I had underestimated) soon made it unpopular. As for a "good" government, it probably was never that to begin with. It was mostly composed of good, highly intelligent men, basic liberals, who had fine, in some cases, heroic records under communist rule. Generally, though, they were not good politicians, least of all the premier himself, Tadeusz Mazowiecki.[23] A Catholic journalist and one of Wałęsa's closest advisers in the old Solidarity days, Mazowiecki presented the image of tired ineffectuality, and his drop in political esteem was reflected in his humiliation in the presidential election in late 1991 when he was pushed into third place and out of the final race by Stanisław Tymiński (see chapter 1).

The short-lived Mazowiecki government has been described as the "nearest to a government of philosopher-kings that Europe has witnessed since the war."[24] It is a description that captures the main weakness—its lack of practicality and the common touch. (Only Jacek Kuroń, minister for labor, was successful in explaining his own, and his government's, policies to the public.)

Besides, rule by philosopher-kings was not exactly what the worker component of the Solidarity leadership had in mind. That component may have fallen sharply since Solidarity's foundation in 1980, but it was still composed mainly of a worker elite, skilled, educated, self-conscious, and proud of its record. Above all, it refused to be patronized, and this it suspected the Mazowiecki government and its supporters of trying to do. Thus, the intellectual-worker alliance that had made the Polish revolution possible came apart amid misunderstandings and recrimination. As for the bulk of the Polish working class—semiskilled or unskilled—which had drifted out of Solidarity, they never had had much sympathy for Mazowiecki, and were suspicious of the radical economic reform plans of finance minister Leszek Balcerowicz (see chapter 5).

The Solidarity consensus, therefore, that had been subject to considerable strain from its very beginning in August 1980 but had still held, now suffered its first big division—between intellectuals and workers.[25] It was to splinter further under the stresses of policy differences, political ambitions, mutual suspicion, and economic crisis. Such a breakup was inevitable. The consensus might, though, have lasted another year, perhaps a year and a half, long enough to give the Balcerowicz economic reform plan time to sink deeper roots, had it not been for the erstwhile personification of Solidarity unity, Lech Wałęsa himself.

Wałęsa's Peeling Glitter

Lech Wałęsa first achieved world prominence in 1980 as the leading figure in the fight for Polish freedom. He received the Nobel Peace Prize in 1983. Then, after five subdued years, he reemerged as the true statesman, first forcing and then negotiating the roundtable agreement in 1989 that began the final end of communist rule in Poland. His greatness as liberator and political leader was conclusively demonstrated in August 1989 when, skillfully, boldly, and with perfect timing, he prevented a communist-led government continuing in power and brought the Mazowiecki government into being. The unemployed shipyard electrician had become uncrowned king of Poland within a decade. He was at the pinnacle of fame and achievement. Still more important now for Poland, he promised well for the future, too. As undisputed head of the Solidarity consensus, he led the worker-intellectual coalition that might lead Poland through the travail of reconstruction.

It was not to be; in retrospect it could not have been. Obviously, the

Solidarity consensus could not last. Its brittle unity needed an adversary; once that had gone, its days were numbered. Many Solidarity intellectuals, true to type, lost no time in claiming that it was *their* hour that had struck, that they were assuming their rightful place in Polish history, that it was brains and not brawn that would rule free Poland, and that Wałęsa and his working-class ilk should step aside. Finally, there was the obvious fact that Wałęsa had worked himself out of a job; in the new political situation he had no relevant institutional position. He was head of Solidarity, but that now meant little or nothing. All that he had was an inchoate mass adulation, which eventually could be harnessed, but for the moment could not keep him in the center of the action or in the national limelight.

Wałęsa had always been swelled-headed and high-handed, but such characteristics largely had been passed over during the years of struggle. Now his bad traits were deemed to be — and actually were — primitive and offensive; too many examples of his egotism and overbearing acts existed for them to be ignored. His behavior may partly have been provoked by wounding intellectual hauteur, but basically no one was to blame but himself. Success, indeed, had spoiled Lech Wałęsa. His arrogance made cooperation with him almost impossible, his conceit made him ridiculous, and it soon was to become morbid. Some observers also commented on his lack of any kind of vision for Poland. One depicted him as "an ordinary man thrust into extraordinary circumstances who now, in the more settled circumstances of Eastern Europe, has become ordinary again."[26]

Behind these destructive personal defects, however, there lay political shrewdness and sensitivity and a readiness to make decisions. One cannot deny the persuasiveness of some of his political judgments or fail to sympathize with his impatience at what often seemed the impasse of Polish politics. His decision in 1990 to break the Solidarity consensus and stand himself for the presidency was widely supported at the time, both at home and by Western observers.[27] Many agreed that the consensus was retarding the development of democracy, that the Mazowiecki government was politically incompetent, and that Wałęsa with his stature, unquestioned political skill, and prestige was needed as president. But, whatever the case's merits, the demagogic means that Wałęsa used to achieve his ends became themselves a degradation of democracy. They loosed a squalor into Polish public life that persisted and proliferated.

After his election as president in December 1990, some of Wałęsa's subsequent suggestions for getting Polish politics out of the blind alley into which it had stumbled were eminently practical. For example, he proposed that a minimum percentage share of the vote be necessary for parties to be represented in parliament—this was already common elsewhere in Eastern Europe—and made suggestions for constitutional reform involving increased powers for the presidency. But any proposal coming from the Belvedere (the presidential palace) was viewed with such suspicion that it was almost certain of rejection—not only, it should be stressed, by the communists and their allies who made up nearly two-thirds of the 1989–1991 Sejm, but by most of the totally democratically elected Sejm after the balloting of October 1991.

This blind alley into which postcommunist politics had stumbled in Poland was strongly reminiscent of the situation some seventy years before in the newly re-created Poland after World War I. Antony Polonsky has described the parliamentary situation prevailing then:

> The different political traditions, together with the introduction of proportional representation and the exuberant individualism of the Polish *intelligentsia,* which played a leading role in all political groupings, led to far-reaching fragmentation. In 1925, for example, there were 92 registered political parties in Poland of which 32 were represented in the Sejm, organized into 18 parliamentary clubs. This extreme political atomization made it most difficult to create a stable and lasting government.[28]

The impasse between parliament and the presidency had similarities between then and now. The presidency—at least until after Piłsudski's coup in 1926—was too weak and the powers of parliament (the "sejmocracy") too strong.

Wałęsa, therefore, was fighting old battles and—manner and methods apart—he unquestionably had a case. He also must be credited for his farsightedness in supporting the radical economic reform program associated with Balcerowicz (see chapter 5). He had no economic expertise, but he had an instinctive grasp of what was needed, and he appears to have been persuaded early on that, however painful, radical reform was the best remedy. His visits to Western Europe and the United States also convinced him that Western financial help depended on the continuation of Balcerowicz's "shock therapy." But although he supported radical reform, he did not do so consistently. Political tactics often seemed more important to him. Sometimes he complained that reform was not going fast enough (he used the charge repeatedly in 1990 against the Mazowiecki government); at other times, especially when addressing a mass audience, he deplored the social hardships involved and virtually promised a slowing down. He was sending conflicting signals to conflicting audiences.

Wałęsa's estrangement from the intellectuals continued well after his break with Mazowiecki's group. Having broken the old Solidarity consensus, he tried, after becoming president in December 1990, to build a new consensus that included a number of more conservative, nationalist, or populist intellectuals, most of them former members of Solidarity but less known than Mazowiecki's circle. They supported his moves to strengthen the presidency and, like him, urged a quicker and more comprehensive "decommunization," differing sharply on this subject with the Mazowiecki group, one of whose main political planks had been the drawing of the "thick line" between communist past and democratic future. This new group also was ambitious for power. But Wałęsa successively cast its members off like so much unwanted clothing. Most conspicuous among them were the Kaczyński twins, Jarosław and Lech, childhood television stars, capable tacticians (especially Jarosław), and for a few months in 1991–1992 two of Poland's most visible politicians.[29] At first, they both were members of Wałęsa's presidential council, which he was building up as a rival seat of power to the government and the recalcitrant parliament. But Wałęsa unmade intellectual aides even more rapidly than he made them, and every new appointment to his "advisory" circle represented another drop in its level of intellect, courage, and political ability. Jarosław Kaczyński, who had built up a political grouping, the Center Accord, to give Wałęsa legislative support, was unceremoniously dropped and was to become one of his former chief's most bitter and unscrupulous enemies. By the spring of 1992 Wałęsa's most confidential adviser (after his priest and confessor) was reputed to be his former chauffeur, Mieczysław Wachowski. Wachowski, whose dim past was soon to be spectacularly exploited, was the ultimate symbol of Wałęsa's self-isolation. He apparently had begun as a factotum, then graduated to majordomo, and was now privy councillor.

Wałęsa's bizarre managerial behavior was being matched by the growing inconsistency of his policy pronouncements. Whether it be economic reform, domestic politics, relations with Germany or with Russia, his somersaults made Polish policy, as enunciated from the

Belvedere, almost impossible to pin down. Wałęsa was not just causing political instability, he had become its epicenter, its outstanding symptom. It was good for Poland that, for most of 1991 at least, such governmental ministers as Premier Jan Krzysztof Bielecki, foreign minister Henryk Skubaszewski, and Balcerowicz himself, presented an image of seriousness and dignity to set against their president's lack of either.

The Level of Public Life

The breakup of the Solidarity consensus and, more specifically, the behavioral precedent set by Wałęsa, signaled a precipitous decline in the standards of political discourse and behavior in Poland. The Tymiński aberration during the presidential election campaign of 1990 has been discussed in chapter 1. But the campaign as a whole was a degrading spectacle, marked by infectious anti-Semitic slurs, which Wałęsa himself only encouraged, against some of his prominent opponents, like the then-Solidarity parliamentary leader, Bronisław Geremek, and Adam Michnik, a former Solidarity tribune and later editor of *Gazeta Wyborcza,* one of the best daily papers in the whole of postcommunist Eastern Europe.[30] (Michnik, himself, though much more sinned against than sinning, also lowered the tone of the campaign by his own intemperance, as did other liberals. Mazowiecki, however, although the target of some of the vilest defamation, never let his standards slip.)

After the presidential elections, with Tymiński's bubble burst and Wałęsa's ambition satiated, there seemed some prospect of, if not public decorum, then at least some public decency. The year 1991 also began with some hope. As Louisa Vinton, a commentator with considerable sympathy for Wałęsa, put it:

> Wałęsa took office hoping to accelerate the pace of change by using his famed ability to sense and steer the public mood. Before his inauguration, he had signaled his determination to be a "synchronizing" president, opening new lines of communication between the government and the public. He soon discovered, however, that his skill as a social seismograph did not always harmonize with the duties and powers of the Presidency. That there was little room for maneuver in the economy Wałęsa had realized well before taking office. He remained convinced, nonetheless, that by taking issues

> directly to the public and signifying his sympathy with the discontented, he could neutralize the force of their dissatisfaction, guide it away from sensitive issues, and shepherd the government through difficult upheavals.[31]

But Wałęsa became immediately embroiled in disputes that illustrated several of the interacting characteristics of Polish politics since 1989: his own overweening personality; the ill-defined division of powers between the presidency and the parliament—notably the Sejm, the lower and more powerful legislative body; decommunization; the unpopularity, yet the indispensability, of drastic economic reform measures; a chaotic parliamentary situation with innumerable squabbling parties, mostly with tiny popular constituencies; public irresponsibility on the part of groups and individuals; increasing public disdain over the antics of politicians—the "them" and "us" syndrome again.

Ironically, the most immediate dispute between Wałęsa and the legislature produced a surprisingly beneficial result for the country as a whole. Mazowiecki had resigned as premier after Wałęsa's victory and his own humiliation in the presidential poll, and the premier-designate, Jan Olszewski, was known to be critical of the drastic Balcerowicz brand of economic reform. Wałęsa, however, insisted on its continuance, rejected Olszewski's nomination, and turned to Bielecki. Bielecki, a firm believer in the Balcerowicz principles, continued the reform against increasing parliamentary and trade union opposition.[32] He gave Poland several crucial months more of economic reform than it might otherwise have received. These months may have made the difference between economic reconstruction and failure. At any rate, if by the end of 1992 the Poles had, indeed, "turned the economic corner," then Jan Krzystof Bielecki is the unsung hero who helped them do it.

Wałęsa, too, deserves some of the credit for keeping the parliamentary, as well as extraparliamentary, opponents of reform at bay. (But he also used Bielecki as a convenient whipping boy on whom populist criticism could be diverted from himself.)[33] However important the economic respite, however, the political damage continued steadily. Wałęsa failed in his efforts to strengthen the presidency, to introduce some order into the parliamentary system, and to devise an election law promoting governmental stability by excluding minuscule parties and splinter groups from the Sejm. He also failed to get the date of new parliamentary elections brought forward so as to end the life of the 1989 parliament in which 65 percent of the seats had been reserved for the communists and their former allies.

Poland's first completely democratic elections since well before World War II were finally held in October 1991. They resulted in what was virtually a hung parliament but which, after much negotiation, eventually produced a right-of-center government coalition strongly under the influence of Catholic political groupings, which were the real winners of the election. The prime minister was the same Olszewski whom Wałęsa had refused to accept a year before and whose appointment he tried, but failed, to block now.[34]

During the election campaign Olszewski, as well as other figures who became part of his coalition, again had spoken strongly against Balcerowicz-type economic reform. But on assuming power they found that dismantling it would prove ruinous, and the main principles of "shock therapy" were grudgingly preserved. What defined Olszewski's governing coalition was antagonism toward Wałęsa and a determination to spread and speed up decommunization.[35] The two issues immediately became intertwined, which led to the continuing decline in the level of Polish public life in the first half of 1992. In resisting the speed, manner, and comprehensiveness of the Olszewski government's efforts to purge communist officeholders, especially in the military,[36] Wałęsa made himself a marked man for the more unscrupulous in the government itself and in politics generally. The depths of degradation were reached in June 1992 when the interior minister produced a large number of former security police dossiers that purported to incriminate Wałęsa himself and other politicians in criminal cooperation with the former communist regime. The documents were palpably unconvincing, but, over the longer term, they achieved what they set out to do: create the whiff of suspicion about a considerable number of public figures, which, whatever the lack of evidence, would not be entirely dispelled.[37] The episode also helped foster the suspicion that those who opposed decommunization and, especially the opening of the old police files, did so out of fear of incrimination. In the short run, however, it became obvious that Olszewski and his associates had overplayed their hands—and played into Wałęsa's. The uproar in the Sejm was such that Olszewski was forced to resign.

Out of office, though, the Olszewski group continued undeterred, repeating their charges that a web of conspiracy was being woven aimed at a communist restoration and a renewal of Russian domination. Poland was in grave danger yet again, and a crusade was needed to save it! The new Suchocka government (see below) was accused of being "crypto-communist," and new patriotic political formations sprang up to "save the republic."[38]

Obviously, once suspicion had been aroused it could not be allowed to wane; with decommunization a popular issue among large sections of the population, and the security police files always a means to put opponents on the defensive, Olszewski and his associates had a handy issue indeed. Some were determined to push it to the extreme, most notably Jarosław Kaczyński and Jan Parys, Olszewski's former defense minister, professedly a fervent believer in the notion of an international and internal conspiracy against Poland. At the beginning of 1993, determined to hit Wałęsa at his weakest point, they unearthed what purported to be evidence that Wachowski had been a security police officer in the communist regime, renewing at the same time their charges that Wałęsa, himself, had actively collaborated with the security police. Thus, in late January, millions of bemused but fascinated Polish television viewers watched a crowd of several thousand, led by Kaczyński and Parys, burn Wałęsa in effigy outside his presidential palace and demand his removal.

Suchocka: The Example

During 1992, especially during the crisis preceding and then briefly following the fall of Olszewski's coalition, Poland was being compared with Italy by several foreign observers: an increasingly strong economy in the private, small-business sector, but with chaotic politics. There was some validity in the likeness. Despite the rhetoric of many politicians and the increasingly threatening attitude of the entire trade union movement, stringent economic reform had continued and was producing results (see chapter 5). But politics were anarchic, and standards of political behavior seemed to have hit rock bottom.

The political anarchy continued after the ousting of the Olszewski government as Wałęsa imperiously tried to impose the Peasant Party leader, Waldemar Pawlak, onto an unwilling Sejm. Finally, after a month of intrigue, brokering, and national drift, a seven-party coalition was stitched together under Hanna Suchocka, whom Wałęsa eventually accepted, but only reluctantly.

Suchocka, a member of the right wing of Mazowiecki's liberal

Democratic Union, was a surprising but inspired choice. She was a skilled, energetic manager and negotiator, a pragmatist and a doer. Coming from a well-known Catholic political family near Poznań, she described herself as having been raised in a home that cultivated "internal discipline, rectitude, and honesty, as well as Polishness and Polish culture."[39]

She radiated a sense of responsibility that had been sadly lacking in Polish politics. Her government was a most unlikely, almost unnatural, combination: its backbone was the liberal Democratic Union and the Catholic, conservative, Christian National Union, two of the strangest bedfellows, especially after the bitterness of the previous few months. Under Suchocka, however, the political polarization generally eased, not just inside parliament but in relations between parliament and president and government and president. The most beneficial results of this easing of tensions was the agreement on a "Small Constitution," a series of constitutional measures strengthening the presidency and the government, something that would have been impossible just a short time earlier.[40]

Suchocka, herself, won her spurs as well as great respect both inside Poland and abroad by her firmness and tact in facing down a series of strikes in the summer of 1992 and an even more threatening outbreak at the end of the year. This skillful assurance earned her "Iron Lady" comparisons with Margaret Thatcher, who had been similarly challenged during her incumbency in Britain.[41] Suchocka, a firm believer in the Balcerowicz principles of economic reform, was determined to cut the budget deficit and conform as far as was possible to the rigorous standards of the International Monetary Fund (IMF). In February 1993 she faced a serious parliamentary threat to this policy, but she kept both her nerve and her equanimity and eventually fought off that challenge, too.

It was always questionable how long she could continue until the unnatural coalition over which she presided collapsed or disintegrated. But she already had achieved a great deal. Above all, she had set an example by showing that political dignity and economic progress were not incompatible. She had restored some respectability to Polish democracy, and she had halted the slide in Poland's prestige abroad. What she needed was *time*, but this she did not get.

Her government was defeated in a confidence vote in the Sejm in May 1993, but she stayed on as premier in a virtual caretaker capacity. Then in September the "postcommunist" parties—the Democratic

Left Alliance and the Polish Peasant Party — won a sweeping victory at the parliamentary elections. Together these two parties got nearly 36 percent of the vote, which, as a result of a new election law aimed at producing parliamentary stability, meant 66 percent of seats in the Sejm and seventy-six seats out of one hundred in the Senate (the upper house). This was a decisive "constitutional majority." They were obviously the big winners. The big losers were the Democratic Union, the intellectual spine of the Solidarity movement, the Catholic groupings, which failed to get any representatives in the new parliament — a sure sign that the Poles may still be Catholic but are not clerical — and Wałęsa's presidential party of "supporters of reform," a party obviously modeled on Piłsudski's interwar party. It was also a devastating blow to Wałęsa's own prestige and political standing.[42]

The Democratic Left Alliance was dominated by a social democratic party that was the direct successor of the old Polish United (communist) Workers' Party (PUWP), the ruling party under communism, and the Polish Peasant Party, the PUWP's satellite party. Ironically, the new premier was the same Waldemar Pawlak whom Wałęsa had tried, unsuccessfully, to appoint the previous year. Just four years after the democratic victory of 1989, the "postcommunists" were in power with an apparently stable majority. Why? The political squalor described in these pages was certainly one reason. So was the social and economic hardship which economic reform had already inflicted and the further hardship it threatened. Disillusion and tiredness, not only with Wałęsa but with the whole Solidarity myth, may have been the main underlying reason.

What now? It was not the end of liberal democracy or economic reform. Poland's new political leaders may be the successors of communist rule but they are not its heirs. They believe in democracy and the electoral process — not just in "one man, one vote, one time." They also have declared their support for economic reform. But there exists a distinct danger here: they support economic reform but are not wedded to it. Intellectually, they know it was inevitable but, instinctively, some of them are suspicious of it. They are wisely aware of the social dangers reform involves; however, just as the former proreform governments may have pressed the accelerator too hard, so the new leftist government may now apply the brake too hard, not just slowing reform but unraveling it. Western financial confidence in Poland, growing apace with the economic successes achieved, might also be shattered and Western investors may think again. It might, however, be precisely the awareness of this that will impel the new government to resist the calls of its supporters for an anti-reform policy. But can these calls be strongly enough resisted? The leaders may be pro-reform but many of the votes that put them in office were anti-reform.

But democracy demands responsibility not only from government but also from opposition. And here, judging from the record since 1989, there may be reason to worry. Wałęsa, his party defeated at the polls, must now preside over the government of the victors. He must cooperate; to undermine them would jeopardize Poland's future. And any attempt to repeat Piłsudski's coup of 1926, or to duplicate President Yeltsin's policies in Russia, would ruin that future. But Wałęsa's record suggests that he rises to big occasions and does the right thing. The record of other Polish politicians, however, on the right of the political spectrum, suggests no such thing. With the left's dominance in parliament so great, and with the right having so little representation at all in it, some rightist politicians could be tempted to resort to extraparliamentary tactics. The real threat to Polish democracy could begin with them.

HUNGARY
The Rustle of Danger

When at the beginning of 1990 neighbors like Czechoslovakia and Romania were still blinking their eyes in the aftermath of revolution, Hungary was steadily consolidating its own evolution toward democracy and the market. Orderly and fair elections just three months later gave the Hungarians their first democratically elected government since 1946, and another major phase in that evolution was thus completed.

The evolution actually had begun as early as 1961 with János Kádár's famous exhortation, "He who is not against us is with us." It continued with the first tentative steps to economic reform in the 1960s, which were then expanded into comprehensive form by the New Economic Mechanism (NEM) in 1968. The decision to continue the NEM even after the crushing of the Prague Spring reforms in August 1968 ensured that the evolution would continue. It slowed and was partly reversed during the 1970s, but gradual change continued to be the most important and recognizable element in Hungarian public life. During the 1980s, especially in the second half, as impulses for reform now quickened in the Soviet Union and as the Hungarian regime realized that the "Sinatra Doctrine" (i.e., doing it my way) had replaced the Brezhnev Doctrine as the guide for East European conduct,[43] significant new economic reforms were enacted.

Obviously, the reforms of the Kádár era were not made with a view to giving Hungary a head start in the race toward liberal democracy and capitalism. They were made to strengthen the workings of the socialist system and to reconcile the Hungarian people with it. But the Soviet socialist system, of which Hungary, despite all of its changes, remained an integral part, had been past strengthening since the fall of Nikita Khrushchev in 1964. As Mikhail Gorbachev was to illustrate so dramatically in the Soviet Union, genuine attempts to strengthen the system only weakened it; the remedy killed rather than cured. In Hungary it was much the same. Most Hungarians became resigned to communism and found its Kádár brand infinitely more tolerable than what they had known before. Hence, many also became reconciled with it. But the communist system always was *faute de mieux,* and when the prospects of something better appeared, it lost whatever legitimacy it once had achieved.

However, the vain attempts to strengthen Kadarite socialism did leave something of value: the rudimentary foundations, in the form of certain institutions and procedures, of a democratic and market system. Kadarite socialism also left a polity with some features of civil society and a population that, however cynical and jaded, was used to certain freedoms and ready for more.

The Political Formations

Hungarians now had to build on the lead that Kádár unwittingly had given them. And they had a political and economic elite that looked capable of doing it. Many members of its former dissident groupings, which had swelled during the later Kádár years, had had considerable experience in the West, were international in outlook, and most of them held markedly liberal sentiments. Most of them were members of either the Alliance of Free Democrats (AFD) or the Federation of Young Democrats (FIDESZ), which, until April 1993, had an age limit of thirty-five. Balancing this support for the AFD and FIDESZ were those supporting the Hungarian Democratic Forum (HDF). Established in 1987, the Forum, roughly, was made up of three political trends: Christian democratic corresponding, say, to West German Christian democracy; national liberal; and national populist. Within each trend, views varied considerably; occasionally, too, the trends could merge, but sometimes they could be sharply differentiated. Finally, there were the reform communists who had done much to initiate the changes in Kádár's Hungary. They now became grouped in the Hungarian Socialist Party and numbered among themselves some of the more able, and certainly the most experienced, political figures in the country. At first their chances of being taken into government anytime soon seemed minimal, but they could (and mostly did) play an important, constructive role in opposition.[44]

Backing up this political potential was a strong economic elite, many of whom had helped spearhead the late Kádár economic and financial reforms. Again, many of these financial leaders were familiar with Western practice and were anxious to continue the change from reform socialism to a market economy, though in some instances an economy more Keynesian than Friedmanite. These economic leaders were supported by an engineering and technical cadre that probably stood above any of its East European counterparts. (The Czech cadre was good, but it had had much less Western exposure than the Hungarian.) As for the general population, many people had developed entrepreneurial habits under socialism, some to keep body and soul together, others to dip their toes into the consumerism that was there for those who could pay. In the countryside the rigors and idiocies of collectivization always had been tempered by various types of capitalist enterprise that had made Hungarian agriculture the most successful aspect of socialist economics in the entire Soviet camp.

The parliamentary elections in March–April 1990 were encouraging, not only because they were free and orderly, but because they enabled a stable majority government to be formed. Again, Hungary was leading the way. The Democratic Forum, although falling somewhat short of a parliamentary majority, emerged strong enough to be able to form a stable government with the Independent Smallholders and the Christian Democrats. And just as important as the creation of a stable government was the agreement (or "pact") reached with the opposition parties about the election of a president and about a code of parliamentary practice and procedures without which proper representative government could hardly have begun.[45]

The new prime minister also seemed to have the background and qualities to lead Hungary through its postcommunist phase into fuller democracy. József Antall had an honorable, if not a particularly active, record as an opponent of communist rule. A medical historian by profession, he leaned toward the Christian democratic trend in the Hungarian Democratic Forum, although there also was an observable nationalist element about him. He had an impressive, unsmiling *gravitas* that went, rather incongruously, with an often bewildering, multitangential loquaciousness. But, above all, he was an honest, almost universally respected figure, a cohesive force, a healer—in short, just the kind of leader a country emerging from even a benevolent communist rule like Kádár's needed. Antall also was a stabilizing force within his own ruling coalition that had a propensity for disunity from the start. Nothing about Antall was inspiring; he was the personification of Aesop's axiom, "Slow and steady wins the race." He was a Hungarian gentleman of the old school, without being overtly reactionary. Not quite a man for all seasons, but apparently a man for most of the situations with which Hungary was likely to be faced.[46]

For more than two years after the spring elections of 1990 Hungary seemed to be developing and broadening its good democratic start. Thanks to the "pact" just mentioned, parliamentary procedures worked more smoothly than anywhere else in the postcommunist lands.[47] This sense of responsibility also was reflected in the crisis arising from the Budapest taxi drivers' strike of October 1990. Caused by sharp increases in the price of oil, this strike could have become more general and bitter had it not been for the sense of responsibility—the "civic-ness"—shown by the government and by the leadership of the parliamentary parties.[48] For the socialists, in particular, it could have been the occasion for attempted disruption. The strike was clearly a temptation, but the socialists chose not to try to undermine the new political system. The crisis marked an important milestone in the postcommunist evolution.

Hungarian democracy also was being served by the careful nurturing of the rule of law in public life. (See chapter 1.) At first, the Hungarian constitution was simply a patchwork of amendments introduced in 1989 and 1990 to the communist constitution of 1949. These amendments did change the character, purpose, and implications of the old document, but they still left a certain vagueness about the delineation of power, especially in the executive branch. Such documentary deficiencies led to serious disputes between the president and the prime minister over their spheres of authority, similar to those in other East European countries. In Hungary, though, the fights had a special sharpness and poignancy because the president, Árpád Göncz, an Alliance of Free Democrats' nominee, not only came from a different party from that of Antall, the prime minister, but was a personality in his own right, a man of strong liberal views, and jealous of what he construed as his sphere of authority. At the beginning, however, disputes like this one, together with the power and courage of the Constitutional Court (see chapter 2), seemed to give an extra zest to political life.

Behind the Image

It was this combination of institutions, procedures, and people that gave Hungary its deserved reputation in the early 1990s for democratic progress. In horse racing terms, Hungary seemed well ahead of the field. Economically, too, Hungary could boast satisfactory performance in several areas. It certainly was convincing Western investors of its promise; by the middle of 1992 more than half of all Western investment in Eastern Europe had gone into Hungary (see chapter 5). Many Hungarians were good at talking business and at persuading Westerners that they meant business. And Budapest, which was the only place in the country that most Westerners ever visited, certainly gave the impression of a capital on the move. Many of its citizens seemed not badly off (some of them seemed demonstratively well-off), and Budapest gave the impression that, though they might not yet be quite Western, its citizens were more ready for the West than was anyone else in the entire former communist empire.

Hungary seemed well-set. But, not for the first time in its history, the country presented an image that was not fully real. Genuine progress had been made in several fields, but some observers suspected that this progress was not so much building on the communist lead as coasting on it, not so much intensifying the previous impetus for change as simply maintaining it.

First, the economy. Despite the progress and the gloss, the Hungarian leadership, unlike the Czech, Polish, and even the Bulgarian, were failing to grasp the nettle of decisive change. Hungary generally was regarded as Eastern Europe's bastion of "gradualism" as opposed to "shock therapy" (see chapter 5). But, allowing for the looseness with which this terminology was often used, it was apparent that "gradualism" in Hungary's case was really hesitation. "Gradualism" was often defended on the grounds of the progress already made under the communist regime. "Shock therapy," therefore, was not so apparently necessary in Hungary as it was in other countries, where no such inherited progress had occurred. This was probably true, but what economic change required in Hungary after 1989 was a bold, new impetus toward the market economy, and this impetus was not forthcoming. Not only was little progress made in reducing the hard currency debt, the largest per capita in Eastern Europe, but no bold ventures in privatization or in financial policy took place, either. In conversation with many Hungarians it was possible in the course of 1991 and 1992 to note a certain complacency in their attitude. While Czechs, Poles, and even some Bulgarians and Romanians were measuring their achievements by *Western* criteria, the Hungarians still were pointing out that they were the most advanced in *Eastern* Europe. It used to be the same under Kádár! In the meantime, the standard of living stagnated; for many, it sank. The rich got richer, and the poor got poorer. Again, the same as under Kádár!

But the political dangers, too, interacting with the economic, could be serious. The early calm sense of political responsibility, and the smooth procedures of parliamentary practice were admirable—especially at the beginning. But were they the reflection of a maturing political process, or had they become by early 1993 a symptom of stagnation? Were Hungarian politics becoming a vacuum in danger of being filled not by the genuine interplay of competing forces but by demagogy, diversion, and strife? The degeneration was becoming evident, and each side blamed the other for it. But the malaise came from much deeper sources than any of the contenders were prepared to admit. Hungarian political life had become isolated from the interests and concerns of the public at large; many Budapest politicians represented little but themselves. Whatever their party affiliation, they owed their positions to the arrangements made for the transition from communism to postcommunism in the course of 1989. These arrangements, immensely constructive for the peaceful, effective, transition, nonetheless took place, if not behind closed doors, then well away from the glare of publicity and without any popular input.

Perhaps this quasi-secretive approach was the only way to achieve these arrangements. But it was an intellectuals' coup rather than a popular revolt. The coup led to a political structure that was neat and tidy, but very much a hothouse plant, in no sense an organic growth. In fact, the Hungarian power transition was probably the least organic of any in Eastern Europe. It had some formal similarities with the Polish transfer insofar as both were preceded or "arranged" through round-table talks. But there was nothing in Hungary like Solidarity in Poland, whose negotiators in 1988 and 1989 were representative of all strands of Polish society and which had shaken the foundations of communism almost a decade earlier. The new Polish political structure was, therefore, organic, in that it had roots in society, in a way that the Hungarian was not. Poland's political groupings, however chaotic, were natural. In Hungary, only the Smallholders really fell within this category — the socialists, to a certain extent. The others, especially the "new" groupings — the Hungarian Democratic Forum, FIDESZ, and the Alliance of Free Democrats — were contrived and artificial. Of course, they presented themselves to the voters for approval, but their bid was on a take-it-or-leave-it basis that might be acceptable in the short run but not permanently.

Thus, the Hungarian party system, as Mária Kovács has pointed out, was structured "alongside the predominant divisions not in society but within the *intelligentsia.*" Kovács continues:

> The other side of the coin then is that today's pluralistic party structure is largely an outcome of the pluralism among the intellectuals and so, more than anything else, this pluralism reflects the special concerns of the intellectuals. In order to illustrate, let me draw a few of the dividing lines: anti-communist cosmopolitan intellectuals in one party, anti-communist populist intellectuals in the other. Anti-communist intellectuals with a record of active dissent in one party, anti-communist intellectuals with a record of passive resistance in the other. Jewish intellectuals in one party, non-Jewish intellectuals in the other, and, bordering on the almost comical, historians in one party, philosophers in the other.[49]

Obviously, it could not be long before the political utility of such a structure began to dwindle. It served the country well in the hazardous period of the transition and early postcommunist phase. Now, though, it was becoming irrelevant, counterproductive, and potentially dangerous. The gap between the political establishment and society as a whole was widening, not narrowing. Again, it was probably wider than in any other East European country, wider even than in Romania, where the ruling Salvation Front did have strong support in the countryside and small towns. The most obvious Hungarian result was a growing disinterest in politics reflected in voter apathy. The voter turnout at parliamentary by-elections after the beginning of 1991 was not so much embarrassing as profoundly disturbing (see chapter 2). In several cases the election had to be repeated because the first turnout had been less than the regulatory minimum.

Disruption and Historical Divisions

The polarization in the political situation, always inherent since 1989 but partially concealed by mutually agreed parliamentary procedures, now emerged clearly in the summer of 1992, that is, midway through the term of its first democratically elected parliament. In the first place, the Hungarian Socialist Party won a parliamentary seat in a by-election and began to climb in the opinion polls.[50] The socialists, it is true, were becoming part of the political establishment, but they were making their appeal to the deprived sections of the electorate, benefiting from a certain "Kádár nostalgia" caused by declining living standards. Second, Hungary's "media war" — the incessant efforts of the Antall government to change the directors, and the direction, of Hungarian radio and television (see chapter 2) — was not only a deeply contested struggle in itself, but it also dramatized the controversy over the powers of the presidency and the prime minister,[51] and, most serious, it raised questions about the government's attitude to some basic political freedoms.

The most damaging polarization, however, was being forced by the political right. Overlooking the rightist fringe parties, which had never made any secret of where they stood, this effort first became evident in the Independent Smallholders' Party under József Torgyán (see chapter 2). His behavior split the Smallholder ranks and brought what had historically probably been Hungary's greatest party into considerable disrepute.[52] The Smallholders, though, kept their constituency in the countryside, and, in any case, their own disruptive antics were soon dwarfed by those inside the Hungarian Democratic Forum (HDF).

It was in the national populistic wing of the HDF that tendencies became apparent which were much closer to fascism than anything even the broadest democratic spectrum could accommodate. These were illustrated and dramatized by an article in the HDF weekly *Magyar Fórum* by István Csurka, a writer of real talent, and a politician who was both a member of parliament and a vice president of the HDF.

In a sense, Csurka rendered a service to Hungarian political life in that he exposed the unreality of the mold in which it had become encased. But he achieved this result in a way that challenged the very values on which democratic politics are based. And, in doing so, he dredged up prejudices that had previously disfigured Hungary's public life and were never much below the surface.[53]

Csurka's article — actually a political manifesto written to mark the fifth anniversary of the HDF's founding and the midway mark of the current parliament — received considerable coverage in the West and set off something of a storm inside Hungary. It was a neofascist tract, with the author reveling in expressions and sentiments that, even to less sensitive readers, recalled the Nazi era. The article also was permeated with suspicions of conspiracy bordering on the paranoid. Hungary, according to Csurka, was still ruled by a communist-Jewish-liberal clique. Anti-Semitic views and innuendoes were mixed with outright racist sentiments. He called for decommunization in terms that unmistakably suggested a witch-hunt. There was a strong irredentist passage and a reference to the Hungarians' need for Lebensraum. "Necessary" violence was emphasized as an integral part of political life. Compromise in politics was dismissed as a symptom of weakness and a recipe for disaster. The text bristled with political malevolence masquerading as patriotism. This statement, however, probably contained the most chilling imperative:

> We can no longer ignore the fact that the deterioration [of the population] has genetic causes as well. It has to be acknowledged that underprivileged, even cumulatively underprivileged, strata and groups, in which the harsh laws of natural selection no longer function because it would do no good anyway, have been living among us for far too long. Society now has to support the strong, fit-for-life families who are prepared for work and achievement.[54]

Though he subsequently denied it, Csurka was referring, at least in part, to Gypsies. If not vintage Ferenc Szálasi, the former Hungarian Arrow-Cross Nazi leader, these words were at least vintage Gyula Gömbös, the prewar prime minister who once established a "Party of Racial Defense" and later led a secret group called the "Hungarian Scientific Race Protecting Society."

It would all have been worrying enough if Csurka had been a crotchety private citizen wanting to get something Nietzschean off his chest. But he was a senior figure in the country's strongest political party apparently making a challenge for the leadership of that party, certainly advocating a drastic change in its policy and political strategy. And Csurka's was by no means a voice in the wilderness, although it might be the loudest and the one carrying the greatest resonance. Other members of the HDF, including members of parliament, were just as aggressively fascist in some of their remarks.

Even more discouraging than Csurka's outburst itself was the reaction of part of the public to it. Many Hungarians were shocked by it, which was reflected in the press and in public and private comment. But many supported Csurka, both at home and in the diaspora. He may have "gone too far" for some, which they put down to "artistic license," but the argument generally was sound. ("In your heart you know he's right.") Most Hungarians, loudly or quietly, supported his sentiments on the "lost territories." Some educated Hungarians realized the damage Csurka might do to Hungary's image abroad and opposed him more for that reason than for any specific thing that he said. Many tended to regard the patronizing remarks he made about Antall as the worst part of the whole tract. (He brought up Antall's lymph cancer—a universally known public secret—as well as castigating Antall's genius for compromise and his conciliatory behavior.) All in all, what was lacking was a strong *moral* outcry. There was a far from massive demonstration in Budapest by opposition politicians and intellectuals which had only a temporary impact in the capital itself or in the country as a whole.

The fact was that Csurka's prejudices had some resonance, and, in terms of the controversy they aroused, they clearly illustrated a classic cultural, political, and social divide in Hungary's history. Writing over a year before the Csurka issue, *Le Monde*'s correspondent, José-Alain Fralon, put it well:

> So two Hungarys appear or reappear. On the one hand there is a traditional, conservative and often rural Hungary, with its sometimes rudimentary sound sense and narrow nationalism, whose representatives flirt dangerously with xenophobia and anti-Semitism. On the other, there is the Hungary of the "modernists," intellectuals, technocrats and businessmen, often as not grouped together in opposition parties, who have always been open to the West and who too see communism as an Asian perversion. In this way arises the old Hungarian division between "populists" and "urbanites."[55]

In the Csurka issue, Fralon's observations also dovetail with those of Mária Kovács, which were quoted earlier. Csurka was reaching over the heads of the establishment intellectual players in Budapest politics and going straight to the "ordinary" voter who was beginning to feel estranged from it all.

This issue presented a serious problem for Antall. At first, he chose to discount the importance of the Csurka incident. He publicly dissociated himself from Csurka's views but refrained from trying to take any disciplinary steps against him. What he was indirectly admitting, of course, was that support for Csurka was too strong; he could be rebuked but not dislodged. He had his own constituency. This reality was confirmed at the HDF conference in January 1993 when Csurka actually challenged Antall for the party's leadership. He lost, but he was noisily acclaimed by most of the delegates and was easily reelected to the HDF presidium, one-fifth of whose members were considered Csurka supporters.[56] The liberal wing of the HDF was routed at the conference. But at least Antall now spoke openly against Csurka, and obviously the breach between the two men could never be healed. Csurka and his closest supporters were subsequently expelled from the HDF and proceeded to form their own party, the Hungarian Justice Party.[57] This development meant that the HDF was shattered, and a calm political climate had become a stormy one. And the man of poise, Antall, was dying.

The reburial in Hungary in early September 1993 of the remains of Admiral Miklós Horthy, Hungary's regent between 1920 and 1944, revealed, as the Csurka case had done, the deep divisions in Hungarian society. The reburial produced a strong wave of nostalgic sympathy for Horthy and an identification in varying degrees with parts or all of the quarter century of precommunist Hungarian history. It was attended, "in a private capacity," by several members of Antall's cabinet, and Antall himself subsequently visited Horthy's grave. But Horthy's reburial also aroused fierce criticism, mainly from liberal and leftist circles which regarded the former regent as antidemocratic, irredentist, and, however personally anti-Nazi he might have been, as pursuing policies that inevitably led to the wartime Nazi alliance. The controversy proceeded on predictable lines, reflecting the gulf in society over public values and over the assessment of Hungarian history. Hungarians were at ease with neither their present nor their recent past.[58]

Hopes and Dangers

The Csurka case has been worth discussing because it exemplified and then aggravated the precariousness of Hungarian public life. Its outward stability was now giving way to a dangerous restlessness. Much would depend on developments both outside and inside the country. The general external situation, with crisis or uncertainty in all of Hungary's neighbors except Austria (and Austria had its own Csurka in the charismatic Jörg Haider), seemed calculated to increase rather than allay restlessness. So did the condition of Hungarian minorities in neighboring countries—Vojvodina, Romania, and independent Slovakia. And the big influx of refugees from Yugoslavia, as well as assorted migrants from Eastern Europe and other parts of the world, strained resources, nerves, and tolerance.

It was unfortunate that the situation of Hungarian minorities abroad and the turbulence across some of Hungary's borders were, of necessity, taking up so much of the government's attention when domestic policy should have been its main concern. Economic and social conditions, after all, affected the majority of citizens who would decide the fate of constitutional democracy in Hungary. Taken in isolation, some elements in Csurka's ragbag of ideas were quite admirable: concern for the aged, for example, and his general concept of developing a large, viable middle class. These would appeal to many, and they could make Csurka's *entire* Weltanschauung all the more acceptable. And part of the democratic dilemma in Hungary and elsewhere in Eastern Europe was that successful economic transformation initially meant a further depression of living standards for most of the population. The vital questions: How long would it all take? How serious the hardship? How many would be affected?

Who would eventually win if the moderate democratic transformation failed or stalled? The left—the socialists or even the unrepentant communists who clung to Kadarism—seemed set to recover some of the working-class support they had lost. But the far right—the Csurka tendency—also stood to gain. Not only was the right's social program attractive, but it would appeal to the sense of nationalist grievance, race prejudice, and xenophobia. It was not likely to have a decisive electoral impact—in fact, that could be relatively small. But it could become a sizable, permanent factor on the political scene.

Hungary needed four things quickly and simultaneously: economic growth with perceptible advances in overall living standards; continued Western investment and support; calm and fairness for Hungarians beyond its borders; a political system combining liberal constitutionalism, responsibility, and responsiveness. Specifically, with regard to the responsiveness, Hungary needed political parties based on sectional interests—business, labor, farmers, etc. For this to happen, important changes in political attitudes and alignments were necessary. Above all, Hungarian democracy had to become inclusive, and it had to promise something.

Antall's death in December 1993 was a severe and untimely blow. His steadiness was needed more than ever. His successor, the former interior minister Peter Boross, was a contested figure whose democratic credentials were questioned by many. Perhaps it was salutary that an election was in the offing. But would it clarify or only confuse, stabilize democratic development or undermine it?

4 COUNTRY POLITICS

SOUTH-EASTERN EUROPE

This chapter deals with three countries: Romania, Bulgaria, and Albania. The countries that once were part of Yugoslavia and are now independent, or struggling to remain independent, are not covered. They form part of the "Yugoslav Tragedy," the title and subject of chapter 7. All except Slovenia are still caught up, in some way and to some extent, in the continuing phases of this tragedy. As for Slovenia, though not exactly a case of becoming free and living happily ever after, it at least escaped the turmoil of its former associates and was making a solid start in developing democracy and the market, even if the question of its longer-term viability as an independent state remained open.

If East Central Europe had been the "triad of hope" (see chapter 3), what could South-Eastern Europe, as represented by Romania, Bulgaria, and Albania, expect to be called? "Triad of despair," a term that many were suggesting, would be prejudging a complex situation that was not without its elements of hope. "Triad of tribulation" would be better, accurate and open-ended, ruling out neither progress nor regression. In all three countries there were signs of both.

The three countries, of course, are ethnically, geopolitically, and historically different. They all were parts of the Ottoman Empire, but they shared a different Ottoman heritage. Bulgaria was a subject nation; what became Romania was mostly under Ottoman suzerainty; most Albanians converted to Islam and led a relatively privileged life, some even as members of the Porte's ruling elite. Under communism, too, although subject to the same structure of rule, all three countries took different courses in foreign affairs. For nearly two decades Albania was an anti-Soviet Chinese satellite. For more than a quarter of a century Romania was semi-independent. For more than forty years Bulgaria was a Soviet dependency.

Now, though, in the postcommunist phase of their histories, some strong similarities exist among them. There are large numbers of ethnic Albanians (Montenegro, Serbia, and Macedonia) and Romanians (Moldova) in neighboring countries. Most Bulgarians would argue that in neighboring Macedonia most of the Slavic population is really Bulgarian. The question of future territorial reunion—Kosovo with Albania, Moldova with Romania—has become potential, if not actual. (Reunion of Macedonia with Bulgaria has looked most unlikely. But never?) Bulgaria and Romania have large ethnic minorities—the Turkish and the Hungarian, respectively—whose treatment and aspirations could cause even more serious domestic and international problems than these countries have had so far. Finally, Albania and possibly Bulgaria could be affected by any spilling over of the Yugoslav war.

In domestic politics there have been some striking similarities. In their first free elections, all three countries returned communist, neocommunist, or former communist governments. The second free elections in Albania and Bulgaria produced governments from the former democratic opposition. Although many observers had expected voters to do the same in Romania, they did not. A similar pattern of postcommunist political violence was present in all three countries. In both Albania and Bulgaria the former communists remained politically strong. During Albania's local elections in the summer of 1992, the communists polled well; in early 1993 the Bulgarian Socialist Party was the strongest single party in the Sŭbranie and had been rising in opinion polls. In Romania many observers would say that the former communists had never lost power, an oversimplification but an important perception in the Romanian political equation. Decommunization, too, not surprisingly, had become an important, virulent, shared issue. All three countries, too, had leaders of considerable substance: Berisha in Albania, Zhelev in Bulgaria, and Iliescu in Romania. But all three were burdened by the ruinous communist economic legacy. Ultimately, in the case of all three—if in varying degrees—the danger arose of the new open society becoming the void.

ROMANIA
The Elusive Middle Ground

In October 1992 Ion Iliescu won the presidency of Romania for the second time, with a clear majority. Iliescu's party, the Democratic

National Salvation Front, also won a plurality of seats in both the senate and the assembly of the legislature. His party's victory, however, was much less clear-cut than his own. His was a personal victory, and he carried his party some of the way with him.

The result was a shock for many Romanians, mainly intellectuals, professional and business people, and students in the larger cities. They had been convinced that these elections would result in the long-awaited breakthrough to more democratic, open government, the final defeat for Romanian communism, and hence a readier acceptance of Romania into the Western comity of nations. It was a shock, too, for many Westerners who, usually on the basis of inadequate Western reporting, tended to see most Romanians as impatiently waiting to cast off the yoke under which they were assumed to be groaning. Iliescu, for most Westerners, was the "former aide" to Ceauşescu. The fact that he fell from Ceauşescu's favor as early as 1971 went unknown or disregarded. Finally, the numerous preelection polls, predicting either a defeat for Iliescu or a very close thing, unquestionably showed that Romanian psephology still left something to be desired.[1]

The election's outcome was not only a shock but a humiliation for many Romanians. Except for Serbia, now Europe's pariah (throw Montenegro in, too), Romania as a result of the election became the only former communist state still led by a leader and a party that, however much both might have changed (and this was hotly disputed), were still of the former vintage. Romania was confidently expected to do what Albania and Bulgaria had done in their second free elections after communism. If the Bulgarians and even the Albanians could do it, why not the historically more "Westernized" Romanians? And the local elections held throughout Romania in February 1992 had given cause for optimism. The opposition scored encouraging victories in Bucharest and some other large towns. One more heave, it seemed, and the breakthrough would be there.[2]

It was not to happen. Disappointed intellectuals then proceeded to ascribe their election debacle to the low political culture of many of their compatriots and to their timidity in emerging from the Ceauşescu cocoon of fear. (The Albanians, though, had had to emerge from an even more enveloping cocoon. The intellectuals had a point.[3] But they naturally were reluctant to admit that one of the main reasons for Iliescu's victory was their own political dilettantism, their disunity, the incompetence of their political leaders, and their remoteness from what most Romanians thought and wanted. The underestimation of Iliescu showed both their lack of acumen and their arrogance. "Iliescu is an idiot"; "He can do nothing but grin and grimace." These were typical of intellectuals' comments about a man who could run political rings around them.

Chronic Polarization

Iliescu, in fact, whatever his limitations and his inability to shed some of his communist psychology, continued to be Romania's dominating political figure and the 1992 elections confirmed this. But what his victory also showed was the degree of polarization—geographical, political, social, and cultural—that still divides Romanian society. Though he polled well in some of the larger cities, retaining some of the worker support he was widely considered to have lost, his main strength lay in the rural areas and the smaller towns. Some observers also detected a historical, territorial polarization: Iliescu did well in the old Regat—Wallachia and Moldavia—with the opposition scoring majorities in most of Transylvania and the Banat.[4]

Several things helped Iliescu in the Romanian countryside. One of them was unquestionably his control of the electronic media, especially television, often the only source of news and opinion in areas where the urban free press failed to penetrate. But this media monopoly could not solely explain his success. He was the closest available approximation to what many Romanians still needed: a father figure. Both he and his name meant something. He deftly played on the conservatism of a culture that was still essentially peasant—the dislike, even fear, of change. He also played on contemporary economic fears. Many workers in small towns were solely dependent for their employment (as, for example, in Slovakia) on one large factory; many of these workers could fall victim to the "shock therapy" type of economic reforms that the opposition seemed to be endorsing. Many peasants, too, satisfied with their private holdings after decollectivization in spite of all the ensuing difficulties and giving credit, rather generously, to Iliescu for this step, were afraid of what the restitution process (the restoring of property to former landlords) might mean to their own security of ownership. Of even greater concern was their desire to get their hands on former state land that the opposition was advocating should also largely be restored to its former owners.

Iliescu, therefore, touched a raw nerve when he raised the bogey of the "boyars' return" and of capitalist-caused destitution in the small towns. While some opposition members were wistfully recalling the "golden age" of precommunism, Iliescu was getting votes by reminding people how tarnished that age had been.

Iliescu also exploited the profound Romanian peasant-worker distrust for metropolitan intellectuals. This attitude had prevailed in precommunist Romania as well as during the communist period, and it also has been alive and kicking since 1989. The distrust usually has been justified. In precommunist Romania the official propaganda depicted the peasantry as embodying the soul and the virtues of the nation. In communist Romania this reverential status passed to the workers. In both cases the homage bestowed was blatantly false; but neither peasants nor workers were much deceived. They despised the purveyors of this propaganda, and as a class they despised the intellectuals for their pampered privileges and their traditional indifference to anybody's condition except their own. This partly explained the fact that in communist Romania no intellectual-worker alliance against communist rule ever developed. (Nor in any Balkan country, for that matter. Such an alliance was essentially an East-Central European phenomenon, and it did not happen there very often, either.) As for the intellectuals, their contempt for the peasants and workers continued unabated.[5] Their explanation for Iliescu's victory was at least partial proof of this disdain.

The extent to which Iliescu exploited nationalism is open to debate. He certainly exploited anti-Hungarian sentiment, though much less crudely than Gheorghe Funar, the presidential candidate for the far-right Party of Romanian National Unity (PRNU), who got more than 10 percent of the vote and whose supporters, as well as those of other right-wing parties, largely rallied to Iliescu in the second round of the presidential election. (On Funar, see also chapters 2 and 6.) Early in his first presidential term Iliescu began to alienate the Hungarian minority and its political representatives in the Hungarian Democratic Union of Romania by reneging on some of the concessions he, or his associates, apparently had promised them immediately after the revolution in December 1989 (see chapter 6).[6] But, the Hungarian minority apart, little evidence has appeared of overt or covert nationalism on Iliescu's part—no anti-Semitism, for example, which is rampant enough in Romanian far-right circles. And on the reincorporation of Bessarabia, he always has been restrained (see chapter 7).[7]

Political and Social Disorders

The 1992 election touched on and reflected some of the most important political issues in Romania's brief postcommunist history. It may have been the first paving stone in the long road to stability. Previously, though, it was disorder and instability that appeared to dominate Romanian public life. The low point was undoubtedly the descent on Bucharest in June 1990 of hordes of miners from the Jiu Valley ostensibly to restore civic order that was being threatened by demonstrating and rioting students. Obviously, some degree of order needed to be restored, and the police were temporarily overwhelmed. But the miners' rampage created a greater degree of damage and disorder, grossly violated any concept of the rule of law, retarded democratic development, and harmed Romania's reputation abroad.[8] It was a ghastly new reflection of the historical polarization already mentioned.

It also indelibly stained Iliescu's reputation, for he had either summoned the miners down or had approved (or condoned) the decision to do so. (He has persistently stated that the miners invaded Bucharest on their own initiative.) But to see the whole episode solely in terms of Iliescu and his alleged infamy, as many Romanians did, was to miss the more important point about social divisions in Romanian society. The Jiu Valley miners, after all, did not have to be press-ganged into swarming over Bucharest and beating up as many intellectuals—real or suspected—as they could lay their hands, or their cudgels, on. They positively relished the idea. But miner power could be dangerous, as was demonstrated in September 1991 when the Jiu Valley once again spilled over into Bucharest in protest against economic conditions for which the miners held Iliescu responsible. One day it could save, the next it could seek to destroy.

The second miners' invasion led, not to Iliescu's fall, but to that of Petre Roman, the capable, slick operator who had been prime minister for nearly two years. It was a textbook example of political manipulation on Iliescu's part. Roman was forced to take the political consequences of a bold economic reform he had piloted and for whose social sufferings he was now being held to blame.[9] Iliescu, therefore, made Roman the sacrificial lamb. Roman and many others were convinced that Iliescu had engineered this new miners' invasion as well, with the aim of breaking their partnership, which already was turning sour.

Roman, whose place was taken by an able, "politically neutral" economist, Theodor Stolojan, subsequently tried to use his own following and organizational strength within the National Salvation Front, of which he was the president, to erode Iliescu's political position.[10] Iliescu then proceeded to form his own breakaway "Democratic National Salvation Front," made up of an increasing number of deserters from the original Front. At the elections in September 1992 Roman was humiliated, his new party's candidate for the presidency doing particularly badly. Although he was young and resilient enough to make an eventual comeback, Roman's short-term political prospects looked dim, indeed. He would have to wait at least until Iliescu's departure.

Securitate and the Conspiracy Mentality

His opponents attributed everything Iliescu did to an unregenerate communism. Much of contention was overdrawn; some of it was grotesque oversimplification. But in one thing—the resilience of Ceauşescu's old Securitate—he was certainly vulnerable. This was a disturbing aspect of his presidency, and it cast a pall over Romanian public life. No one knew for certain how powerful the old Securitate and how comprehensive and integrated its activities still were. But no doubt existed about its considerable Mafia-like presence. Probably there was no countrywide security web as such; rather, there were larger and smaller pockets, sometimes acting independently, sometimes cooperating.[11] Securitate business interests developed, sometimes picking off the plums in the privatization of industry and business, and former members also were believed to be active in semilegal and totally illegal activities. Telephone tapping was common, sometimes blatant enough to be comic. (There is an apparently true story of a telephone tapper interrupting a conversation and asking the interlocutors to stop while he changed the tape.) But nothing was comic about threats of death or bodily harm that were by no means uncommon. Some opposition writers and journalists were beaten up and intimidated. Many old Securitate officers also joined the new intelligence service, helping to give it a sinister reputation that it did not wholly deserve. To suggest, as some did, that the Securitate were Iliescu's unseen praetorians was ridiculous, but he undoubtedly could have been more forceful in trying to stop these persistent abuses of citizens' freedoms and privacy, and he could have been more frank in acknowledging that a problem existed. To some extent he was helpless, incapable of ending all the abuses even if he were aware of them, and the new intelligence service was not likely to move resolutely against people it regarded as part of its old boy network. It would be years before even a semirespectable new intelligence organization could emerge, and many more years before the public accepted it as such.

The Securitate's buoyancy was grist to the Bucharest rumor mill. Suspicion bordering on paranoia has clouded Romanian public life throughout recorded history, and communist rule only strengthened the tendency. It was not surprising that the December revolution of 1989 and the National Salvation Front's coming to power spawned new conspiracy theories. The full story of this episode still remains to be told. There will always be enough loose ends, though, to keep the conspiracy theorists going. But, for the sake of perspective, it might be mentioned that other great events in Romanian history have not been above suspicion. Two eyewitnesses reported as follows on King Michael's coup of August 23, 1944, against Antonescu and the Nazi alliance: "A careful analysis of all the evidence obtained on the spot reveals that on the night of the King's proclamation there were so many plotters plotting, conspirators conspiring, traitors committing treason and cheaters cheating that nobody knew who was who and what was what. We traced nine separate plots all striving for the same goal."[12] Obviously, many things are not as they seem to be, and throughout Eastern Europe communist rule strengthened the tendency to conclude that *nothing* is as it seems to be. In postcommunist Eastern Europe, with open societies replacing closed societies, there would seem to be much less reason for suspicion now. But the new open societies are confusing societies, without the grim predictability that some aspects of communism had. And the confusion only reinforces suspicion. Nowhere has this suspicion been more evident than in Romania—with Poland sometimes a close second. In both these countries, parts of the educated sections of society, which should have known better, have been as guilty as anybody in sowing suspicion and spreading confusion.

It was this state of affairs that so lowered the level of public life in both countries. In Romania, especially, a snide, back-biting triviality about so much of political discourse was unparalleled in Eastern Europe. Again, the intellectual class was largely to blame. It was as if they were continuing the games that many of them had played under Ceauşescu — and which he deliberately let them play — in a new and much more permissive setting. In this regard, the media set a particularly low standard. Even a courageous, "quality" newspaper like *România liberă,* a pillar of the opposition, often demeaned itself by petty point-scoring, at being clever rather than constructive. Exceptions existed, but they tended to be few.

Filling the Void?

After Ceauşescu, political development in Romania had to start from scratch. Always excluding Albania, Romania was in this regard the worst-placed of all the former East European communist countries. The power vacuum that emerged after Ceauşescu was largely filled by the National Salvation Front, with a speed either fortuitous or suspicious, depending on how far one accepts the conspiracy theories about its assumption of power.[13] But plot or no plot, and no matter how distasteful some aspects of the Front were and continued to be, it brought some stability into a dangerously volatile situation. Without it, the vacuum would have become void until a deus ex machina appeared in the form of overt dictatorship.

Facing the large, inchoate, but dominating Front, a huge number of oppositional groupings dotted the political scene, expressions more of political exuberance than political significance. Some of those emerging as real political players tended, however, to recall the precommunist past rather than point to the postcommunist future. Among them were the National Peasant Party, a famous prewar party, which added the Christian Democratic appellation to its title. Led by Ion Raţiu, who had spent the whole of the communist period in Western exile, it demanded a return to the institutions set up by the 1923 constitution, which, of course, included the monarchy. The Liberal Party, a reincarnation of the most famous party in Romanian history, also demanded a return to 1923. It was led by Ion Câmpeanu, another figure who had spent many years in exile.[14] Both parties were based on sound principles and contained some worthy leaders. Nor were all of these figures nostalgic reactionaries idealizing a precommunist past. But their general direction tended to be backward rather than forward, to draw inspiration from the past instead of taking into account that, for better or for worse, Romania had changed irreversibly since 1945.

Not surprisingly, these parties strongly urged the reunion of Moldova into a greater Romania. But it was their agitation for the return of the monarchy that best demonstrated their nostalgia. King Michael's triumphal return to his native country for a short visit in 1992 raised the two parties' hopes and increased their pressure for the monarchy. But Michael, always a brave and deservedly respected figure, was seventy in 1992 and was clearly a tired man of yesterday, out of touch with the reality of his own country and of the political world at large. Comparisons by his supporters with King Juan Carlos and the success of the monarchical restoration in Spain ignored the difference in age and energy between the two men and the differences between Franco's Spain and Ceauşescu's Romania. Even more important, though, was the likelihood that any restoration of the monarchy in Romania would not be a cohesive solution, as the monarchists were claiming, but another divisive element in a country that was divided enough. Besides, most public opinion surveys indicated relatively little support for a restoration.[15]

However, other groupings in the democratic opposition were not so rooted in the past. Their problem was that they were inadequately led and found it hard to both cohere and settle on a specific political program. (In all of these respects they strongly resembled the Union of Democratic Forces — UDF — in neighboring Bulgaria). These groupings first attempted to unite in November 1990, when the Civic Alliance was formed, to evolve a few months later into the Party of Civic Alliance (PCA), led by Nicolae Manolescu. In November 1991 the PCA joined with other democratic opposition parties, including the National Peasants and the Liberals, to form an umbrella organization, the Democratic Convention. The Convention did well in the local elections in February 1992, and it was hoped that it would remain, however loose, a united formation on the political scene. But the subsequent defection of Câmpeanu's Liberals seriously hurt it, and, although the Convention did fight the presidential and parliamentary elections later in the year, some doubted that it could survive the aftermath of its defeat. Romanian democracy would be well served if it did.

On the far right of the political spectrum were the nationalist groupings and parties, some of which are discussed further in chapter 6. The most important of these competing in the 1992 elections were the Party of Romanian National Unity (PRNU) and the yet more extreme Greater Romania Party. Neither made a significant impression, but the former's presidential candidate, Funar, did get more than 10 percent of the vote. The PRNU, however, was an organized political expression of something much bigger: *Vatra Româneăsca* (Romanian Cradle), which claimed a membership of more than 6 million, although this figure was certainly an exaggeration. It was xenophobic, violently anti-Hungarian, opposing whatever rights had already been granted to the Magyar minority, but not so rabidly nationalist or overtly racist (anti-Semitic, anti-Gypsy), as the Greater Romania Party. Generally, the extreme right's leadership consisted of two elements. First were the former communist writers and intellectuals who had served the Ceauşescu personality cult. Some had shown strong anti-Semitic tendencies then. Now they continued, in a much more uninhibited way, the nationalist ethos that Ceauşescu had propounded. Second was a group whose radical nationalism, including virulent anti-Semitism, extended back to the precommunist period—mainly to the Iron Guard ethos, which itself began to attract more devotees. This movement has been dubbed by one expert as the "radical return."[16] Fortunately, neither group yet had a strong following among the electorate, but each was aggressive and noisy, apparently well-financed, and growing.

On the far left, former communist Premier Ilie Verdeţ had founded the Socialist Labor Party, which received just over 3 percent of the votes in the 1992 election. Its program was reform communist, and its main preoccupation was to try to capitalize on the growing social and economic hardship rising from economic reform and the general overall frustration.[17] Its prospects were not to be entirely discounted. Though it hardly threatened to take power in the foreseeable future, it could reap a considerable "dissatisfaction dividend" as things got worse before showing much sign of getting better.

A Possible Evolution

The National Salvation Front itself was never coherent, always precarious. It contained something of almost everything—communists in various stages of reconstruction, socialists, social democrats, nationalists, populists, liberals. Unquestionably, it included many former servants of the old regime, to whom it gave shelter and an avenue of rehabilitation. These elements soon turned some liberals away from the Front, defections it could ill-afford to suffer.

For almost two years the Front was more motivated by power—gaining and retaining it—than by any issues of policy. Its official profile was leftist—not neocommunist but more social-democratic. Subsequently, though, it became riddled with dissent, mainly through issues concerning personality and power but also to some extent on policy lines. Iliescu, elected president in Romania's first postcommunist elections in May 1990, was no longer formally leader of the Front. This post, as mentioned, had been assumed by Roman, prime minister of the first Front government. After an initial period of edgy cooperation, the Front began to divide between the followers of Iliescu, clearly left of center and suspicious of the comprehensiveness and pace of the economic reforms and the privatization program, and Roman, whose government was espousing this reformist line. After being ousted from premiership, Roman was able to retain leadership of the Front mainly because of his control of the organization's patronage and press.

For Romania's political future, the most hopeful institutional aspect of the Iliescu-Roman split was that a genuine, modern party system might evolve from it. Iliescu's new Democratic National Salvation Front, later to be called Social Democracy of Romania, was emerging as the only serious left-of-center party or coalition in terms of electoral support. The original National Salvation Front would, it was expected, become the party, or coalition, of the center. The former would embrace general social-democratic principles, the latter would stress free market principles, although tempered by social justice—the *soziale Marktwirtschaft* of Germany. If such groupings were to emerge, and if the main components of the Democratic Convention could hold together, then a fairly stable, if loose, party system could evolve.

This scenario, however, might be too optimistic. Roman's National Salvation Front could continue to lose strength to the Social Democracy of Romania. This decline in strength would not be too serious—in fact, it might be beneficial to democratic development—if the Democratic Convention became an effective political coalition. But the Convention might not become that effective, and, in the meantime, Iliescu's new Front could become a still stronger political force. The Front already showed some characteristics similar to Latin-American movements like the Peronistas in Argentina and the old Institutional Revolutionary Party (PRI) in Mexico, and even without Iliescu the Front could stay relatively united on the basis of the perquisites and patronage it could dispense. That development certainly would be discouraging, but it still would be better than a chaos from which only the right-wing nationalist parties and perhaps the far left would benefit. Then the polarization, to which Romanian politics traditionally have been prone, would have reached its dangerous climax.

BULGARIA
Oasis or Mirage?

"The Kirghistan of the Balkans." This was how a Central Asian friend, with a knowledge of South-Eastern Europe and obviously not without a touch of irony, described Bulgaria in early 1992. He was referring to the stability obtaining in both these countries relative to the chaos raging in their immediate vicinity. Not only that. He was implicitly wondering how long it would last, how long it would be before Kirghistan and Bulgaria lost their enviable distinctiveness and assumed the characteristics of their turbulent environment.

The comparison was not altogether inapt, though hardly one that many Bulgarians would have appreciated. Bulgaria did offer, and continued to offer, a contrast to the other former communist Balkan countries — the bloody anarchy of much of former Yugoslavia, the neurotic politics of Romania, and the bedlam of Albania. Parliamentary democracy was in place. How well it was working was another matter, but it had survived the difficult transition from the quasi-totalitarianism of communist rule. Rudiments of the rule of law also had appeared, most notably in the workings of Bulgaria's new constitutional court.[18] Having been tied to the Soviet economy for so long (see chapter 5), its own economy might have seemed close to collapse. But it was at least undergoing the beginnings of systemic reform — so far without the unbearable social disruption that some had predicted.

The long road toward democracy had begun with the communist palace coup that ousted the veteran leader, Todor Zhivkov, in November 1989. This step moved, not toward democracy, but toward perestroika — Gorbachev reform communism. But, unlike Gorbachev, the post-Zhivkov Bulgarian leadership, dominated by the former foreign minister, Petŭr Mladenov, had no political concept of its own other than staying in power and avoiding a popular revolution that would overturn the entire communist system. To maintain control, the leadership was prepared to make political concessions. But these concessions were nowhere near enough for the activist youth of the larger Bulgarian cities, especially Sofia, who wanted root-and-branch change and were not prepared to wait for any slow evolution of the communist system toward democracy. With the fall of Zhivkov, they had had one bite of the cherry; now they wanted the whole cherry—and quickly.

The political impact of the anticommunist sections of the Sofia populace since 1989 should not be underestimated. Its first success was in getting rid of Mladenov in July 1990. In response to continuous street demonstrations, Mladenov had semiprivately referred to the possible need of "bringing in the tanks." This fatal remark was taped and, occurring soon after the Tienanmen Square catastrophe in Beijing, was a propaganda gift to the demonstrators. Mladenov had to resign and disappeared from public life.[19] The power of the streets, therefore, became evident at an early moment in postcommunist Bulgaria. This form of power was to become still more evident a few weeks later, at the end of August 1990, when a large crowd attacked the communist party building in the center of Sofia and set parts of it on fire.[20] Finally, in November–December 1990 the socialist (former communist) government of Andrei Lukanov, which had been returned to power the previous June in Bulgaria's first free election since 1946,[21] was toppled as a result of nationwide strikes and demonstrations in Sofia. Its place was taken by a coalition government including socialists and members of the opposition Union of Democratic Forces (UDF), led by Dimitŭr Popov, a political independent.[22] Yet again, in June 1993 large crowds led by UDF leaders repeatedly demonstrated in Sofia in an unsuccessful bid to force the resignation of President Zhelev.

These examples of extraparliamentary pressure and violence should be kept in mind when praising Bulgarian progress toward a peaceful constitutional and parliamentary system. Politics were often violent, and the violence stemmed from the refusal of a section of the urban population to accept democratic election results. The ousting of Lukanov in December 1990 looked to some observers rather like Prague, February 1948, in reverse—more street democracy than parliamentary democracy. The remarkable thing was that no one was reported killed in the series of tumults, a feature that makes Bulgaria unique in the postcommunist Balkans and one new to Bulgarian history itself. But unless it became established practice that election results are accepted, somebody certainly would get killed.

Political Groupings

One of the most successful elements of Bulgaria's postcommunist reconstruction has been Zhelyu Zhelev, the president who succeeded Mladenov in the summer of 1990.[23] A former communist party member, an academic who had become disillusioned with the system and had written a soon-suppressed study, ostensibly about fascism but actually about communism, for which he suffered both professionally and personally, Zhelev became president as part of an informal pact between the socialist government and the democratic opposition. With the situation in the country tense, it was an astute move, a good example of constitutional compromise. Zhelev had been the acknowledged leader of the Union of Democratic Forces (UDF) before his elevation, and he made no secret of the fact that, as far as moral and political values were concerned, the UDF was where his sympathies lay. But as president, he did his best to steer a middle course between the competing political groups. In doing so he incurred the wrath of many UDF members, especially after the UDF came to power with its election victory in October 1991, for his alleged favoritism toward "the communists." But some of the differences between him and the UDF government arose from a lack of constitutional clarity over the powers of the president and the government (here, the similarities with Poland and Hungary are evident).

Other differences, however, resulted from the UDF leadership's utter refusal to compromise — or more correctly, their unawareness of what compromise was. The UDF was the Bulgarian counterpart of the anticommunist consensus groupings that had arisen throughout Eastern Europe. An umbrella organization, it originally covered seventeen different parties and groupings. It had political moderates, ideological dogmatists (mostly young), and more than its fair share of unpredictable eccentrics. Like its counterparts elsewhere, it sharply divided over how much to try to retrieve of the precommunist past and how much to retain of the communist legacy. On economics, it was divided between Reaganaut-Mont Pélerin free-marketeers, social liberals of the German variety, and Western-type social democrats; on politics, between monarchists (the exiled Tsar Simeon, waiting in the wings in Madrid, was the most capable and presentable of Eastern Europe's ex-royalty),[24] neofascists, conservatives, liberals, social democrats, and opportunists without either affiliation or principle. In fact, the UDF had something of everything—except mutual tolerance. And it was this deficiency that was to weaken its government seriously when it tried to cope with the problem of reconstructing Bulgaria.

Its lack of tolerance was most evident at the very top, in the cabinet of Filip Dimitrov, the intelligent young UDF leader who became premier after the October 1991 election victory.[25] Dimitrov's was probably the most ideological leadership in all of East Europe. And the implacability of some members was very much in the historical tradition of Bulgarian politics. As a leader, Dimitrov aimed to pursue a thoroughgoing free market reform based more firmly on Western theory than practice; politically, he was bent on a comprehensive decommunization campaign that could result only in dividing society further (see below, pp. 111–112). Altogether, the Dimitrov government had a callow, primitive, air—principled, certainly, in its determination to get away from communism, not all that aware, however, of what the democracy toward which it claimed to be moving was really about.

In the country as a whole, the communists-turned-socialists were not nearly as discredited as their record since 1948 should have condemned them to be. While the main UDF support came from the intelligentsia, the students, and the growing number of small entrepreneurs, together with considerable sections of organized labor, the socialists, like their Romanian counterparts, were strong in the countryside, small towns, and among some older workers. Aside from the numerous Brezhnevite-Zhivkovite antiques, still convinced that reform was both destructive and unnecessary, the post-1989 party was divided mainly between those who, instinctively and ideologically, could not move beyond Gorbachev's early reform communism, and those edging close to Western social democracy. Lukanov, for a brief period the outstanding figure in postcommunist Bulgaria, did see the need for basic change, and so did several of the younger, emerging socialist leaders. But the bulk of the leadership remained relatively conservative.[26]

The socialists lost Bulgaria's second free elections in October 1991 to the UDF, but only by a narrow margin. They remained a powerful force, obviously hoping that the economy would deteriorate to the point where they could regain a nationwide majority and that the social hardships of economic reform would bring more workers into their fold. It was probably these hopes that played into the hands of the more conservative leadership, posing as the champions of social welfare. If, though, the economy began to show signs of consistent progress, with the attendant social hardships not as bad as many feared, then the social-democratic tendencies would prevail in the party. In the future, therefore, despite the protests of practically everybody in the UDF that they would never cooperate with "the communists," a merger of like-minded social-democratic elements across the political spectrum could take place. Democracy in Bulgaria would be strengthened by such a merger in that working-class representation on a democratic basis would be assured in the political process.

The "Turkish Question"

The third major component of Bulgarian political life was the Movement for Rights and Freedoms (MRF), an almost exclusively ethnic grouping representing the more than a million-strong Turkish minority. This minority had suffered severely under the Zhivkov regime,[27] but after the downfall of communism its situation markedly improved. The name-change laws were repealed and the restrictions on the use of the Turkish language lifted. About half the more than 300,000 who had emigrated to Turkey returned, and, although many had difficulties recovering their land and property sold to, or appropriated by, ethnic Bulgarians, it seemed that by the end of 1992 most of these difficulties had been removed.

Indeed, after November 1989 the Turkish minority appeared to be entering its best period since the end of Ottoman control over Bulgaria in 1878. The key to its recovery lay in the political influence it now acquired. The Movement of Rights and Freedoms, after overcoming strenuous objections on constitutional grounds to its very existence, returned twenty-three representatives to the Bulgarian parliament in October 1992. And, because of the closeness of the election result, it was precisely this group that held the balance between the victorious UDF and the defeated socialists. It was their support that made the UDF government possible, and it was their withdrawal of support from Premier Filip Dimitrov that led to his final resignation in November 1992. Their political leader, Ahmed Doğan, was an authoritative, able political strategist. Some diplomats in Sofia considered him the best politician in Bulgaria.[28]

Bulgaria's Turks, therefore, had made a remarkable comeback

since 1989. They were the only minority of any size in Eastern Europe, and probably the former Soviet Union, too, that felt safer, more confident, and more powerful *after* the communist period than *during* it, not to mention *before* it. Take any other member of the former Warsaw Pact, plus Yugoslavia and Albania, and the Turks in Bulgaria were markedly better off than any of the minorities there. Could it last? On an everyday, individual basis, relations between Bulgarians and Turks often have been good. But that also had been the case with relations among many ethnic groups throughout Eastern Europe and the old Soviet Union, and good relations had not subsequently prevented the fiercest antagonisms and, as in Yugoslavia, the most atrocious violence. Clearly, there was no cause for complacency in Bulgaria. Many Bulgarians had been shamed by Zhivkov's brutal discrimination of the 1980s, but these were mainly residents of cities and towns some distance from the main Turkish settlements in the country's northeast and southeast. It also was these Bulgarians who were most sensitive to foreign outrage over Zhivkov's policy and to the fact that Bulgaria's relations with "Europe" and its hopes of eventual acceptance into the European Community depended in part on its treatment of its minorities.

But in those areas of the country where Bulgarians and Turks lived in close proximity, tension continued. Disputes over the property rights sometimes still rankled, but the most serious issue since 1989 had been the opposition of many local Bulgarians to legislation granting minority children the right to Turkish-language instruction in the public schools.[29] The socialists tried to stoke the fires by stirring up anti-Turkish sentiments with nationalist propaganda, most of it at the local level, where it usually went unreported. In the presidential elections in January 1992, although Zhelev was victorious, he was strongly challenged by the socialist-backed candidate who unashamedly played the nationalist card.[30] Some perceptive Bulgarians began worrying about a possible nationalist backlash, especially in view of the kingmaker role the Rights and Freedoms Movement was now exerting in parliament. And overshadowing this domestic anxiety was the growing strength and influence of Turkey (see chapter 8). Official Bulgarian-Turkish relations were improving considerably, but many Bulgarians feared growing Turkish power, saw their country as a bulwark against Turkish expansion, and their large Turkish minority as a potential fifth column.

Revenge or the Rule of Law?

Vengeance, bitter, bloody, and widespread, has been a depressing feature of Bulgarian history. The dying Ottomans set the tone immediately before liberation in 1878 with their "Bulgarian atrocities" in suppressing the uprisings of 1876. After liberation, it was the turn of many local Turks to suffer Bulgarian revenge. In 1923 the fall of the peasant leader, Aleksandŭr Stamboliski, and the failure of the communist uprising of that year, led to fearsome reprisals against both agrarians and communists. More than twenty years later, after the Soviet "liberation," it was the turn of the communists to wreak terrible vengeance on their real or imagined enemies.

This violent tradition in Bulgarian politics continued during the communist period, not in the form of mass slaughter but in inexorable repression of all forms of opposition. It was, after all, a regime based on coercion, with violence as its ultimate guarantee. The system eventually was overthrown without serious violence and largely by means of the ballot box. However, the question that many people were now asking was, how much, and what kind of, revenge would the new victors exact over their vanquished?[31] Nobody, of course, expected the bloodletting on the scale of the early part of the century, but many were concerned about the extent and type of Bulgaria's own decommunization.

The Dimitrov government, dominated by the "dark blue," radical anticommunist faction of the UDF, was determined to pursue decommunization rigorously. (The UDF color is blue. The socialists' color remained red, but their emblem now became the red rose.) The prosecutor-general, Ivan Tatarchiev, a strong nationalist, and a man not prone to compromise, set about preparing cases against top leaders of the old regime. Bulgaria thus became the first East European country to prosecute the topmost former regime leaders. These included not only Zhivkov, whose trial had begun more than a year earlier, but also Georgi Atanasov, the last communist premier, Lukanov, the first postcommunist premier, who, though never a Zhivkov favorite, had held important governmental posts in the last years of the old regime, as well as other communist luminaries. The problem was, however, that the defendants were charged either with relatively minor pecuniary offenses or for policy errors, which, however grave, were hardly indictable in any judicial sense. Zhivkov's trial in 1991–92 was the most notable and ended in September 1992 with a prison sentence. It hardly enhanced the reputation of Bulgarian justice.[32] Some Bulgarians who hated the role Zhivkov played in Bulgarian history nevertheless thought his trial a farce and shaming for Bulgaria. On the decommunization issue as a whole, Zhelev took a moderate position. He realized three things about Tatarchiev's campaign: it set back the acceptance of the rule of law; it polarized society further; and it hurt Bulgaria's international reputation. But many in the top UDF leadership appeared to have become oblivious to such considerations.

Deeper into Confrontation?

Dimitrov's confrontational policy only could have worked with a united party and a clear majority in parliament. He had neither. His policy actually aggravated the divisions inside the UDF, and the implacable attitude of his "dark blue" hard-liners made compromise impossible. The "dark blues" had made some powerful enemies: Zhelev, the president; the Movement of Rights and Freedoms, which had, indeed, become more assertive but with which, had the proper spirit been shown, some compromise could have been reached; the *Podkrepa* free-trade union movement whose strong but erratic leader, Konstantin Trenchev, originally had been a pillar of UDF support; the officer corps, upset by the extensive purges being planned; and, finally, the moderates within the UDF itself, many of whom were faced with the ultimatum of "conform or get out."[33]

The Dimitrov government had been in office scarcely six months before its first big tremor of personal instability occurred in May 1992. The government went through a serious crisis the following July and then lost its parliamentary authority in October when the Movement for Rights and Freedoms finally withdrew its support. Within a short time, thanks to defections or expulsions from its own ranks, the UDF had lost its plurality in parliament, which now was regained by the socialists, who had watched the developing shambles on the other side with gleeful anticipation.

A new government, composed largely of "technical experts," finally was installed under Lyuben Berov, a nonparty economist who had been an adviser to Zhelev. It achieved parliamentary support through a combination of votes from Socialist Party members with those from the Movement of Rights and Freedoms, and a few UDF "heretics."[34] No one was prepared to wager how long it would last. But if the Berov government collapsed, the only recourse was to elections, which were not officially due until 1995. Both personally and politically, the eclipse of the "dark blues" under Dimitrov, and Berov's appointment, were a victory for Zhelev. The new government was essentially a presidential one, and considerable speculation arose about a new "centrist" party forming around the presidency. If this happened, and if the new government or Zhelev himself were not forced out by extraparliamentary means, then Bulgaria could return to something like the political stability it seemed to have had for a short time after 1989, a stability that it then steadily lost.

Certainly, Zhelev needed to exert the authority of his office and his own personal prestige. The debacle of the Dimitrov government, the first noncommunist government in Bulgaria for nearly half a century, cast a pall over political life, with only the socialists happy. As one West European commentator put it:

> It is, of course, normal when such a heterogeneous creation like the UDF, with 17 different parties or groupings belonging, or having belonged, to it, eventually falls apart. But it is the way this happened that gives pause for thought. In the devious craving for power and influence no holds are barred and it is often a matter, much less of political controversy as of personal revenge, of settling accounts, and strong personal economic interests. It is a matter of intrigue and rummaging in the past. Mutual recriminations fly around; people accuse one another of collaboration with the old security police or of being involved in one or another dirty business deal. Stories of betrayal abound and new conspiracy theories are constantly being put into circulation.[35]

It was a damning indictment of political standards in Sofia in early 1993. However, the former communists (now socialists) were not the ones most to blame; instead, "totalitarian" anticommunists had threatened to run riot.

The political situation, therefore, was less than promising. But the damage could be offset by an upturn in the economy. Predictions about the economy were impossible to make, partly because estimates of the actual situation varied. The Bulgarian economic stabilization program called for: price reform involving the freeing of most prices; the creation of a unified, flexible, and market-based exchange rate; limited growth of nominal wages; restricted domestic demand; high interest rates; and severe budgetary discipline (see chapter 5). By the end of 1992 some Western observers considered the economy to be working reasonably well. Everyone, though, was worried about the eventual social implications of the initial downturn, especially the unemployment figure that was well above half a million (more than 13 percent) as early as September 1992 and was rising rapidly. The socialists were confident that, if this figure increased appreciably, their return to power, in 1995 or before, was assured.

It remained to be seen, too, how Bulgaria would be affected by the chaos around it in the Balkans. Except in the unlikely event of Bulgaria being attacked, itself, the government was determined not to become involved in the Yugoslav debacle. In view of the role Macedonia had played in its modern history, Bulgaria had shown commendable restraint (see chapter 6). But apparently there were some differences within Sofia's political establishment over Macedonian policy. The strong support for the new Macedonia was being challenged by those who did not want to spoil the excellent relations with Greece that had been built up over twenty-five years — Greek firms, too, were investing heavily in Bulgaria — and who also feared separatist agitation in "Pirin Macedonia" within Bulgaria itself. In any case, the forty years of tension between Sofia and Skopje was remembered by everybody. The socialists, in particular, were not pro-Macedonian, but neither were some UDF members. Finally, there was Turkey, its relations with the Movement for Rights and Freedoms inside Bulgaria and the broader role it might play, or be forced to play, in the Balkans as a whole.[36]

There still was much hope in Bulgaria as well as hope for it. But at least the postcommunist illusions had gone. Internally, dangers had arisen for which Bulgarian political forces themselves were much to blame. External dangers could arise that would not be their responsibility. But in early 1993 Bulgaria was still an oasis, the Kirghistan of the Balkans. Cold comfort, perhaps, in view of the disorder around it. But in the Balkans, even cold comfort was a pleasant change from the usual no comfort at all.

ALBANIA
The Beckoning Void

Journeying through the west of Ireland, travelers in the nineteenth century came upon totally deserted villages, their residents having left because of hunger, poverty, and desperation. In 1994 some villages in southern Albania presented the same prospect. Their residents either had gone to the big towns in Albania itself, or to Greece. The parallel is neither unfair nor fanciful — and if the opportunity did present itself to go to the West, many more men under thirty-five, and some older, would have left. The boatloads that got to Bari in the summer of 1991 (see chapter 8) would have been only the shape of things to come. All the East European countries were beset by the problem of potentially large-scale emigration, but none to the relatively massive and crippling extent of Albania.

Why was this so? Put simply, because the material condition and the morale of many Albanians had gone beyond the point of social and patriotic constraints — in many cases of moral constraints, too. Misha Glenny has put it well: "The Albanian revolution was accompanied by the rapid atrophy of the social infrastructure countrywide, such that living standards had dropped below the level at which normal social psychology begins to function. To a large degree, this has led to the temporary suspension of nationalism as a pertinent ideological motivation among large sections of the population in Albania."[37]

No other East European country had been affected in this way, not even Romania. There, the depredations of Ceauşescu's rule had been similar in some respects to those of Enver Hoxha in Albania, although they had not gone nearly so deep. And even in Ceauşescu's worst years, fairly extensive contacts with the West, China, and the countries of the Soviet alliance still were taking place. Only a relatively few Romanians enjoyed these contacts, but such outlets did have a leavening effect on other parts of the community. But in Albania's isolation, contacts with the outside world, while never totally cut off, were reduced to a minimum, and these were exclusively official contacts. Moreover, the humanly erosive impact of Hoxha's long rule, then the anticommunist revolution that shattered the stabilizing constraints that existed, and then the horrendous economic conditions — these put Albania back into something close to Hobbes's state of nature. The public hanging of two men after the gruesome murder of a family in the summer of 1992 was a reflection of the state of Albanian society.[38]

In *Eastern Europe and Communist Rule,* I argued that, whatever the evils of Hoxha's rule might have been, he did make a basic contribution to the molding of an Albanian national consciousness. I argued that Hoxha was rounding off the work begun by King Zog between the two world wars.[39] This argument is much in tatters today. Any national consciousness Hoxha molded was ephemeral and superficial and will be revived and spread only when a basic economic and social stability can be secured. In the meantime, it is in Kosovo and the Albanian parts of Macedonia, where Albanians are repressed or challenged by the Serb and Macedonian nations of state, that most Albanian national feeling is to be found. This struggle of Albanians abroad eventually could have an important effect on restimulating national sentiment in Albania itself.

One Year Late

Albania's anticommunist revolution occurred a year after the upheaval throughout the rest of Eastern Europe. Ramiz Alia, Hoxha's anointed successor in 1985, was never a Stalinist in the sense that his master was. He soon realized that Hoxha's isolationism was untenable, and he gradually set about reintroducing his country to the outside world. In 1987 the technical state of war with Greece was ended. That same year diplomatic relations with Bonn were established. Albania edged closer to the Balkan conference and actually hosted a meeting of its foreign ministers in 1990. Likewise in 1990, Albania reestablished diplomatic relations with the United States and the Soviet Union and joined the CSCE process. Alia, however, was intelligent enough to know that going into Europe, no matter how gingerly, meant being affected by it. More immediately threatening to the Hoxha legacy was the revolution going on in Eastern Europe and the Soviet Union, as well as the disintegration of neighboring Yugoslavia. All along, Alia had seemed inclined to relax the system in a comprehensive way. But, like several of his "transition" counterparts in Eastern Europe, and like Gorbachev himself, he never intended to touch the essentials: one-party rule could be diluted, but it still had to be preserved.[40] Alia certainly never intended to hold genuinely free elections. But growing communist party disunity, serious intellectual restlessness, spearheaded first in Tirana and then in self-chosen French exile by Ismail Kadare, Albania's world-class novelist,[41] and, most of all, popular discontent, manifested in rioting and street demonstrations, especially in Shkodër in northern Albania, forced him and the regime leadership to think the unthinkable.

The result was that Albania's first free election since the early

1920s took place in February 1991. The Albanian (communist) Party of Labor, now transmogrified into the Albanian Socialist Party, won a clear majority. The party's victory was part of the Balkan post-communist electoral pattern mentioned earlier and was a serious rebuff for democracy in Albania. Slightly more than one year later, though, the Albanian Democratic Party swept to a convincing victory. Communist Albania, the house that Enver built, almost the last of its type still standing, had fallen.[42]

What happened in between the two elections also had become familiar in the Balkans. The socialist victory in February 1991 had not been accepted by many Albanians, and rioting in several cities ensued. This violence was particularly serious in Shkodër, historically the most politically conscious of the Albanian cities, where several people were killed by the police and security elements (*Sigurimi*) that were only too glad to show their tenacity. Alia, who remained president, and the ministers serving under him, did initiate market reforms in the economy and warily introduced some privatization in agriculture. An entrepreneurial frenzy burst forth in petty trade, much of it on the windy side of whatever law existed. This occurred, of course, not just on the Balkan pattern, but on the entire East European pattern. But in terms of what was needed to cope with the country's appalling economic situation, the government's efforts were risible. In any case, however revolutionary they may have seemed in terms of Alia's own ideological ground rules, these efforts still bore the communist hallmark. Still, this may not have made much practical difference, anyway. If the government, say, had been more enthusiastic about agricultural privatization, it simply would not have had the means to supply the necessary loans and the machinery to have given the new holdings a chance to become viable. Albania was simply in a destitution trap.

It was this destitution, plus the lack of a moral and civic sense of restraint (as well as the lifting of the former terror) that caused the almost total breakdown of law and order during 1991. Hoxha's ban on religion, imposed in 1967, meant that now no clergy or religious institutions—Muslim, Orthodox, or Catholic—could serve as a societal anchor. This ban had been lifted by Ramiz Alia but it would take some time before the social impact of religion could be felt. The result was a massive increase in crime of all kinds. What struck Western visitors the most forcibly was the vandalism: sometimes planes could not land at Tirana airport because runway lights had been smashed; seating in many trains was entirely ripped out. Most symptomatic of all was the plundering of shops suspected of having even minimum amounts of provisions. The situation was apocalyptic. Hardly surprising, then, that young people attempted to leave on a massive scale. Hardly surprising, too, that the West was thought of as an idyllic spot to be reached at all costs. Nowhere was this fata morgana more vivid than in Albania.

Alia and Berisha

Politics between the two elections were dominated by two men: Alia and the Democratic Party leader, Sali Berisha. When this book was being written, it seemed distinctly possible that Alia would spend the rest of his life in jail on assorted charges of felony while he held office. (After his electoral defeat in 1992, he retired from active politics.) Hoxha's aging widow, Nexhmije, was another prime victim of Albania's mounting decommunization drive,[43] which later engulfed practically the entire former communist leadership. But whatever were to happen to Ramiz Alia, he would go down in Albanian history as a key figure of transition (see also chapter 2). More precisely, he would be remembered as the man who led the move away from Hoxha's Stalinism. Such a transition would have happened, anyway, but the change could have been much more violent and even slower than was the case.

The point of departure — Hoxha's Stalinism — was clear. And there Alia's role ended. But the destination for Albania? This was now in the dynamic Berisha's hands. A young cardiologist, scion of a communist family who had enjoyed postgraduate education in France, "Salu" was a whirlwind leader whose devotion to democracy, the market, and his compatriots, was genuine.[44] The strong powers with which the Albanian presidency was invested gave him an authority unique among East European presidencies, and Berisha was bent on using every ounce of it. Largely as a result of his exertions and his example, the public disorder that had been rampant in 1991 eased somewhat the following year. (Private crime, however, continued to mount.) Berisha also embarked on a relatively radical economic reform in agriculture and in industry, and both he and his program made a favorable impression in Western Europe and the United States.

But, again, what was there to reform? A basic Albanian economy was needed before reform could begin. Such an economic foundation once had existed, but it had been so undermined during the 1980s that what was needed was rudimentary reconstruction rather than Western-oriented reform. Throughout the Balkans, but most especially in Bulgaria and Albania, the tendency was to try to run before learning to walk—in economics, in particular, to go for the most sophisticated Western nostrums when simpler ones would do.[45] (Under communism, their regimes had shown the same impatient tendencies.) Such an inclination reflected a rooted backwardness, which even the most educated sections of society basically shared. Berisha was a case in point. The danger of his approach was that, in his spectacular impatience, he would try to make the economy leapfrog over stages of development vitally necessary for its proper advancement. Thus, just as Alia's earlier reforms had been too timid, Berisha's might be too bold.

The Recidivist Danger

Berisha's impetuousness could undo the dedication and ability he brought to his task. The warnings were there. In the summer of 1992 the Albanian Socialist Party made impressive gains in local elections, just a few months after their parliamentary election debacle.[46] The remedies the former doctor Berisha was prescribing might be not only too sophisticated but also deadly for a country of Albania's backwardness. Berisha also was beginning to show a high-handedness and arrogance in dealing with subordinates that was losing him valuable support. And if the socialists came back to power, they probably would be more recidivist in Albania than any of their counterparts elsewhere might be. Not that they would reinstall terror; rather, they would try to curry favor with a "socialism" that assured a bit of the basics to everybody. This—and here again the Balkan pattern obtrudes—could be the appeal of the more conservative communists and/or socialists in Romania and Bulgaria, too. And the old nomenklatura, much of it still in place, would be more than ready to serve them.

Albania probably would not survive that kind of regression, even if a new socialist regime would be prettier than Hoxha's. Albania's future could be assured only by the sensible introduction of a mixed economy (Albania's mineral resources are not inconsiderable) and of representative and judicial institutions that might enable the country's society eventually to capture the democratic essence. Time also was pressing because, despite emigration, Albania's population, as many observers have pointed out, was increasing rapidly and could still approach 4 million by the year 2000. If it did so, and if no effective economic reform had been carried out and/or no large-scale emigration had been possible, then Albania would be threatened by famine, a European counterpart to Somalia.

Albania was an obvious case for outside aid. And, *relatively,* not much would be needed to help put it on the right course. Here, there was, at least, a brighter aspect. Albania was not solely dependent on *Western* aid; as a 70 percent Muslim country it could look to Islam as well, which it appeared to be doing with some success. Ties to wealthy Muslim countries were increasing, and by early 1993 they were being reflected in increased economic aid.[47] The dangers of Albania becoming a bridgehead for Islamic fundamentalism were negligible. (Albanian Muslims were generally too relaxed for such a prospect.) But if the perception of this danger were such as to stimulate more aid from the West in competition, then Albania might benefit from both sides. Albania joined the Conference of Islamic States at the end of 1992. At the same time, it formally applied for North Atlantic Treaty Organization (NATO) membership, and was already an object of covert protective attention from the American military and the Central Intelligence Agency. It obviously was aware of its room for maneuver.

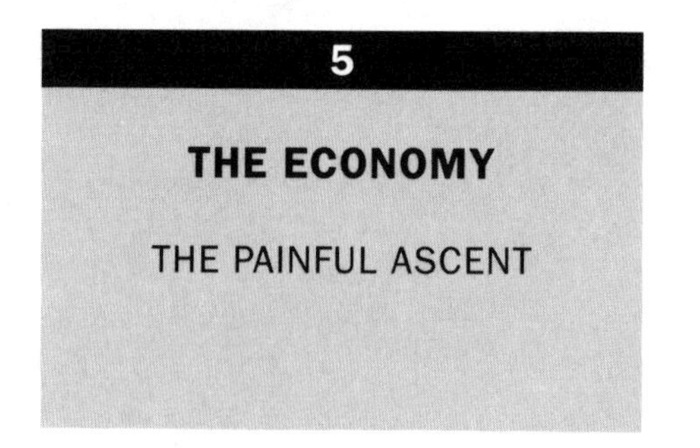

5 THE ECONOMY

THE PAINFUL ASCENT

The basic failure of communism may have been moral, but its most immediately evident failure was economic. The system had advertised itself as being much better-equipped than capitalism to bring industrialization and modernization to less-developed societies in a relatively short time. True, a large number of people might have to suffer in the process, but this pain was the unavoidable sacrifice to be made for the millennium that beckoned.

The promise of communism was spurious, but for a time it held some credibility. During the so-called extensive phase of economic development, when the building of heavy industry, virtually synonymous with "socialism," was proceeding apace, the basic weakness of the entire concept could be hidden behind a smoke screen of impressive material progress. (However self-serving the statistics were, they did convey a general trend.) Subsequently, when during the 1960s extensive economic development was no longer viable, some degree of reform, timid in retrospect but novel at the time, was introduced by most East European countries. For several years after 1968, however, with the Brezhnev counterreformation effacing the reforms of the Prague Spring, economic reform, except in the special case of Hungary, became both heretical and risky. The socialist economies of Eastern Europe, as a result, went into terminal decline. For a while during the 1970s and part of the 1980s the seriousness of economic conditions could be masked by the fraud of consumerism, the populist escapism that raised living standards to a degree inconsistent with the real state of the economy. Consumerism was essentially political. It marked the end of the ideological counterreformation and the beginning of the materialist diversion aimed at passive popular tolerance rather than active support. Whereas the counterreformation had the mark of Suslov, consumerism was quintessentially Brezhnev. Anything for a quiet life; buy them off! It worked for a few years while

Western credits gushed into Eastern Europe (with Czechoslovakia the big exception). These investments originally had been designed to spur modernization and export-led growth, but they increasingly went into keeping the consumerist carousel in motion. (In Ceauşescu's Romania, though, the merry-go-round slowed down very quickly.) But by the end of the 1970s the rise of Solidarity showed the game was up in Poland, and by the middle of the 1980s it was up everywhere. The consumerist bill had to be paid; the only recourse was for the whole system to declare bankruptcy.

This bankruptcy became the postcommunist inheritance after 1989. It was multidimensional. Even the strongest East European economies were in crisis. The true condition of the East German economy, reputedly the strongest in Comecon, became evident only under the cold scrutiny of German reunification. The Czechoslovak economy was described several times by Václav Havel and others as not just a house badly needing repair (as the new government had expected), but a ruin. The deterioration of the Czechoslovak economy (the Czech, especially) since World War II was a tragedy in itself. Before World War II the Czech economy, once the powerhouse of the Habsburg Empire, had remained proportionately one of the strongest in Europe. A Swiss who grew up near the old Zurich airport in the late 1930s and watched Czechoslovak planes flying in recalls how the Swiss considered Czechoslovakia an "advanced" country compared with their own. A half-century on, Czechoslovakia was advanced only in terms of the international wreckage of which it was a part.

The truth was that Eastern Europe (and the Soviet Union, for that matter) had been subject to massive *misdevelopment.* As Paul Marer puts it: "In terms of the structure, modernity, and marketability of the goods they were producing, communist economies were falling further and further behind much of the rest of the world, which was not revealed by statistics. Falling behind also had the effect of reducing their people's standard of living."[1] This is not to say that some countries, overall, had not done better than others. Hungary's economic reforms, beginning in the early 1960s, had made its economy probably the most effective in Eastern Europe, and Yugoslavia's economic reforms, also initiated in the 1960s, also had worked well for several years. But by 1984 most indicators in the East European economies had become danger signals: stagnating production, rising budget deficits, concealed and open inflation, declines in hard currency trade, severe food shortages in some countries, rising foreign debt in others.

Overall, in Eastern Europe in 1989 the increase in industrial production was only 0.1 percent, the lowest ever in communist history. In gross agricultural production, the overall increase was slightly more than 1 percent; in national income it also was stagnating and actually decreasing in Poland, Bulgaria and Hungary. Table 1, prepared by the Vienna Institute for Comparative Institutional Economics, shows the development of net national income throughout the 1980s.[2]

Poland, Hungary, and Bulgaria also had amassed huge hard currency debts. (Romania, through the Ceauşescu-obsessed policy of throttling imports and maximizing exports, had finally paid off its debt in 1989. Czechoslovakia borrowed relatively little.) The Polish debt received the most publicity, but Hungary's became the biggest on a per capita basis, and Bulgaria's, as the result of reckless borrowing in the second half of the 1980s, also became extremely onerous. Table 2 gives the development of East European debt in the second half of the 1980s.[3]

As many East Europeans were facing harder times because of the economic failure, their social "protection" had become increasingly suspect. Social welfare had for a long time been touted by the East European regimes as proof of socialism's advantage over bourgeois democracy. It encompassed, they claimed, those essential human rights without which the West's concept of human rights—covering free speech, freedom of association, movement, etc.—was a propaganda diversion. But the East European social welfare systems had been deteriorating rapidly since about the end of the 1970s. By the end of the 1980s many aspects of them had become more a scandal than a showpiece.

Pin the Tail on the Donkey

In view of their inheritance and the socialist experience, the postcommunist governments in Eastern Europe had no choice but to move from state socialism to a market economy. The problem was how? It never had been tried before, except partially in some undeveloped countries.[4] The mechanics of switching from capitalism to socialism forty years before had been relatively simple. But making the opposite switch recalled the children's party game, Pin the Tail on the Donkey. Blindfolded, children were given a piece of cardboard shaped like a tail, which they then had to pin into the paper figure of a tail-less

Table 1. Net National Income at Fixed Prices in Comecon and Yugoslavia (average annual percentage growth rate)

	1981–85	1986	1987	1988
Bulgaria	3.7	5.3	5.1	2.4
CSFR	1.8	2.6	2.1	2.4
GDR	4.5	4.3	3.6	2.8
Hungary	1.3	0.9	4.1	0.3
Poland	0.8	4.9	1.9	4.9
Romania	4.5	7.3	4.8	3.2
Eastern Europe[b]	2.1	4.5	3.3	3.1
USSR	3.2	2.3	1.6	4.4
Comecon[b]	2.9	2.9	2.1	4.0
Yugoslavia	0.6	3.5	−1.2	−1.7
Comecon and Yugoslavia[b]	2.8	2.9	1.9	3.8

[a]Gross national income.
[b]Estimate.

donkey placed on a wall. The object of the exercise was to pin the tail closest to that part of the donkey's anatomy which nature had deemed most appropriate. After 1989, however, Eastern Europe was the child, the tail, and the donkey. It has not been short of advice. Western advice, in fact, has rained down on the East Europeans, some of it sound, some naive, and some downright self-serving. What it has been totally short of is experience; it has been groping for the market in the dark. The market meant free prices, the dismantling of subsidies, privatization of ownership, convertible currencies, an end to all unprofitable economic activity. Defining it was simple. Attaining it would be difficult.

The Two Strategies: "Shock Therapy" and "Gradualism"

There appeared to be two ways to attain the market. The first became known as "shock therapy," the second "gradualism." (At the outset, it should be stated that some East Europeans, with good cause, find the expression "shock therapy"—with its medical associations—downright insulting. Another example, perhaps, of Western patronizing tactlessness! I use it, therefore, regretfully but with little option of

1989 Plan	1989 actual	1990 Plan	1986–90 Plan
6.2	0.4	−3.7	5.4
1.8[a,b]	1.7[a]	2.5	3.5[a]
4.0	1.9	−4 to −5	4.6
−1 to −2[a]	−1 to −2[a]	0.0 to 0.5[a]	2.8 to 3.2
4.2	0.0	−10[a,b]	3.0 to 3.5
8 to 9	0[b]	9 to 10	9.9 to 10.6
4.1	0.5	−2.3	4.8
5.7[b]	2.4	4.4[b]	3.7 to 4.2
5.2	1.9	2.5	4.2
1.5	0.8[a]	−2.0	4.0[a]
5.1	1.8	2.3	4.2

avoiding it.) Both of these approaches were inspired by liberal economics. "Gradualism" was sometimes described by Western observers as if it were akin to the old "third road" doctrines, a mixture of socialism and capitalism, popularized by István Bibó and others some forty years earlier. This Western interpretation was a mistake. "Gradualism" was as much bent on the market as "shock therapy."[5] It just moved more incrementally. But "shock therapy" should not *exclusively* be associated with speed. It means "introducing and sustaining, until the objectives are achieved, a package of economic policy measures that (1) allow prices (initially mainly those of goods and services) to become determined primarily by market forces, and (2) bring under control severe inflationary pressures, whether inherited or newly generated as prices become market clearing."[6] These measures include price and market reforms, macrostabilization involving control of wages and other enterprise spending, reducing the budget deficit, and privatization. (Under "shock therapy," such measures would be introduced as a package.) Gradualists tended to argue that a step-by-step approach would be less costly economically and would reduce the danger of social and political unrest.

The differences between the two strategies, therefore, were not basic, stemming from opposing economic doctrines, or philosophies

Table 2. Hard Currency Debt of the Comecon States and Yugoslavia (in millions of dollars at the end of each year)

	1985	1986	1987	1988	1989	1990[a]
Bulgaria						
Gross	3,240	4,671	6,139	8,186	9,201	9,804
Net	1,149	3,290	5,054	6,406	8,025	9,604
CSFR						
Gross	4,608	5,567	6,657	7,281	7,915	8,100
Net	3,597	4,350	5,059	5,610	5,724	6,557
Hungary						
Gross	13,955	16,914	19,592	19,625	20,605	21,270
Net	11,678	14,773	18,088	18,238	19,440	19,788
Poland						
Gross	29,300	33,500	39,200	39,200	40,800	47,000
Net	27,705	31,779	36,205	35,581	36,871	38,902
Romania						
Gross	6,634	4,395	5,740	2,899	582,000	1,000
Net	6,265	5,756	4,353	2,086	−1,254	800
Eastern Europe						
Gross	57,737	67,047	77,328	77,191	79,103	87,104
Net	50,394	59,948	68,759	67,923	68,806	75,581
USSR						
Gross	25,177	30,486	40,208	46,755	52,392	52,502
Net	12,115	15,644	26,073	31,444	37,716	47,502
Comecon						
Gross	82,914	97,533	117,536	123,946	131,495	139,676
Net	62,509	75,592	94,832	99,367	106,522	123,153
Yugoslavia						
Gross	18,407	19,196	20,459	18,891	17,320	17,300
Net	15,454	16,883	18,229	15,086	10,420	10,500
Comecon and Yugoslavia						
Gross	101,321	116,729	137,995	142,837	148,815	156,976
Net	77,963	92,475	113,061	114,453	116,942	133,653

[a]Estimate.

of life. They reflected more the differences in the carryover from the communist era. If in Hungary there seemed little need for "shock," in Czechoslovakia, Bulgaria, Romania, and Albania, where the command economy had been comprehensive and no "capitalist" groundwork had been laid, the case for shock—at least in purely economic terms—was strong. In Poland, where about three quarters of the arable land had been privately owned and some vestiges of previous reforms had survived in parts of the economy, a case could have been made for a certain gradualist restraint. But it was precisely in Poland where, largely because of political circumstances, and the pressure of world financial opinion, "shock therapy" was first introduced and became a dominant national issue.

What follows is a five-country review of the type of reforms being introduced and their early effects. (Neither Albania nor most of the states of former Yugoslavia are included because, as of late 1993, accurate and coherent estimates of progress were not available.)

"Shock Therapy" in Poland

This became national policy in Poland at the beginning of 1990 after Solidarity's huge victory in the parliamentary elections of the previous June. At first it was supported by all sections of political opinion except the defeated communists. By many Poles, though, it was supported for the wrong reasons, being seen as a capitalist strategy that would quickly raise Poland to Western standards. Within only a few months many were to be disabused of this notion. The best-known Western advocate of "shock therapy" as a remedy for the East was Jeffrey Sachs of Harvard University. Sachs advised both the new Polish government and the Yugoslav federal government under Premier Ante Marković on economic strategy. Sachs's role initially led many in the West to believe that he was the real architect of the Polish plan to restore liberal economics. The fact was that for several years a growing number of capitalist economic theorists had existed in Eastern Europe itself, impatiently waiting to put theory into practice. Leszek Balcerowicz was to become the most famous of these, the eponym of "shock therapy" in Poland. Sachs certainly advised Balcerowicz, but Polish economic strategy was mapped out in Warsaw, not in the Harvard Yard.

Balcerowicz, a youngish academic partly American-educated and with teaching experience in several European countries as well as in India, was an early Solidarity enthusiast but never with a fixed political profile. He was not a former communist, nor after 1989 did he identify with any political grouping. His devotion was to capitalism, and his ambition was to get there as effectively as possible. Already in the early 1980s he and a number of like-minded young men and women had thought the economic reform plan—the Reformed Economic System (RES), devised by Solidarity experts and largely shelved after martial law—was much too timid and socialist-tainted.[7]

Nine years later, in 1990, Balcerowicz could at last practice what he preached. His specific proposals were formulated in the three-month period beginning in October 1989. They were essentially a combination of macroeconomic stabilization and liberalization. Price liberalization went hand in hand with a tough budgetary and incomes policy. Wages were tightly restricted through a variety of financial means. Privatization was a crucial part of the whole process, as, indeed, it was in gradualism. The establishing of small businesses and private entrepreneurship was encouraged through financial concessions, and it was hoped to break down and sell off the huge enterprises that had dominated the socialist economy. The złoty was at first made only internally convertible, but Polish citizens, Polish firms, and foreign tourists could buy and sell foreign exchange, and by the middle of 1991 foreign firms were permitted to repatriate złoty earnings in hard currency. As for Poland's foreign hard currency debt, it was hoped that repayment could be deferred and that a large part of it, owed to Western governments, could be forgiven.[8]

The "Balcerowicz plan," as it came to be called, got off to an impressive start. Its most obvious success was in the fight against inflation. Inflation had rocketed in the last years of the communist regime, especially under its last prime minister, Mieczysław F. Rakowski, who allowed a wage-price indexation policy. After retail prices had increased by nearly 250 percent in the last quarter of 1989 alone, the increase had been reduced to less than 1 percent a month by the middle of 1990. (It was about 40 percent per year at the end of 1992,[9] which was worrying, but not alarming, to Polish economic officials.) This reduction was achieved at a time of extensive price liberalization. As a result, many goods came back into Polish shops, and, at least in the larger cities, the lines of shoppers, one of the hallmarks of the communist period, virtually disappeared. Wages were meant to be kept under control by high taxes on wage increases in the big state firms.

Two other important successes were scored in the first year of the Balcerowicz plan. Small-scale private entrepreneurship—small shops, stalls, etc.—succeeded phenomenally. Any occasional visitor to Warsaw, Gdańsk, or Cracow was almost overwhelmed by the ferment of small-scale capitalist enterprise. By mid-1991, retail trade had been largely privatized, and more than 38,500 private companies had been formed in the country as a whole, compared with just a few hundred in 1987.[10] This trend continued. Already at the beginning of 1992 the Polish state statistical office reported that the private sector had accounted for 20 percent of total exports in 1991 and 46 percent of imports. Also in 1991, the output of privatized industry rose to 48.6 percent, while output from the state sector had declined by almost one-fifth. Excluding agriculture, most of which had always been in private hands, about one quarter of the total work force was now in the private sector. Some 62 percent still worked in the state sector, the rest in the cooperative sector.[11]

The other important success was in international trade. In 1990 a $3.8 billion trade surplus was recorded along with a 6.6 billion transferable ruble surplus in trade with the Soviet Union. As Ben Slay has noted, these were the biggest surpluses recorded in Polish history, and Poland's surplus with the Soviet Union practically eliminated its total debt.[12] These trade successes were achieved by cuts in real wages, which reduced demand for imports, at the same time making Polish exports more competitive, and by devaluing the złoty to a stable rate against the dollar. This also increased Polish exports.

These achievements brought Poland much favorable international attention and, for some, created the impression that, either through accident or design, the Polish government was set for success and might become a model for other former socialist countries. Poland became for a time a favorite of the International Monetary Fund (IMF) and World Bank. These two organizations granted Poland $1 billion for a stabilization fund to support the convertibility of the złoty as part of an overall aid package of $2.5 billion awarded in 1990.[13] But the most spectacular sign of international favor came in April 1991 when Western government creditors agreed to forgive half of Poland's publicly held debt, provided that Polish debt servicing resumed (Warsaw had unilaterally suspended such servicing in late 1989) and that the IMF targets for the Polish economy continued to be met.

But while Balcerowicz was becoming highly esteemed abroad, he was becoming very controversial at home. A growing number of

Poles were unprepared for the pain inflicted by his remedies, especially those who thought the jump from socialist penury to capitalist plenty would be a short one.[14] This reaction partly explained the extraordinary turnout for Stanisław Tymiński in the presidential elections of November–December 1990 (see chapter 3). A sharp recession already had set in. By the end of 1990, real wages had fallen by 20 percent and the gross national product by 11.6 percent, while unemployment was mounting ominously. Real wages tended to stabilize during 1991, but by the end of that year unemployment had reached well above 2 million, or about 11.4 percent of the population, and many of these Poles were now genuinely unemployed, not school-leavers or housewives registering as unemployed.[15]

In February 1992 the Olszewski center-right government, which had formed after the elections, announced a plan to reflate the economy by increasing the money supply in real terms.[16] This approach was striking at the very heart of Balcerowicz's strategy, and many now considered Poland's "shock therapy" at an end. Poland, in fact, was entering into a full half year of troubles in which national morale plummeted and the prospects looked dim for progress to both democracy and market prosperity. But Poland was not yet lost, nor was its economy. The premiership of Hanna Suchocka, which began under unfavorable auspices in July 1992, saw the gradual steadying of both the economic and political situation. Her government successfully faced down a strike at the beginning of her term and a serious miners' strike at the end of 1992. In the meantime, economic progress in some key indicators had been proceeding, undemonstratively and practically unnoticed. But by the end of 1992 it was noticed, and the outside world and even many Poles began thinking that Poland might make it after all.

Some of the end-of-year results were indeed impressive. Industrial production that had been dropping strikingly, was picking up, and inflation seemed under control and was expected to drop to about 38 percent in 1993. Poland had run up a good trade surplus with the West and again was looking attractive to foreign investors. (Suchocka's firm hand with social unrest was a big attraction here.) More than 60 percent of the work force was now employed in the private sector, which produced about 45 percent of the gross domestic product. There were about 200,000 registered private companies (plus a great many that were unregistered), of which about 7,600 were receiving some foreign capital.[17]

The truth was that the political chaos of those few months in 1992 had hidden the fact that some important economic progress continued to be made. Just as important, the Olszewski government's bark turned out to be worse than its bite. Whether the government found on coming to office that there was really no alternative to "shock therapy," or whether it was too busy with political battles to get round to its economic promises, is not clear. But the fact is that little was done. Reports about the death of the Balcerowicz "shock therapy" had been greatly exaggerated. Balcerowicz himself might be (politically) dead; his plan, as such, had been diluted, but his principles remained strong.

There was some cause for optimism, therefore. But reason dictated that optimism must be cautious. The year 1993 promised to be the worst one yet in terms of social distress and possible disruption as reform hit the big state-owned heavy industrial centers. The government itself was saying that 3.5 million people could be out of work by the end of the year.[18] (The figure for the end of 1992 was 2.5 million.) It was indeed worker discontent, plus political irresponsibility in the Sejm, that brought down the Suchocka government (see chapter 3). Then, in September 1993, the left-wing groupings won the parliamentary elections on a program of slowing economic reform in order to mitigate social discontent. They won mainly because in Poland, as in every other former communist country, many people, while intellectually supporting the market, still instinctively crave the welfare state. Balcerowicz himself, however, as well as many others, had always stated that slowing down reform would mean killing it. How the new government managed its balancing act would be crucial.

CZECHOSLOVAKIA
"Shock Therapy" with Complications

The Czech and Slovak Federative Republic (CSFR) also adopted the "shock therapy" strategy and began putting it into practice in January 1991, one year after the Poles. There were both simple and complex reasons for the delay. Communism was overturned in Czechoslovakia as late as November 1989, and, though this was only four months after the rout of the communists at the polls in Poland, the starting point for the two countries was significantly different. Communism's terminal illness in Poland had been diagnosed several years before, and the end came quietly through the ballot box. Communism's demise in

Czechoslovakia was a much shorter process and came about through revolution—however "velvet." The ground for the economic transformation was prepared sooner in Poland. The Czechoslovaks needed more time, and they took it.

They needed time for other reasons, too. The new democratic ruling elite was much more divided than the Polish over the right course to follow—"shock therapy" or "gradualism."[19] Many new Czechoslovak politicians and economists were former reform communists of the Prague Spring vintage and favored a gradualist approach toward a left-liberal or social-democratic type of economic structure. As in Budapest, considerable sympathy existed for the old "third road solution." Václav Havel, as well as others who had not been communists, also was reported as preferring something milder than "shock therapy."[20] And many of the people around Havel, former communists or not, had been heroes of the dissident movement and at first enjoyed both influence and prestige.

The other important factor was Slovakia. As soon as the velvet revolution was over, Slovak nationalism (as discussed in chapter 3) began complicating Czechoslovakia's economics as well as its politics. This divisive element meant that the consensus necessary for launching a coherent economic strategy became all the harder to reach—especially in the case of "shock therapy," with its unavoidable social hardships. And soon after "shock therapy" began, the Czech-Slovak relationship became so strained that every issue became a national one for many Slovak politicians. Every step, therefore, in the economic transformation of the federation was dogged by the national question; the two intertwined in a destructive embrace.[21]

"Shock therapy" was adopted partly because the "West"—the European Community, IMF, World Bank, and private credit institutions—was virtually demanding it, and partly because Czechoslovakia, right to the end of communist rule, had maintained a highly centralized command economy. In contrast for example with Hungary, much ground had to be made up. With difficulties anticipated from Slovakia, grasping the nettle was probably seen as the wisest course. It also was seen as the most effective way of breaking down communist bureaucratic resistance to the reform. But another reason was exemplified by the role that personality played in postcommunist Eastern Europe. This reason was Václav Klaus (see chapter 3). Emerging as Czechoslovakia's most prominent *Vollblutpolitiker,* Klaus helped bully and maneuver the federal government into accepting "shock therapy." His concept of economics and his capitalist fervor were similar to those of Balcerowicz. But there the similarities ended. Their personalities were totally different. Balcerowicz shied away from politics as much as possible. The abrasive, self-confident Klaus reveled in the public forum, using it to advance both his policies and himself.[22]

Klaus was contemptuous of gradualism — the "third way" and the market socialism of Gorbachev's perestroika.[23] He saw all of these approaches as bars to radical reform. In the event, some of Klaus's policies were not as unflinchingly radical as he tried to make out. Like Balcerowicz, he was forced to allow some "excessive" wage increases and kept some large factories from liquidation on social grounds, when economic criteria dictated their closure. Still, largely due to his efforts, Czechoslovakia's reform, along with Poland's, began as the most radical in the entire region.

A document called "Scenario for Economic Reform," adopted in September 1990 by the Federal Assembly, outlined ways of dealing both with macroeconomic principles and the microeconomic measures arising from them.[24] These measures were broadly similar to the Polish. Stabilization was to be achieved through restrictive budgetary and monetarist policies. The plan set itself the twin tasks of controlling inflation, at the expense of economic growth and full employment, and the fullest possible price liberalization. Liberalization of prices began at the beginning of 1991 and entailed introducing internal convertibility for the Czechoslovak crown, or *koruna.* (This internal convertibility was similar to, but not as extensive as, the measures applied in Poland to the złoty.) Against the hazards of convertibility, Czechoslovakia received about $800,000 from the World Bank to form a stabilization fund.[25]

Klaus's self-confidence aside, the Czechoslovak government introduced its reform program with some trepidation, aware that the economic situation would get worse before it got better and that difficulties obviously would cause popular resentment. In anticipation, the government already had prepared an outline of its strategy for 1991 and 1992 (not to be confused with its scenario for reform). This document was more directly practical, with specific policy points, statistical forecasts, and four different scenarios that could unfold during the next two years. It already had been approved in November 1990, but publication had been delayed to avoid public unease. Its publication just a few weeks later seemed to indicate the government's eagerness to reassure the public that a firm and knowing hand was at the tiller.[26]

Briefly, the four scenarios ranged from "favorable," through two that could lead to situations of "economic collapse," to a fourth of "total breakdown." The "favorable" scenario foresaw regular and adequate sources of Soviet energy and raw materials and an unhindered implementation of Klaus's radical reform program. The years 1991 and 1992 were divided into three periods: price shock, adaptation, and recovery. The price shock phase would see inflation increasing by up to 40 percent, food prices by as much as 50 percent. Prices would, in fact (and this was vintage Klaus), go up to the point where people no longer could afford to buy certain goods. To check a price-wage spiral, less-than-inflation wage agreements throughout the economy would have to be reached and kept. At the same time, interest rates on bank deposits would be increased by at least 30 percent to stimulate savings. Once this storm had been weathered, the economy would enter the calmer seas of the adaptation period. Now, firms (whether privatized or not) would be adapting to the level of demand set by the price shock phase, lowering prices when necessary or turning to alternative production lines for which there was a demand. In this moment of truth, some firms would adapt, others would go to the wall.

During the adaptation period unemployment could rise to between 10 percent and 20 percent of the total work force, and appropriate unemployment expenditures would have to be set aside. Unemployment could best be checked by restrictive wage policies and speedy adaptation to market conditions. The "recovery" phase after 1992 was self-explanatory; unemployment would have dropped to about 3 percent, a necessary minimum to keep prices down; inflation, after being under 30 percent in the 1991–92 period would decrease steadily.

This favorable scenario has been worth discussing at some length because it is generally representative of the optimistic scenario being depicted, including the three phases, at the time in other East European countries, most notably Hungary and Poland. The two intermediate, "close to collapse" scenarios were based on different degrees of falloff in the Soviet supply situation, imperiling the radical economic reform. A considerable falloff would not necessarily kill the reform, but it would involve serious drops in the standard of living for an indefinite period. A drastic reduction, on the other hand, would put the Czechoslovak economy on a "war footing."

Czech Optimism, Slovak Doubts

Opinions were soon to vary about the condition of the Czechoslovak economy and the impact radical reform was having on it. The controversial personality of Klaus himself sometimes led to hyperbolic criticism. One Czech-born American economist, for example, accused him of rank incompetence.[27] At the other end of the spectrum was Klaus himself, acknowledging difficulties, but never doubting the rightness of his policy or its eventual success.

Amid such controversy, the report published by the Organization for Economic Cooperation and Development (OECD) in early 1992 sounded a note of qualified optimism.[28] The OECD thought that the Czechoslovak reform, on the whole, had made a good start—certainly in terms of beginning to dismantle the almost total command economy left by the communists. It particularly praised the progress of price liberalization. Although already by October 1991 only 5–6 percent of prices remained state-controlled, the price explosion that many feared had not materialized, thanks to tight monetary and fiscal policies. The inflation rate had risen to about 55 percent in 1991, some 20 percent higher than in the government's "favorable" scenario, but still far from being runaway. And it was expected to come down to 10 percent in the course of 1992. The OECD warned that tight monetary policies were still essential, as was a firm lid on wage increases. It praised the government's foreign trade liberalization and urged Western Europe to respond with fewer restrictions on Czechoslovak exports. Its predictions were generally in line with the Czechoslovak government's own in that they foresaw important signs of recovery by the end of 1992. But the OECD still expected, in the course of the year, rising unemployment—up to 12 percent for the whole country (this meant an even higher rate for the more vulnerable Slovak economy), and further, if slower, reductions in industrial production and in gross domestic product.

The Czechoslovak economy, therefore, seemed to have the chance of turning the corner in 1992 or, at least, 1993. But two imponderables clouded the future. One was the same as in the Polish case: the popular reaction to the hardships caused by the reform. So far the government had been much luckier than the Polish. The Czech working classes had not been seriously hit, and, though conditions were considerably worse in Slovakia, even there the reform had not begun to bite deeply.

In any case, Czechoslovak unemployment relief and social welfare generally provided a soft enough cushion—too soft in the view of some. And, as mentioned, the government, despite Klaus's tough talk, had not been as draconian on wages as it had threatened and was trying to avoid factory closures involving massive layoffs. The Czechoslovak arms industry, and especially the Slovak, was the best case in point. It became an international issue as well as adding another difficult dimension to the Czech-Slovak relationship. On moral grounds, the Czechoslovak government, and especially President Havel, originally planned a quick phaseout of this key industry. But the unemployment that a phase-out threatened, particularly in Slovakia, with its political repercussions crowding in, inevitably had led to yet another victory of realism over idealism: the arms industry would survive till further notice.[29]

The question of arms exports was just one aspect, or symptom, of the other big imponderable: Slovakia itself. The Slovaks were much more severely hit by economic reform than the Czechs. In Spring 1992 the unemployment rate in Slovakia was well above twice that in the Czech lands, and the gap would widen. In this situation, many Slovaks saw both the confirmation and continuation of the alleged Czech discrimination against them. As Vladimír Dlouhý, the federal minister of economics and himself half Slovak, put it: "My impression is that the Slovak colleagues have come to the conclusion that the impact of the reform on Slovak regions will be more severe and that, consequently, Slovak interests will not benefit at all from a rapid reform."[30] His was a tactful way of expressing what many Czechs and Slovaks were thinking. Some of them were much less tactful.

The truth was that the Slovak economy, because of communist policy, was much less resilient than the Czech. As one government minister described it:

> Slovakia, due to the fact that its industry was built mostly during the last 40 years, is industrially monocultural, since almost every region is dependent on one large factory, while in the Czech lands there is a much greater diversification due to an industrialization process lasting for more than 150 years, and in every region there is some substitute activity for almost everyone.[31]

Perhaps even more basic was the fact that many Slovaks did not see economic reform in as pressing a way as many Czechs did, since they did not feel the same overall economic decline over the previous forty years.[32] Slovak living standards had improved steeply during this period. Then again, many sections of Slovak industry had been located in Slovakia because it was geared specifically to Soviet needs. (The armaments industry has been mentioned. But this was not the only one.) Therefore, with the demise of Comecon, followed so quickly by the collapse of the Soviet Union itself, the shock had been all the greater.

Slovak nationalism became a crucial factor in the whole economic reform question. The Slovak economy had a separate identity from the Czech, but it was by no means independent of it. They shared a common market, a common currency, a common set of laws and standards, a common privatization policy, etc.—that is, a comprehensive mutuality that demanded one center. Had the Slovak demand for confederation been accepted, therefore (see chapter 3), it would have disrupted the whole economic reform package that was being introduced. And Klaus and his followers preferred total separation to the economic *Schlamassel* that would have resulted from any confederation.

Already by the end of 1992, the Czech situation seemed both to be bearing out Klaus's economic policy in general and, at least from an economic point of view, his rejection of Slovak notions of a confederation. According to a *Los Angeles Times* review at this time, the Czech Lands had a "balanced budget, a trade and current account surplus, Eastern Europe's lowest inflation rate (10–12 percent), a stable currency, and an unemployment rate (2.5 percent) that is less than half that of the United States."[33] Karel Dyba, the Czech minister for economic policy and development, with some justification could claim that his new country was the best off economically in the whole of Eastern Europe,[34] and there was a good chance of its keeping that position indefinitely.

The situation in newly independent Slovakia was much less clear. Vladimír Mečiár, its prime minister, had consolidated his power as much on his opposition to "shock therapy" for Slovakia as on any claims to independence for the new government. As was being promised, there would be no going back to a planned economy, but considerable state intervention would be used to prevent unemployment from going much beyond the rate of nearly 11 percent at which it stood at the beginning of 1993. How in the long run many of those huge "socialist" factories could be maintained was open to question. Mečiár could well have been raising expectations that he simply could not fulfill.

HUNGARY
Gradualism with a Good Start

Unlike the other two members of the East-Central European "triad"—Poland and Czechoslovakia—Hungary's economic transformation has captured few Western headlines. Abjuring "shock therapy," the Hungarian government opted for "gradualism," less arresting but arguably more appropriate to its unique circumstances. It quietly has insisted on going its own way, attentive to, but not overawed by, the preferences and the patronage of Western financial institutions.[35]

Gradualism came easy to the new democratic government elected in March 1990. This occurred because, as discussed in chapter 3, some of the essential groundwork already had been laid by the Kádár regime. The privatization of small concerns, shops, and businesses, for example, started in a modest way in 1982. In January 1987 a crucial banking reform was begun that involved breaking up the central bank and its monopolistic power. The several new banks emerging from this reform were not, of course, private banks. They still were state-owned and controlled, but they did generate some "socialist competition" in a critical sphere. "Demonopolization," a war cry of the radical reformers, at least had begun. In 1988 an unprecedented reform introduced income tax in a socialist country. It was about as popular in Hungary as it is anywhere else—"Ethiopian wages, Swedish taxes" was the Budapest lament—but it was an indispensable ingredient of fiscal reform. After Kádár, but still in the communist era, the Budapest stock exchange opened its doors in June 1989—not a particularly vibrant institution but an essential feature of the unfolding capitalist landscape. An accountancy law, with tough bankruptcy provisions, brought Hungarian accounting standards up to Western standards and was another earnest of businesslike intent.

So much for communism's capitalist groundwork. The new democratic government passed a basic privatization law in September 1990 and small-scale privatization began in earnest the next year. The new government also pruned government spending and began removing subsidies "salami style."[36] But its signal success by the end of 1991 had been its ability to liberalize about 90 percent of all prices and yet keep inflation within bounds. Inflation was about 40 percent in 1991, and it was hoped to reduce this figure to 30 percent the following year.

Unlike Poland, Hungary had not importuned forgiveness of its Western debts, an abnegation that only increased its creditworthiness. The hoped-for breakthrough in foreign investment still had not occurred, but Hungary easily was leading the East European field in this regard. By the end of 1991 Hungary had received half of the total Western investment in Eastern Europe, but this financing underscored only how sluggish Western investment had been. In 1989, when still under a communist regime, Hungary had attracted $300 million in foreign investment. This amount increased to almost a billion in 1990, and in 1991 the figure topped $1.5 billion.[37] As to national income, it had not plummeted as it had in other reforming countries: in 1991 it fell by only 6 to 7 percent.[38] This slide, though, was worrying Hungarian economic officials. Gross Domestic Product dropped nearly one-fifth between 1989 and 1992.[39]

Still more worrying was the fact that Hungary's gradualism had not been able to avoid the social hardships that shock therapy also involved. As early as the end of 1991, 350,000 men and women, or about 7 percent of the work force, were unemployed. Foodstuffs, too, were becoming extremely expensive. In 1992 it was estimated that 70 percent of "average family" budgets went on food.[40] Most Hungarians in 1992 would say that, materially, life was better under Kádár.

Hungarian officials, however, like many Western observers, were optimistic. Their predictions roughly corresponded with the Czechoslovak three-phases scenario: 1992, turning point; 1993, recovery; 1994, upswing.[41] By the middle of 1993, as in the Polish and Czech cases, some hope showed itself that the worst was over. The economy, as a whole, was expected to start expanding; between 3 and 5 percent was the estimate for 1993.[42] Exports had been especially strong, and Hungary for 1992 was expecting a current annual surplus of between $800 and $900 million, an increase of about two-thirds above 1991. Hungary's foreign debt still was formidable, but it was still being managed: The *gross* debt was more than $23 billion, but reserves had increased rapidly, and the net debt stood at about $13 billion.

Stiff obstacles still needed to be overcome, however. Unemployment was expected to hit 15 percent by the end of 1993, a rise of 3 percent above 1992, and inflation would hover around 20 percent.[43] These were the kinds of statistics that meant more to ordinary Hungarians than encouraging figures about trade and other such "abstractions." Most Hungarians were convinced they were worse off. A noted German journalist in early 1992 already referred to the dangers of "serious social tension and sensitive public reaction."[44] It was this that could swell the socialist vote in the 1994 elections.

ROMANIA
The Consequences of Reform

Nowhere in Eastern Europe, with the possible exception of Albania, were the social and political consequences of economic change in the early postcommunist period more dramatic than in Romania. In September 1991 thousands of coal miners from the Jiu Valley, the biggest coal-mining region in the country, made another of their periodic descents on Bucharest and, by means of riotous demonstrations, forced the resignation of Premier Roman, who was perceived as the architect of the economic reforms that were beginning to bite (see chapter 4). The liberalization of prices, one of the "shock therapy" aspects of Romania's reform, bit the most deeply and was the ostensible cause of the miners' insurrection.

Before the miners' action, strikes in many sections of industry had become commonplace and have continued to be so. What the miners did was simply to rivet attention on a situation that threatened to descend into chaos, into disorder approaching Albanian proportions. Nowhere else was the interaction between economics and politics more patent. The pauperization under Ceauşescu and the debasement of the country's already primitive political culture, the lack of political and social consensus, the pervasive suspicion, all combined to form the worst possible climate in which to launch economic reform. Western attitudes also weighed heavily on Romania's reform efforts. Postcommunist Romania encountered not just Western indifference but, except in the case of France, open Western hostility. Romania's big international problem, therefore, was how to disarm Western antagonism, especially to qualify for whatever Western aid might be available. A determined economic reform was one way, and, since the keepers of the Western purse strings showed a predilection for "shock therapy," the government, led by Petre Roman, made some efforts to oblige. The economy may well have needed "shock therapy," anyway. But Romania was the clearest example so far of an economy needing something that society simply could not stand.

At first, the miners' invasion of September 1991 appeared to give the death blow, not just to "shock therapy," but to any meaningful reform. Roman was toppled, and Western cynicism about Romania only increased. Within the ruling National Salvation Front, the rift between fast reformers, slower reformers, and nonreformers increased. But in this situation the Romanian trait of savvy resilience showed itself yet again. In international terms, economically (and politically, too) the only way to go was forward. Roman's successor as prime minister, Theodor Stolojan, was a convinced reformer with an austere reputation and an apolitical profile.[45] His new government showed its hand almost immediately in November 1991 with a major currency reform that made the leu, the Romanian unit of currency, internally convertible.[46] This reform was an earnest of the new government's intentions, an international as well as an internal signal.

In a sense, the Stolojan government was politically lucky in that the previous Roman government had taken the most unpopular moves by imposing the drastic price increases that led to its fall. The first of these was in November 1990 and had been followed by three more. There were safeguards for staple foods, on which some subsidies were retained, and there also was a wage-indexing scheme designed, unsuccessfully as it turned out, to take the edge off higher living costs. Stolojan thus could assure the public that at least part of the worst was behind them. But the previous measures had taken, and would go on taking, a heavy toll. The overall inflation rate toward the end of 1991 peaked at 252 percent.[47] The official unemployment figure rose to nearly 1 million, or about one in ten of the total work force,[48] and the figure continued increasing substantially.

In the spring of 1992, though, some brighter features came forward. The government, facing elections in the summer, began to sound bullish about some economic indicators. Coal extraction was on the rise, as was production of several light-industrial items. But food production still was declining, and a small trade deficit existed. At the same time, there were some encouraging figures on small-scale privatization. About 36 percent of domestic trade was now in private hands,[49] a figure that was increasing rapidly; the Romanian entrepreneurial spirit was undoubtedly reviving. Price liberalization also had put goods in the shops for those able to buy them; the social and political danger, of course, was that few Romanians could do so.

What of the future, then? The more specific question—applicable throughout Eastern Europe, but most poignant of all in Romania—was whether politics and people would let the reforms work.[50] In 1993 most Romanians were pessimistic. So were most foreign visitors, who, often unfairly, compared the situation with that in the East-Central European countries. Some Western economists, however, were more optimistic. They admired the scope and progress of the economic reform, especially in view of the social and political volatility and of Ceauşescu's legacy. Over the longer term they saw Romania emerging as the prosperous country its human and natural resources, and its geography, could enable it to be.[51] Over the shorter term, however, it was evident that many Romanians were in no position to take the kind of medicine their economy needed. This factor won Ion Iliescu the presidential elections in September 1992. He had run on a platform of slower, modified reform aimed at lessening the social hardships involved (see chapter 4). The new Romanian prime minister, Nicolae Văcăroiu, appointed after the parliamentary elections, while insisting on the market economy as the continuing goal, was constantly at pains to stress that it must be a *social* market economy. This position was not surprising in view of the inflation and unemployment levels. Clearly, the state in future would be playing a bigger role in the economy than in either 1991 or 1992.[52] The danger was that it would undermine whatever good economic effects the reforms had so far achieved—for example, by unduly supporting, as in Slovakia, the big state firms with financial handouts.

BULGARIA

Hesitancy, Boldness, and Doubts

In the last two decades of communist rule, the Bulgarian economy went through two distinct phases. During the 1970s the apparent success was such, and the general increase in the standard of living so marked, that some visitors were inclined to speak of the "Bulgarian economic miracle."[53] This progress carried through into the early 1980s, but it was followed by a precipitous decline. All talk of a miracle stilled; the rates of increase of all of the main economic indices fell sharply; and living standards virtually stagnated. Foreign borrowing increased dramatically with nothing constructive to show for it. This decline unquestionably played a part in the downfall of president and party leader Todor Zhivkov in November 1989.[54] But, again, a certain degree of Balkan perspective is necessary. Zhivkov's economic legacy, however unsatisfactory, amounted almost to bonanza when compared with Ceauşescu's. Romania's only clear advantage has been the absence of foreign debt, whereas, in 1992, Bulgaria's debt amounted to about $12 million.[55] Bulgaria's debt had been declining sharply in the early 1980s when Zhivkov appeared to be following the same policy as Ceauşescu in cutting it down. But the policy then sharply reversed, mainly to keep living standards from falling too severely.

Had Bulgaria begun a meaningful economic reform soon after the fall of Zhivkov, it might by early 1993 have been looking forward to an eventual recovery. But real progress toward the market began only at the beginning of 1991; a year, therefore, had been lost. The Bulgarian Socialist (former communist) Party that then dominated the government, torn by internal strife, with even reformers unable to shake off their old collectivist complexes, squandered precious months in procrastination. Only in the fall of 1990, when the communist government was ousted, was comprehensive reform accepted as the only counter to economic collapse, especially now that it was clear that the command economy no longer could be propped up by Soviet support.[56] Bulgaria, which formerly conducted 80 percent of its trade with Comecon — 60 percent with the Soviet Union — was especially affected by the collapse of both. It was later to suffer severely, as was Romania, from the commercial effects of the Gulf War and the international embargo on Serbia.

Under a new stabilization program encouraged by the IMF, the first priority was strict monetarism, reducing both the budget deficit and inflation. The stated intention was to stabilize the lev and make it domestically convertible. At the same time, it was necessary to liberalize prices by lowering or abolishing most subsidies. In their struggle to find the right balance between austerity, which meant as great a degree of wage control as possible, and letting prices rise, which meant social hardship, the Bulgarians achieved a level of success that surprised many observers. In early 1991 inflation was estimated as high as 370 percent per year, but by June it was down to about 3.5 percent per month.[57] Although it then started to rise slowly, the Bulgarian rate still was comparing favorably with that of other postcommunist East European economies. A prohibitively high interest rate and the fact that most Bulgarians incline to save rather than spend partially explain this creditable performance. Already by the spring of

1992, therefore, there were encouraging signs of financial stabilization, and Bulgaria was beginning to win praise in the West for its combination of boldness and good husbandry.

But these steps toward financial stability continued to be dogged by the foreign debt. Standing at $12.2 billion in early 1992, this meant about $1,300 per capita, second after Hungary.[58] For almost two years the Bulgarians had made no payments on the debt principal or, for a somewhat shorter time, even on the interest. A rescheduling had been arranged with Western creditors as early as spring 1990, but this move was of little help since the bulk of the Bulgarian debt was with private Western institutions. This failure to meet its obligations made Bulgaria for a time something of an outcast from the world financial community. Talks in early 1992 brought some return to its Western creditors and some respite for the Bulgarian economy.[59] But the situation continued to be unsatisfactory. What Bulgaria wanted was an upturn in its overall economic situation that would secure the financial progress made and make the country attractive for foreign investment.[60]

In the course of 1992 there was promise of distant improvement, but the immediate impact of the reforms was painful. Inflation again was rising very sharply and domestic consumption was dropping. Unemployment, 500,000 (more than 10 percent) at the end of 1991, began to rise again.[61] The social consequences of this jobless rate were not difficult to imagine. In 1991 there had been almost continual labor unrest, including serious coal miner and transport worker strikes, and the unrest was continuing.[62] Nothing like the disruptive violence in Romania occurred, but the situation was tense enough. The Bulgarians' reputation for patience was being sorely tried. Tension on the labor front continued throughout 1992 and into 1993. Although inflation dropped in 1992 (at one point in 1991 it had topped 500 percent), it was still very high, and unemployment now stood at 13.2 percent. The year 1993 promised to be another bleak one. Toward the end of 1992 the democratic government under Filip Dimitrov, which had looked determined to pursue reform, however unpopular, was replaced by a mainly technocratic government that looked likely to slow some of the reforms.

Again, the balance might be tilting away from economic necessity toward social appeasement. The correct balance might be as elusive as ever. One essential for eventual success was Western sympathy and forbearance. Dimitrov's evident determination had made a good international impression[63] but it had not produced much help. What was needed was continuing determination on the Bulgarians' part and the West's realization that economic support for Bulgaria could be an important element in preventing further chaos in the Balkans.

The Debate Over "Shock Therapy"

Opinions were strong on the subject:

> We don't think much of the radical attempt to switch from a command to a market economy. Certainly, one can by decree introduce the internal convertibility of the currency, as well as liberalize prices and foreign trade, but the real foundations for a market economy are still missing. Neither private ownership nor the business orientation of managers is at hand.[64]

This was the considered view of Friedrich Levcik, director of the Vienna Institute for Comparative International Economics, toward the end of 1991. His was an opinion being more loudly voiced by many others, especially as the social impact of "shock therapy" began to be evident. There probably was no more vociferous critic than Valtr Komárek, a reform-minded economist in the last years of communist rule in Czechoslovakia, briefly a deputy premier in the first post-communist government, but subsequently very much a political outsider—and one of Klaus's personal enemies. For Komárek, "shock therapy" was out of touch with reality. The issue, he maintained, was one of time. Everybody agreed on the need for the market. The question was "whether it should be done in two years or 10."[65] Melvin Fagen, a former director of the UN Economic Commission for Europe, in an article in the *International Herald Tribune,* strongly urged Boris Yeltsin not to administer "shock therapy" to Russia. He disagreed with Komárek apparently only on one point. Komárek had dismissed "shock therapy" as being untested "beyond the economic laboratories of Cambridge, Massachusetts," an obvious, if laborious, thrust at Jeffrey Sachs. According to Fagen, it had been tried in many places, "especially in those undeveloped countries that have suffered street riots and lower living standards as a result of the requirements imposed on them by the International Monetary Fund."[66]

The IMF was, in fact, cast as the villain by many opponents of "shock therapy." After the miners' riots in Romania in September 1991, for example, many thought the financial measures that had caused the miners' wrath had been introduced to please the IMF.[67] The president of the National Bank of Hungary, Péter Ákos Bród, stoutly defended gradualism at a Washington, D.C., conference organized by the IMF at the beginning of 1992, indirectly criticizing the IMF while doing so.[68] Komárek thought some Western bankers had a "heavier approach than the Marxists."[69] Zbigniew Brzezinski put it more tactfully, but no less forcefully:

> the West, including its financial institutions, must show greater sensitivity to the social problems of the ongoing transition in Central Europe. It is politically and morally inacceptable for the West to insist that post-communist countries deliberately accept prolonged, massive and painful unemployment. Yet, that is in effect what both the IMF and foreign private investors are demanding. . . .[70]

His point was clear: without political gumption, "shock therapy" would kill the patient.

On the other side the "shock therapists" were not only unrepentant but continued confidently didactic. Despite all of his political tribulations, Balcerowicz was convinced of its success.[71] Away from the firing line, so were Jeffrey Sachs and several others. In a speech in Frankfurt toward the end of 1991, Sachs shrugged off the falling production figures in Eastern Europe. The positive nature of the economic reforms already undertaken, he argued, was hidden behind gloomy governmental statistics and showed the "predictable and necessary dismantling of an overdeveloped industrial economy that was created to serve the Soviet Union." The "booming new service sector" was cushioning the shocks of dismantling the big industrial concerns. "A decline in industry and growth in the service sector should be expected, and that is just what is happening." What was needed now was quicker and more extensive privatization — sorting out the morass of property rights, or finding out definitively who owned what.[72] The privatization issue was becoming crucial to the "shock therapists' " arguments. As one Hungarian economist bitterly put it: "Today, self-interested, short-sighted elites are mishandling the most crucial aspect of the [economic] transition — the transfer of state-owned assets to private hands."[73]

It was an argument likely to go on for a long time, without ever being decisively settled. Despite the dogmatism displayed by both sides, it was too early in 1993 to say which approach suited Eastern Europe best. The "shock therapists," at least at the beginning, had seemed too one-dimensional in their approach, ignoring or making light of the interaction between economic, social, and political issues. But the evident successes later being achieved in Poland and the Czech Republic could serve to vindicate what they had been claiming.

The Essential Privatization

Privatization — breaking up the monopolistic state sector and putting it into private, competitive ownership — has been regarded as an — or *the* — essential component of any market-oriented reform program. Two kinds of privatization, large and small, have emerged. Small refers to the private shops, trade outlets, small businesses, and service centers that have proliferated throughout Eastern Europe since 1989. One of Václav Klaus's much-used debating points on the subject was that his two sons, who before 1990 had never known private shops, now were able (and eager) to patronize nothing else.

It was not small- but large-scale privatization that presented the real problem. As a writer for the *Economist* put it: "a lively sector of small service firms cannot upset the dead weight of thousands of big manufacturing companies remaining in state hands."[74] But here, inevitably, progress has been much slower. Toward the end of 1991, between 75 and 90 percent of industrial output in Eastern Europe still remained in state ownership,[75] and in June 1993 experts were agreeing that "privatization results have fallen short of expectations."[76] Few domestic purchasers were rich enough or bold enough to buy. True, the nomenklatura capitalists — usually former communist managers who had quickly bought chunks of the old state monolith, especially in Poland — caused great indignation, giving the whole privatization process a bad name. But although politically an issue, these purchases were economically marginal. Foreign buyers, on whom considerable hopes were initially placed, were moving steadily into the three East Central European countries. At first, they seemed mainly interested in the few big "plums," like Škoda, or Budweis beer, in Czechoslovakia,[77] and Tungsram in Hungary, but later they quietly began acquiring many smaller properties. Generally though, the early, too-confident expectations had not been fulfilled. The restitution of state property to former owners or their heirs also was proceeding slowly (and, even so, was causing political and social dissension), but this hardly affected the larger industries. The truth was that the great bulk of these industries were not worth buying, and the few prospective buyers were turned off by chicanery, bureaucracy, and interminable legal delay. In addition, there were strong, entrenched interests in the status quo, not only from the old regime managers but from many sections of the trade unions and, in Poland and Hungary, from the workers' representative councils in the factories. These workers' councils, which had been seen politically as a considerable step forward during the communist era, were now, in an era when basic economic change was imperative, mostly behaving as a vested interest opposing change.

In the second half of 1991 the progress of privatization had been so disappointing that a new mass privatization approach was made by Poland, Czechoslovakia, and Romania. The Polish and Romanian approaches were similar in principle in that they involved the free distribution of company shares to all adult citizens.[78] Polish citizens were to get shares in a relatively small number of large investment companies, which assumed the ownership of hundreds of state-owned companies. These investment companies were to be controlled by Polish directors but managed by Western appointees. In Romania a law of August 1991 stipulated the privatization of about six thousand state-owned enterprises over a period of seven years. Thirty percent of the capital of these enterprises would be distributed to all adult citizens (about 17 million) in the form of vouchers (or "property certificates")—about 85 million in all.[79]

The Czechoslovak scheme, promoted by Václav Klaus, was the most spectacular, and perhaps most risky, of all. It involved the *sale* of investment vouchers to all adult citizens for the nominal sum of 1,000 crowns (about $32), or about one week's salary. Stock, initially in more than a thousand companies, or some 40 percent of state-owned property, was to be sold for the vouchers at the beginning of 1992. It first was expected that about 2 million people would join the scheme. Actually, 8 million people subscribed, and it became the most famous privatization venture in history. What made the difference was the gold rush atmosphere generated by the emergence of numerous private funds that offered to buy the citizens' vouchers with the promise of a handsome profit—over tenfold in a year being offered in some cases. Some private funds, with their seductive television commercials and foot-in-the-door salesmen, were refreshingly or repulsively novel in their methods, depending on one's point of view. The most spectacular was the "Harvard Capital and Consulting Company" (see chapter 2). Its only connection with Harvard was its Czech returnee president Viktor Kozený, who was later embroiled in an espionage scandal. Its title and techniques suggested a combination of American prestige and push that ordinary Czechs and Slovaks found irresistible. How irresistible they would find it in the future remained to be seen. Bonanza or South Sea Bubble? And, if the voucher plan succeeded, what would the relationship be between ownership and direction of industry? This question was just one of many to be answered. There could be no doubt that the Czechoslovak voucher scheme got off to a flying start. But where to? Many economists were predicting success, others failure. The Czech-Slovak split complicated the matter. But despite all the difficulties, Klaus, whose political future depended on its success, continued to be genuinely confident.[80]

During much of 1992 Polish privatization seemed bogged down in popular apathy, justified doubt about the Polish industry's stability, huge corruption scandals, and political controversy. But what may have been saving the situation was a kind of privatization that smacked of genuine Polish improvisation. In early 1933 the *Economist,* in a favorable review of Polish economic development, wrote:

> In the event, privatisation has worked, but not in the way that free-market purists and western advisers envisaged. Privatisations by liquidation, worker/management buy-out and joint venture have proved much faster and more successful. They could be conducted by local authorities, and were therefore much less affected by the vagaries of Polish politics. By the end of 1992, over 1,500 privatisations of this sort were either completed or in progress, away from the hassles of Warsaw ministries.[81]

There was also increasing pressure in Poland for adopting the Czech voucher method of privatization; but it was doubtful how much the idea would prosper under the new post-September 1993 Polish government.

Hungary had—perhaps surprisingly in view of its promising start—been a laggard in privatization.[82] It had looked initially to a quick selling-off campaign. Its "State Property Agency" had more than two thousand companies to sell off, but progress was extremely slow, and in mid-1992 only a tiny fraction of these were in private hands. The whole policy was at an impasse. A new one was needed, and it came in April 1993 when the government announced what it called its "mass privatization" program, which had some of the characteristics of the voucher scheme introduced in Prague. It did so with one eye (or both eyes) on the upcoming parliamentary elections due in early 1994.[83]

Bulgarian moves toward privatization had been fumbling and feeble from the start. The socialists when in power had been halfhearted, or less, about it. The Union of Democratic Forces (UDF) when in opposition had promised that privatization would be its top priority when in power. But the UDF was slow in keeping this promise. By the spring of 1992, however, it had a plan in place. Like the Hungarians initially, the Bulgarians wanted to avoid the Czechoslovak voucher plan. Instead, they opted for a comprehensive hybrid scheme. It was ambitious but complicated and susceptible to bureaucratic clogs and chokes.[84] At best, it would be slow, and this very slowness might inflict irreparable harm on it.

All in all, large-scale privatization of many of the old state-owned factories did not give grounds for much optimism. Perhaps, though, privatization was becoming the wrong term, or too narrow a term, for what was taking place. *Creating a private sector* would be better. This effort involved the creation of *new* privately owned firms in sectors that showed promise. And not just on a small scale — this already was happening — but on a medium and even large scale, preferably with, but possibly without, Western involvement. Most of the huge socialist creations would simply have to crumble, leaving desolation and destitution in their wake. As in Western countries, old industries and once booming areas would simply decay, while other "new" parts flourished. The fate of Eastern Europe in this regard would not be much different from that of other industrial regions — Western Europe and the United States.

The Safety Net

In these painful transitions from socialism to capitalism, with the high percentages of unemployment involved, the new East European governments realized that one crucial addition was necessary to the social welfare mosaic inherited from their predecessors: unemployment benefits. Since, under communism, unemployment was alleged to have been, by definition, impossible, the new governments had to scurry around to get compensation schemes in place — all the more so as unemployment began to rise rapidly. The provisions varied somewhat from country to country.[85]

> *Albania:* Initially, unemployment benefits amounted to 80 percent of former wages. But in April 1992 the government announced it was changing this to 60 percent for the first six months of unemployment and then gradually would phase out benefits.
>
> *Bulgaria:* About 60 percent of the average wage for eight months.
>
> *Czechoslovakia:* set at 65 percent of average salary for the first six months and 60 percent in the following six months.
>
> *Hungary:* for the first year, 70 percent of average salary; 50 percent for the second year.
>
> *Poland:* payment of 70 percent of average salary for the first three months; 50 percent for the next six months; 40 percent for the next three months.
>
> *Romania:* set at 50–60 percent of average salary for the first nine months, plus another three months in case of illness.

These are the essentials of the different national systems, all of which contain exceptions, conditions, and qualifications. In Bulgaria and Romania the benefits were considered scarcely adequate, but in Poland, Hungary and Czechoslovakia some considered them more than adequate, constituting a disincentive to find other employment.[86] Voices were being raised in all three of these countries demanding a lowering of the benefit rates. But at a time of rising unemployment and deteriorating living standards, it would have been political suicide to do so.

The Shrinking of the Soviet Trade

The point is made in chapter 8 that the newly freed East European states, contrary to their hopes, simply could not shake off their neighbor to the east. The USSR no longer was imperial, and within a short time it was no longer united. But, whatever the condition of its successors, and however successful some East European states might be in redirecting their trade westward, the former Soviet Union, especially Russia, would continue to play an important role in Eastern Europe's economic future.

After the years of Stalinist exploitation, the East European countries settled into a relatively advantageous pattern of economic relations with their Soviet masters. The Soviets supplied cheap energy and raw materials and provided a huge, undiscriminating market. This comfortable state of affairs was severely jolted by the world oil price explosions of the 1970s. The Soviets responded to the OPEC price increases by charging the East Europeans more for their own oil. Soviet oil remained generally cheap by world standards, but the increases gave most satellite economies a shock from which they never recovered. In the 1980s Soviet supplies of energy were reduced in volume for a while but then picked up again. In the meantime, the Soviet market, despite louder grumbles about the quality of East European exports, remained firm.[87]

Eastern Europe's energy dependence on the Soviet Union amounted (except for Romania) to 100 percent for natural gas, 80 percent for crude oil and petroleum products, and more than 70 percent for hard coal.[88] Romania, a considerable oil-producing country itself, but whose industrialization program made its own supplies inadequate, first tried to make up the ever-increasing difference by supplies from the Middle East. But in the 1980s Romania began importing Soviet oil, and by the end of the decade it was getting nearly one-fifth of its energy supplies from the Soviet Union.[89]

The region's dependence, therefore, was obvious, and nothing underlined it more than the prospect of the supplies being endangered. It would take years before alternative sources could be found and adequately financed. And, already in 1990, supplies to Eastern Europe dropped by 30 percent.[90] Just as serious as the actual drop in supplies was their unreliability. No country now knew how much oil was coming its way through the pipelines. As the Soviet Union began falling apart in 1991, the East European states scrambled to make whatever arrangements they could to meet the crisis. The main strategy was to negotiate directly with the Russian republic, where most of the oil and natural gas deposits were located. A number of different arrangements were made, none of which looked as if it would stand up for long.[91]

For example, Poland had been among those East European states forced to return to barter dealing with the Russian republic at the end of 1991. Russia promised to meet all of Poland's natural gas and half of its oil needs for 1992 in return for Polish exports of foodstuffs, medical supplies, and coal-related products. But immediately in the new year Russia began to renege on its commitments, as it did to other

East European states.[92] Indications were that they all would have to get used to it. By 1992 Russian oil deliveries appeared to have improved,[93] but the stability of Russia itself was so doubtful that absolutely no guarantee existed of future reliability.

The *entire* economic relationship between the East European states and the Soviet Union was disrupted by the decision to switch to hard currency commercial finance at the beginning of 1991. The East Europeans already had been affected, not just by the crisis in Soviet energy supplies, but by the loss of the GDR trade caused by the disappearance of the GDR itself. An important segment of the old Comecon mosaic of economic interdependence had been pulled out. Comecon was not formally disbanded until September 1991, but it had ceased functioning effectively at least a year earlier. Its demise caused few regrets, but some of its consequences were painful, none more so than the conversion from transferable ruble to hard currency accounting. The transferable ruble was merely a bookkeeping convenience allowing Comecon's barter trade to be reckoned and recorded. It was Moscow's own idea to discontinue it and go over to hard currency, signifying the end of the old economic relationship; no more subsidized energy exports from them and no more shoddy exports to them. For one thing, the Soviets no longer could afford the old relationship; for another, no political incentive existed to do so.

The shift to hard currency had immediate effects. For example, Hungarian and Czechoslovak exports to the Soviet Union dropped 80 percent in the first quarter of 1991 compared with the same period the previous year, while Polish exports dropped 60 percent.[94] By the middle of 1991 it was estimated that Soviet exports to Eastern Europe were falling by 60 percent and Soviet imports from Eastern Europe by 50 percent.[95] This was a commercial revolution, a consequence of, and complement to, the political revolution of 1989. It also was part of the whole economic revolution engulfing the East European states. It was painful and likely to be protracted. This upheaval roughly coincided with the losses caused by the Gulf War in 1991, which were particularly severe for Bulgaria and Romania. Both of these countries subsequently asked for UN permission to resume importing Iraqi oil.[96] Later the sanctions against Serbia also severely hit Bulgaria and Romania.

Finding new markets was as difficult as finding new sources of supply. In terms of both variety and quality, Eastern Europe seemed to have little to offer to a selective Western market. And where it could compete — in some agricultural products and a few consumer goods like textiles — it found the European Community, its proximate and prized market, largely unreceptive.[97] The collapse of the Soviet market had been too swift and comprehensive. "Gradualism" in this regard would have been much better for the East Europeans! Dogmatic shock therapists might argue that the swifter the collapse, the swifter the East Europeans would have to find new markets and sources of supply; in the end, therefore, like "shock therapy" at home, it would have been not just beneficial but essential. But the domestic "shock therapists" had been depending on steady supplies of Soviet raw materials to back up their programs (see above, pp. 133–134, and the discussion of Czechoslovakia in chapter 3).

However, it is precisely in this area of alternative markets that some real success stories can be recorded. In spite of all of the Western barriers, the three East Central European countries made surprisingly good progress in redirecting their trade westward. Taking 1988 as a base, Czechoslovakia and Hungary in 1992 looked set to increase the value of their exports to the European Community countries by well above two and a half times, with Poland not far behind.[98] This success admittedly was precarious, and, for their part, the Balkan countries were making little progress. But it was encouraging. Much now would depend on Western vision and liberability. Further prospects, though, were not all that encouraging. Western Europe was simply not prepared to meet Eastern Europe halfway (see below, pp. 158–159). Some experts already were talking of a new "Iron Curtain" descending.[99]

Statistics: Different Perceptions, Clashing Interpretations

Communist statistics always were open to question; in the case of some countries — Romania and the GDR most notably — they were often totally unreliable. But *post*-communist statistics also have a credibility problem, if of a different sort. Many economists have pointed out that statistics on the economic progress during the early phases of reform often are so distorted as to be useless. Falls in production are measured solely within the framework of the old centrally planned economy. Thus, while the production of the state firms might be accurately assessed, that of the firms in the burgeoning private economy is underestimated, usually because private sector firms, with an eye on the tax man, seldom say that they are doing as well as they really are. Some of the smaller private firms simply fail to say anything. Overall figures for the decline in East European output are, therefore, too high, although nobody knows by how much.[100]

Still more basic is the argument that statistics on the decline in production are not just misleading but irrelevant. Under socialism, the plan—not demand—dictated production. Much of what was produced was neither wanted nor needed; it was, in fact, part and parcel of the whole problem now in the process of solution.[101] Therefore, what is now considered a loss in production simply represents that percentage of useless production that could not be sold. Now the market is taking care of things, and what seems to be a loss is actually part of the healing process of reform. Similarly, drops in real wages should not be taken too tragically because, under socialism, part of wages earned was useless because few or no goods could be bought. Now, shops are full, and wages can be spent according to demand and desire. The same argument also applies to the rises in unemployment. For one thing, many of those officially classified as unemployed are working in the second economy. Many more did not really work under socialism, anyway, and it is only technically correct to call them unemployed now. Now, they get unemployment relief, a more direct form of governmental help than the nominal paid employment in which they used to indulge.

From an economic point of view these arguments were well taken. But they ignored the popular perceptions on which the success of the transformation under way could depend. Many people in all of the East European countries were convinced that their standard of living was becoming worse. They saw a small number of private entrepreneurs getting arrogantly richer, while they were getting sheepishly poorer. This situation went against the grain of a strong egalitarianism, or social jealousy, throughout the region, which had existed before 1945 but which communism strongly reinforced. (As the saying went, the race should not just start even but end even.) Most galling of all was the fact that among the new capitalists were some members of the old nomenklatura, riding high on the new wave of the future. Then there was the corruption. It had been rampant under communism, but now it was obvious, growing lucrative, and publicized. This was the underside of capitalism that could give the whole system a bad name. And it was unfortunate that many new genuine businessmen who were contributing to the national wealth and who would become part of the new middle class tended to be tarred with the same brush by the public as the antisocial wheeler-dealers.

The crucial question was how long people would have to wait before the reformers' confident projections came true. Or how long could the reformers go on blaming the former system for the ills of the new one. The answer was that the time was getting short.

The Transition in Agriculture

East European agriculture under communism presented a mixed picture. Poland, where about three-quarters of the arable land remained in private hands, had a resilient agriculture but not a very efficient one, suffering many of the drawbacks of scattered strip farming. Czechoslovak agriculture was almost totally socialized, but some of it was relatively efficient and many farmers did well. Hungary's largely collectivized agriculture, flexibly and administratively administered, was the most efficient of all. In Bulgaria, where "big is beautiful" dominated communist thinking, the huge collectives and then the "agro-industrial" complexes were impressive in everything except results. Agriculture in both Romania and Albania presented examples of misrule and mismanagement.[102]

Now the task was to create, for the first time in history, a large, prosperous private farming class, to bring back the kulaks and spread them. Land reform legislation was enacted throughout the region. But legislation was one thing, implementation another. Not only the feasibility but the wisdom of doing away entirely with the state and collective farms became a subject of debate. But generally the governments pressed ahead with plans to privatize the socialist, especially the collectivized, sector. Where this shift could not be made, cooperatives were to be encouraged.[103]

The difficulties were formidable. Many state and collective farm workers were reluctant to give up their security and relatively easy life for the hazards of private farming. The mystic communion between peasants and their land had been broken by communist rule. Moreover, much bureaucracy, inefficiency, and confusion had to be broken through before a would-be private farmer could acquire the necessary legal status. Technical problems of getting credit and the proper equipment and machinery also arose. And all of these difficulties had to be confronted against the opposition and chicanery of many local bureaucrats—communist hangovers who were against private farming, sometimes for ideological reasons, more often because it threatened their positions and privileges.[104] All of these problems were compounded by the advanced age of most socialized farmers. Moreover, despite the huge exodus from the land to the cities over the last forty years, by Western standards too many people still were engaged in agriculture. In relatively advanced Czechoslovakia, for example, 794,830 or 10.4 percent of the employed population still worked on the land in 1990.[105] In Bulgaria the percentage was 22 percent.[106]

One of the principal means of land privatization in postcommunist Eastern Europe has been the restitution to its former owners of land confiscated by the communists and then socialized. Different governments have planned to accomplish this restitution in different ways, and their laws regularly have been amended and liberalized since 1991.[107] In Poland, where small private ownership had predominated, the government announced its intention of compensating originally expropriated owners with coupons to be used for buying shares in privatized companies. In Czechoslovakia a law was passed allowing claimants to reclaim up to 150 hectares of arable land. Bulgaria allows compensation in the form of land; the maximum amount at first was niggardly, but it later was increased. In Hungary the reconstituted Independent Smallholders' Party strongly pressed the restitution issue, which resulted in legislation allowing for compensation either in land or company shares. In Romania a radical restitution law was passed allowing land up to one hundred hectares eventually to be reclaimed.[108] In Albania, in what the *Economist* called a concession to the "nationalists," former owners can reclaim land even if it has been built over.[109] Generally speaking, numerous methods for land compensation have been applied. But the long and arduous procedures and the certain prospect of applicants getting much less than they considered themselves entitled to made the whole operation highly controversial. The results often were dulled hopes, raised tempers, and endless frustration.

Results and Prospects in Agriculture

In December 1991 Germany's best-known commercial newspaper carried an article pointing to the dramatic drop in the use of fertilizer in both East European and Soviet agriculture. Taking fertilizer use as a measure of the condition of agriculture, it concluded that the serious fall reflected a close to catastrophic harvest that would result in serious short-term food shortages throughout the region.[110]

Allowing for a certain one-dimensional exaggeration, this appraisal fell not far short of the mark. Agriculture in most countries was, and continued to be, in serious difficulties. The transition to the market in the economy as a whole, especially in Hungary, Czechoslovakia, and Poland, where the process was further advanced, was having a serious initial impact on agriculture—especially the partial discontinuance of agricultural subsidies. In Hungary, for example, subsidies were reduced by almost half in 1991; when inflation was included, the reduction amounted to almost 75 percent. From the beginning of 1991 almost all agricultural subsidies in Czechoslovakia were removed. The same was true for Poland, which also abolished tariffs on Western food imports. In the pan-European context the irony and unfairness of this situation were not lost on the East Europeans. The West Europeans were exhorting them to turn to free markets and free trade, and they, eager pupils, were responding by demolishing subsidies and lowering tariffs. All of this was occurring at a time when agriculture in Western Europe was often heavily subsidized and protected by high tariffs.

Agriculture also was suffering from the depressed standard of living, aggravated, even if only temporarily, by the economic reforms. In Poland in 1990, for example, personal consumption reportedly dropped by nearly a quarter compared with the previous year.[111] The prices of food and other agricultural produce fell. At the same time, throughout the region, agricultural input prices were rising rapidly, and farmers were caught in the classic "scissors" syndrome—high costs, low prices—that had plagued much of East European agriculture between the two world wars. The short-term future promised little relief; if anything, more of the same could be expected. As the overall economic reforms continued, domestic demand for agricultural produce would continue to fall,[112] prices would drop, and farm profitability and incomes would stagnate. The loss of traditional Comecon markets, especially the Soviet, would aggravate the situation.

Such a prospect made the potentially large and lucrative West European market all the more important. Exports to Western Europe from Poland, Czechoslovakia, and Hungary did increase considerably through 1991 and 1992. But they still remained relatively small. The breakthrough, for which the East Europeans had been hoping and on which their future would partly depend, was still far away. In fact, because of tariff liberalization in some parts of Eastern Europe, West European foodstuffs were making bigger inroads there than the reverse. (In the course of 1992 President Wałęsa had begun complaining about this problem.)[113] It was not entirely a case of Western hypocrisy. As Timothy N. Ash points out, if Western markets were opened further, "the costs of helping the East European economies will be borne disproportionately by individual sections of the Western economies in lost jobs."[114] The question, though, was how big these sections were and whether no ways could be found of compensating members of them.

It would be absurd if a minitrade war ever were to develop between West and East European farmers at a time when *all* of the East European countries were bent on the quickest possible admittance to the European Community. But the prospect could not be dismissed entirely. Toward the end of 1991 both Hungary and Poland reimposed some quotas on livestock and other forms of agricultural produce. One widely touted suggestion for relieving the situation was for West European countries to purchase East European produce and supply it to some of the Soviet Union's successor states and to countries like Albania.[115] It was an idea that could take hold, but it would far from fulfill the East Europeans' desire to get into the Western market.

In December 1991 Poland, Czechoslovakia, and Hungary finally signed accords with the European Community giving them associate status from the beginning of 1992. Romania and Bulgaria followed a year later. After hard negotiations the Community made concessions in several commodities, including a considerable range of agricultural produce.[116] These agreements certainly were a start, but, in spite of the brave face East European officials put on them, a distinct disappointment. In June 1993 it looked as if further concessions from Brussels were on the way.[117] Such concessions needed to be big if some East European countries were not to feel forced to extend and increase some of the modest price subsidies that they already had been forced to reintroduce, thereby "going into reverse" in their reform intentions.

Western Assistance and Investment

Western assistance to, or economic involvement in, Eastern Europe is being conducted through different but sometimes interacting channels. These are (1) international institutions, like the IMF, the World Bank, or the European Bank for Reconstruction and Development (EBRD), created specifically for aid to postcommunist Europe, with its (palatial) headquarters in London; (2) Western governments, either severally or collectively; (3) private business capital; (4) philanthropic organizations, like foundations, supporting educational, environmental, and numerous other sociocultural-educational causes. The first three of these channels will be discussed below.[118]

International organizations like the IMF are in the best position to coordinate financial aid aimed at achieving macroeconomic stability. One example is helping a country — for example, Poland — to set up a stabilization fund to cushion against losses incurred when its currency is made convertible. Western governments and, in many cases, Western banks provide loans to postcommunist governments. In the 1970s and 1980s, in the communist period, although Western credits included some tied loans, that is, bound to a specific project, they more often were untied and in the end virtually wasted. Western lending and the profligate way the loan money was used caused the huge hard currency debts with which some East European countries are now burdened.

Private Western capital is best suited to stimulate economic recovery at the microeconomic level. It can aid both in the privatization of industry and in providing much-needed technical assistance. It is targeted on those sectors of industry having the likeliest economic prospects, and in these industries it can also promote management expertise. Western investment, therefore, so far has mostly found its way into those countries that have initiated meaningful market reforms and have indicated their will to persevere with them in spite of difficulties. Serious Western investment is also long-term, distinguishing it from the carpetbagging Western entrepreneurs who swarmed over Hungary, Poland, and Czechoslovakia in 1990.

The availability of "opportunistic" Western investment (using the adjective in the constructive economic sense) should depend, not only on the outlook for serious reform in Eastern Europe, but on two other factors: the speed and consistency of the privatization campaign, and the legislation governing foreign investment. Regarding foreign investment, the following is a country-by-country glimpse of the most important legislation as obtaining in 1992.[119]

Poland: No restrictions on foreigners setting up subsidiaries or investing. Foreigners could completely own Polish companies, have a three-year tax holiday and exemption from import duties. No curbs on repatriation of profits.

Czechoslovakia: No restrictions on percentage of equity held in Czechoslovak companies nor on repatriation of profits. (The situation arising from the splitting of the country into the Czech Republic and the Slovak Republic is likely to be similar, although perhaps with restrictions in the Slovak case.)

Hungary: Profit and unlimited capital repatriation of capital in hard currency are allowed. Progressive tax reduction for foreign participation in Hungarian companies. Total foreign ownership allowed.

Romania: Total foreign ownership allowed, and foreign investors could freely repatriate profits made in convertible currencies. Tax and customs concessions to foreign investors.[120]

Albania: Virtually the same as for Romania.

Bulgaria: A January 1992 law allowed foreigners to repatriate profits from investments (no limits on size) in hard currency without limit. Foreigners could set up business and acquire property, including land for building (but not for farming).[121]

It was likely that regulations on foreign ownership and participation would continue to be eased in most, if not all, East European countries. But foreign ownership already was becoming a most sensitive issue. Economic interest, which certainly would be served by increasing foreign ownership, clashed with what many East Europeans considered to be a sense of national dignity and, partly, of national survival. The clash was particularly strong in Poland and Czechoslovakia with regard to the injection of German capital. Volkswagen's taking control of the famous Škoda plant in Mladá Boleslav was the occasion for some soul-searching among Czechs—and more than a little nationalist posturing,[122] an attitude sharply criticized by a group of Czechoslovak reformist economists in a memorandum to the government in September 1991. This attitude reflected, they said, an unholy alliance of socialist and nationalist aversions to foreign capital. They ridiculed the notion that foreign capital could "buy up the entire Czechoslovak national economy in a single afternoon,"[123] and they ended by urging still greater concessions to foreign capital. But nationalist unease on the subject probably would grow in Eastern Europe. In Hungary, for example, István Csurka was bent on making it a political issue (see chapter 3) and his views were shared to some degree by many Democratic Forum members.

Joint ventures sometimes were seen as a convenient halfway house in terms of Western participation, a means of getting a foot in the door. By the end of 1991 the number of joint ventures had increased impressively, but already in early 1992 considerable pessimism was being expressed, particularly in Germany, about the future of this form of collaboration.[124] Joint ventures, it was being argued, had been useful when the communists were in power to help break into some East European markets. But now, except in a relatively small number of cases, their role seemed to have been played out.

It was foreign investment that in the end would make the difference. But how much difference? Many observers stressed the value of foreign investments in reviving Eastern Europe's economies and in acting as a catalyst—accelerating development through the transfer of business skills or new technology and boosting trade. But the *Economist,* for example, warned that foreign investments alone were far from enough. Even "on the most optimistic assumptions," it considered that Eastern Europe would get only about $7 billion in direct foreign investment by 1995 (plus about $21 billion from international aid agencies like the IMF and from Western banks).[125] This investment would be only a small percentage of what was needed, and the balance would have to come from domestic sources. This balance posed the great question for the future of the East European countries: Could they generate anywhere near what was needed from their own resources? It was too early to give an answer. The Czech Lands, Hungary, perhaps Poland had a chance. For the rest, the outlook was bleak. International support would be needed for an indefinite time.

Finally, a word about who was leading in the Western investment stakes, or which country was getting most. As mentioned, by the end of 1992 Hungary was clearly ahead of the receiving field. Between 1989 and the end of 1992 it had drawn more than half of total Western investment in Eastern Europe. But Czechoslovakia confidently had been expecting to overtake Hungary. With Czechoslovakia's demise in 1993, it was probable that the Czech Lands would get increasing investments, but Slovakia relatively little. Reliable figures for Poland were not available, but it certainly would rank third after Hungary and Czechoslovakia. Romania, Bulgaria, most of the successor states of Yugoslavia, and Albania were—not surprisingly—attracting very little by comparison. Albania, though (as mentioned in chapter 4), eventually could receive some Muslim investment.

Regarding Western *investors,* some figures published at the end of

1992 caused something of a surprise. Earlier, the United States had been considered as making a relatively strong showing only in Poland, but, even there, while American companies invested more than $62 million between 1989 and 1991, German companies invested $153 million.[126] In Czechoslovakia American investment in early 1992 was said to be trailing behind that of even Switzerland.[127] Italian, French, and British investment was disappointing, but that of Austria was substantial in Czechoslovakia and particularly in Hungary.[128]

However, the figures for 1992 showed not only that Western investment was increasing, in spite of earlier pessimism, but that the United States had been playing a bigger role than earlier figures had indicated. A New York-based East European investment magazine reported that American firms not only had maintained their lead in Hungary, but had led all other foreign investors in Czechoslovakia in 1992.[129] Overall, in investments in the Soviet successor states and in Eastern Europe together, the United States had outstripped Germany. (The largest number of American deals, however, and those amounting to the greatest value, were made in Russia.)

This was surprising, especially after the figures for 1991. But some factors had to be kept in mind:

First, the figures did not include the former German Democratic Republic (or the five new provinces of reunited Germany), where the major German investment effort had now begun to concentrate.

Second, some analysts were claiming that the leading American role in 1992 was really because of a few "big ticket items," like a General Motors deal with Poland.

Third, some analysts also thought that the greater numbers of medium and smaller investments being made from countries like Germany and Austria would have a bigger economic influence in Eastern Europe over the long run.

Fourth, Germany still had a clear lead in government trade, aid, and financing.

Fifth, statistics are often inadequate and unreliable, not necessarily because those giving them are guileful, but because some investment figures often are partly included in trade statistics and because of the difference between money *committed* and money that finally ends up being *invested.* Still, the American lead was there, however temporary.

And, most important, Western interest in Eastern Europe — or parts of it — was not sagging but increasing.[130]

It was Japan that remained the most conspicuous near-absentee. Immediately after 1989 it had showed keen interest in Eastern Europe. In January 1990 the Japanese prime minister at the time, Toshiki Kaifu, visited Poland and Hungary, and his visit was seen as preparing the way for considerable investment. But this did not happen. The Japanese evidently decided it still was too risky and that too much attention to Eastern Europe might impair their chances in a steadily integrating Western Europe.[131] Suzuki, the auto manufacturer, did move into Hungary (where, apparently, there was a sharp cultural clash between Japanese and Hungarian work habits),[132] but, in general, the Japanese have been prepared to sit and wait, satisfied that they were not missing much.

The Overall Prospects

At the end of 1991 two distinguished Western news dailies carried articles on the same day with totally opposing predictions for Eastern Europe's economic future.[133] The coincidence was a fitting reflection of the disunity in the expert camp on the subject, a disunity caused partly by temperament but mainly by differences in the interpretation of trends and statistics and in the emphasis given to them.

One of the more serious early predictions was made by a respected Basel economic research institute. Future economic development in Eastern Europe was divided into three phases: "contraction"; "orientation" (growth of production up to 4 percent): and "growth" (growth rates above 4 percent). For Hungary, the prediction was "orientation" beginning in 1992 and "growth" from 1995. For Czechoslovakia, both "orientation" and "growth" would begin one year later than in Hungary; for Poland, the dates were 1993 and 1997. For both Bulgaria and Romania, the "orientation" phase was seen as beginning only in 1995, with "growth" as yet nowhere in sight.[134]

In an accompanying comment to these predictions, the *Neue Zürcher Zeitung* made the point that has been the constant theme of this chapter: that social and political factors would profoundly affect economic forecasts of this kind.[135] The same also could have been said about the OECD report issued almost a year later. It predicted that overall output in all East European countries would continue to drop in 1992 but at a much lower rate than in 1991. Like most observers, the OECD was relatively optimistic about Hungary, where it thought production might bottom out in 1992. For Czechoslovakia and Poland there was guarded optimism, for Bulgaria and Romania relatively little. Generally, though, the OECD surprised many Westerners, and East Europeans, with its optimism. But many observers now emphasized the threatening impact of social and political factors on the economic reforms under way. The OECD report, while praising most reform efforts as truly radical, fell back on bureaucratese in referring to their noneconomic impact: "Behavior changes have been less evident and implementation problems have been pervasive."[136] A report by the Geneva-based UN Commission for Europe, also at the end of 1991, was more direct about the future dangers. Uncertainty ruled, it said, on how much longer East Europeans would peacefully tolerate their declining living standards. Accurately predicting increasing social unrest in 1992, the report also predicted popular pressure on the governments to dilute their reform programs. "Reform fatigue" would set in soon.[137]

At the end of 1992 the overall forecasting was still the same, although more optimism now existed about Poland. With Czechoslovakia being no more, there was optimism about the Czech Lands, gloom about Slovakia. Hungary, because of political doubts and economic hesitancy, could steadily lose its early lead. As for the Balkans, war was crippling all the former Yugoslav states except Slovenia. Romania had problems on an intimidating scale, and political and economic doubts similar to those in Hungary could assail Bulgaria. Albania continued to be an economic swamp.

Some perspective was needed, though, in the optimism beginning to surface. Even when (or if) an East European country bottomed out and then entered into positive growth, this would be cause more for quiet satisfaction than for jubilation. The baseline obviously had to be considered. In all, 1991 was the most disastrous year for the East European economies since the 1940s. Such a recovery, therefore, would be something in the nature of a "dead cat bounce," to use a stock market expression.[138] The projected growth might indeed occur, representing hope. But the going would be long and rough. What was happening, and would likely continue, was that reform economists in Eastern Europe and large sections of the population would be talking past each other, each pointing to different aspects of the economic situation to support their case.

By early 1993 the first stage of economic reform — the macroeconomic adjustment, begun in 1990 — was well-advanced throughout the region. Prices had been liberalized, and, with the introduction of at least internal convertibility, a big step toward currency exchange liberalization had been taken. The steep inflation that initially had accompanied these moves had been checked, if not contained. Czechoslovakia, Poland, and Hungary also had achieved considerable success in redirecting their trade toward the West and away from the former Soviet and Comecon markets on which they had depended for so long. But before the macroeconomic changes could be fully secured, the large-scale privatization process needed to be extended and accelerated. As one expert put it, "if privatization goes wrong, it endangers the entire reform process."[139] But, again, privatization was just as much a political and social process as an economic one, and its pitfalls were numerous. One of the biggest of several privatization dilemmas concerned future ownership: to whom should state ownership be transferred — foreigners, former owners, former members of the old communist nomenklatura (as was often the case in all of the countries concerned and which aroused great indignation), the workers of the company concerned, or the population at large? And then there was the distinction, not unknown in the capitalist West, between ownership and control.

Equally urgent for every country — even Hungary, where such reforms had begun toward the end of the communist era — was the need for banking reform. The region's banking systems were largely dominated by state banks whose assets were either nonexistent or dubious. But state banks still were giving fictitious loans to state enterprises, which, in turn, gave credits to each other, all in the never-never-land way of the old socialist system. The answer was to establish private banks, but where was the capital to do this? It also was necessary to conduct case-by-case evaluations of the firms to be privatized and to be financed — but there was little incentive to do so. This constituted a huge problem that needed to be tackled quickly, even if an early solution was impossible.

And, however successful Eastern Europe's capitalistic reforms appear to be, they will come to nothing without the right attitudes and skills to make them work. Two distinctly contrary trends have been evident so far. On one side, there has been the remarkable burgeoning of small-scale entrepreneurial activity, leading some observers to question whether forty years of communism had done as much to dull the edge of enterprise as had originally been feared. On the other side, the persistence of socialist sloth among large sections of the industrial and agricultural work force also has been evident.[140] Industrial managers, too, need Western-type training.

Finally, almost as serious as the deficiencies in the work ethos is the deficiency in industrial skills in Eastern Europe. Many observers rather surprisingly refer to the region's work force as "well-educated." By global criteria — compared, say, with Bolivia or Peru — they certainly are. But by the standards of Western countries and the NICs (newly industrialized countries) of Asia, most East European workers are at best half-educated. Nor, by these standards, are they skilled. Even the Czech working class, which was once up to the highest world standards, is now inferior in terms of the standards of skills that count. Even with the most rigorous training standards, how long would it take to bridge the gap?

The Environment: No Worse, No Better

A Reuters correspondent, attending an environmental conference in Budapest in October 1992, summed up the situation well: "If there is one bright light in the economic misery gripping Central and Eastern Europe, it is that the depression has slowed the rate at which the region is spewing pollution into the environment. But that is small comfort for countries where air, soil, and water rank among the world's filthiest, a health threat to millions . . . ."[141]

The environmental legacy of communism was not only depressing but extremely dangerous. In the concluding chapter of *Surge to Freedom,* I described the issue not so much as relating to the quality of life as to life itself.[142] As a whole, the region worst affected was the broad curve embracing practically the whole of the German Democratic Republic, northwestern Bohemia, southern Poland, and eastern Slovakia. The major culprits were brown coal and official inefficiency and neglect, which left cities like Prague, Cracow, and Budapest with world records in air pollution and made some smaller towns virtually uninhabitable by even the most basic standards of health and hygiene. Czechoslovakia was officially condemned as "one of the most polluted countries in the world,"[143] with 70 percent of its rivers seriously affected and 70 percent of its forest trees damaged. As one expert put it: "The state acted as economic planner, employer, and environmental authority—all three together. And in the event of conflict it was mostly the environmental aspect that was sacrificed to economic production."[144]

After 1989 all of the East European countries were faced with the problems of going over to a market economy, restructuring their industries, and cleaning up the environment. Generally, the environment stood to improve in the pursuit of these goals. The huge heavy industrial concerns would be phased out; energy, under free market conditions, would become much more expensive and hence would be more economically used. (The use of energy under communist rule had been profligate in the extreme.) Some experts also were concluding that much of the existing pollution, although presenting a serious problem, was "superficial" in the sense that, with the right resources, leadership, and effort it could be appreciably reduced fairly quickly.[145]

On paper this may have been true, but it sounded too optimistic. Over the long term, if and when levels of prosperity were to be reached in the East European countries that approached Western levels, then the number of automobiles, for example, would markedly increase and hence cause more environmental problems. In the short run, any improvements in the environment were bound to be associated with serious drops in heavy-industrial output and the resulting unemployment. Those affected, therefore, could hardly be enthusiasts for environment protection. Since popular awareness and support were essential for eventually overcoming environmental damage, this missing support could be a serious handicap.

Generally, East European popular attitudes have not been conducive to an early solution. Ecology, of course, had been one of the early planks in the platform of many dissidents in their struggle against communist rule—especially in Bulgaria, Czechoslovakia, and Hungary. Once newly elected governments came to power after 1989, they passed wide-ranging legislation protecting the environment. Czechoslovak, Polish, and Hungarian laws were modeled on European Community guidelines, although target fulfillment dates were roughly set at the end of this century or the beginning of the next. But, as has often been the case in the West, although most people were as much in favor of clean air as they were in favor of love, kindness, and other virtues, it tended to take a backseat when jobs were at stake and costs of cleaning up the environment became evident. Thus, environmental questions so easily become politicized and hence neglected. Paradoxically, the environment to many citizens is something that, no matter how urgent, always can be postponed. Nothing much changes from day to day, and, since 1989, so many problems seem to have arisen that simply cannot wait. And if, say, five thousand workers in a particular town could be thrown out of work overnight, it is a courageous citizen indeed who will point to the ecological benefits of their factory's closure.[146] Ecological consciousness only improves when *per capita* income rises.

The costs of ecological retrieval must seem staggering to even the most enthusiastic environmentalists. The World Bank, for example, reportedly estimated that more than $50 billion would need to be invested to bring the Czechoslovak environment up to "acceptable" standards. Poland's own estimate is that $260 billion will be needed over the next ten to twenty-five years to bring its environmental standards to the European Community level of 1992.[147] Even allowing for the Polish estimate being (calculatedly) too high, these are huge sums, and East European governments and the growing private sector have so many other demands on their resources.

However, the East European governments, themselves, are one of the main sources of funds in the campaign to save the environment. Poland and Czechoslovakia also have introduced "Environment Bonds," with the Poles imaginatively suggesting that part of their foreign debts be converted into such bonds. Another important source of funds is in the form of Western official credits as, for example, from the European Community's PHARE program (*Pologne-Hongrie: Assistance à la Restructuration Economique*), from its European Bank for Reconstruction and Development, the World Bank, and directly from some Western governments. Environmental problems often affect more countries than those that cause them. Hence, Germany, for example, and at the Land level, Bavaria, have seen it in their own interests to help neighboring Czechoslovakia. Just how dangerous the situation in Bohemia can be was shown in early 1993 when Prague and several smaller towns were enveloped for days in a gray-yellow smog.[148]

Western investors are seen by many as another important agent in coping with the environment problem. Some Westerners are put off by the problems they face,[149] but, in the case of those who are not, the modernizing and technically advanced production processes they introduce are powerful weapons in themselves. But, as many environmentalists were predicting from the beginning, Western investment has not been an unmixed blessing. Attracted to Eastern Europe not only by relatively low costs but by slacker environmental regulations than obtained in the West, some investment has become as much a part of the problem as its solution. This applies particularly to those Western firms quickly going into the energy and raw materials sector and into, for example, the cement industry, during the interim period before the stricter environmental regulations come fully into effect. On the other hand, uncertainty about new environmental protection has been an impediment to Western investors, as has the insistence of some governments that when a Western firm takes over a local company, it must also be prepared to foot its environmental bill.[150]

The Nuclear Reactors

There is one huge exception to the generalization just made about environmental questions and their perceived urgency: the ever-present danger from some of Eastern Europe's nuclear reactors — the danger, in short, of another Chernobyl. This problem is not just East European; in terms of the numbers of nuclear reactors involved, it is more a problem of some of the successor states of the Soviet Union. And, of course, it could become a worldwide problem. But Soviet-*built* reactors, wherever they are located, are the problem and, as Chernobyl showed, only one is needed to cause disaster.

The Economist put the problem baldly:

> Virtually all the 58 Soviet-built civilian nuclear reactors, a seventh of the world's total, strung across four countries and three former Soviet republics, lack basic safety equipment. Their operators have technical ability, but neither the will nor the resources to maintain safety standards. Western engineers believe that at least 26 of these reactors should be closed as soon as possible. The rest need refitting, as do another 21 new reactors under construction.[151]

In Eastern Europe one of the most dangerous nuclear stations — certainly the one receiving the most attention from 1990 onward — was Kozloduy in Bulgaria. Safety standards were improved there in 1992, but not to the satisfaction of many Western experts. Some stations in Czechoslovakia, particularly some reactors at Jaslovské Bohunice, in Slovakia, also had been considered suspect, especially by officials and scientists in neighboring Austria. The Bulgarian and Czechoslovak governments gave assurances about the safety of these stations and were sensitive about the criticisms made of them.[152] The economies of both countries were very dependent on them, and spokesmen in both Prague and Sofia insisted that they could not materially reduce, still less scrap, them. But much uneasiness remained, and it was legitimate. The state of the former Soviet Union suggested that even less attention than ever would be given to protective safeguards there. Slovakia, independent from 1993 on, might be less well-equipped to "cover" Jaslovské Bohunice than Czechoslovakia was. (This, by the way, is a potential threat from Slovakia that could make Gabčikovo [see chapter 6] a secondary matter.) In the new Czech Republic the government was determined to press ahead with the new Temelín nuclear station despite Austrian protests. It argued that the only alternative to nuclear power was the notorious filthy brown coal.[153] As for Kozloduy, even with the improvements and the assurances, nervousness was persisting.

The point is that neither the Soviet successor states, nor the East European states, can themselves do what is necessary. Western help is needed on a scale that dwarfs what so far has been given. A type of Marshall Plan approach was needed—urgently. It could already be past five minutes to twelve.

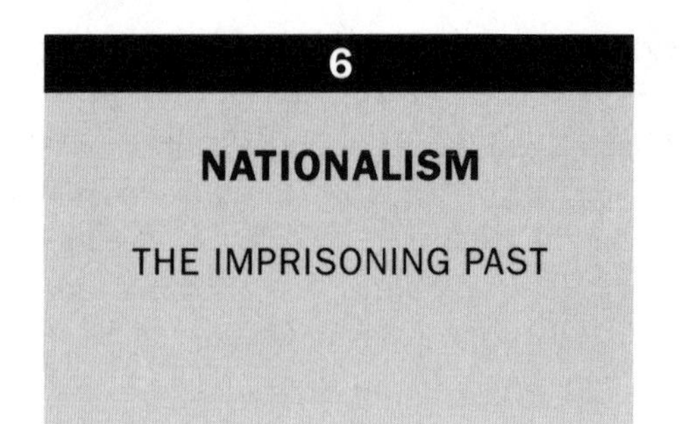

6

NATIONALISM

THE IMPRISONING PAST

The revolutions in Eastern Europe in 1989 made it clear that the whole post-World War II international order and diplomatic settlement were unraveling: the East-West division of Europe, the brittle international stability provided by the Cold War, communist rule in Eastern Europe, and Soviet domination of the region. Very soon afterward, the linchpin of the post-World War II order, the division of Germany, was removed. Germany became reunited, and the GDR disappeared.

This stage was only the first in a still more comprehensive unraveling—not just of Yalta and Potsdam, but of some of the post-World War I settlements. Two of the most important states to emerge after 1918, the Soviet Union and Yugoslavia, disintegrated. Czechoslovakia, another synthetic creation of the Paris treaties after World War I, ceased existence at the beginning of 1993. The significance, scope, and speed of these developments destroyed the underpinnings that had sustained the eastern half of the continent for much of the twentieth century. The other half, Western Europe, through its overall political order, economic prosperity, and collective institutions centered on the European Community, remained stable. But it could not remain immune to the upheavals occurring in the East. The assumptions on which its plans for further unity were originally made now had radically changed, and Western Europe became increasingly vulnerable to the dangers of the situation in the continent's other half.

As the doubts and debates over the Treaty of Maastricht showed, the West European states were not as immune to the pull of nationalism as their previous efforts toward unity may have suggested. But, except in the case of fringe groups, nationalist violence had burnt itself out in the West. In the East, after nearly a half-century of repression, it seemed to be making up for lost time. Isaiah Berlin put it with insight and vigor:

> a wounded *Volksgeist* . . . is like a bent twig, forced down so severely that, when released, it lashes back with fury. Nationalism, at least in the West, is created by wounds inflicted by stress. As for Eastern Europe and the former Soviet Empire, they seem today to be one vast open wound. After years of oppression and humiliation, there is liable to occur a violent counterreaction, an outburst of national pride, often aggressive self-assertion, by liberated nations and their leaders.[1]

This contrast with Western Europe is worth exploring. As one analyst states:

> Whereas nationalism in Western Europe accompanied social, economic, and political changes caused by the Enlightenment, in Eastern Europe nationalism preceded such changes. Just as applying new Western ideas to the different, less advanced, conditions in German-speaking lands led to the chauvinistic and aggressive German nationalism, applying Western ideas in the even more backward conditions and institutions in Eastern Europe led to the emergence of nationalism based on irrational and pre-Enlightenment concepts, founded on myths of the past and tending toward exclusiveness. Because a biased interpretation of history caused nationalists of Eastern Europe to believe that a special creative genius of their nations had been stifled by foreigners or by foreign ideas, East European nationalism became a force aimed at creating conditions suitable for this genius to reappear. The task was to be accomplished by eliminating all foreign influence and convincing the members of a given nationality of their genius by making them aware of their supposed greatness. As a consequence, xenophobia, historicism, and a forced feeling of superiority emerged as decisive forces . . . .[2]

Joseph Rothschild, in his *Ethnopolitics,* written several years before the revolutions in Eastern Europe and the collapse of the Soviet Union, argued:

> ethnic nationalism, or politicized ethnicity, remains the world's major ideological legitimator and delegitimator of states, regimes, and governments. A state's legitimacy depends heavily on the population's perception of the political system as reflecting its ethnic and cultural identity. Indeed, at the margin of choice, today most people would rather be governed poorly by their own ethnic brethren than well by aliens, occupiers, and colonizers . . . .[3]

Later in his book, Rothschild touched on the developmental factor necessary to promote nationalism and give it coherence. Arguing that "primordial" characteristics were not sufficient for the consolidation of ethnic groups, he sees as essential for the evolution of the decisive phase of nationalist development elites with a capacity and an interest (religious, economic, social, or political) in "mobilizing" those people who share these characteristics into a self-conscious group.[4] The emergence of these elites in Eastern Europe began in the nineteenth century, continued into the twentieth, and, perhaps paradoxically, was given a great boost during communist rule. The Czech national movement of the nineteenth century is a case in point.

The Czechs, of course, had had a strong national consciousness in late medieval and early modern times, but this consciousness began to be suppressed early in the seventeenth century. The best example in East-Central Europe, though, is probably that of the Slovaks. The first stirrings of Slovak national consciousness, after over nine hundred years of Hungarian domination and co-optation, also began in the nineteenth century, although the Slovak movement was, for several reasons, much weaker than the Czech. The real molding of a Slovak elite took place with the founding of Czechoslovakia, despite justified Slovak complaints about Czech domination and condescension. The catalyst, however, no matter how distasteful its auspices, was the puppet Slovak state during World War II. The ruthless communist purge of Slovak "bourgeois nationalists" after 1948 silenced for a time but could not eradicate a Slovak national communist elite that reemerged in the early 1960s and laid some of the groundwork for the Prague Spring. While the Czech reformers saw reform in 1968 as largely a matter of liberalization, their Slovak counterparts saw it principally as a national movement, aimed at securing equality with the Czechs. After the Soviet-led invasion, Slovakia, now with federal status, further developed an elite of its own and its own sense of identity. After 1989 it was largely that elite that led it to independence (see chapter 3).

Communism, which by definition was supposed to make nationalism irrelevant, did the opposite in both the Soviet Union and Yugoslavia. It led to the establishment of local elites which, despite strong centralizing pressure from the center, were often bent on strengthening their own power base. Moscow often resorted to sending proconsuls or to depending heavily on trusted, dependent locals to check the centrifugal trends. In Yugoslavia, local elites were gradually given increasing leeway, and the republic, rather than the federal level, became the one on which, for the most part, real power was considered as resting. Most Yugoslav political figures came to consider service at the federal center in Belgrade as a means of strengthening their power in Zagreb, Skopje, or elsewhere. To get some symmetrical national balance in his new Yugoslavia, Tito set about stimulating national sentiments in Macedonia, Bosnia-Hercegovina (where he eventually introduced a Muslim nationality), Montenegro (where the emphasis was on more Montenegrin and less Serb), and in Slovenia.[5] For this purpose he helped create or revive new national elites. It was somewhat different in the case of the Serbs and Croats, the two major Yugoslav nations. Both nations had had traditional elites that had been largely wiped out in, or immediately after, World War II. The communist order imposed new elites, which, however, came to adopt the mutually hostile nationalisms of their two different states. And it was the renewed clash of Serbian and Croatian nationalisms that initiated Yugoslavia's collapse.

Ernest Gellner has a definition of nationalism that is worth reproducing:

> Nationalism is primarily a political principle, which holds that the political and national unit should be congruent.
>
> Nationalism as a sentiment, or as a movement, can best be described in terms of this principle. Nationalist sentiment is the feeling of anger aroused by the violation of the principle, or the feeling of satisfaction aroused by its fulfillment. A nationalist *movement* is one activated by a sentiment of this kind.[6]

Gellner then refers to a situation that has particular historical relevance:

> But there is one particular form of the violation of the nationalist principle to which nationalist sentiment is quite particularly sensitive: if the rulers of the particular unit belong to a nation other than that of the majority of the ruled, this, for nationalists, constitutes a quite outstandingly intolerable breach of political propriety. This can occur either through the incorporation of the national territory in a larger empire, or by the local domination of an alien group.[7]

Since the demise of empires in Eastern Europe, however—the Ottoman and the Habsburg—and then the collapse of the Soviet imperial system, the most acute national problems in the successor states have concerned ethnic minorities. These minorities have been mainly of two kinds. The *first* consists of those ethnic groups that were formerly the ruling imperial groups, smaller segments of larger nations. These minorities then often become subject to a unifying or assimilative process by the majority ethnic group that is now the *Staatsvolk,* or "nation of state." Most of Eastern Europe's post-1989 minority problems—indeed, post-1918 problems—stem from such groups. These minorities are parts of nations that have come down in the world. The *second* kind comprises those ethnic groups, minorities, or nationalities that, to paraphrase Karl Deutsch, have the aspiration, but usually not the power, to become nations. They are sometimes, but not always, located in distinct parts of the states of which they are formally citizens. The former Soviet Union presents one of the most striking examples of such nationalities.

In Eastern Europe, as a whole, but especially in the Balkans where it has taken on its most virulent form, nationalism has assumed several aspects, all distinct, although some are similar, and many interactive. They can be summarized as follows:[8]

(1) *Ethnic or national minorities.* Serbs in Croatia and Bosnia—and potentially in Kosovo. Hungarians in Vojvodina as well as in Romania, Slovakia, and even Ukraine. Poles in Lithuania, Belarus, and Ukraine. Jews in Hungary. Germans in Poland. Ukrainians in Poland. Turks in Bulgaria, Greek Thrace, and Macedonia. Albanians in Macedonia. Greeks in Albania. Gypsies virtually throughout the region.

The most common official demand, or aspiration, of minorities in Eastern Europe and elsewhere, articulated by themselves and/or the mother country on their behalf, is for *autonomy.* Autonomy, though, can mean several things: (a) "cultural" and "functional" autonomy—separate schools at different levels, as well as higher educational institutions up to university level, self-managing churches, social organizations, etc.; (b) "local" autonomy: self-government for *all* local bodies of government within a state irrespective of ethnic considerations; (c) "territorial" autonomy: essentially home rule for a specific region in which one ethnic group is in a clear majority, although forming only a minority in the state as a whole. The Hungarian Autonomous Region in Romania in the 1950s would be an example.

(2) Ethnic minorities give rise to *protective nationalism,* concern of the "parent" or metropolitan nation for its nationals beyond its borders. Present Hungarian policy is the best example. Serb aggression in

Croatia and Bosnia is ostensibly based on it. Turkish concerns in Bulgaria and Greek Thrace derive from it. So do Poland's for its nationals in Lithuania, Belarus, and Ukraine, and Germany's for its nationals in Poland (and Russia's for Russians everywhere).

(3) *Territorial/Irredentist.* Serbian aggression in Croatia and Bosnia, though ostensibly to protect fellow nationals, can fall within this category. Eastern Europe has no other *actual* examples. Possible future examples could be Hungarian efforts to retrieve some of the Trianon losses; Bulgarian or Serb designs in Macedonia; Greek efforts to recover Northern Epirus in Albania; Turkish designs on parts of Bulgaria and Greece.

(4) *Defensive nationalism,* wholly or mainly. Bosnian Muslims are a clear example, fearing the carving up of their republic between Serbia and Croatia. Macedonian nationalism at present is largely defensive—against Serbia and, potentially, Bulgaria, Albania, and Greece. So is that aspect of Bulgarian nationalism based on fear of Turkey. Albanian nationalism in Kosovo is partly defensive against the oppression of a small minority Serb *Staatsvolk.* Albanian nationalism vis-à-vis Greece is mainly defensive.

(5) *Reunification of divided nations.* The two potential cases here are Albania with Kosovo and Romania with Moldova. Possible eventual Bulgarian ambitions toward Macedonia could be included. All three recognize the territorial integrity of the states in which their kith and kin (actual or claimed) live, but refuse to recognize their distinctiveness as a nation. In the case of Bulgaria with Macedonia, this refusal eventually could be a crucial distinction.

(6) *Religious nationalism,* or religion as an expression of nationalism, could play a big role in Balkan developments. In the case of the Muslims of Bosnia and Hercegovina it already is doing so. It also has affected Muslims in the Sanjak, in Macedonia, and in Bulgaria, where Turkish-Muslim nationalism is strongly affected by the proximity of Turkey. To a lesser degree, this is the case with Greek Thrace. Religious nationalism, affecting both Muslims and Christians, could become a decisive factor in the Balkans. It is in this context that Turkey could assume a major role. In East-Central Europe the tensions between Roman and Greek Catholicism, Roman Catholicism and Orthodoxy, and Greek Catholicism and Orthodoxy in Poland, Slovakia, Belarus, and Ukraine have a considerable nationalist component.

It should be noted that the *economic factor* in contemporary East

European nationalism has played little or no direct role. Obviously, it exacerbates nationalism of different kinds, and dissatisfaction over economic conditions could well be exploited or diverted by nationalism. But economics has not *caused* nationalism nor has it been an expression of nationalism in the current period. Nor would any firm economic revival cure the virus of nationalism, although revival might mitigate it. In former Yugoslavia nationalist passions have passed the point of no return. There, economics have become irrelevant.

The Points of Crisis

What follows is a checklist of actual or potential crises and of crisis points in Eastern Europe that had emerged by early 1994, *or that could emerge in the future,* from unsettled issues related to nationalism. The list is not intended to be a Doomsday roster or a jeremiad, but rather a guide to conflict situations and tension spots, a list of bills that history is now presenting for settlement, if not full payment. No attempt is made to calibrate the seriousness of the different issues or their potential for conflict because, as events since 1991 have shown, conflict can flare up in the less likely cases and places, while the apparently more likely ones remain smoldering. Better, therefore, to be on the qui vive for all of them and ready for the distinct possibility of new ones appearing. It also must be emphasized that this checklist is essentially a catalog, not a full discussion, of the crises concerned. Such a discussion would require a book in itself—and undoubtedly several are in preparation.

It was the crises affecting or potentially radiating from the former Yugoslavia that had caused or threatened the most serious violence. The origins and early development of these crises are discussed in chapter 7. In this chapter, only those actual or potential crises affecting parts of former Yugoslavia that could spill over into neighboring South-East European countries are taken up. These are Kosovo as it could affect Albania; Macedonia as it affects, or may be affected by, its neighbors; and Vojvodina. This choice may seem arbitrary. The Bosnian crisis certainly has had international ramifications and could have more. But a distinction can be made between international and purely regional, and, in any case, for reasons of continuity the course of the crisis in Bosnia-Hercegovina is best confined to the Yugoslav chapter. Similarly, the Turkish problem in Bulgaria is discussed in the

Bulgarian section of chapter 4, since it is essential to the analysis of Bulgarian politics. Some overlapping, of course, is unavoidable since all the crises interact.

Albanian-Related Crises

The victory of the Democratic Party in the Albanian parliamentary elections of March 1992 appeared temporarily to increase the pressure, both in Albania itself and in Kosovo, for union. Subsequently, though, enthusiasm and optimism on both sides of the border cooled, especially when Albanian and Serbian military power were compared, and the possibility of the Serbs using theirs was obviously increasing. Also, the more the Kosovars and the Albanians saw of each other through increased border traffic, the less they seemed to like one another. Kosovars, who had been considered the most backward of all the Yugoslavs, were appalled at the backwardness of Albanians. As for the Albanians, they found Kosovars much the same as, say, Bavarians used to find Berliners. The result was that both sides—with some pressure, too, from the Western powers—began to stress independence for Kosovo. Nothing about union was mentioned—at least for the moment.[9]

But silence about union was on the assumption that Serb repression in Kosovo did not worsen. If it did, if Serbs began a wholesale expulsion of Kosovars in the direction of Albania itself in a new bout of "ethnic cleansing," or if they began mass exterminations of the Kosovar population, then Tirana, as it has made clear, would have to intervene. As it was, evidence was growing of a creeping ethnic cleansing campaign by the Serbs in Kosovo. Some Albanians privately were even estimating that, in the course of 1991 and 1992, about 200,000 Kosovars had left Kosovo.[10] In case of a full-scale collision, Albania would demand Western help, and, unless the Western powers concerned went back totally on their declarations, it was likely to get some.

Some observers discounted the probability of the Serbs, militarily and economically stretched, opening up another front and still further antagonizing world opinion. But, especially when it came to Kosovo, the totally irrational was always possible with Serbia. Slobodan Milošević, the Serbian president, despite of, or because of, the untold damage he had already done, might hesitate. But Vojislav Šešelj, a more extreme nationalist even than Milošević and greatly strengthened after his Radical Party's successes in the Serb elections in December 1992, would not (see chapter 7). Priština, too, Kosovo's capital, had become the headquarters of the notorious Zeljko Ražnatović, "Captain Arkan," and his irregulars. "Arkan" entered the Serb parliament in late 1993. Therefore, anything could happen regardless of what Belgrade might, or might not, consider prudent.[11] In any case, violence might begin, not through any specific Serb action, but through the action of Kosovars provoked beyond endurance by continuing Serb repression. Then there would be the danger of massive Serb retaliation, including a full attempt at "ethnic cleansing."

But potential crisis existed not only on Albania's borders with Serbian-ruled Kosovo—and by extension with Montenegro, which had historic claims on parts of northern Albania, including Shkodër;[12] it also was present on its borders with both Macedonia and Greece. The large Albanian minority in Macedonia, already chafing at what it considered discrimination by the Slavic "nation of state," was becoming increasingly restive for this reason alone. But its leaders had indicated that many Macedonian Albanians felt themselves involved, not only with the future of Albania, but especially with that of their compatriots in Kosovo. Although few Macedonian Albanians were seeking early reunion with Albania, they were aware that the tide of postcommunist history was tending toward bringing Albanians more together and making them more conscious of both their disabilities and their opportunities.[13] And the map showed that the largely Albanian-populated county of Tetovo in Macedonia was right on the frontier with Kosovo. Many in Albania were aware of this fact, too, and some saw both as *Albania irredenta,* a complicating element without much relevance at present but likely to acquire more.

Albanian-Greek relations always had been testy. There has never been any love lost between the two nations, as indicated by the old Greek saying: "Don't despair, God is not an Albanian." After World War I Athens eventually became resigned to Albania's existence, but, officially or unofficially, Greece had territorial claims on "Northern Epirus" and has always been rightly concerned over the condition of the fairly large Greek minority there—probably about 100,000. The Albanians later responded by bringing up the fate of their "Cham" minority in northern Greece. Official relations between the two countries improved markedly from the beginning of the 1970s, but, after twenty years of relatively good relations, they plummeted again at the beginning of the 1990s.[14] The overthrow of the communist system in Albania had opened the frontier with Greece, thus enabling a massive exodus of Greek Albanians. In the ensuing anarchy and economic destitution, however, many thousands of non-Greek Albanians slipped over the Greek border, straining the Greek economy and adding to that country's growing crime problem.[15] In the summer of 1993 the Greek authorities began mass expulsions of these illegal immigrants. Also, in the overall context of insecurity and the international unraveling that affected the whole region, some Greeks, acting unofficially, wanted to bring up the Northern Epirus question again.

Some members of the Greek Orthodox Church hierarchy were militantly irredentist,[16] as were certain sections of the military. There was also a well of popular irredentism to be plumbed by the politicians. A future situation is by no means inconceivable where a type of pre-World War I bargaining might reemerge. In such a case, if Albania were invaded by Serbia or Montenegro or seemed in a totally irretrievable situation of domestic disarray, Greece actually might try to regain Northern Epirus by force. Or in the event of the new Macedonian state collapsing and, say, Tetovo and other parts of it reverting to Albania, then Greece might demand the restoration to it of Northern Epirus by way of "compensation," especially if the other parts of Macedonia went to Serbia and/or Bulgaria, with Greece getting nothing. Back to 1912 and 1913!

Macedonia: Focus of Crisis

Tito appeared to have solved at least part of the historic "Macedonian Question." By giving Macedonia republican status inside the post-World War II Yugoslav federation, he helped insulate the territory from the external pressures that always had threatened it, and by establishing (or reestablishing) the status of the Macedonians as a nation, he undoubtedly fostered a sense of national spirit among them as well as creating a governing elite with a vested interest in the republic of Macedonia. At the same time, he ensured reasonable protection for the minorities in Macedonia, most notably Albanians and Turks, in the same way that other minorities throughout the Yugoslav federation were officially protected.

This solution was further proof of Tito's statesmanship, but it did not please Macedonia's neighbors, especially at first. Serbia considered the territory rightfully its own; it had been south Serbia in interwar Yugoslavia. Bulgaria had historic claims and regarded the Macedonians as Bulgarian. Greece, in which most of historical Macedonia was now located, resented both the creation and the name of this new republic. In the Greek civil war, the new Macedonia also was one of the bases used for supporting the communist cause. As for Albania, though at first Tito's puppet state with no foreign policy, it was mindful of the large Albanian minority there and how in the Ottoman Empire those Albanians had not been separated from those who lived in what became modern Albania. After Hoxha threw off Tito's tutelage in 1948, Tirana's relations with Skopje deteriorated, but Albania never felt strong enough to challenge Tito's Macedonia.

Its neighbors simply had to get used to the new Macedonia, and the importance of its location was such that it could not be ignored. Although not recognizing the Macedonian nation as such, both Greece and Bulgaria acknowledged its existence as a Yugoslav republic. As Greek-Yugoslav relations improved after Tito's break with Stalin in 1948, so relations between Athens and Skopje improved. For many years the Bulgarian attitude evidently was dictated by the vagaries of Soviet-Yugoslav relations, but later the regular rows between Sofia and Skopje over Macedonian history indicated the freer rein that Bulgaria had begun to assume in this matter.[17] As for the Serbs, they were just biding their time. Many eventually came to accept the new situation. But as Serbian frustrations grew and then became articulated in the 1980s, Macedonia became one of the Serbs' grievances. It by no means was at the top of the list, however—Kosovo, Croatia, and Bosnia clearly took priority. With a recognized Serb minority of only just above 40,000 in Macedonia itself, only the most overweening Serb would see it as an imperative. Many others simply saw it as yet another desideratum that, in the circumstances, could wait.[18]

The new, independent Macedonia is both paradox and dilemma. For regional stability it would have been better if its creation could have been avoided—better had it been able to remain in a smaller, more equitable, Yugoslav federation. In 1990 and 1991 both its own leaders and those of Bosnia-Hercegovina were eager to stay within Yugoslavia, regardless of what Croatia and Slovenia did. But Serbian policy killed the idea of a smaller, genuinely federal Yugoslavia and made independence the only option for both republics. The sole alternative was Serbian domination. And now that an independent Macedonia has been created, maintenance of its independence is crucially important to Balkan stability.

But by early 1993 Macedonia's existence was being seriously threatened. Domestically, it was never a viable economic proposition, with its economy one of the bazaar variety; its politics were unstable, and its ethnic relations were becoming more tense mainly because of the demands for more equality by the Albanian population and the unwillingness of the Slav majority to grant it.[19] Macedonia was fortunate to have as its president Kiro Gligorov, erstwhile friend of Tito, and the most moderate, able, and statesmanlike leader in the Yugoslav successor states. But too much depended on this one man. Vassil Tupurkovski, now retired into academic life in Skopje and the United States, but formerly a member of the Yugoslav presidential presidium, is also a man of breadth and vision. But Macedonia is seriously short of leadership ability. If Gligorov were to go, it would be desperately lacking.

The greatest single threat to Macedonia's existence, however, has come from Greek nonrecognition. Taking the name Macedonia was seen as representing a usurpation of something essentially and historically Greek. Even more—and this was the "Macedonian Question" revived—taking the name Macedonia implied, the Greeks argued, that the new republic had territorial designs, if not currently then perhaps eventually, on the whole or parts of Greek Macedonia. As evidence supporting these fears, the Greeks cited the statements by—indeed, the very existence of—the revived IMRO (see chapter 7); also named were the design of the new Macedonian flag, and the motif on new Macedonian bank notes, both of which supposedly were symbolically irredentist, as well as passages in the Macedonian constitution. The Greeks also went back to Tito's designs on Greek Macedonia immediately after World War II and the real threat they then constituted to the territorial integrity of Greece.[20] What the Greeks tended to omit in this connection was that, whereas after World War II Yugoslavia seemed very strong and Greece weak, now Macedonia had a risibly minuscule military while Greece, for its size, had a very powerful one.[21]

The government in Athens had no difficulty in stirring up the entire Greek nation, both in Greece itself and in the diaspora, to an extraordinary pitch of national fervor over this question, so much so that the Greek leaders became hostage to it, and their diplomatic maneuverability became severely restricted by it. But, though Greek nonrecognition was serious enough because of the economic consequences it had for Macedonia, its real importance was in Athens's initial ability to induce its European Community partners and the United States not to recognize Macedonia either. Neither the Americans nor the West Europeans were happy about this restriction—and the Western media were overwhelmingly against it—but they were persuaded on the grounds of solidarity with an ally and to save the Mitsotakis government, which, with its slenderest of majorities in the Greek parliament, was likely to be unseated if he either wavered or lost Western support on the issue.[22]

The "Macedonian Question" in the early 1990s generally seemed to boil down to a choice between two evils for the West and the international community. The *first* choice was recognizing and then buttressing Macedonia—militarily, economically, and politically—and thereby risking not only the collapse of the Greek government and the return of a populist socialist government under Andreas Papandreou, always considered the Western, and particularly the American, "nemesis." Some observers also feared that Western support for Macedonia might lead to serious instability inside Greece, even to a revival of some degree of political involvement by the military. Any new government emerging from this process might be considerably more pro-Serb than Mitsotakis had become, and a growing Serb-Greek alliance in the Balkans of the 1990s could only perpetuate and spread the conflict.

The *second* choice was continuing to accept the Greek position and, thereby, perhaps literally forcing Macedonia out of existence. For if Macedonia continued to be *considered* nonexistent, it *would become* nonexistent. Macedonia could not survive what was, in effect, an international boycott; nor could it survive being forced to change its name. (Some Western governments, particularly the American, in spite of their ongoing *official* attitude, acted on their awareness of the danger and were strengthening their unofficial relations with Skopje. But even over the short run, this kind of surreptitious support was no substitute for official recognition.) Certainly, democratic government could not survive in Macedonia if the international boycott were continued or the change of name enforced. One or the other alternative might lead to an IMRO nationalist takeover, making the new state as aggressive and unpredictable as the Greeks were claiming it already had become. Domestically, it would rouse intense alienation among the Albanian minority, causing that group to look more and more to reunion with Albania. The approximately 100,000 Turks in Macedonia also could look to Turkey for protection. As for the government, representing only the Slavic Macedonian majority, its anger and its fears, it would probably seek protection from Bulgaria or even Serbia, or it also might appeal to distant Russia. Perhaps to all three! It was not surprising, therefore, that by the spring of 1993 Western governments changed their policy and almost began lining up to recognize Macedonia. With its large and persuasive Greek-American lobby, the United States might take more time. But now it was becoming evident that, in trying to isolate Macedonia, Greece was isolating only itself.

The situation seemed even more complicated by the phoenix-like return of Andreas Papandreou to power in Greece after his election triumph in October 1993. Papandreou's election rhetoric had been militantly chauvinistic on Macedonia, Albania, and Turkey. But in previous periods of power he had been considerably more moderate—for example, on NATO, the European Community, and relations with Washington—than many of his utterances had indicated he would be. And it was now possible that this might be the same with regard at least to Macedonia. In early 1994 Papandreou seemed to want to ease the tension with Skopje, realizing, hopefully, that Greece should behave like a European country at the end of the twentieth century and not like a Balkan country at the beginning of it.

Bulgarian official policy toward Macedonia continued to be responsible and restrained. Bulgaria recognized the new state, giving it much sympathy and some help. The main political parties in Sofia ostensibly disavowed any reversion to irredentism. But nationalism was growing again in Bulgaria. It was directed mainly at the Turkish minority, but it also could be drawn again to Macedonia.[23] As for Russia, the powerful nationalist forces there would, as they showed in their loud support for Serbia, be in their element reconstructing the Slavic alliance and pronouncing Russia's leadership of it. The whole situation could indeed lend itself to shifting international entanglements, alliances, and crises. Not just the Macedonian Question, but the Eastern Question, might be back![24]

Vojvodina

With its mixed population mainly of Serbs and Hungarians, but also of Croats, Slovaks, and Ukrainians, Vojvodina was always one of the most fascinating and controversial parts of Yugoslavia. (Before its expulsion after 1945, a large German community also lived there.) At the beginning of the 1990s this agriculturally rich region had a population of about 2 million, of whom about 57 percent were Serbs and about 19 percent Hungarian. Up to 1918, large parts of Vojvodina were in Hungary, but Baranya, Bačka, and parts of the Banat were then ceded to the new Yugoslavia.

In Tito's Yugoslavia, Vojvodina became, like Kosovo, an autonomous province of Serbia. The treatment of minorities in the province was relatively enlightened, with the large Hungarian minority enjoying rights, privileges, and a sense of security no other Hungarian minority enjoyed in Eastern Europe. The majority Serbs tended to be divided between descendants of those who had settled there in the seventeenth and eighteenth centuries, and relative newcomers who settled there after 1918 or again after 1945. The older settlers tended to be more mellow, more tolerant toward the Hungarians and others. Socially, they regarded themselves as a cut above the newcomers, who were rougher, more aggressively Serb and correspondingly less tolerant of the Hungarians. The 1974 Yugoslav constitution gave Vojvodina, as it did Kosovo, considerably increased powers of autonomy, including the right of veto at the federal level. But this relative autonomy did not affect Vojvodina in the same way as it did Kosovo. After all, Serbs were in a majority in Vojvodina, not a 10 percent minority as in Kosovo, and most of them approved of their province's newly gained powers. In particular, the ruling Serb elite in Novi Sad, the capital, seemed to revel in its post-1974 status. The rulers now could cock a snoot at Belgrade, not only in its capacity as capital of Yugoslavia, but also as capital of Serbia. The Serbian government itself was clearly less happy about the situation, but it realized that the potential problem posed by the 1974 constitution lay in Kosovo and not in Vojvodina. Still, with the accession to power of Slobodan Milošević in Belgrade, the measures he took against Kosovar autonomy (see chapter 7) also applied to Vojvodina, which quickly became virtually an integral part of Serbia.

The relationship between Serbs and Hungarians in Vojvodina had been far from idyllic, but it was tolerable. The condition and the security of the Hungarians, however, changed quickly for the worse once the Serb-Croat war began in 1991.[25] As citizens of Serbia, young Hungarians began to be conscripted to fight what they considered to be a Serb war of aggression. The traditional Hungarian sympathy for Croats was strengthened by what they considered the justice of the Croatian cause. Their resentment only increased when it appeared that they were being called to the Serbian colors in greater numbers than their proportion of the population warranted. Considerable numbers of young Hungarians began to leave Vojvodina, going mainly to Hungary.[26]

But, beginning in late 1991, this exodus was dwarfed by a massive influx of refugees into Vojvodina. At first, most of these were Serbs fleeing Croatia and parts of Bosnia-Hercegovina as hostilities began there. Some were encouraged to move into villages lived in by Croats, Slovaks, and Ukrainians, who often were brutally expelled. But the real deterioration started after April 1992 when the war in Bosnia-Hercegovina truly began. Not only did the influx of refugees into Vojvodina strikingly increase, but the Serbs began, on a small scale, the kind of "ethnic cleansing" there that had become familiar from parts of Bosnia and Croatia. In spite of denials from Belgrade, it seemed, as Hugh Poulton says, that many Serb refugees were "given a free hand to terrorize minorities, forcing them to flee and taking over their homes."[27]

Many members of the Hungarian minority also began to feel their existence threatened by Serbian plans to settle refugees in some predominantly Hungarian villages. Serbian refugees were now, therefore, becoming colonizers. The Vojvodina Hungarians also were faced with Serbian government plans to whittle away further their ethnic compactness by redrawing administrative boundaries and transferring Serbs into overwhelmingly Hungarian districts.[28] (The Romanian government, beginning in the 1960s, had done this to some predominantly Hungarian districts in Transylvania.)

It remained to be seen how far the Serbs would go in their repression of the Hungarians in Vojvodina. They already had been able to go so far in Croatia and Bosnia without being stopped that some elements in Belgrade could lose all sense of restraint.

As for Hungary, it was, already in 1993, very nervous about the situation. President Árpád Göncz, known as a moderate in Budapest politics, in October 1992 described the situation in Vojvodina as a powder keg, with the sheer survival of the Hungarian minority there being endangered.[29] Indeed, if the Hungarians in Vojvodina were being directly threatened by the spreading violence and if, as would certainly be the case, there was a massive influx of refugees into Hungary, then no Hungarian government would have a chance of survival if it did not take some action.

Romanian Crisis Points

Two nationalist crisis points affect Romania, one relating to Moldova (Moldavia), the other to Transylvania and the situation of the Hungarian minority there. From the Moldovan crisis Romania could eventually derive possible, if problematic, advantage in the form of reunification. The Transylvanian situation, on the other hand, presents problems that appear to be intractable.

Reunion with Moldova? In World War I the Western allies, in their attempts to enlist Romanian support, offered Transylvania, the Banat, and Bukovina to the Bucharest government in the event of victory. Romania, flouting its previous alliance obligations, swallowed the bait and came into the war in 1916. Its forces were badly mauled by more powerful German armies, and it was forced to make a humiliating peace. But at the end of the war, humiliation turned into jubilation when Romania acquired not only everything that had originally been offered but also secured Bessarabia, under Russian rule since 1812.

During the interwar years Romania's gains became the target of its deprived neighbors, and in the late 1930s its foreign policy was dominated by frenzied attempts to avoid or minimize territorial dismemberment. But in 1940, as part of the Molotov-Ribbentrop agreement, it had to surrender Bessarabia and Northern Bukovina to the Soviet Union. The loss was not as serious as that of northern Transylvania to Hungary during that disastrous year, but it was acute and humiliating enough. During the war, Romania temporarily recovered Bessarabia but, with the advance of the Red Army and the allied victory, Bessarabia returned to the Soviet Union.

In the Moldavian Soviet Socialist Republic, Stalin initiated a policy, continued by his successors, of trying to create a new Moldavian nation, using all historical, linguistic, cultural, anthropological, and coercive, means at his disposal. His aim was to separate, once and for all, the Romanians on the east bank of the River Pruth from those on its west bank—that is, those in Romania—to preclude forever the possibility of reunion. Whatever success he achieved was almost entirely through force, and his success, therefore, was artificial and fragile. He was much less successful than Tito was in Macedonia. But Tito was working with more promising material. Macedonian history made Tito's Yugoslavia an attractive proposition. The Soviet Union was a decidedly less attractive proposition for the Romanians in Bessarabia. Socialist Romania, of course, hardly generated enthusiasm, but at least the Romanians would have suffered with their own kith and kin.

The number of Romanians, or Romanian-speaking citizens in Moldova, varies, like population statistics in disputed areas always do, according to which side is giving the information. The most reliable observers put the number at some 3 million out of a total population of nearly 4.5 million. Some Bucharest sources claimed 5 million Romanians alone.[30]

To the beginning of 1990 the prospect that Bessarabia ever might be restored to Romania, or even that Romanians on both sides of the Pruth would be able to conduct relatively normal relations with each other, seemed so remote as to exclude consideration. The Romanian regime, under Gheorghiu-Dej and then Ceauşescu, despite all of its anti-Soviet nationalism, was usually circumspect with regard to Bessarabia. Although rejecting the notion of a separate Moldavian nation, Romania did so quietly. At the same time, it officially abjured irredentism and accepted the postwar frontiers.

But toward the end of the 1980s, developments, first in the Soviet Union and then in Romania itself, changed the whole picture. Gorbachev's introduction of perestroika and glasnost and the concomitant transformation of Soviet political life led to the revival of nationalism in Moldavia and demands for greater political and cultural autonomy. It also led in 1989 to a discussion of the Ribbentrop-Molotov pact. The impact of this pact was strongly felt in Moldavia. Open resentment about the incorporation of Bessarabia into the Soviet Union began to mount. And this resurgence of Moldavian nationalism quickly attracted attention in Romania.

There, the fall of Ceauşescu in December 1989, while not leading to the open, democratic society most of its citizens wished, did lead to an unprecedented freedom of discussion—and this discussion soon included Moldavia. There was an enormous wave of sympathy for the Romanian-dominated Popular Front, established in Moldavia in the spring of 1989, and which for several months became the dominant force in Moldavian politics. The Front not only pressed for more freedom from Moscow for the republic of Moldavia, but it organized demonstrations repudiating the Nazi-Soviet treaty that had led to Bessarabia's incorporation into the Soviet Union. Already by the end of 1990 Moldavia was demanding independence from Moscow and declaring its right to secede. In August 1991, after having changed its name to Moldova a few months earlier, it did declare independence and later, also, its right of secession from a Soviet Union that was now collapsing.[31]

As the aspirations of the Romanian majority in Moldova evolved toward independence, so the links with Romania grew stronger. Cultural ties multiplied and, with them, Romanian concern generally about Moldova, which now could be visited with little difficulty. A spirit of indivisibility began to develop on either side of the Pruth. Iaşi, the capital of Romanian Moldavia, and Chişinău (Kishinev), the capital of the Republic of Moldova, were becoming virtually twin cities, even by early 1990.[32]

But those Romanians and international observers who had been expecting a quick, or perhaps a gradual but still inexorable, move toward reunification were disappointed. In 1992 Moldovan attention was preoccupied with the Trans-Dniester question. In December 1991, only a few days before the demise of the Soviet Union, leaders of the Russian minority on the left bank of the River Dniester, still determinedly and unreformedly communist, proclaimed the Dniester Moldavian Soviet Socialist Republic, and a state of civil war ensued involving many casualties.[33] The rebels were supported by the 14th Soviet Army stationed in the region and, explicitly and implicitly, by most shades of political opinion in Moscow. Most Russians not only came to regard this territory as Russian soil but were adamantly opposed, as was the Ukrainian government in Kiev, together with most Ukrainians, to any reunion of the rest of Moldova with Romania.[34]

In the meantime, though, whatever support among the Romanian Moldovans for reunion that initially had existed was evaporating rapidly. The Moldovan Popular Front, under Mircea Druc, which stood for reunification with Romania, was becoming increasingly marginalized as a coalition of parties led by the Moldovan president, Ion Snegur, rapidly took control of political life. In his opposition to reunification, as well as his insistence on total secession from the Commonwealth of Independent States (CIS), Snegur was now undoubtedly reflecting the opinion of the majority of Moldovans.

Why the unwillingness? Why one nation, two states, when Moldovans were at last free to make it one nation, one state? Several reasons are ably summed up by Vladimir Socor in his running coverage of Moldovan affairs. First, it was obvious that the condition of Romania was hardly such as to set off a mass stampede to join it. Ethnicity counted for much, but not that much. Deeper reasons existed, however. For one thing, there was a potentially dangerous lack of economic complementarity; Moldova was almost exclusively agricultural, generally producing the same kind of crops as Romania. Becoming part of Romania inevitably would lead, therefore, to agricultural recession in Moldova. Moreover, many Moldovans were convinced that their country, given a not too discouraging international environment, could succeed on its own. Among the newly emerged independent states from the former Soviet Union, Moldova by no means was the smallest. It also had some of the best arable land in Europe, a relatively well-educated population, and a reasonably competent ruling elite, which had no wish to sink itself in a greater Romania.

Most Moldovans also knew that reunion with Romania could well lead to an invasion by the 14th Soviet Army from across the Dniester. At best, it seriously would aggravate their old problems with their own minorities: the Russians, Ukrainians, and the Gagauz, a group of Turkic Christians numbering about 3.5 percent of the population, and with Moldova's Bulgarian citizens. Also—and this came as something of a shock to many Romanians—reservations still lurked in the Moldovan folk memory, dating back to the interwar period when Bessarabia was part of Greater Romania. Corruption, inefficiency, brutality, exploitation—it was a record not forgotten. The Soviet record also was damning, but now there was a third way for Moldovans: their own, and the majority wanted to try it.[35]

As for the Romanians, opinion polls in 1992 suggested that a majority wanted reunification and were at a loss to understand the Moldovan attitude.[36] Iliescu and his Democratic National Salvation Front associates generally referred to the inevitability of reunion and castigated Russian attitudes on the question. Iliescu, himself, surely realized the international dangers of reunion. But extreme nationalist opinion, flouting Moldovan wishes, pressed for early and, if necessary, forcible reunion. The democratic opposition groupings also were for reunion, with some groups prepared to be more patient than others. But, however unrealistic the proposition might be, it made good politics for Romanians to accuse each other of a lack of patriotism about

Moldova—or any other issue.[37] Certainly, there was not much political future for anyone publicly rejecting reunion.

Up to the end of the century, Moldova on its own looked set, rather like Macedonia, to become an unwitting focus of regional problems and instability. Romania would, presumably, continue to wait, and assist what it considered the unavoidable process of reunion. Inside Romania itself, reunion could become yet more grist for the nationalist mill. Hungary, too, would be watching closely for any international border-changing precedent that reunion with Romania would involve. (A precedent, perhaps, for Transylvania or parts of it.) With nationalism gaining further impetus there, Russia might become more explicitly militant on the subject of Trans-Dniester and of Moldova as a whole. And then there was Ukraine, with a considerable minority in Moldova itself and a latent territorial dispute with Bucharest over part of Bukovina, which Romania surrendered in 1940 and now wanted back. Moldova, therefore, presented a scene of crisis in which Romania played a crucial, but by no means the only, part.

The Hungarian Minority in Transylvania. The historical dispute between Romania and Hungary over Transylvania, the bitterness and passion it has aroused, the manipulation of evidence by both sides, need no recapitulation here. It is one of Europe's most familiar and intractable disputes, the claims and arguments of each side as predictable as the dawn, and the prospects of a settlement satisfactory to both as dim as dead of night. It is a dispute that at best can only be contained, never solved.

Transylvania over the last three-quarters of a century, since it was awarded to Romania under the Treaty of Trianon in 1920, has inexorably been becoming more Romanian and less Hungarian and German, the two nations that formerly dominated it and gave it its unique and appealing character. Through emigration and atrophy, the German presence is but a shadow of what it was, while the Hungarian has been heavily diluted by repression, assimilation, and especially by large influxes of Romanians into Transylvania. Yet Transylvania remains radically different from the rest of Romania (the *Regat*).

Transylvania is Central European, not only in character but in "problem linkage." The fate of the Hungarian minority there will affect not only domestic politics in Romania itself and neighboring Hungary but could influence the fate of Hungarian minorities in the rest of Central and Eastern Europe—in Slovakia, in Vojvodina, and in Ukraine. Transylvania, therefore, could have an important bearing on the whole Hungarian future, stretching across several borders, and on the stability of parts of both East-Central and South-Eastern Europe.

Serious rioting, with some deaths, occurred in March 1990 in Tîrgu Mureş, the old capital of the former Hungarian Autonomous Region. Just how the rioting started, and who started it, were inevitably the subject of controversy between Romanians and Hungarians, and among Romanians themselves. Some opposition Romanian politicians blamed the Securitate. These charges perhaps were plausible, but they reflected a shortsighted tendency on the part of some politicians, especially in the *Regat,* to avoid facing up to the depth of Transylvania's ethnic problem. Probably the profoundest explanation was given—however unwittingly—by the commission of inquiry into the rioting set up by the Romanian government. The commission concluded: "The large gap between the previous stifling of people's aspirations and the suddenly won freedom, as well as certain shortcomings in democratic culture and in adequate civic behavior of all socio-professional categories (another aftermath of the totalitarian communist inheritance) are causes of the chain of extremist manifestations in the last few months."[38] It was as fitting an analysis for many of Eastern Europe's other flashpoints as it was for Transylvania.

The Tîrgu Mureş incidents also were partly a reaction to the illusion that the fall of a tyrant like Ceauşescu would replace tension with racial harmony. The truth was that more ethnic harmony prevailed in Romania in the last years of Ceauşescu than ever was likely to be seen again. It was, though, a "negative" harmony, predicated on a common hatred of the man and his brand of communism. It had its culmination in the "spirit of Timişoara" uniting Romanians, Hungarians, and other national groups in the opening of the December 1989 uprising. But once Ceauşescu had gone, the harmony evaporated in the freedom and chaos of the new era. In the first half of the 1990s, the historic tensions returned in all their ugliness.

The new National Salvation Front (NSF) government in Romania had apparently begun with relatively liberal intentions toward the Hungarian minority (see chapter 4). But the government soon found it was far ahead of its constituency. And in this context its constituency was not only the numerous former Ceauşescu loyalists who switched their allegiance to the Front, but the mass of the Romanian people. What the Front leaders balked at—but what they had first seemed to promise — were special rights to Hungarians *by virtue of their recognized minority status.* They soon were insisting on the classic nationalist unitary concept that exclusively debarred special minority treatment.

In the excitement of their liberation from Ceauşescu the Hungarians in Romania had indeed been expecting, however vaguely, many more rights than Bucharest was prepared to give. It was this clash of Romanian determination and Hungarian frustration that basically produced the violence of March 1990. In Transylvania there was the same feeling as in other parts of Eastern Europe: that the end of an era, even of a whole century of history, had arrived. Therefore, if Yalta was passé, why not even Trianon? For Hungarians, it might be now or never for this historical injustice to be rectified, especially with the Soviet Union having disintegrated in the East. Such yearnings may never have been publicly articulated — the more responsible spokesmen for the Hungarian minority energetically rejected them — but, both consciously and subconsciously, they were part of the public mood and affected people's emotions and reactions. (March 15, the day that the Tîrgu Mureş incidents occurred in 1990, was a Hungarian national holiday marking the revolution of 1848.)

Revisionist notions about Trianon usually were not articulated by responsible politicians in Hungary either. All were publicly resigned to its irreversibility. But, unquestionably, preoccupations about Transylvania became much more evident in Hungary than they had been since before World War II. The former irredentism now was sublimated in an aggressive concern. Invoking both the spirit and the letter of the Conference on Security and Cooperation in Europe (CSCE), all political groups in Hungary were demanding de jure recognition for the minority in Romania. All considered a Hungarian concern for the minority to be appropriate and legitimate. But this concern often was expressed ambiguously, conveying the idea, perhaps deliberately, that more was intended. Premier József Antall, for example, described himself as the "spiritual prime minister" of all Hungarians,[39] and some of his colleagues made statements similar in spirit, but occasionally even more tactless. (Antall's statement worried the Slovaks, too.) In this context it is worth comparing the official Hungarian stand on Transylvania with that of Bulgaria on Macedonia. Both formally accepted the loss of the provinces, renounced irredentism, and denied territorial claims. But each in different ways maintained its involvement: Bulgaria denied the existence of a Macedonian nation; Hungary indirectly hinted at a *droit de regard* in Transylvania (rather in the same way as the Republic of Ireland does in Ulster.)

Moreover, despite Hungary's recognition of the 1947 Paris peace treaty provisions, which confirmed Trianon, and its adherence to the CSCE tenets about the recognition of existing borders and their not being changed except through mutual agreement, Budapest still was unwilling to sign a bilateral state friendship treaty with Romania specifically recognizing the existing borders. Such a treaty would be similar to the one signed between Germany and Poland in 1991, for example, in which Bonn finally recognized the Oder-Neisse frontier. The German government had tried to obtain assurances about the German minority in Poland before agreeing to the recognition, but eventually these demands were dropped. Hungary also pointed to the necessity to improve the condition of the Hungarian minority in Romania as its reason for delaying the treaty, but Hungary was not specific about what it wanted. It also was insisting that the minority itself participate in negotiations on the subject.[40]

Official attitudes like these, and unofficial demands regularly made by Hungarian public figures or appearing in the nationalist Hungarian press, fed Romanian paranoia about Transylvania, a paranoia many politicians across the spectrum were only too ready to exploit. But there was more to it: there was the historic Romanian dislike, fear of, and inferiority complex toward Hungarians stemming from the centuries of oppression in Transylvania. For their part, many Hungarians despised Romanians almost as much as Serbs despised Albanians, and the Hungarians seldom were diffident about showing it. Even the most moderate expressions of concern about Transylvania in Budapest, therefore, or of hope by members of the Hungarian minority in Romania, were greeted with serious suspicion by most Romanians. It was this suspicion that sparked so much of the virulent anti-Hungarian nationalism that reappeared in 1990. The *Vatra Românească* (Romanian Cradle) movement thrived on the atmosphere of ethnic suspicion. *Vatra* had the capacity to poison relations between the nations as well as many other aspects of Romanian public life.[41]

An extreme illustration of Romanian aversion to Hungarians was provided by Radu Ceontea, a member of the Romanian senate and a former chairman of *Vatra.* In a magazine interview in early 1991 he was asked what he thought about Hungarians. His reply:

> I come from a pure Romanian village in the Mureş Valley. My village suffered in every possible way under the Hungarians. My father was the village butcher, and my mother had four years of schooling. The only book I knew before my school textbooks was the Bible. Even as a small child, I was told by my father not to trust Hungarians. He told me that "every single Hungarian carries a rope in his pocket." The cord with which they would strangle Romanians. All my life I have never trusted Hungarians, but I have maintained correct relations with them. I even learned their language to a certain extent. It is a horribly complicated language. In 1968, following the invasion of Czechoslovakia, I was afraid that the Hungarians would occupy Transylvania, so I fled to the Regat. Having seen that nothing happened, I went back to my native country in 1977.[42]

Ceontea then said he lived in constant fear in his hometown of Tîrgu Mureş, where his apartment was guarded by two policemen "because I would not like my wife and daughter to be raped and murdered." He was, to repeat, an extreme case, but he was chairman of *Vatra* when he spoke, and many Romanians in Transylvania would empathize with him.

The question of how far the anti-Hungarian mood was condoned by the new Romanian government was difficult to answer. The democratic opposition charged Iliescu and company with stimulating it. But this opposition had its own share of chauvinists, and, in any case, it knew that fairness toward Hungarians, however useful it might be with a foreign audience, was not a great vote-catcher at home. The government's attitude toward *Vatra* was ambiguous at times; it seemed unwilling to risk offending it too much. At the local level, there appears to have been much collusion between the National Salvation Front and *Vatra.* The proliferation of chauvinist magazines like *România mare* and *Europa* also must have needed some official support. Amid a widespread shortage of newsprint, the fascist, chauvinistic press seemed to be doing suspiciously well.

Just how divisive Transylvania was in Romanian-Hungarian relations was illustrated by the ceremony at Alba Iulia on December 1, 1990, commemorating the meeting there on the same date in 1918 when, by popular acclaim, the province of Transylvania was declared part of Romania. The new government in Bucharest declared this anniversary to be the new Romanian national holiday, replacing August 23, the anniversary of the Soviet Union's "liberation" of Romania in 1944. This switch was supported by all sections of Romanian public opinion. To Hungary, however, it was an affront, and to many members of the Hungarian minority a humiliation. And the first Alba Iulia celebration was marred by Romanians in the crowd, egged on by none other than premier Petre Roman, himself, who booed representatives of the Hungarian minority participating in the celebration. Some of the disturbance obviously was organized. Part of it may have been spontaneous, nationalistic hooliganism. Whatever, it made a tense situation even worse.[43]

A deceptive quiet prevailed in Transylvania during 1991. So much so that, with the violence in parts of the Soviet Union and the mounting crisis in Yugoslavia, some Western observers were tempted to conclude, not that a modus vivendi had been reached, but that both parties, resigned to an impasse, were at least ready to make it a peaceful one. But developments in 1992 only showed how complacent such reactions had been. Not that any new outbreaks of serious violence occurred, but many people clearly sensed how close such violence and, hence, an international crisis might be. The reason had to be sought, not in any change in the Hungarian position, but in the growing nationalist influence in Romanian politics. It was not a surprising development. The very bumpy progress away from the long misrule of Ceauşescu toward economic promise and political democracy, as well as the continuing ostracism of Romania by most of the international community, all provided fertile ground for the aggressive nationalism that, even when not determining policy, never had been far below the surface of Romania's politics throughout its history.

A new figure now appeared on the political scene to galvanize this aggressive nationalism. Gheorghe Funar in February 1992 was elected mayor of Cluj. (See also chapters 2 and 4.) It was no surprise that this personification of prejudice came to power in Cluj (Kolozsvár, Klausenburg), Transylvania's chief city, where, formerly, Romanians had been relatively few and submissive but now were an assertive majority. And, for many of them, all that was needed to make their assertiveness vindictive was a man like Funar. As mentioned in chapter 4, Funar became head of the Party of Romanian National Unity (PRNU), a party of Romanian national paranoia. Its success, not only in Cluj but in other towns, even outside Transylvania, cast a cloud over the striking successes that the opposition democratic parties gained in the February 1992 local elections at the expense of the ruling National Salvation Front. What happened most notably in Cluj was that many previous NSF voters turned, not to the Democratic Convention, the alliance of democratic opposition parties, but to the PRNU.[44]

Funar, a dynamic man in his early forties, became known by some as the Romanian counterpart to Serbia's Slobodan Milošević. He was apparently on record as making several racist remarks about Hungarians, revealing his own mentality and helping to stir up ominous signs of intercommunal hatred. In an interview with the Associated Press, for example, he called Hungarians a "barbarian migratory people who still have barbarian genes."[45] His bite, too, could be equally bad. Not content with refusing even the more reasonable demands of the Hungarian citizens of Cluj, he was bent on reversing practices that had come to be accepted as customary by the vast majority of Cluj's population—Romanians included. Hungarian-language street signs were banned, as were Hungarian posters. Conferences in Cluj scheduled by Hungarians were forbidden. The statue of Mathias Corvinus, the medieval Hungarian king, had a Romanian-language inscription imposed on it saying that he was Romanian.[46]

Most of Funar's provocations were the result of demagogy and the fertile field in which it was being practiced. But they were facilitated by the vagueness of the new Romanian constitution of December 1991 as well as by certain laws pertaining to minorities. For example, a law on public administration stated that, in localities where a minority makes up a "significant" part of the population, official transactions affecting members of that minority should be conducted in their own language. In 1992 there were about 80,000 Hungarian nationals of Cluj, or about 22 percent of the population. Funar, however, rejected the notion that this constituted a "significant" part of Cluj's population, insisting that more than 50 percent would be significant.[47]

Funar got a worrying 10.87 percent of the national vote in the 1992 presidential elections. In the parliamentary elections at the same time, his Party of Romanian National Unity increased its representation fourfold with 7.71 percent of the vote for the Chamber of Deputies and 8.12 percent for the Senate. Such support still would seem to be containable, but, as mentioned in chapter 4, xenophobia was also an important plank in some of the other smaller parties on the far right and on the far left, and nationalism, in varying degrees of intensity, ran right across the Romanian political spectrum. This ultranationalism on the far left is a phenomenon ably analyzed by Michael Shafir.[48] It was nostalgic for Ceauşescu and his "Romania first" ethos. Funar, too, was on record as describing Ceauşescu as a "good Romanian."[49]

A situation might develop where he could unite all strands of Romanian nationalism into a powerful unit—the most serious threat of all to the Romanian struggle for democracy.

This prospect is apocalyptic, a worst case scenario, but not inconceivable. A violent disturbance, spontaneous or orchestrated, could lead to a chain of bloody incidents. Ethnic strife on a large scale could ensue, and some of the nightmare of Bosnia might be repeated. Hungary obviously could not stand aside, and conflict with Romania could result.

The problem might be insoluble, but perhaps it was not wholly uncontainable. It is necessary to slow down and then reverse the spiral of distrust and then begin with the sort of confidence-building measures that the Helsinki process once had been preoccupied with. Such measures would need to be drastic but not inescapably utopian. First, Hungary must swallow the bitter pill and formally, in bilateral treaty, renounce all territorial claims on Romania. Romania must swallow its own bitter pill by renouncing the concept of the unitary state and granting the Hungarian minority collective rights, as a minority. The European Community, or the United Nations, should guarantee the maintenance of these rights. It would be a gamble, of course, much more on the Hungarian side than the Romanian, and would need leadership and courage in Budapest. It also might create awkward precedents. But if each side kept its word and the West took an active role, the distrust could erode, and the Funars and Csurkas gradually would lose their demagogic opportunities. Finally, Romania, the whole of it, should receive greatly increased quantities of Western economic aid, both as a reward and an insurance. Unlike the actual conflicts in the former Yugoslavia and the former Soviet Union, the potential conflict in Transylvania was not yet beyond economics. It could, indeed, be ripe for them.

Hungarian-Slovak Relations

On January 1, 1993, Slovakia became a truly independent sovereign state for the first time. Until the creation of Czechoslovakia after World War I, it had been an integral part of Hungary—Upper Hungary—for a thousand years. For much of this time, Slovaks had accepted Hungarian domination as something in the natural and inevitable course of things. Only during the nineteenth century did national stirring begin. And, for the Slovak cultural elite that started to acquire national consciousness, the enemy was Hungary and its Hungarian masters. In *Eastern Europe and Communist Rule,* I wrote the following about Slovak resentment against Hungarians:

> Hungarians in Slovakia were generally contemptuous of Slovaks, and the official pre-1914 Budapest policy of assimilation through "Magyarization," though it brought considerable benefits to those prepared to submit to it, aroused a humiliated resentment among the steadily growing Slovak intelligentsia, which had to accept "Magyarization" or vegetate—or emigrate. Thus "anti-Hungarianism" became one of the mainsprings of Slovak nationalism. This was true of the clerical fascists of the Father Tiso variety, of democratic nationalists, as well as of communists like Clementis and Husák. Vladimír Mináč, an elderly Slovak writer, put it poignantly and emotionally in 1964: "Should one touch healed wounds? Are the wounds really healed? National antagonism is a tough flower; if we do not talk about it, that does not signify it does not exist. Our relationship to the Hungarians not only molded our national fate but also formed our way of thinking; it formed the soul of our nation."[50]

In some respects, especially psychologically, the Hungarian-Slovak relationship was similar to that between the English and the Irish. Insensitivity was met by a growing resentment.

After 1918 the relationship between the nations shifted decisively. Slovakia was part of the huge losses that Hungary incurred at Trianon, losses that made a once dominant state into an irredentist state. For most Hungarians, Slovakia's loss was not that of a possession but rather of part of their own country, part of themselves. And they left behind in Slovakia several hundred thousand of their own countrymen, who became a discontented and an "arrogant" minority.[51] Not only that: much of the Hungarian minority was concentrated in south Slovakia, adjacent to the post-Trianon border, and many localities that by any criterion of self-determination should have remained in Hungary were given to the new Czechoslovak state for reasons of "strategic security."

Hungary's inglorious role as an irredentist state during the interwar period, steadily and irretrievably falling into the hands of the Axis powers, need not be described here. It recovered a part of Slovakia right on the eve of World War II and lost it again at war's end. During the communist period Czechoslovakia and Hungary were Soviet minions and "friends" by ideological definition. Hungarian resentment certainly did not disappear but was muted for many years. Class solidarity ostensibly replaced national antagonisms. But during the 1980s, with Slovakia having enjoyed a degree of federal status within Czechoslovakia since 1968 and the besetting myth of socialist "brotherhood" noticeably slackening, signs of Slovak national assertiveness began to proliferate. Almost inevitably, one of its targets was the Hungarian minority, now numbering about 600,000.

More specifically, it was the Hungarian minority's educational facilities, *in their own language,* that became the target of encroachment. These facilities were a matter of life and death for the Hungarian community because they ensured the survival, not only of Hungarian culture, but of a distinct Hungarian identity. Hence, the Hungarian minority's concern was easily mobilized, and the strength and clamor of its opposition to proposed changes in a Slovak education law in 1985 prevented measures being enacted that could have begun the gradual abolition of Hungarian higher educational facilities.

After 1989 many of the safeguards that had existed for minorities throughout Eastern Europe (and, soon, in the former Soviet Union) no longer existed. And in Slovakia the Hungarian minority had particular reason to feel exposed. Czechoslovakia began to fall apart as soon as the velvet revolution of November 1989 was over (see chapter 3). But, however much exhilaration the Slovaks themselves derived from their increasing sense of fulfillment, the minorities in Slovakia had reason to worry. Any loosening of Czechoslovak control from the Prague center always had tended to mean less security for them—Jews, Ruthenes, as well as Hungarians. Now, of course, almost all of the Jews were gone and most of the Ruthenes were in Ukraine. The Hungarians remained—and the Gypsies (see below pp. 224–228).

It was not long until the anti-Hungarian edge of Slovak nationalism began to be apparent. The new Slovak constitution, for example, referred to the "Slovak nation" and not to the citizens of Slovakia. (Minorities, after all, constituted about 17 percent of the population.) Then there were the pinpricks—for example, the prohibition of street signs in the Hungarian language—most notably by local authorities, without central permission but clearly with central connivance. In 1990 Slovak nationalist groups made a concerted effort to discontinue totally the use of the Hungarian language in public transactions in which members of the Hungarian minority were participating. In October of that year the use of Hungarian in such cases was restricted to localities where 20 percent of the residents were Hungarian; otherwise, regardless of who the participants were, the language had to be Slovak.[52] These changes were a model of liberalism compared with what Gheorghe Funar was prepared to tolerate in Cluj, but they were restrictive. And many Slovak nationalists were determined to restrict further.

Since independence in 1993 the omens have not been good for the Hungarian minority. With the wraps of more than forty years well and truly off, and with separation from the Czechs consummated, the tone of much Slovak official utterance was now anti-Hungarian, and none was more blatant in this regard than Premier Vladimír Mečiár, himself. International relations, as well as domestic politics, were for Mečiár simply a broader extension of the boxing ring into which, as a younger man, he often had climbed. He needed somebody to hit, apparently because—and this went for many Slovak nationalists—he expected somebody to hit him. For three years after inception of the velvet revolution, he was after the Czechs; now the Hungarians were the punching bags. Among Mečiár's first words after Slovakia achieved independence was that he "distrusted" Hungary.[53] And, of course, apart from anything else, Hungarians served as a good diversion from the enormous domestic problems that independent Slovakia faced.

Seen through the Slovak prism, some aspects of Hungarian behavior did seem provocative. Statements, attributed to senior Hungarian officials (and then denied, or explained), that Hungary surrendered Slovakia at Trianon to *Czechoslovakia* alone, made at a time when Czechoslovakia was obviously in the process of disintegration, carried implications that were grist to the mill of Slovak nationalists and made even moderate Slovaks nervous. So did the frequently made Hungarian proviso that they accepted Europe's existing frontiers, "irrespective of whether or not they are just." The behavior of some Hungarians living just inside the Slovak side of the border also was deemed provocative by many Slovaks. But the great majority of Hungarians in Slovakia behaved responsibly during the Slovak transition to independence, and apparently no massive urge gained strength to be reincorporated into Hungary.[54] It was the irresponsible few who made the headlines and who tended to make the assertive, though far from confident, Slovak nation nervous and the life of its demagogues that much easier.

As if there were not enough trouble—past, present, and potential—between Hungary and its new neighbor, Gabčikovo arose to add some more. In the last quarter of 1992 no East European topic, except the Yugoslav disaster, got more Western press coverage than the Gabčikovo hydroelectric power dam on the Danube running between Slovakia and Hungary. Briefly, it began as a monument to Hungarian-Czechoslovak "fraternal" cooperation in the late 1970s and ended as an unseemly dispute between two independent states in the early 1990s. Hungary, which under the agreement had been obligated to build a dam a few miles downstream on its own territory at Nagymaros, stopped construction on its dam in 1989 under growing public pressure. The Hungarian argument was that this new example of socialist monumentalism would be an ecological catastrophe. The Czechoslovak government, however, continued building Gabčikovo, denying that the ecological damage would be so serious.[55] But what was becoming evident in the course of 1992, as the work neared completion and Slovakia was moving toward independence, was that, for many Slovaks, Gabčikovo was assuming a symbolic importance intertwined with their identity and their independence. Gabčikovo, therefore, became a national issue. What the National Theater had been for the Czechs (vis-à-vis the Germans) in the second half of the nineteenth century, Gabčikovo was becoming for some Slovaks (vis-à-vis the Hungarians) in the last decade of the twentieth. The Hungarians' insensitivity made them largely unaware of this aspiration or indifferent to it, and Budapest seems to have expected that its intensive diplomatic activity against Gabčikovo, together with general Western reservations about the scheme, would make the Slovaks back down.

But the greater the pressure, the more determined the Slovaks were to proceed. In October 1992 Slovak engineers blocked the flow of the Danube and diverted its waters two kilometers northward into artificial canals for a distance of twenty-five kilometers on the border between Slovakia and Hungary. What was left of the mighty Danube on this stretch was nothing but a miserable little creek. Technically, the Slovak action had slightly altered the border between the two countries, which was midstream in the Danube, and the Hungarians strove to make a "breach of international law" out of this act, which, strictly speaking, it was.[56] The whole issue, a complicated one in which each side's case had some merit, went to the International Court of Justice in The Hague to assess. But Slovak nationalism gave

Gabčikovo a dimension that would probably defy legal adjudication. It had made it a matter of pride.

Poland and Its Eastern Neighbors

National disputes in Eastern Europe since 1989 have generally followed familiar meteorological rules: the more northerly they are, the cooler they are. In parts of the Balkans they boiled over into violence; in other parts they have seemed perilously close to doing so. Moving north, the crisis points have posed less of a violent threat, although Transylvania was becoming a dangerous flash point. The dangers at which Poland was the center, although serious, were still in that no-man's-land between potential and actual crisis, with violence not a factor to be expected, but not entirely to be ruled out.

The potential crisis (optimists might still see it only as a potential problem) centered on Polish minorities in neighboring countries. The following table gives the official numbers of Poles in lands east of Poland:[57]

Lithuania	257,994
Belarus	417,720
Ukraine	219,179
Russia	94,994 (60,000 in European part)
Latvia	60,416
Kazakhstan	59,957

Many unofficial but reliable sources consider these figures much too low. But, taken as they are, they add up to 1.1 million. Those for *Lithuania* already have added to crisis.

Such were the misgivings, real or imagined, of the Polish minority in Lithuania that many of them preferred the old Soviet Union, where the real authority had been distant, to the new Lithuania, where authority was now but a stone's throw away. The misgivings are embedded in the long history of the association of the Polish and Lithuanian nations between the end of the fourteenth and the eighteenth century, an association about which most Lithuanians were much less enthusiastic than all Poles. More recently, in the twentieth century, Poland's seizure of Vilnius (Wilno) in 1920, after it had been awarded to newly independent Lithuania, was a bitter and lasting humiliation.

The Polish minority, about 7 percent of the whole population, is concentrated in two districts—one around Vilnius, where Poles make up 65 percent of the population, and the other in Šalčininkai (Soleczniki), bordering Belarus, which has an 80 percent Polish population and is one of the most impoverished parts of the country. Supported since 1989 by nationalist elements of varying shrillness in Poland itself, Šalčininkai has demanded increased autonomy, but the situation generally had been quiet until the attempted putsch in Moscow in August 1991. The putsch was supported by some leaders of the predominantly Polish administrative districts—communist, ethnic Poles. This action brought the wrath of the Lithuanians against the Poles in general, most of whom always had been suspected of being less anti-Russian than anti-Lithuanian. The central government in Vilnius disbanded the Polish district councils in Vilnius and Šalčininkai and replaced them with Lithuanian "proconsuls."[58] The Polish minority protested against these measures, saying they implied the collective guilt of the entire Polish community. But the government stuck to its point, and the proconsuls remained. The result was that practically all Polish Lithuanians opted out of public life altogether, refusing to vote in local elections in November 1992 that could have reinstalled their own ethnic administrators. The impasse, therefore, remained.

By overall East European standards the Polish minority in Lithuania was far from downtrodden. There were, for example, 125 Polish schools in 1992, full and clear access to Warsaw television, and a selection of Polish newspapers financed by the state.[59] But the situation was vitiated by mutual distrust. The worst construction was put on the intentions of the other side. And just as Romanians and Slovaks never had lost their inferiority complex vis-à-vis Hungarians, neither had Lithuanians vis-à-vis Poles. And the Lithuanians' attitude scarcely could be softened by some of the chauvinist outbursts heard on occasion in Warsaw. "There can be no doubt," pontificated one Polish academic, "that, from the cultural, ethnic, and legal point of view, Wilno [Vilnius] is Polish." Most Poles thought so, too, but usually kept it for private conversation. But, however sotto voce, this viewpoint hardly was likely to reassure Lithuanians. Nor were the constant nostalgic references to Wilno as one of the centers of Polish civilization, the birthplace of some of Poland's greatest figures, and a reminder of the "good old days."[60] (Similar Polish references to Lwów (Lviv) infuriated Ukrainians in the same way.) Unofficial Polish demands for autonomy for the Polish districts frightened Lithuanians. As one of them tellingly put it, when referring to possible autonomy for the Polish district around Vilnius: "How would the Poles like a German autonomous district around Warsaw?"[61]

But it was not just a case of Lithuanians nervously responding to Polish demands, or to Polish tactlessness. The Polish minority had genuine fears about Lithuanian national exuberance, their dislike of Poles collectively (though often not at the individual level), and a general "it's our turn now" attitude common to all formerly repressed nations. The Poles feared "Lithuanianization" through a gradual erosion of the privileges they already had, especially in education. In early 1993 what Poles immediately feared were administrative-territorial inroads into the districts of Vilnius and Šalčininkai. These inroads would be made through the familiar tactic of the Lithuanians altering the boundaries and bringing in more of their countrymen.[62]

If these inroads were to occur, a potential crisis would turn into an actual one. Lithuania was the only one of Poland's former Soviet neighbors (Russia, Belarus, and Ukraine are the others) with which Warsaw had not signed a state treaty of friendship. It was not hard to see why — although mutual fear of reviving Russian nationalism (see chapter 8) could make their differences look small indeed.

The Polish Minority In Belarus

In June 1992 the first Belarus embassy ever was opened in Warsaw. In the Polish capital to mark the event, the head of the Belarus parliament, Stanislau Shushkevich, said that all problems between the two countries could be settled within the short term. His optimism, however, was not shared by the Minsk Metropolitan, Filaret, who accompanied Shushkevich. Filaret criticized the Polish Roman Catho-olic Church for interfering in the internal affairs of Belarus and for what amounted to "religious imperialism" generally. He specifically criticized the Polish Church's appointment of Catholic bishops in Belarus, without the permission of either the government in Minsk or the Orthodox Church, which was the national Church of Belarus.[63]

Many Belarusans would agree with Filaret. They saw the 400,000-strong Polish minority, galvanized by Poland's Roman Catholic

Church, as a foreign wedge, undermining Belarusan sovereignty. The more fearful of them saw a Polish fifth column awaiting the day of irredentist fulfillment. Such fears were idle, but there was no doubt about the Polish Church's determination to regard the Poles in Belarus as parts of its own flock, both spiritually and organizationally. And this effect obviously had nationalist implications, which could undermine Belarusan sovereignty. Further, in any dispute that arose, the Belarus minority in Poland, over 200,000 in number and concentrated in Poland's northeast county of Białystok, bordering Belarus, certainly would become involved.[64] In short, no grounds existed for complacency. A bit more Polish tact and a bit more Belarusan maturity might head the problem off. And, in the shadow of Russia, it was in Poland's interest to have Belarus survive.

Poland and Ukraine: Enemies Become Allies?

Polish and Ukrainian enmity dates back at least to the middle of the seventeenth century. It has simmered for more than three centuries, punctuated by outbursts of violence giving new impulses to the enmity. The most recent of these outbursts occurred during and especially after World War II. In 1942–43 massive slaughters of Poles by Ukrainian troops and irregulars took place in Volhynia in what was clearly an "ethnic cleansing" operation. After the war, in 1947, in the so-called Operation Wisła, Polish security forces brutally expelled more than 150,000 Ukrainians from their homelands in southeastern Poland, mainly forcing them into Poland's newly acquired western territories. The move ostensibly was aimed at breaking the back of the Ukrainian Insurrectionary Army, which still was fighting a guerrilla war against Polish and Soviet forces. But it also was designed to ease Poland's "Ukrainian problem." This time, therefore, it was Poles who were doing the "ethnic cleansing," and obviously the memories of both of these terrible episodes still rankle in both nations today.[65]

There were about 5 million Ukrainians before World War II in Poland, which then possessed large territories in what are now independent Ukraine and independent Belarus. (Many of the Polish residents of these territories were resettled after World War II in Poland's new western territories taken from Germany.) Today, there probably are no more than 300,000 Ukrainians in Poland, dispersed and without much political influence. Still, since 1989 the Ukrainians have made demands that have been only partly met by Polish authorities, including a formal condemnation of "Operation Wisła" (made by the Polish senate but not the Polish Sejm) and compensation for property lost after World War II. Organized religion is also an obstacle to better relations, as is true in the case of Polish-Belarus relations. As it is in western Ukraine, the Uniate (Greek Catholic) Church is strong among Ukrainians in Poland, and one of their demands is that its status in Poland be regularized, as should that of the Polish Autocephalous Orthodox Church. The restitution to the Uniates of more than 250 of their churches in Poland that had been confiscated in 1947 and taken over by the Roman Catholic Church was part of the reconciliation process. Pope John Paul II who, as a Pole, was acutely aware of Polish-Ukrainian history, had begun a series of conciliatory steps in 1987 and was anxious that as many Uniate churches as possible should be restored. In 1991 he ordered the restoration of the Cathedral of St. Theresa in Przemyśl to the Uniates, but this move was strongly—and forcibly—resisted by Roman Catholics in the city and became the occasion for much anti-Ukrainian feeling. It only showed how brittle the rapprochement was and how it would take many years of leadership and hard work—and without serious incident—to make it secure.[66]

The nearly 220,000 Poles in Ukraine, not forming any sizable geographic unit but scattered over the western and southwestern parts of the country, did relatively well under the old Soviet dispensation in terms of education, press, and—except during the Solidarity period in 1981—contacts with Poland itself. Since then the rights of the Polish minority, as well as other minorities, including the Hungarian population of 150,000, have been safeguarded by legislation, and Poles probably can look forward to a dignified existence in the new, independent Ukraine. This legislation does not result from any sudden flush of Ukrainian goodwill toward the Poles but because of the problem of Russia and the Ukrainian preoccupation with it. Ukraine's future as a nation-state depends on regulating its relations with Russia. It is a complicated task, fraught with danger. Between 11 million and 12 million Russians live in Ukraine, more than one-fifth of the country's total population. This huge minority makes any questions relating to either the Polish or the Hungarian minorities something of an insignificant sideshow as far as the authorities in Kiev are concerned. Yet the Russian minority helps much smaller minorities like these because the concessions granted to it, mainly in order to give Russia no excuse for meddling, obviously have to apply to other minorities, too. Of course, it also makes good political and international sense—an earnest of Ukraine's good intentions in Europe and a reflection of its hopes of being accepted by the West. But when all auxiliary reasons are exhausted, it is Russia that the Polish, and the Hungarian, minorities have to thank for the concessions they are getting.

But it is not only the minority question that now leads Ukraine to want better relations with Poland. If, as many Poles aver, Poland's road to Europe goes through Germany, then Ukraine's road to Europe goes through Poland (as does Belarus's). And "Europe," more specifically the European Community, is needed by Ukraine to help serve as a counterweight to Russia. In a small way, too, a developing partnership with Poland is also seen as a counterweight to Russia. In this context, the entire Ukrainian attitude to Poles might be changing. This changed attitude applies, not only to the traditionally unfavorable stereotype of Poles, but to a Ukrainian revision of the interpretation of some key events in the history of relations between the two nations. Not, of course, of atrocities like "Operation Wisła," but of more distant events like Khmelnytsky's (Chmielnicki) rebellion in the middle of the seventeenth century that turned Ukrainians against Poles and on the road to Russian submission. Therefore, the prospects for a deep and far-reaching rapprochement between the two countries are there. Both nations need it and realize it.[67]

Kaliningrad: Last Russian Outpost

The former Soviet oblast of Kaliningrad is the only part of Russia bordering Poland. Small, certainly, but militarily bristling. Out of an oblast population of nearly 900,000 in early 1993, some 500,000 were members of the Russian armed forces and their dependents. (Kaliningrad city has about 400,000 inhabitants.) It is not only an important army center, but the site of a large naval facility.[68] Formerly the German Königsberg, but now totally Russified—looking more like Irkutsk than the old Hanseatic city—it was part of the historic province of East Prussia, divided after World War II between Poland and the Soviet Union, with the former getting most of it but with Stalin insisting on holding the strategic port of Königsberg and its environs. The Kaliningrad enclave is the last bit left of Stalin's massive East European land grab after 1945. A rabbit-shaped creation, it fronts onto Poland, Lithuania, and the Baltic Sea. Reunited Germany also might assume an important role in its future. In 1992, with the rumors that the former Volga Germans might be resettled in Kaliningrad, it looked as if Germany already was acquiring a key role. (Apparently many locals expect this to happen—even that Germany will literally buy it, and rename it Königsberg.) These rumors had little to them, but they were enough to upset the Poles. Better Russians there than Germans, many Poles averred. Better neither, of course, for the Poles were continually uneasy about the inordinately strong Russian military presence. At a lower level, though, contacts between Kaliningrad and the neighboring Polish districts of Olsztyn and Suwałki had begun to proliferate as never before. There were a number of joint ventures and some Polish investment. In a small way, too, Poland was Kaliningrad's window to the West.[69]

In the best of all *possible* worlds Poles obviously would like Kaliningrad to be part of Poland. Many of them would privately admit it. But, officially, Polish relations with Russia took a promising turn between 1991 and 1993, and Warsaw would like to maintain this progress. Lithuania, though, and this was another worrisome prospect for the Poles, would, if the situation ever became propitious, also stake its claim for Kaliningrad. Obviously, the government in Vilnius has kept a tactful reserve on the subject, but some sections of the Lithuanian press were candid about the "need" eventually to acquire this territory and about their concern over suspected Polish designs on it.

Not just the acquisitive instinct is behind Lithuania's attitude to Kaliningrad. Security factors also are involved. Lithuania might be the state most concerned, but all three Baltic states have regarded Kaliningrad as a security threat, and their fears hardly were calmed by the fact that some of the Russian forces being withdrawn from their own territories were posted there. For Lithuania, Kaliningrad also represents a tie to Russia it could well do without. Surface transit between it and Russia proper goes through Lithuania, and the Lithuanian nuclear station at Ignalina provides much of Kaliningrad's energy requirements—just two reminders that Kaliningrad is very much part of Russia. The real danger for Lithuania is that, if Russia keeps Kaliningrad—and no Russian government in the foreseeable future would let it go—pressure on Lithuania will grow to concede a "Russian corridor" ensuring access. The dangers implicit in this situation are obvious, not only to Lithuania, but to Europe.

Poland's Relations with Germany: Uneasy but Mellowing

Like virtually all European nations, Poland did not greet Germany's reunification with enthusiasm. Indeed, its particular reaction was one of distinct unease: once again, so soon after shaking off communist rule, Poland could find itself in the German-Russian nutcracker. This nervousness about a reunited Germany explained its initial hesitation about the dissolution of the Warsaw Pact. But after the Polish-German treaty of June 1991, with its finally unequivocal recognition of the Oder-Neisse frontier, Poland accepted the reality of the new Europe and the new Germany's part in it. Relations between Bonn and Warsaw, therefore, improved. But however much they improved, they always would be characterized by a certain unease on Poland's part. Much of this unease centered on the sensitive issue of the German minority in Poland.

David McQuaid has said in his excellent essay on Poland's minorities that "until 1989 the communist authorities maintained that Poland had more Greeks and Macedonians (4,500) than Germans (2,500)."[70] The Polish authorities simply considered—and most Poles wanted to believe—that all except a handful of the former German minority and the former German residents of the new western Polish territories had made their exit, forced or voluntary, in the years after World War II. The real number always was difficult to estimate. Immediately after the war many Germans who could, passed themselves off as Poles. Subsequently, with the *Wirtschaftswunder* in West Germany and communist reality in Poland, it was the other way round: many who could claim German ancestry tended to do so; *Volkswagendeutsche* was the term often applied to them by contemptuous (and envious) Poles.

The real figure in early 1994 was probably about 300,000, concentrated in Silesia. The Polish-German treaty recognized the right of each minority in either country to its ethnic, cultural, linguistic, and religious identity, and it stressed the impermissibility of any attempt to assimilate a minority against its will. Leaders of the German minority had demanded more, including autonomy in the Opole (Oppeln) district, where there was the strongest concentration of Germans, dual citizenship, and the right of those expelled during World War II to return. These demands were rejected by the Poles, as was the German request for minority rights to be encoded in the constitution or in a special law.

Within two years after 1989 the Germans clearly had become the best-organized, most articulate, and politically influential minority in Poland. This development was largely the work of Johann Kroll, a farmer from Opole, founder of the Social and Cultural Society of the German Minority. The organization fielded candidates in local elections in May 1990, winning majorities in almost half of the district's municipal councils. In the parliamentary elections in October 1991 the German minority won seven seats in the Sejm. The group took 26 percent of the vote in Opole, the best percentage showing of any single party competing in the Polish elections.[71] In the September 1993 elections it received about the same percentage of total votes but, because of changes in the electoral law, it got only four seats.[72]

Such solidarity and organizational ability frightened many Poles. So did the close links that Kroll and his organization kept with the vocal expellee organizations in Germany, including those who had opposed the treaty with Poland and who still referred to the Polish Western Territories as "East Germany." After the treaty was concluded in June 1991, relations between Poles and the German minority improved. Many of the German minority's members had been hoping that Bonn would demand greater privileges for them before finally conceding on the frontier question, as Chancellor Helmut Kohl at first seemed to be insisting. But after the treaty and the recognition of the border, many seemed prepared, if rather fatalistically, to accept what they had. The Germans had tried to get more but had failed. Many on both sides were now hoping that, like the frontier question, the minority question also had been solved and that minorities would perform the task of being the bridge between the nations.

The optimism lasted for several months; then, in 1992, some members of the German minority got caught up in the nationalist wave sweeping Eastern Europe and parts of the old Soviet Union. A few also became involved in the nationalist violence that, on a small scale, was affecting parts of reunited Germany. Gang fights between German and Polish skinheads and hooligans broke out, with the Poles apparently as much to blame as the Germans. That was serious enough, but even more serious, in what it signified and symbolized, was the appearance in November 1992—obviously marking All Saints' Day (November 1) when Germans commemorate all their dead—of war memorials in Silesia commemorating local members of the Wehrmacht who had died during World War II.[73] A combination of deliberate provocation and arrogant insensitivity, the memorials aroused anger throughout Poland and elicited a public warning from President Wałęsa himself.

Still, in one highly important sense, Poles and Germans obviously were coming together. In 1992, 30.7 million Germans visited Poland, mainly on brief shopping expeditions.[74] (The figure for Germans visiting Czechoslovakia in 1991 was 26 million.)[75] German bargain hunters do not necessarily make Polish friends, but a certain mutuality here could help mellow the past. More important, so could renewed Polish fears and German concern about Russia and the surge of nationalism there. Some of the past, if not forgotten, could recede because of fears for the future. For many Poles, Germany had now genuinely changed. But Russia continued to be the "inhuman land."

Pivotal Countries

From the crisis points just discussed, five countries emerge as *pivotal* to the future stability or instability of Eastern Europe, not always because of any intrinsic importance in terms of population and power, but in terms of either their geostrategic locations or their situation as parent/metropolitan states with considerable minorities beyond their borders:

Hungary: Hungarian policy in both East-Central and South-Eastern Europe will affect a whole range of national and minority issues in Romania, Serbia (Vojvodina), Ukraine, and Slovakia. Hungarian restraint, evident so far, could have an important stabilizing effect throughout the entire region. Lack of it could be incendiary. Some signs, both domestic (growth of nationalism) and external (threats to Hungarian minorities), could point to an eventually more assertive Hungarian regional policy. The strong opposition in the Hungarian parliament in the Spring of 1993 to the ratification of the Hungarian-Ukrainian state treaty was a case in point. Rightist deputies objected to a passage stating that neither side had territorial claims on the other. A new and most unusual mutual interest with Russia also was developing, based on the fact that both countries had large numbers of their nationals in neighboring lands.

Ukraine: Ukrainian policy will have a direct impact on its four neighboring East European states: Poland, Slovakia, Hungary, and Romania. Its relations with Moldova also will indirectly affect Romania. Its pervasively important relations with Russia will affect its interaction with all of these states.

Serbia: Serbs are responsible for war, horror, and misery in parts of the old Yugoslavia and could inflict still more damage, leading to a wider Balkan war and Serbia's own eventual destruction.

Albania: With Kosovo 90 percent ethnic Albanian in population and Macedonia at least 25 percent, with its tense relations with Greece, and its developing relations with Turkey, Albania is the focus of much potential instability. Internally and externally, it could be deeply affected by developments in its three neighboring countries — the rump Yugoslav federation (Serbia and Montenegro), Macedonia, and Greece.

Turkey: Turkey could be of decisive importance in the Southern Balkans if more Muslims there become directly involved, or even as a result of the situation in Bosnia. (See chapters 7 and 8.)

Finally, there is *Russia.* At present its influence is small, sought after by some in South-Eastern Europe, feared by many others. Its potential for good or ill is daunting. One thing is certain: it has not waved a permanent good-bye.

Cooperation: Long-Lived or Short-Lived?

The enumeration of all of these crisis points in Eastern Europe makes a disturbing scenario. But it is not the whole picture, at least as far as *East-Central Europe* is concerned. There, from 1990 until the beginning of 1993, serious and at least partly successful efforts were made by Poland, Hungary, and Czechoslovakia to form a political, diplomatic, economic, and security alliance among themselves. The Visegrád Triangle, called after a town in Hungary where the Bohemian, Hungarian, and Polish kings had met in 1335 and where Havel, Wałęsa, and Antall (with Göncz) met in conference in February 1991 became a sign of hope in otherwise gloomy surroundings.[76]

The years 1991 and 1992 saw encouraging development in various forms of cooperation between these three East-Central European countries — so much so that they were looked on as setting an example to others in cooperating toward regional stability. This effort was all the more notable because in the first few months after 1989, little sign of a willingness to cooperate had been shown, especially between Czechoslovakia and Poland. Zbigniew Brzezinski's proposal in January 1990 of a federation between Poland and Czechoslovakia (actually, the revival of an old idea), though received quite well in Poland, had practically no support at all in Czechoslovakia where, especially in the Czech Lands, Poland always had been regarded with some suspicion.[77] Later, there was an obvious personal coolness between Wałęsa and Havel. Between all three countries there also began something like a "race for Europe" — to be accepted into the European mainstream — with an accompanying devil-take-the-hindmost attitude.

But this rivalry, based partly on past antagonisms, partly on present exigencies, mellowed considerably and began to be replaced by a certain cooperative sincerity. It became obvious to all three countries that the European Community, and "Europe" generally, was not nearly as keen on accepting any of them as they had been expecting. Second, the conservative putsch in Moscow in August 1991, fiasco though it turned out to be, was a reminder to everybody of how precarious their newly won freedoms might have been, or might still be. This, therefore, served to strengthen the cooperation that the Visegrád meeting had established earlier in 1991. Third, the West — the European Community and the United States, both through public and private channels — strongly supported the Visegrád concept. In the mood then prevailing, therefore, anything that both Europe and the United States approved was taken as virtually mandatory by the East Europeans involved.

In perspective, 1992 might well be seen as the high point of Visegrád. Practical cooperation continued in different fields at a number of levels, and, though joining the European mainstream remained the main objective for all three countries concerned, this triangular substitute was considered both a practical interim measure and a good thing in itself. On a more intellectual level, some also saw it as the partial embodiment of the old Mitteleuropa concept — not exactly what its early enthusiasts had in mind but, in the circumstances, better than nothing.

However, it was precisely during 1992 that shadows and complications appeared which increasingly made Visegrád — in its original form, at any rate — irrelevant. Both Poland and Czechoslovakia were preoccupied with serious domestic difficulties. For the first half of the year Poland was convulsed in political chaos. Czechoslovakia, though, was the real problem; it was heading for its demise and division into two separate countries. Could the Visegrád Triangle, then, become the Visegrád Quadrilateral? It was more than doubtful. As discussed in chapter 3, Slovakia's political and economic future was in doubt from the start, as was its international orientation. It was at loggerheads with Hungary over the Gabčikovo dam issue and, potentially, over the treatment of its Hungarian minority. But even more serious was the future Czech attitude. Václav Klaus, now the Czech premier, had never been a Visegrád enthusiast, and at the beginning of 1993 he again made this viewpoint clear in a number of statements. Visegrád, he maintained, had been an artificial creation virtually imposed by the Western powers.[77] For Klaus, the future of the new Czech Republic lay unequivocally with the West, and nothing should be allowed to divert it. His impatience with anything that smacked of regional cooperation along Visegrád lines also was shown by his lack of enthusiasm for the Central European University, founded by George Soros, the main part of which was located in Prague.[78] Klaus's Western preoccupation caused much waggish comment. A story, apocryphal but wickedly perceptive, was circulating in Prague in 1993 about his own suggestion for the Czech Republic's new name: East Germany.

But developments within the region itself also were damaging Visegrád's prospects. The very concept of "Central Europe" (or East-Central Europe) was expanding after the collapse of both the Soviet Union and Yugoslavia. A regional concept of three states—or even four with Slovakia—now seemed provincial and obsolete. Two, perhaps three, former Soviet republics now had claims for admission to the club—Ukraine preeminently, Belarus, and possibly Lithuania. From the old Yugoslavia, Slovenia's claims were obvious, and Croatia's were strong, too, despite the Balkan tug of its Serb-populated regions. Any regional concept now had to be dynamic, not static; it had to take into account the geopolitical revolution that had taken place and its consequences for international relations. Obviously, too, the situation and prospects of Russia, looming in the Eastern background, would continue to affect the East-Central European (as well as the Balkan) region. Russia's relations with Ukraine would affect the degree to which Ukraine could conduct a Western diplomacy and develop its relations with Poland, on which the future stability of East-Central Europe could well depend.

The original Visegrád concept now looked too narrow. In such a dynamic and unsure situation a *firm,* institutionalized alliance, between Poland, the Czech Republic, and Hungary, forming a single entity in relation to the principal regional issues, could have been advantageous to its members and a stabilizing force. But there was never much hope, intention, or chance of Visegrád ever being that.

The fact was that East-Central Europe, as well as South-Eastern Europe and the former Soviet Union, had become crowded with larger and smaller new states that had emerged at the end of the twentieth century. And they all wanted to assert their identity and their independence. Afterward they probably would be ready for associations of various kinds—that is, if they all survived. In this context a conversation between Churchill and Stalin, recalled by Z. A. B. Zeman, is even more relevant now than it was in 1944, when it took place:

> The shadows cast by the Habsburg Empire were sharply etched. . . . In October 1944, Churchill suggested to Stalin that Poland, Czechoslovakia and Hungary should form a group which would be more than an entente: it would be a customs union, a *Zollverein:* "The evil in Europe was that travelling across [it] one used too many currencies, passed a dozen frontiers, many customs barriers and all this was a great obstacle to trade." Stalin replied that the Hungarians, the Czechs and the Poles would first want to build up their national life without restricting their rights by combining with others; "later, economic feelings would prevail, but in the first period they would be purely nationalistic and therefore groupings would be unwelcome."[79]

No one can question Stalin's insincerity. But no one should question his realism.

Era of Uncertainty

The Balkans are likely to remain a threat to European peace for at least a generation. But, as the previous summary of crisis points has indicated, the *East-Central Europeans* can have no grounds for complacency. Hungary looks particularly vulnerable; geography makes it impossible to avoid Balkan concerns (Vojvodina, Transylvania) and the effect of Balkan conflicts. As of the end of 1992, more than 50,000 refugees had poured into Hungary as a result of the Yugoslav conflict,[80] and the number was increasing. Hungary, in fact, was virtually surrounded by tension or unpredictability. Apart from its reassuring border with Austria and its short, relatively harmless one with Slovenia, Hungary has Croatia, Serbia (Vojvodina), Romania, Slovakia, and Ukraine as neighbors — all either dangerous, unfriendly, or uncertain. Some of its neighbors — Romania, Slovakia, and Serbia — considered Hungary a threat (or appeared to do so), and toward the end of 1992 vague talk was heard about the desirability of an updated "Little Entente," now to be composed of Slovakia, Serbia, and Romania to counter this alleged threat. But Hungary's leaders were genuinely insulted at the notion that it could be a threat to regional stability. Between the wars, supported by Germany and Italy, it had been a threat, which brought the historical Little Entente (Czechoslovakia, Romania, and Yugoslavia) into being. But such a threat today, the Hungarians argued, existed only in the paranoid minds of some of their malevolent neighbors.

Poland, too, found itself swimming in a new sea of international uncertainty. Before 1989 it had had three neighbors, in a relationship marked on every side by mutual suspicion and disdain. But, at least, the Soviet Union, the GDR, and Czechoslovakia were familiar and, within certain known parameters, predictable. Now, however, Poland has seven new neighbors — Germany, the Czech Republic, the Slovak Republic, Ukraine, Belarus, Lithuania, and Russia. Of these, the Poles feel relatively at ease only with Germany, the Czech Republic, and Slovakia. With all the others, some degree of worry exists. With Belarus there might be a particular reason to worry. The Minsk parliament's decision in April 1993 to join the Russian-dominated Commonwealth of Independent States (CIS) collective security agreement and later to opt for virtual economic union with Russia led many Poles to fear that harmless Belarus was being, in effect, replaced on its eastern border by a not so harmless Russia.

Even before Vladimir Zhirinovsky's nationalist surge at the Russian elections in December 1993, many Poles (Like many Westerners) had been doubtful about Belarus's future as an independent state. But now fears of Russia's return intensified. Not entirely without reason, many Poles were also predicting a Lithuanian drift toward the status of a Russian satellite. These dangers they viewed against the background of the massive Russian military presence in Kaliningrad. Finally, there was the increasing political, economic, and ethnic instability in Ukraine. Many Ukrainians themselves had already lost their exuberance and were becoming gloomy about their country. Some put the blame entirely on Russia but a few were ready to blame their own mistakes as well. Few Poles expected an early military threat from Russia, but most feared that the freedom to breathe which they had so recently won might become unacceptably circumscribed.

In the meantime, though, any specter of the Bear's return was being overshadowed on Poland's eastern border by the Wild West type of lawlessness that was prevailing there. While millions upon millions of German shoppers were invading western Poland, thousands upon thousands of gangsters, killers, and brigands, from almost all of the Soviet successor states, were operating in and often terrorizing eastern Poland. The Warsaw *Polytika* on May 29, 1993, published a map showing the worse-affected areas, plus a "do's and don'ts" guide for those who have to travel there. The Albanian apocalypse had come to Białlystok.

In sum, what Poland's and Hungary's situations demonstrate is that the East European countries need a *tous azimuts* foreign policy. Total preoccupation with the West, with "rejoining the European mainstream," even if it ever met with a fully welcoming Western response, would be dangerously one-sided. Full membership of the European Community, even membership of an invigorated NATO (see chapter 8), would not preclude the necessity of aiming for satisfactory arrangements with the East as long as this remained possible—with Russia, mainly, but also with Ukraine, Belarus, Lithuania, and Moldova. Most of the East European countries realized this fact and by the end of 1992 had concluded various kinds of agreements with these Soviet successor states. These agreements now needed to be filled with real substance and meaning.

"Pinned to the Wall of Nationhood"

It is worth continuing with a few sadly relevant thoughts of the Croatian novelist, Slavenka Drakulić. She speaks specifically about a collapsing Yugoslavia, but her remarks have a general application. She refers to the old transnational anticommunism that united her with many similar-minded young people in Yugoslavia and other parts of Eastern Europe. But now:

> At the end, all of that didn't help me. Along with millions of other Croats, I was pinned to the wall of nationhood—not only by outside pressure from Serbia and the federal army but by inside na-

> tional homogenization in Croatia. That is what the war is doing to us, reducing us to one dimension: the Nation. The trouble with this nationhood, however, is that, before, I was defined by my education, my job, my ideas, my character and, yes, my nationality too. Now I feel stripped of all that. I am nobody because I am not a person anymore. I am one of 4.5 million Croats.[81]

Before, she said, she had felt a certain individuality. But now:

> I am not in a position to choose, not any longer. I think no one is. Just as in the days of brotherhood-unity, there is now another ideology holding people together, the ideology of nationhood. It doesn't matter if it is Croatian, Serbian, Czech, Slovak, Georgian or Azerbaijani nationhood. What happened is that something that people cherished as a part of their cultural identity — an alternative to the all-embracing communism, a means to survive — became their political identity and turned into an ill-fitting shirt. You may feel the sleeves are too short, the collar too tight. You might not like the color, and the cloth might itch. But there is no escape; there is nothing else to wear. One need not succumb to this ideology of the nation — one is sucked into it.[82]

Many were not just being sucked into it but being murdered by it.

Slavenka Drakulić's cri de coeur brings to mind the manifest humanity and good sense of Lord Acton more than 130 years ago in his essay on nationality, where he warns of the nation-state:

> It overrules the rights and wishes of the inhabitants, absorbing their divergent interests in a fictitious unity; sacrifices their several inclinations and duties to the higher claim of nationality, and crushes all natural rights and all established liberties for the purpose of vindicating itself. Whenever a single definite object is made the supreme end of the State, be it the advantage of a class, the safety and power of the country, the greatest happiness of the greater number, or the support of any speculative idea, the State becomes for the time inevitably absolute. . . . The co-existence of several nations in the same State is a test, as well as the best security of its freedom. It is also one of the chief instruments of civilisation; and as such it is in the natural and providential order, and indicates a state of greater advancement than the national unity which is the ideal of modern liberalization.[83]

Acton was writing in the middle of the nineteenth century. At the end of the twentieth, nationalism had helped destroy communism, but in parts of Eastern Europe and the former Soviet Union it could destroy the hopes of democracy, too.

A Note on Anti-Semitism, Old and New

Anti-Semitism—the "socialism of the dolt," as August Bebel described it—is alive and even kicking in some corners of Eastern Europe today. As in the case of the nationalism of which it was so often an expression, it never disappeared under communism but was just submerged—and then often not too deeply. It had been a major part of the broader culture in several East European countries for far too long for it to disappear immediately when the red banner was unfurled.

In Eastern Europe the issue of anti-Semitism under communism was complicated by the fact that many of the "Muscovite" leaders returning after exile in the Soviet Union were Jewish. The fact that they were Soviet-imposed and then proceeded to impose the Stalinist reign of terror in their own countries only exacerbated the existing anti-Semitism and even gave it a specious coat of respectability. Communism was a "Jewish conspiracy"; thus, anti-Semitism could be identified with anticommunism! This sort of logic was particularly evident in Hungary, where Jewish "Muscovite" rule was especially murderous. But it was conveniently forgotten that many of the "home" communists, later to be persecuted by "Muscovites," had been murderous enough themselves in stamping out their anticommunist opponents after World War II. The Jewish communist leaders in Eastern Europe had no monopoly on viciousness. But they threw out another bone for the anti-Semites to gnaw on.

Anti-Semitism in public life simmered throughout most of the communist period. It boiled over in 1968 in Poland where it had been a political plank in one or another of the communist party factions for a number of years. Elsewhere it was generally present, often tangible but rarely assertive. The Holocaust, of course, had left few Jews in Eastern Europe. In Hungary, estimates of the number of Jews were between 80,000 and 100,000, by far the largest community. But, compared with the approximately 6 million before World War II in the region as a whole, probably fewer than 200,000 survived after it. Still, as Paul Lendvai describes in *Anti-Semitism Without Jews,* the phenomenon persisted.[84] The "Solidarity" movement in Poland had its anti-Semitic elements, and the Polish Catholic Church's exemplary record as the incarnation of the national spirit was more than once blemished by regurgitations of its own traditional prejudice.

It would be wrong, though, to single out Poland. It was the least closed of all the communist societies and, therefore, the most closely examined by Western media. Its warts were the most visible. But there were warts everywhere, even in the Czech Lands, where the Stalinist trials of the early 1950s had been marked by the most primitive anti-Semitism. In Romania, Ceauşescu, in his assiduous courtship of the West, was liberal in allowing emigration to Israel and in other gestures toward the rapidly diminishing Jewish community. But, particularly as his own domestic rule degenerated, the cloven hoof became more apparent in the anti-Semitic outbursts of some of his more sycophantic courtiers. In Hungary, the Kádár leadership tried, generally with success, to keep the lid on the unofficial anti-Semitism pervasive throughout the country. But in 1989 the lid was off everything, everywhere. More than forty years of repression were quickly stripped away, and in the ensuing emancipation the prejudices of centuries burst forth. Prominent among them was anti-Semitism.

"Anti-Semitism without Jews" conveys the right notion in terms of Eastern Europe's contemporary history. But some Jews *have* survived, and not only in Hungary. Paradoxically, the fewer they are, the more noticed they often become. Some of them, prominent in the dissident movements in Hungary, Poland, and Czechoslovakia, became national figures. At first, they were heroes. Later, though, when the dissidents had had their day, the fact that some of them were Jewish only made resentments against them worse.

After 1989 anti-Semitism became immediately apparent. It first surfaced in a serious way in the Polish presidential campaign at the end of 1990 (see chapter 3) when it attracted considerable international attention, particularly because of Lech Wałęsa's innuendos and evasions. Wałęsa is no more instinctively anti-Semitic than many Poles; he had worked well in Solidarity with intellectuals of Jewish background like Bronisław Geremek and Adam Michnik, and he was, in any case, acutely aware of the international suspicions about Polish anti-Semitism. At electoral meetings he did not initiate anti-Semitism but rather responded to it. He acted, though, in a way that went along with the anti-Semitic mood instead of repudiating it. In doing so, he not only gave himself a reputation that, despite his redemptive efforts later, has been hard to shake off, but he also tended to confirm the anti-Semitic reputation of his country in the eyes of the world.

In the meantime, anti-Semitism had become assertive in chaotic postcommunist Romania. Here, very few Jews remained in public life to serve as targets, although, of course, lack of Jews has never deterred resolute anti-Semites. (If they do not exist, invent some; if there are too few, think up some more. One of the more egregious cases of this attitude, though, was not in Romania but in Czechoslovakia, of all places, in December 1992 when a far-right Prague newspaper published a long list of alleged Jews in public life headed by Václav Havel!) Extreme nationalist Romanians specialized in cosmic and local Jewish conspiracies to which hapless, honest, Romania was falling victim. Their prejudices sometimes were expressed in ways reminiscent of Julius Streicher in the Nazi *Der Stürmer*. Petre Roman, prime minister in 1990 and 1991, and partly Jewish (in spite of his evasions), was one of their prime targets.

The Csurka factor in Hungary has been discussed at some length in chapter 3. Csurka's type of anti-Semitism was shared by a considerable number of Hungarians. Sometimes it was even more crudely expressed; more often, though, it was used with more subtlety. The traditional Hungarian preoccupation with national survival was understandable and had much pathos. But the constant stress on the Hungarian national "essence" was exclusionary as far as Jews were concerned. It was to be found, not only among the extreme right parties, but among strong elements of the Hungarian Democratic Forum, the Smallholders, and the Christian Democrats. In neighboring Croatia the murderous racism of the Ustaša state of World War II had by no means been extinguished in the nearly fifty years separating it from the newly free Croatia. President Tudjman himself apparently embodies some of the xenophobic, anti-Semitic propensities of his predecessors. So do many members of his ruling Croatian Democratic Party. To the right of it, the Croatian Party of Historic Rights, the new expression of the Starčević-Frank-Ante Pavelić tradition, is impregnated with anti-Semitism. Still, in Croatian nationalism today, anti-Semitism occupies a relatively small place. The Serbs and, in a different way, the Muslims are the targets.

Excesses apart, most of the anti-Semitism in Eastern Europe today remains indirect rather than overt, wrapped in code words that are easily understandable to the initiated mass of East Europeans. Any accusations of anti-Semitism are almost always indignantly and energetically denied. In many cases these denials are sincere. It often comes down to the question of what anti-Semitism is or is not. For many East Europeans (as well as Germans and Austrians for that matter), anti-Semitism means approving or condoning Auschwitz. But anything that falls short of that, anything this side of the *Arbeit Macht Frei* archway, correspondingly falls short of anti-Semitism.

In this context it is worth quoting the conservative German historian, Ernst Nolte, who, in his book about Martin Heidegger, goes into moral and intellectual contortions trying to explain away Heidegger's commitment to Nazism. In doing so, Nolte defines what a "real" anti-Semite is, as against one of the more ordinary variety. A "real" anti-Semite, according to Nolte, is one who "opposes Jews and tries to get rid of them *as* Jews, with no exceptions allowed. . . . [Thus:] The only person who qualifies as an anti-Semite is the one for whom the aversion to Jews or the struggle against them stands at the center of his thought and activity."[85] The less obsessed variety, presumably, if not "anti-*Semite*," might be considered as "anti-*Semitic*," that is, somewhat less obsessed by the subject, or "Sunday anti-Semites," or anti-Semites "*nur nebenbei*," as one German journalist, in all seriousness, put it to me in conversation! Perhaps before World War I one could distinguish between religious, political, economic, and racial anti-Semitism and between various shades of anti-Semitism. But Hitler and the Holocaust made all such distinctions not just misleading but vicious.

The anti-Semitism that has surfaced in Eastern Europe since 1989 is also a reflection of disappointment and frustrated hopes. Breaking the bonds of communism has not resulted in the promised land that so many expected. In many cases, economic conditions are worse, life has become uncertain, often incomprehensible and threatening. Hence, the need for scapegoats, as mentioned in chapter 1, and such is East European history that Jews must be on the list. It cannot be much comfort for them to know that they are not the only ones on it.

Racism and the Gypsy "Problem"

It was, in fact, not the small and dwindling number of Jews that were bearing the brunt of the reviving racism in Eastern Europe; it was the huge and proliferating number of Gypsies. (This, of course, is not counting the dark-skinned residents or transients from Asia and Africa, part of the new stream of global migration.)

It is dangerous to attempt even approximate estimates for the number of Gypsies (or Romanies, as they now mostly prefer to be called) in Eastern Europe. Zoltan Barany, in an informative essay on the subject, suggests that the following figures, published in 1990, were probably the most accurate at that time:[86]

Albania	62,000
Bulgaria	800,000
Czechoslovakia	800,000
Hungary	600,000
Poland	50,000
Romania	2,000,000
Yugoslavia	800,000

In the whole of Eastern Europe, therefore, at the beginning of the 1990s there were more than 5 million Gypsies, between half and two-thirds of the entire world Gypsy population. The increase in the number of East European Gypsies over the previous ten to fifteen years had been between 35 and 40 percent. This increase occurred during a period when most other ethnic groups in Eastern Europe were either stagnating or decreasing. And those that were increasing, like the Bulgarian Turks, were not doing so at such a high rate.

From their arrival in Eastern Europe from the thirteenth century into the fifteenth century, the Gypsies always had been persecuted. But whatever the persecutions of the previous six hundred years, they were as nothing compared with the genocide under the Nazis. About half a million Gypsies, mostly East European, were killed in the death camps during the war. Afterward, some German Gypsies were "compensated" for their sufferings. As for the rest, as Barany says, "no one has as much as apologized to them."[87]

Under the communists, at least the organized killings stopped, and, in all countries, considerable efforts were made to ameliorate their hard, often desperate material lot. By and large, though, these efforts were inconsistent, ideologically based, and fundamentally misguided. The straitjacket that the communists sought to impose on the whole of society was grotesquely unsuitable for the Gypsy mentality and way of life. (In fact, Gypsies embodied exactly that kind of spontaneity that was anathema to all good Leninists.) They probably were treated most flexibly in Tito's Yugoslavia. Still, throughout the region, Gypsy educational and literacy levels rose remarkably during the communist period and an embryonic Gypsy intelligentsia began to emerge.

The downfall of communism was greeted favorably by most of the few politically conscious Gypsies. The straitjacket now could be entirely thrown off. Nonetheless, most Gypsies lost the sense of physical security that the communist states had given to most of them. The racism to which they had continually been exposed at least was restrained during communist rule. Now they were fair game to the spirit of violence let loose on the fringes of East European society. Organized and spontaneous attacks on them became frequent in every country. These attacks usually were by disaffected youths of the skinhead variety and mentality, but they were sometimes supported, often condoned, by other sections of the population. What went on in 1992 in parts of the reunited Germany also went on in many parts of Eastern Europe, on a far bigger scale and with much less publicity.

But the Gypsies were not just the target of thugs on the social fringe of East European society. Prominent politicians were making indirect racial slurs regarding them. István Csurka's remarks have already been quoted (see chapter 3, p. 88). In September 1993 the Slovak premier Vladimír Mečiár made similar remarks about Gypsies.[88] These two men, divided by so much, clearly had some basic instincts in common! And at a lower level, local officials in every country were making similar, though more direct, anti-Gypsy statements. They knew that it was good politics, that there always had been anti-Gypsy prejudice, and that now many people were understandably concerned about the apparent profusion of Gypsies and the burgeoning crime associated with them.

The atrocities against Gypsies were probably the worst aspect of the entire disturbed social scene in Eastern Europe after 1989. But there also was no question that some Gypsies were posing a serious problem to orderly society. They were responsible for a disproportionate amount of crime throughout the region. But it must be emphasized that Gypsy crime was largely petty crime, not serious or violent crime. They also were heavily involved in black-marketeering, although in Eastern Europe after 1989 the point where capitalist entrepreneurship left off and black-marketeering began sometimes has been difficult to identify. A few Gypsies made fortunes out of the new opportunities and flaunted their success in their own spectacular way. At the other end of the social pole, the number of Gypsy beggars increased alarmingly, recalling for some veterans the depressing everyday scenes characteristic, say, of Bucharest before World War II. Now, however, the Gypsies were not confined to the Balkans alone. A steady stream of them was trying to get to Western Europe. From 1993 onward, as West European countries made entry more difficult, this Gypsy migration would tend to back up in East-Central Europe—in the Czech Republic, Slovakia, Poland, and Hungary. That is, until the portcullises were lowered there, too. The dilemma seemed never-ending.

In many ways, therefore, the Gypsies were a growing problem. But the *real* problem was the prejudice and violence that were being directed against them. Some governments had become aware of this situation, most recently the Hungarian and the Czechoslovak; Hungary, in fact, passed enlightened legislation designed to help Gypsies. But things were likely to get worse, not better. In Balkan countries like Romania and Bulgaria, the official policy was considerably less liberal. Authorities there seemed eager to truckle to the prejudices of the majority.

Many Gypsies faced a grim economic future, too. In this regard, their situation had been worsening because the skills and trades in which they used to excel—basketry, weaving, tinkering, carpentry, horse breeding, etc.—no longer were in demand. This lack of opportunities would increase the pressure for migration. But not only economics were weakening them; even more damaging was their own lack of unity. In 1991 forty Gypsy organizations were registered in Hungary and more than twenty in Czechoslovakia. This diverse profusion partly reflects the numerous different Gypsy tribes existing in Eastern Europe, particularly in the Balkans, and their numerous dialects. Also, many Gypsies cannot speak any kind of Romany language at all, communicating only in the language of the country where they live. The Gypsy temperament, too, is maverick. Hence, the difficulty in creating any kind of umbrella organizations that would facilitate political action. A real "Gypsy lobby" is something for the distant future.

But a Gypsy political consciousness and self-respect *are* developing. The late Cyrus Sulzberger recalled a Macedonian Gypsy before World War II telling him: "There are 77½ religions in the world. Ours is the half."[89] Far fewer Gypsies now would be so self-deprecating or fatalistic. The Gypsy intelligentsia is expanding, becoming politicized, and acquiring leaders of some stature. Its prime aim must be to attain national minority status for its people. Such national stature always has been withheld from them. Gypsies were not considered a minority but an "ethnic group," without homeland, history, or common language. It is tragically typical that the only East European state since 1989 to grant them minority status has been the doomed Bosnia-Hercegovina. But one can expect pressure for minority status to continue. And, despite the obstacles, this pressure will become better-organized. The East European governments would be well-advised to grant such status. It would not be just the right thing to do, but the wise one. Eventually, Gypsy violence, even terrorism, is by no means an impossibility; the Gypsies, indeed, could be the new Eastern Europe's time bomb. If that bomb is not defused in this century, it could go off early in the next.

7
THE YUGOSLAV TRAGEDY

Joseph Rothschild states in his book on prewar Eastern Europe: "by every relevant criterion—history, political traditions, socioeconomic standards, legal systems, religion, and culture—Yugoslavia was the most complicated" of the new states created after World War I. It was made up of larger and smaller pieces of both the former Habsburg and Ottoman empires, with only Serbia, the Piedmont of the new Yugoslavia, and Montenegro previously having enjoyed independence in the modern era. Rothschild is worth quoting again to emphasize Yugoslavia's uniqueness.

> Thus, unlike Czechoslovakia, the new Yugoslav state did not emerge in its entirety from the deceased Habsburg Empire; unlike Romania, it was not simply an enlargement of a prewar core kingdom; unlike Poland, it was not a restored, but an altogether new, state; unlike interwar Hungary, it lacked ethnic homogeneity. Its several parts had over the centuries been subsumed within Byzantine, Ottoman, Hungarian, Germanic, and Italian cultural zones. Indeed, the so-called Illyrian Provinces along the Adriatic and in the northwest had for a brief interval even been attached to Napoleonic France. Each part had interwoven the culture of its particular zone with indigenous South Slav institutions and styles. The ancient and tenacious Theodosian line that divided the Western, Roman (Catholic and Protestant) world from the Eastern, Byzantine (Orthodox and Ottoman) one ran right through the new Yugoslavia.[1]

He continues:

> Populated as it was by sundry antagonistic communities of widely divergent cultures, who worshipped in several different religions, had inherited eight legal systems from their former sovereignties, and wrote the basic Serbocroatian language in two orthographies (not to mention their several other Slavic and non-Slavic languages), Yugoslavia was bound to be subjected to profound cen-

> trifugal pressures which were to overwhelm her elite. Furthermore, areas of mixed population, such as the Vojvodina, Bosnia, or Macedonia, functioned less as bridges than as barriers, aggravating rather than easing these centrifugal pressures.[2]

All in all, it would be difficult to imagine a more adept way of explaining why, right from the beginning, Yugoslavia had little chance for survival. But it also must be emphasized that, despite all of their cultural and historical differences, the Serbs and the Croats, who formed the matrix of Yugoslavia, were in many respects very similar. These similarities made the conflicts between them almost fratricidal, hence all the more bitter. And in the Bosnian war, beginning in 1992, the three combatants — Serbs, Croats, and Muslims — were, ethnically and linguistically, virtually the same. Again, the similarities were an important reason for the hideousness of that war.

The failure of the first Yugoslavia seemed to confirm fears that many always had about its very survival. True, its initial destruction and dismemberment were at the hands of external powers, and this foreign determination not to let Yugoslavia survive was the main reason for its downfall. But it was not the only one. It interacted with internal weaknesses that always had existed but were gravely exacerbated by subsequent misrule.

During World War II, though, there occurred the miracle of Yugoslav resistance. *Yugoslav* resistance, it should be noted, not exclusively Serbian. In the flood of historical revisionism after the collapse of communism generally and then the disintegration of Yugoslavia itself, attempts have been made to extol the Serb Chetnik resistance and to discredit Tito's Partisan movement.[3] A judicious rescue of the Chetniks and their leader, Colonel Draža Mihailović, from the web of communist-woven infamy was overdue, but the effort hardly justified the unbridled disparagement of the Partisans' historic role in saving and reviving Yugoslavia. The fortitude and general unity that the country displayed in supporting Tito's defiance of Stalin in 1948 was evidence enough of the cohesive impact the wartime experience had made.

The Fatal Complacency

In the event, of course, the unity shown in 1948 was deceptive. The successful defiance of the Soviet Union only reinforced the complacency on the part of the Yugoslav leadership that contributed to the eventual collapse of Yugoslavia at the beginning of the 1990s.

The complacency had been there from the start. Imbued with the conviction that Marxism-Leninism held the key to both social progress and ethnic harmony and was the remedy for their country's prewar failures, the Yugoslav communists saw themselves as alone capable of defying the odds that had been so strongly against Yugoslavia from the beginning. And this conviction was strengthened by three stunning successes: their successful revolution, their victorious wartime resistance, and the epic of 1948.

But, taking the half-century of Titoist Yugoslavia as a whole, it now seems that it was sustained, not so much by any solidity of achievement, as by a series of mutually interacting myths, part genuine, part concocted. Very briefly, these were:[4]

(1) *The socialism-federalism myth.* This myth held that a combination of socialism and federalism could overcome ethnic differences in a multinational state, even differences as sharp and deep as those that had been present in the interwar kingdom and had reemerged so violently during World War II.

(2) *The Tito myth.* The heroic, warrior-statesman, *pontifex maximus* myth unquestionably had a genuine basis, but it also was robustly propagated by Tito himself and by the propaganda machine of the communist party-state.[5]

(3) *The "Club of 41" myth: The wartime partisan legend.* Again, as an inspiration in the early days of the republic, this was a creative, binding force.[6] The break with Stalin would have been impossible without it. Later it was an obstacle to progress.

(4) *The myth of 1948 itself.* The unique defiance of Stalin helped change the course of East European history.

(5) *Self-management: The ideological myth.* This myth was Yugoslavia's own (controversial) contribution to the "treasure house" of Marxism-Leninism. It was a short-lived propaganda triumph and a long-lived economic catastrophe. Its deficiencies could be hidden in the artificial prosperity of the 1960s and 1970s. Later, they could not.

(6) *The myth of nonalignment.* This myth was Tito's illusion, a mixture of geopolitics and ego. Even before his death, most Yugoslavs recognized it as unsustainable. When the choice came between East and West, the Yugoslavs wanted West—Western Europe, in particular.

All of these myths, except the Tito myth, lost their potency several years before Tito's death in 1980, but his charisma sustained them. With the first Croatian crisis in the early 1970s, cracks began to appear; these were widened by the global economic downturn of the 1970s. Like all of the East European communist countries, Yugoslavia never recovered from it.

At present, with the memory of Yugoslavia's death throes still all too fresh, there has been little chance for "perhaps if" retrospection or for discussion of whether Yugoslavia might have been saved in some form. Probably it was beyond saving. But perhaps if Milovan Djilas's social-democratic proposals of the early 1950s had been applied instead of anathematized, a democratic political system might have evolved. The economic system, though, however reformed, still would have remained essentially etatist and, as such, could hardly have survived the rigors of the 1970s. (As it was, the self-management delusion precluded the possibility of real reform until it was too late.) In brief, Yugoslavia like the Soviet Union, as Gorbachev was to find, could not reform itself, or even preserve itself, if it remained tied to the premise and spirit of Leninism. Tito, the creator, was in this sense also the destroyer of federal Yugoslavia. He never could shed the Leninism of his formative years. He was keenly aware of the basic and ongoing dangers threatening Yugoslavia, but his instinctive response (always stronger than his intellectual response) was not to branch out in search of new solutions but to retreat into his Leninist *querencia.* As I have written elsewhere:

> Tito remained true to Leninism throughout his life. He could broaden its framework and in the minds of the purists play fast and loose with some of its tenets, but he could never break that framework. In his last years he became its prisoner. The single remark that best revealed his true political convictions was made regarding the Sixth Congress of the Yugoslav League of Communists in 1952. It was this congress that recommended the party withdraw from active, everyday direction of the political life of the country into a guiding, teaching, arbitrational role, persuasive rather than coercive. Some 18 years afterward Tito said he had "never liked the sixth Congress." It went againt the grain of everything that meant sense and order to him.[7]

The sixth congress was held just four months before Stalin died. Had Tito liked it, there might have been hope.

It was ten years later, in 1962, that Tito was flatly to declare that the national problem in Yugoslavia had been solved.[8] This statement expressed not just the official Yugoslav leadership line, it was what many of them sincerely believed by then. They were not so much behind the curve of history as they were ahead of it. But their mistake was not simply the result of the fallacy of their ideology. Yugoslavia seemed to be doing fairly well in 1962—internationally, politically, and economically. As for its nations, it was too much to speak of harmony, but a developing Yugoslav cooperation was noticeable. The horrors of wartime and the rigors of the late forties and fifties seemed to be behind them. The future looked more promising.

But within a few years, what once had seemed banished reestablished itself as Yugoslavia's fatal malady. In 1968 came the first serious Albanian demonstrations against Serbian rule in Kosovo, and in 1970 the Croatian crisis began. Tito was realistic and experienced enough to understand that the Kosovo and Croatian crises signaled the return of the national problem. The devolution, therefore, contained in the new constitution of 1974 was meant to preempt it. So was his promulgation in 1978 of the collective leadership system, to take effect after his death. This system's main aim was to establish and perpetuate strict equality among the nations of Yugoslavia in party posts and in the executive organs of federal government. After Tito's death, his own posts of president of the Yugoslav state and of the League of Communists of Yugoslavia (LCY, the party) would be rotated annually on an ethnic basis. Hence, a new state and party leader from a different republic or province would be elected every year. It eventually proved an ineffective expedient, exacerbating, not easing, the problem. But it was an attempt at a solution as well as further evidence of how the national problem was preying on Tito's mind in the last years of his life.[9]

Economic Decline and Fall

Economic decline may not have caused the Yugoslav disintegration, but it certainly hastened it. As the economy fell from the beginning of the 1980s into terminal decline, so nationalism irresistibly gathered pace. The economic decline was so precipitous because, until it was too late, it was tackled by conservative, or Leninist, methods rather than by the more liberal methods some Yugoslavs advocated and of which there were already examples in the rest of Eastern Europe.

Indeed, the crisis of the early 1980s again brought to the fore the seesaw struggle between reformers and reorganizers that was one of the main themes of Yugoslav (and of East European) communist history. And—again a familiar pattern—it was the reorganizers who won.

In 1982 the Yugoslav government introduced its "Stabilization Program," which had the makings of a genuine market reform program allowing for a wide range of free enterprise activity and also had the potential for further development.[10] This Stabilization Program could have been the last chance for Yugoslavia, but it was not taken. The timidity of its proponents and the well-organized vigor of the political and economic vested interests opposing it combined, not so much to kill it, as to neuter it. In 1986 the Bosnian Croat, Branko Mikulić, became federal premier; with his ascendancy Yugoslavia's fate was sealed. With too much bustle and too few brains, Mikulić was essentially a product of the red Tammany. He neutralized rather than implemented the Stabilization Program; by the time he resigned, nothing was left between the covers. At least he made history by *resigning* at the end of 1988, but it was more like a prizefighter throwing in the towel than a statesman taking the honorable course.

It was ironical that Yugoslavia, like the Soviet Union, got its Gorbachev when it was much too late—and, because it was too late, both leaders accelerated collapse rather than prevented it. Ante Marković, the new Yugoslav federal premier, a successful Croatian economic official and former factory director, instituted a program of economic reform that partly resembled the "shock therapy" methods of the Mazowiecki government in Poland at the beginning of 1990. (Both Marković and Leszek Balcerowicz, the Polish finance minister, had the same American adviser—Jeffrey Sachs of Harvard.) The early period of Marković's program was severe. The first few months of 1989 were almost as disastrous as anything under Mikulić. But by the end of the year, real promise was apparent. The dinar had been made convertible with surprisingly few ill effects, and inflation began to drop dramatically. These successes gained approval from the IMF, checked the pessimism in the West about Yugoslavia's survival, and boosted popular morale in the country itself. Realizing the inseparability between economic and political reform, Marković strongly supported political liberalization. The multiparty system had, in fact, begun to sprout in several republics before it was legalized by the federal government in April 1989.

Economically and politically, Marković was actually much more "liberal" than Gorbachev. He could sweep away the ideological cobwebs more willingly and thoroughly than the Soviet leader. His essential similarity with Gorbachev (strange for a Croat, not so strange for a Russian) was in his failure to gauge the true strength of small-nation nationalism and to understand it, let alone sympathize with it. In the summer of 1990 Marković founded the Alliance of Reform Forces of Yugoslavia, a supranational political party aimed at saving the federation. It attracted some of Yugoslavia's best and brightest but, well before they came together, their cause was lost.

The Gathering Storm of Nationalism

Tito died in May 1980, and the fears of many observers that disintegration would soon follow seemed to be justified by the serious riots in Kosovo the following year. But for several years thereafter, a period of almost unbroken but deceptive quiet prevailed. To most people's surprise, the succession system Tito had devised in 1978 seemed to work for a time, as the faceless annuals (the Yugoslav presidents who alternated each year) passed through the revolving door of Yugoslavia's leadership—and then into oblivion.

We now know that this quiet period was the calm before the cataclysm. And the calm was shattered mostly by the Serbs. Many Serbs had always resented Tito's Yugoslavia, not so much because it was communist, as many were subsequently to claim, but because it was not Serb enough. It was the Serbs' efforts to make Yugoslavia an extension of Serbia that largely had undermined it before World War II. Now, Tito, half Croat, half Slovene, taking the lessons of the interwar kingdom to heart, built the new state partly on the principle of cutting Serbia down to size. In geopolitical terms, this meant hiving off Montenegro and Macedonia as separate federal republics. An independent Montenegro was something that the Serbs could accept; ethnically, Montenegrins were Serbs and could be depended on. Besides, Montenegro had a history and proud tradition of independence, which Serbs did respect. The Macedonian republic, though, they took as an insult. "South Serbia" in the prewar kingdom, Serbs considered it theirs by right. Neither the Bulgarians nor the Greeks, they contended, had any right to it. And certainly not the Macedonians themselves, because they were not a nation. (At least on this point, Serbia, Greece, and Bulgaria agreed.) The Serbs also were distinctly uneasy over Kosovo and Vojvodina becoming autonomous provinces — within the republic of Serbia, it is true, but not essentially of it. The status of Kosovo, particularly, the sacred historical Serb heartland, they took as a particular insult. The fact that Albanians had formed the majority there for centuries made absolutely no difference. Hence, to Serbs, Tito built his new country on the principle of "strong Yugoslavia — weak Serbia." It was a conviction that always rankled.[11]

For nearly a quarter of a century, however, Tito's Yugoslavia had its consolations for them. Although a federation, the country retained strong centralizing characteristics, and most of the federal civil bureaucracy was Serbian-run. The fact that Belgrade was both the federal and Serbian capital in itself gave Serbia a certain preeminence. (This was something that the other republics came to resent more and more, regarding Belgrade as the Serbian, not the Yugoslav, capital.) In terms of real power — security, police, military, and finance — the Serbs had much more than they proportionately deserved.

But after the mid-1960s the Serb position in the federation began to suffer serious reverses. In 1965 "the Reform," a packet of liberalizing measures, was approved, which had the effect of loosening the conservative Serb grip on power. One year later came the purge of Alexander Ranković. The symbol of Serb nationalism, ideological conservatism, and police power, Ranković also had been a reassurance to many Serbs because he controlled Yugoslavia's internal security. They had proudly hailed him as the "hammer" of the Albanians in Kosovo. In 1968, though, spurred by Ranković's purge and the restlessness in parts of Eastern Europe and other parts of Yugoslavia, serious Albanian student disturbances occurred in Kosovo. They were the first significant warning to Serbia that things in Kosovo were changing forever — a warning that the Serbs refused to take to heart.

The Croatian crisis of 1970–71, the most serious in Tito's Yugoslavia since 1948, also had a strong anti-Serbian edge. Serbs could take some comfort from the way it ended, with the Croatian nationalists temporarily routed, but the more perceptive of them knew that, regardless of its outcome, the crisis signified Serbia's increasing isolation. The more perceptive *Yugoslavs* (i.e., *believers* in Yugoslavia) also feared that this was not the end of something but the beginning of the end. Nationalism still was Yugoslavia's fire bell ringing in the night. It would prevent the Yugoslav dream from ever becoming reality, although no one could have suspected that the nightmare of World

War II would ever be repeated. Most thought that the very ghastliness of that nightmare would itself be the deterrent. Instead, it proved to be just a recurring act in the Balkan grand tragedy.

The Croatian crisis of 1970–71 reminded everybody that the Croat-Serb relationship always had been Yugoslavia's nexus. But Kosovo for many years continued to be its flashpoint. Nothing roused Serbs to anger and stoked the old fires of resentful solidarity more than the upgrading of Kosovo's status in the Yugoslav federation by the new constitution promulgated in 1974. On the national issue, it reflected typical Titoist tactics—or temperament. After cracking down, he often would concede practically all that the victims had ever asked for. Hence, after cracking down on Croatian nationalism in 1971, he proceeded to make considerable concessions to all the republics at the expense of the federal center. In doing so, he made a major concession to Kosovo—and Vojvodina—by giving them veto rights at the federal level equal to those of the republics. Legally, at this level, the two provinces became virtually the equals of Serbia. Vojvodina was affronting enough, but politically it hardly mattered, with well above 50 percent of the population Serb and less than 20 percent Hungarian. But in Kosovo, where Serbs and Montenegrins were slipping down to about 10 percent of the population against the Albanians' 90 percent, it mattered comprehensively—as much emotionally as anything else. It brought home to Serbs the distinct possibility that one day they could lose their sacred heartland to a people that they not only despised but regarded as "criminal interlopers." As long as they could rule Kosovo through faithful Albanian front men, backed by Serb military and police, they were all right. But, if colonialism were collapsing the world over, the same could happen here.

Serbian discontent simmered for several years before exploding. After Tito's death, it grew ominously. The Albanian riots in Kosovo in 1981 were a direct challenge to Serbian dominance. Incidents of violence and intimidation grew throughout the province, and the Serb minority dwindled further, partly because of the violence, partly for economic reasons, partly out of fatalism. Fury and panic were whipped up in the Serb media with reports about Albanian murder and mayhem in Kosovo. Many of the stories were invented or distorted, but by no means all. Even some of the true ones were chilling.[12]

By the middle of the 1980s Serbian resentment about the ungrateful way history was allegedly treating them burst into the open. In 1985 the Serbian government had tried to get Kosovo's right of veto abolished, but the other republics rejected its demand. All except the Montenegrins would have liked Serbia's power reduced further, and, anyway, they enjoyed its discomfiture. In September 1985 a book appeared in Belgrade by a well-known Serb historian that virtually saw the whole of Yugoslav communist history as an anti-Serb conspiracy.[13] In the autumn of 1986, in a more significant and demonstrative event, many members of the Serbian Academy of Sciences, inspired by the famous novelist Dobrica Ćosić, about whom more was to be heard after Yugoslavia's collapse, prepared a memorandum with strong nationalist overtones complaining about the "Vietnamization" of Serbia.[14] This document was a key in the unfolding Yugoslav tragedy. It gave rising Serb nationalism both rationale and respectability. Certainly by the end of 1986, practically the whole Serbian nation—politicians, intellectuals, and common folk—were united in their resentment. A proud nation felt itself at bay. Add to these resentments the Serb *Herrenvolk* complex regarding the Albanians (as well as everybody else in the Balkans), and Yugoslavia had its most highly charged situation since the Croatian crisis of 1970–71.

Slobodan Milošević

All that was needed was a leader to embody and articulate Serb fury and frustration. In *Surge to Freedom,* I put it this way:

> He appeared in the unlikely person of Slobodan Milošević. A senior federal bank official before he catapulted himself to political fame, Milošević was well known to members of the Western banking community who negotiated loans and payments agreements in Belgrade. He struck them as a competent enough bureaucrat; none of them suspected the inner flame that lay concealed, awaiting its cause. Milošević, the classic people's tribune, told the Serbs what they wanted to hear with a simple, direct eloquence. To compare his speeches with those of any of his Yugoslav contemporaries was like comparing night and day. Though Milošević's speeches were imbued with Serbian patriotism, he also declared himself strongly for Yugoslavia ("What kind of Yugoslavia?" asked the Slovenes, Croats, and sundry others). He seldom ranted, and often seemed at pains to be fair to his opponents. His demagogy lay in his ability to stir audiences by depicting the problems that worried them, but without suggesting solutions that even remotely took into account

> the complexities of the situation. His modesty of manner could be disarming, and his almost Spartan life-style contrasted with the corruption festering throughout Yugoslav public life.[15]

That was written in 1990. Two years later, Milošević was held in infamy throughout the world—even nudging out Saddam Hussein as the biggest global villain since Pol Pot. But not much more was really known about him—except for two not always disconnected characteristics: he was a consummate politician and a pathological liar. Several of his unblinking, demonstrable lies about the fighting in Croatia and Bosnia between 1991 and 1993, for example, suggest not only intentional cunning but also a condition of some morbidity. His only real ideology was Serb nationalism; his only politics were Serbia. It was misleading to call him a bolshevik, Stalinist, or "hard-line communist." He was certainly no Jeffersonian; and his experience of Western banking and its practitioners had not converted him to capitalism. But within the Leninist framework he was ready for pragmatism in diplomacy and politics, as well as in economics. He went along with the multiparty system when no other option was available, but he made sure he controlled the media. "Peronism" was the term often used to describe his style and substance of rule. In economics, although keeping the commanding heights for the state, he was prepared to let the rest go to private enterprise. But all of these traits were secondary; what counted for Milošević was rescuing his country from the humiliation and impotence into which he and all Serbs were convinced it had drifted. In doing so, he blundered into a catastrophe for which he must take most of the personal blame.

Having secured power in Serbia in 1987, he set about saving, as he saw it, the endangered freedom and dignity of Serbs throughout Yugoslavia. Securing his hold on Serbia was only the first and much the least dangerous part of his policy. He virtually assumed patronage of all Serbs, not just those in Serbia itself, but also those outside it, somewhat loosely called *prečani,* numbering nearly 2.5 million. This concept was dangerously new, sweeping aside what Christopher Cviic has described as the "Titoist 'feudal' principle that had firmly tied each leadership to a particular territory."[16] Many Serbs, in a Yugoslavia that was disintegrating, its different nationalisms gathering strength, and its old certainties disappearing, began to look to the new messiah in Belgrade who was telling them what they wanted to hear.

In view of the oncoming disaster, it is ironical to recall now that, early in 1990, Milošević, although reelected president of Serbia by a big majority only a few months earlier, had suffered a number of reverses at the federal level as well as in Kosovo. His high-handedness as well as his opposition to Ante Marković's economic program offended many liberals in Belgrade. He was beginning to look like an old-fashioned nationalist who was losing his way in a new environment he could not understand. Many (including myself) thought he had "peaked."[17] What we did not foresee was that Yugoslavia would collapse so rapidly. Nor did we anticipate that its collapse would jerk some parts of it back into such primitive tribalism, that is, into the kind of situation made for a primitive nationalist.

Slovenia: The Prelude to Collapse

Slovenia began the collapse. The last phase of Yugoslav history probably began in 1986 when dissident elements there began agitating for sovereignty—at first not sovereignty with independence *outside* Yugoslavia, but sovereignty in a looser form of Yugoslav "confederation."

Slovene nationalism had never played much of a role in either prewar or postwar Yugoslavia, except for the economic nationalism that was bound to affect the most prosperous member of an association that mostly included sponging, insatiable bankrupts. But by the end of the 1980s a broader Slovene nationalism was growing almost in spite of itself, propelled by events both inside and outside Yugoslavia, by the collapse of communism in the Eastern European countries and their liberation from Soviet domination, and by the failure of the Yugoslav nations to devise a new formula for living together. In Slovenia, though, even as nationalist impulses quickened, political liberalism always was uppermost. First, socialism with a human face, then the blossoming of civil society, and finally a liberal democratic system and the transition to the market economy.

When the Slovenes did set their sights on full independence, they got it inside of a year. After a mounting series of crises that began in 1989, the Slovenian assembly in Ljubljana declared sovereignty. In a plebiscite the following December the Slovene people in overwhelming numbers voted for independence. Both the Slovene and Croatian governments already had put forward their proposals for what they called a Yugoslav confederation "organized like the European Community." Actually, there was much vagueness and some disingenuousness in this proposal. Essentially, in the developing Yugoslav context, it meant full independence. The European Community analogy was a fig leaf. The Serbs realized this sleight of hand, and the confederation idea got nowhere. Subsequently, in the first few months of 1991 the Slovenes assumed an unaccustomed role of nationalist pacesetters in the crumbling federation. Slovenia, not Croatia, could act in this way because it mattered much less to Yugoslavia's survival than Croatia did. Nor did Slovenia's economic strength count for much in a situation that now had gone beyond economics. Even more important and fortunate for Slovenia was the fact that it was ethnically almost homogeneous, or, more to the point, it had, unlike Croatia, no Serbs to speak of. Slovenia was compact and situated right at the northwest tip of Yugoslavia—ripe enough and ready to drop off the edge. Culturally, too, Slovenes had often felt closer to Austria than to any of their South Slav bedfellows, many of whom had resented the Slovenes' "Germanness." "The only Slavs who yodel," was their unbrotherly scoff.

Still, Slovenia did not drop off without a struggle of sorts. Proclaiming complete independence in June 1991, the Slovene government administered and took over all Yugoslav rights and responsibilities on its territory, including the control of federal frontier posts. After a series of encounters and skirmishes in which Yugoslav ground units performed dismally and federal airplanes bombed Slovene targets unnecessarily and ineffectually, the war of independence was won. Slovenia was free. It could leave before the tragedy began.[18]

The Revival of Croatian Nationalism

More than Kosovo, far more than Slovenia, it was the increasingly bitter interaction between Croatia and Serbia that presented the biggest danger to Yugoslavia's survival. Relations between the two nations had been blighted by jealousy, hatred, and the most atrocious violence. But both nations had known that for as long as there was a Yugoslavia, their fates were intertwined. They were hostage to Yugoslavia's survival. Both also knew that separation, however desirable it might seem to many, might be impossible without serious bloodshed.

Croatian nationalism had ruined the prospects of the Serb-dominated interwar Yugoslavia, and, as mentioned, the outburst of Croatian nationalism in 1970–71 had caused communist Yugoslavia's worst domestic crisis till that time. After 1971, Croatia had retreated into hibernation. Politics became conventional and conservative, and the nation as a whole lapsed into one of its familiar bouts of moody introspection. But the crises in 1989 in Kosovo and Slovenia shook the Croats out of their languor.

Unlike in Serbia, where nationalism revived under orthodox communist rule, it was democracy that helped revive nationalism in Croatia. The Slovenes were first in the race for democratic elections, but the Croats ran them a close second. Croatia's first free general election in more than half a century resulted in an overall majority for the Croatian Democratic Community coalition, led by Franjo Tudjman. A young Partisan general under Tito during the war, Tudjman eventually moved to strongly Croatian nationalist positions and had been imprisoned after the crisis of 1971. He had been a controversial figure for several years largely because of what some considered a rabid anti-Serb attitude and for statements smacking of the Ustaša-type nationalism that had ruined Croatia's reputation during World War II. After his election, he moderated his language but not his prejudices. As for democracy, he preached it, and benefited from it, but has shown few signs of real conversion to it.[19]

Tudjman's election victory, his own reputation, the anti-Serb passions of many of his supporters, and the whole atmosphere of extremism in which Croat politics now seemed to be engulfed, thoroughly alarmed Croatia's large Serb minority—some 12 percent of the total population, numbering between 500,000 and 600,000. Many of them lived in and around Zagreb, but most lived in districts on the border with Bosnia-Hercegovina that were for the most part ethnically homogeneous: Knin-Benkovac on the Dalmatian coast, Lika, the Kordun, and Banija. (These Serbs, mainly of peasant stock, generally were tough and uncompromising, whereas those in Zagreb were more sophisticated and integrated into the Croatian way of life. Indeed, Tudjman's first great mistake may have been to think that all Serbs in Croatia were like those in Zagreb.) The dual effect of Milošević's one-nation mind-set and Tudjman's electoral victory made these Serbian enclaves ripe for disruption. The first serious case of it occurred in Knin in the summer and autumn of 1990. The details were widely reported at the time.[20] Basically, the disturbance stemmed from demands from all of the Serb communities for cultural autonomy, and eventually political autonomy, inside Croatia. But few doubted that many Serbs hoped for detachment from Croatia. In the late summer, disturbances spread to other Serb enclaves but soon petered out without serious bloodshed.

These disturbances in the summer of 1990 were minor compared with what was to come. But most Yugoslavs already were aware of their serious implications. Serb-Croat distrust was as deep as ever, and the memories of a half-century before came flooding back. Next time the incidents could be major ones. If civil war came to Yugoslavia, it would begin here.

The Bosnian Background

The incidents in the Serbian enclaves in Croatia reminded everyone of the role that Bosnia-Hercegovina might play in the future of Yugoslavia—either in its reconstruction or in its dissolution. The southern Slav republic par excellence, multiethnic and multireligious, Bosnia-Hercegovina had played a relatively subdued role so far in Yugoslavia's history. But most observers always had seen it as the key to the country's future.

The very artificiality of Bosnia-Hercegovina gave it both its significance and its weakness as a nation-state. Its ethnic composition was about 43 percent Muslim, 33 percent Serb, and 18 percent Croat. This mixture and the fact that no ethnic community had a decisive majority were the basic reasons for Bosnia-Hercegovina's vulnerability, even more so than its overall economic, social, and cultural backwardness. Serbia had historical and ethnic claims to large parts of it; Croatia had similar claims. Both claims were being aired with increasing persistence (although ostensibly unofficially) at the end of the 1980s. And the claims overlapped, with Serbs and Croats sometimes claiming the same territory and ever-higher numbers of ethnic kinsmen. In the crossfire of these claims were the Muslims. The descendants of converts to Islam during the Ottoman occupation, the Muslims of Bosnia-Hercegovina (though not the Muslim Albanians of Kosovo) were allowed by Tito after 1968 to become members of the new Yugoslav Muslim nation.[21]

Bosnia-Hercegovina had been created to keep Serbs and Croats apart, an essential precondition for a stable Yugoslavia, and the decision regarding Muslim nationhood was, in part, a further step toward this end. For a while, this arrangement seemed to be succeeding, but as the promise of Tito's Yugoslavia faded, it was only a matter of time before the hollowness of the Bosnia-Hercegovina solution became apparent, only a matter of time before the Serb-Croat scramble for both its territory and its citizenry began. And, finally, there were those crucial Serbian enclaves in Croatia, mostly separated from Serbia by Bosnian territory. As Yugoslavia continued to disintegrate, it made Bosnia-Hercegovina ever more vulnerable. Whereas Slovenia could escape at the edge of Yugoslavia, Bosnia was captive in the middle.

In these circumstances, how stable was the republic internally? How much Bosnian or Hercegovinan consciousness could survive? Such a consciousness had been seen as essential to the development of the Yugoslav consciousness. But whatever Yugoslav consciousness that had existed was fast disappearing in 1990. How much of a Bosnian-Hercegovinan consciousness had, indeed, *ever* existed? Mainly among the Muslims. It gave statehood to their religion; it legitimized their sense of nationhood; it gave them dignity and power. They had to share their power, but they still had enough to feel relatively secure for the first time since Ottoman rule. Besides, power brought place and patronage, which those Muslims who benefited had no difficulty in accepting. For the Serbs and Croats it was different. For most of them Bosnia-Hercegovina was a political arrangement made by Tito after World War II. For them, it was not a nation-state as it was for the Muslims. The Bosnian Serbs, in particular, always had been known for their strong Pan-Serb sentiments, a fact that was to be shown in their resistance in 1993 to the Vance-Owen plan (see below, p. 262). This difference in attitude became more marked as the tensions within Yugoslavia increased. The Muslims started caring even more about Bosnia-Hercegovina; its Serbs and Croats even less.

Serbia's Back to the Wall

The Serbian position on Slovenian and Croatian demands for sovereignty and confederation was quite clear. The federal system still had, a coordinating, if not a unifying, role to play.[22] The Yugoslav people as a whole, not by republics, should be consulted about Yugoslavia's future in the form of a countrywide referendum. (The Serb position on this issue was exactly like Gorbachev's in the Soviet Union.) If, eventually, Yugoslavia were to break up, then there must be a revision of the republican borders established by Tito after World War II. (Some Serbs were saying that the borders were as arbitrary as those drawn by the imperialist powers in Africa and the Middle East.) This revision would, in effect, mean the incorporation of virtually all Yugoslav Serbs in Serbia. It was this insistence, totally unacceptable to all other republican governments and contrary to accepted international principles and practice, that soon was to lead to the Yugoslav tragedy. The Serbs argued that theirs was a special case, that the borders in question were not international but internal Yugoslav and had been deliberately designed to weaken Serbia. Coming more to the substance of the issue, they claimed that the safety of Serb minorities, particularly in Croatia, could not be guaranteed. The situation, in fact, easily could return to that of World War II when hundreds of thousands of Serbs were massacred in Croatia and Bosnia.[23]

The Serbs unquestionably had a case, and there was some international understanding for it. But behind the rationale of their position was a psychological and emotional basis that would find little support anywhere. Serbs instinctively refused to accept the "indignity" of minority status in any potential Yugoslav successor state. Toward all other Yugoslav nations, as well as several others in the region, their attitude ranged between lofty superiority and outright contempt. Minority status might be for others, but not for them. Many Russians soon were to feel the same way. Many Hungarians had, too, after Trianon. So had many Germans after World War I. Minority status was not for major nations.

It was clearly not just Milošević and his political followers who argued and felt this way. Practically every Serb throughout Yugoslavia (not to mention the worldwide diaspora) shared his conviction. A relatively small number of liberals in Belgrade might deplore the demagogy and the crudity of the demand, and some of the Serbs in Zagreb were distinctly uncomfortable about it, but by this time they were of little importance. The opposition parties that had crept into political life in Serbia during 1989 also were strongly nationalistic. In fact, Milošević sometimes began to seem restrained, at least in public, compared with some of his domestic opponents. His most notable opponent at the time was the writer Vuk Drašković, leader of the Serbian Movement for Renewal, a party that made its appeal to anticommunist nationalists. Even if the Yugoslav federation were to survive, Drašković and his followers argued that at least two autonomous districts should be carved out of the Serbian majority areas in Croatia.

In Bosnia-Hercegovina, more Serbian autonomous districts should be created. Furthermore, the city of Dubrovnik, once part of Serbia but now in Croatia (and with only about a 10 percent Serb population), should have a "special status." Here, the claims were vague, but somehow Serbia's historical ownership should be recognized.[24] Later, though, for reasons of political expediency and perhaps out of sincere revulsion at the cruelty and carnage, Drašković was to change his course radically and, though remaining a Serb nationalist, strongly opposed "Milošević's War" and became a focal point for Serbia's democratic opposition. The Serbian Chetnik Party (later renamed Radical Party) leader, Vojislav Šešelj, a man of evident psychopathic tendencies, was the crudest of all, deliberately invoking the past in stirring up anti-Croat passions.[25] And, not coincidentally, in the course of 1991 it was Šešelj who began drawing bigger and bigger crowds. Although on a higher plane, Dobrica Ćosić also was an adamant nationalist Serb, especially on the Kosovo issue, but he, too, became much more restrained as the mayhem got out of hand.

All the Serbian political leaders, as well as their followers, were inspired by the old Serbian medieval empire that reached its height in the fourteenth century and then finally fell gloriously at the Battle of Kosovo—the earthly defeat by the Turks in 1389, which, through Serb faith and legend, became transfigured into a heavenly victory and an eternal inspiration. This legend, the subject of a large body of epic poetry and passed down the generations by song or recitation, had sustained Serbs through the long dearth of Ottoman domination, through the struggle for liberation in the nineteenth century, and then through the struggles and privations of two world wars in the twentieth. Now, once more, with Serbia perceived as being in peril and with lurking passions whipped up by demagogy, fear, and hatred, the legend's power, as the essence and touchstone of "Serbianism," was restored. Everybody, outside and inside Yugoslavia, underestimated this dynamic—including, probably, many Serbs themselves at first.

By the middle of 1990 many Serbs were itching to plunge into the post-Tito free-for-all that had been a decade in coming. And they were ready with their demands: if the borders of Stephen Dušan's fourteenth-century empire might seem a little too much, then they would self-sacrificingly settle for those of December 1, 1918. This would mean the inclusion, not only of most of Bosnia-Hercegovina, but the whole of Macedonia, and perhaps of Montenegro. As for Kosovo, it should not just revert to being an integral part of Serbia, but the remaining elements of Albanian autonomy should be abolished or curtailed. (If necessary, recalcitrant Albanians should be deported.)

Much of this old-fashioned nationalism was fueled by a traditional Orthodox religiosity, and it was demonstratively supported by the Orthodox hierarchy, which had played a major role in the revival of Serb nationalism and at first showed no hesitation in allying with communist nationalists on this issue. Indeed, the role played by the Serbian Orthodox Church in fomenting and sustaining recent Serb nationalism should not be ignored. Regarding itself as the true, eternal bearer and representative of "Serbianism," it always had been ready to give its blessing to whatever secular leadership was seen to serve this sacred cause. Hence, it supported the atheist, Milošević, at first. It always had been resentful of what it considered Tito's pro-Albanian, anti-Serb policy in Kosovo, the province that historically symbolized the intertwining of Serbian church and state. "Kosovo is our Jerusalem," intoned Amphilocius, bishop of Vršac,[26] and the meaning of the parallel was lost on nobody. Subsequently, the Church supported Belgrade's policy in Croatia, some of its leaders insisting as strongly as the political leadership that, with the disintegration of Yugoslavia, all Serbs should now live under their own roof. Subsequently, however, in the spring and summer of 1992 the Church turned sharply against Milošević and joined the political opposition in demanding his removal. But while there was no doubt that many church leaders, including the new Patriarch Pavle, found the dictatorial substance and style of Milošević's rule deeply offensive and were seriously concerned about the prospect of civil war in Serbia itself, what also disturbed some of them was his lack of success in pursuing the Serb cause to a surgically swift conclusion. One fiery dignitary made no bones about it:

> Ask the likes of Milošević, Adžić (the former federal defense minister), and others what they were thinking of when they began that war. . . . Now they have all become peacemakers. But in reality they are capitulators before the AVNOJ (the Anti-Fascist Council of National Liberation of Yugoslavia) borders, the AVNOJ grave of this people. . . . They betrayed the Serbs in Macedonia . . . in Krajina . . . in Bosnia and Hercegovina. What will become of the Serbs in Kosovo, in Old Raš, in northern Bačka?[27]

As for the Roman Catholic hierarchy in Croatia, its leaders showed rather more polish. They obviously supported the cause of Croatian independence but their reservations about Tudjman and his style of leadership as well as about subsequent Croatian behavior in Bosnia-Hercegovina, evolved into strong opposition to the Croatian president. Such concern, though, was not always noticeable among many of the lower clergy. Some parish priests identified with extreme nationalist positions in a manner that was bound to recall the Croatian Church's largely wretched record in World War II.[28]

The Serbs in rural Croatia were particularly responsive to the militants in Belgrade. They were vulnerable, and they knew it. Many Serbs throughout Croatia had been part of a privileged governing elite under Tito. To avoid physical extinction by the Ustaša during the war, many had flocked to Tito's banner. And after the war, they were rewarded for their services. Constituting only 12 percent of the population, they numbered a much higher percentage among the Croatian communist party, party officialdom, the bureaucracy, and especially among the police.[29] Tudjman and the Croat nationalists had relished telling them and everybody else that this privileged position would last as long as it took them to win power. But the Serbs in Croatia had other, more genuine grievances after Tudjman came to power. Tudjman made no attempt to placate them; on the contrary, he seemed bent on provoking them. In a book on Balkan nationalism I criticized Tudjman in the following terms:

> The new Croatian constitution of December 1990 was strongly nationalist, giving the Serbs no collective rights as a minority and containing no hint of political autonomy in areas where Serbs are the majority. Moreover the adoption of the traditional Croatian flag, which carried bitter memories for Serbs as the emblem of the fascist *Ustaša* republic of the Second World War, as well as the toleration, even quiet encouragement, of other symbols, reflected at best an insensitivity toward the Serbian minority, at worst a deliberate attempt to humiliate it. To the right of him (Tudjman) in the Croat political spectrum were some virulent and unabashed nationalists. . . . And the extremists in Croatia, as in Serbia, were loudly (and, in many cases, financially) supported by their fellow-nationals in the West. The truth probably was that concessions at the outset to the Serbian minority would not have reconciled it to Croatian independence, but they would have made the Croatian case that much stronger.[30]

The leadership of the Serb minority in Croatia, almost certainly echoing the views of most of its constituents, refused to accept the recently floated idea of a Yugoslav confederation, still less the notion of an independent Croatia. They simply said what Milošević had been saying: the republican borders would have to be revised. And if a single Greater Serbia could not be formed immediately, a second Serbian state would have to be established in the west of what had been Yugoslavia. The Croatian Serbs lost no time in acting. Almost immediately after the promulgation of the new Croatian constitution in December 1990, an "autonomous region of Krajina" was declared in ten areas where Serbs were in a majority. This action was to lead directly to war between Serbia and Croatia the following summer. But the intention behind creating the "autonomous region of Krajina" was that it should link up with Serb regions in Bosnia-Hercegovina to become the new state of West Serbia. This new state would be twice as big as Slovenia, with a population of 3 million to Slovenia's 2 million. After Serbia and Croatia, it would, in fact, be the third largest of the Yugoslav successor states. And the eventual merger of this state with Serbia was seen as a certainty.

The Fatal Link in Bosnia

This idea of linking up Serb-majority areas in Croatia and Bosnia with Serbia proper was to lead to the Bosnian catastrophe. It meant the deliberate breaking up of Croatia and Bosnia-Hercegovina, which was bound to lead to war. But it also led to the barbarism that later was to be inflicted on the Bosnian Muslims who stood in the way of securing the Serbian regional links. "Ethnic cleansing" was the brutal consequence. So were the detention camps that in the summer of 1992 caused outrage in the entire civilized world, not to mention the accompanying brutalities that became part of everyday life in Bosnia-Hercegovina. Of all the atrocities, though, it was the mass rapes of Muslim women—between 20,000 and 50,000—that aroused the worst horror. It was calculated, cynical, and subhuman.[31] And the fact that many of the individual atrocities were committed by alcohol-soused Serb irregulars only compounded the bestiality. Here, however, it must be emphasized that, although the most culpable, the Serbs were to have no monopoly on crimes against humanity in Bosnia-Hercegovina. Enough ghastliness was committed, especially by Croats but also by Muslims, to show that it was a matter of degree rather than of essence.

The horrors almost certainly were intensified by Serb popular contempt for Bosnian Muslims. Many Croats, too, despised and resented the Muslims. Croatia, too, had claims on parts of Bosnia-Hercegovina, certainly the part of western Hercegovina that was adjacent to its borders, several parts of which had Croat majorities. But some Croats, occasionally including Tudjman, previously had claimed the whole of Bosnia-Hercegovina on remote historical grounds and, even less defensibly, because it had been part of the puppet state of Croatia during World War II.[32] On the political and personal levels, though, the Croat-Muslim relationship in Bosnia-Hercegovina had been better than the Serb-Muslim one. The Muslim political community, such as it was before the end of World War II, had generally supported the Croats. The Croats may have had little respect for the Muslims—some thought they were really Croats gone religiously wrong—but they were a useful buffer against the Serbs.

The Serbs' contempt for the Bosnian Muslims was in some ways even greater than what they felt for the Albanians in Kosovo. The Serbs had never forgotten how many Muslims readily joined the slaughter of Serbs by the Ustaša in World War II. But it went even deeper: the Muslims were traitors who had forsaken their (Christian) religion and their (Serb) nation. As Muslims, they also had become the local ruling class in Ottoman times, while the Serbs had been in thrall. The Albanian Kosovars, "criminal interlopers" on sacred Serb territory though they were said to be, were at least not traitors in that they had never had the privilege of being Serbs. Many Serbs at the beginning of the 1990s still would sympathize with the feelings of Stoyan Protić, a leading Serb politician in the 1920s. When asked immediately after World War I what was in store for the Bosnian Muslims, he reportedly replied: "As soon as our Army crosses the Drina (i.e., into Bosnia), it will give the Turks (i.e., Bosnian Muslims) twenty-four—perhaps forty-eight—hours to return to the faith of their forefathers, and then slay those who refuse, as we did in Serbia in the past."[33] Beyond sympathizing with Protić, many Serbs were prepared to do more or less as he suggested.

In the meantime, however, a sea change had come over the Muslims. For many years after the Ottoman collapse they had been docile and head-hanging, asking nothing more than an unnoticing tolerance. Now, at least the younger generation was proud, prickly, and ready to stand toe-to-toe with any Serb or Croat. Being granted nation status after 1968 obviously had played a role in this change, but it also resulted from the growing assertiveness and power of Islam worldwide. The Muslims soon were to put their political and cultural stamp on Bosnia-Hercegovina, and in the November 1990 elections they gave Europe its first Muslim head of state, Alija Izetbegović. Generally, the Bosnian Muslims reflected Islam at its most easygoing, and they were more moderate and tolerant in their religion than either the Serbs or the Croats were in theirs, although Izetbegović himself had earlier been associated with fundamentalism and had spent some years in jail under the communist regime for his writings. But, however moderate the bulk of Bosnia's Muslims were inclined to be, they certainly were not going to be abused in the way that they had been. In 1993 in Sarajevo there were, indeed, signs that some Muslims might be deserting their traditional moderation. Fundamentalism was on the increase and was likely to gain more adherents. And, although they had considered themselves loyal Yugoslavs—they were, in fact, probably the most loyal Yugoslavs of all—many Bosnian Muslims had always preserved a kind of ultramontane affection for Turkey as "heir" to the Ottoman empire. A University of Sarajevo professor used to recall an occasion from the early 1970s when some Muslim road workers were putting up national flags to mark the visit of a dignitary from Ankara. "One of ours" was their chorus when a Turkish flag went up; "one of theirs," when a Yugoslav one did.[34] For any Serbs seeing this display, it only would have confirmed what they had felt all along.

And, as if Muslims beyond their borders were not problem enough, the Serbs had a potentially serious Muslim problem within the borders of Serbia proper. About 250,000 Muslims resided in the Sanjak (formerly called the Sanjak of Novi Pazar), most of them in Serbia and some in Montenegro. Already in 1991 they were demanding autonomy and showing the same kind of assertiveness that Muslims elsewhere in Yugoslavia were displaying. In case of a general Muslim conflagration in the Balkans, they could represent Serbia's most vulnerable point.[35]

The Serbs, therefore, now found themselves confronted with a different kind of Muslim than they were traditionally used to. And this may explain one aspect of the Bosnian war that often went unnoticed: the deliberate effort on the part of some Serb forces to wipe out the new Muslim intelligentsia. Many of the Muslims who were executed—as opposed to being killed in action—by the Serbs were members of this intelligentsia, leading some journalists to coin the expression "elitocide."[36] What Stalin had tried to do with the Katyn massacres in the case of the Poles in World War II, some Serbs were trying to do in Bosnia a half-century later.

The Yugoslav Military and the War

The Serbian strategy of regional linking in both Croatia and Bosnia-Hercegovina was what made war inevitable. Ironically, it was the train of events in Slovenia that precipitated conflict, more specifically the failure of the Yugoslav People's Army (JNA) to stifle Slovenian independence in the summer of 1991. The attempt itself showed the army was prepared to use force. The army's lack of success had two effects, both of which brought war nearer: general fear of the Yugoslav military was reduced, while the resolve of the army's largely Serbian high command to avenge its humiliation in Slovenia by a show of strength in Croatia was strengthened.

The Yugoslav military generally had enjoyed a high reputation throughout the federation. Like that of the Red Army, its prestige dated from World War II. Because of this prestige, the military also came to be regarded as the great unifying factor in the federation, particularly when the few other such factors—Tito himself after 1980; the Soviet threat; the secret police; and the party—had faded into oblivion. The military always had a privileged position and always had pursued an active role in Yugoslav politics. But this role never had been a grossly interfering one. The closest that military force ever came to being used in communist Yugoslavia was when Tito threatened it in the Croatian crisis of December 1971. This threat, plus Tito's towering prestige, brought the crisis to an end. But even in 1971, with Yugoslavia relatively strong and Tito still at the height of his powers, doubts were expressed about how effective military intervention would have been. Some suspected it could have led to civil war, meaning that—even then, in this most supranational of all institutions—nationalist, ethnic centrifugalism would have led to an implosion engulfing the country. By 1990 such suspicions had become near certainties. But many politicians and citizens continued to be wary of the army. It still could daunt and intimidate them.[37]

An increasing number of senior officers in the second half of the 1980s began to voice concern over the state of Yugoslavia, and some of them evidently were prepared to act to prevent further corrosion. This developing concern coincided with a recentralization of the structure of command of the federal army. In the 1960s and 1970s the command, to a considerable extent, had been decentralized along national lines. Thus, most frequently, a Croat general commanded federal units in Croatia, a Macedonian in Macedonia, and so on. During the 1980s, however, this trend was reversed, and Serb generals tended to move back into command positions in other republics. This shift was to be of considerable significance when civil war broke out in 1991. Early in 1988 in Slovenia, when communist power was beginning to disintegrate, the Military Council in Belgrade apparently devised a contingency plan for intervention in case "counterrevolutionary" disorder broke out. Exposure of this plan actually proved a boost to Slovene nationalism.[38] It also strengthened anti-Serb feeling in the republic. The possibility of military action, therefore, contrary to what many expected, stiffened rather than softened national resistance. The power to daunt was waning.

Tension between the military and nationalists in Slovenia continued, and as nationalism gathered strength in Croatia, civil-military tension increased there, too. The trouble in Knin in the summer of 1990 has been discussed. In view of what was to happen the next year, the most disturbing aspect about it was the refusal of federal military units to help the Croatian police in dealing with the rebellious Serbs. (The Croats complained that their police actually had been *prevented* by federal units from taking necessary action.) This naturally strengthened the conviction in Zagreb that the military was simply the tool of Serbia.

An even more serious incident took place in Ljubljana at the end of September 1990. An amendment to the republic's constitution transferred control over Slovenian territorial defense forces from the federal to the state presidency. The Yugoslav federal secretariat for national defense denounced the measure as unconstitutional and threatened steps to prevent it from being implemented. But the Slovene authorities announced that they were replacing the federally appointed general who commanded the republic's territorial defense forces with a Slovene officer. The dispute became centered on the control of the territorial defense force headquarters in Ljubljana. Tension was eased, at least temporarily, when the Slovenes set up their own defense force headquarters. Now, therefore, Slovenia had two such establishments—one federal, one republican! There was an opéra bouffe aspect to the whole affair, very Slovene in its practical way out and its avoidance of bloodshed. But this first big challenge to their sovereignty aroused much emotion, even among the placid Slovenes.[39] If a new incident occurred, it might not be managed with such finesse. And if something similar were to occur in Zagreb, it might not be handled with such maturity.

The unsuccessful effort by Yugoslav army units in the summer of 1991 to nip Slovene independence in the bud was the last genuine action by the Yugoslav military as such. From then on the Yugoslav federal government quietly disintegrated, and what remained of it became totally identified with Serbian national interests. Behind the fiction of Yugoslavia, there now stood only the reality of Serbian power. For its senior officer corps, 70 percent of which continued to be Serb (and Montenegrin), this was no problem. But for the rest of the army, especially the enlisted men of various nationalities, it became a major question of allegiance, which many of them solved with their feet. Some 12 percent of these men were Albanian, and in 1988 one new recruit in four was reported as being Albanian.[40] Desertions of "other nationalities" were to increase sharply as the Yugoslav civil war intensified. The Yugoslav People's Army, heir to the Partisans and the "Club of 41," had melted away—with Yugoslavia itself.

As the federal army became more and more identified with Serbia, the question of its relation with the government of Serbia—with Slobodan Milošević, in effect—became more acute. What were civil-military relations in Serbia? Who was running whom? Did the army have an agenda different from, in defiance of, Milošević? Was it more to blame than Milošević for what eventually happened?

The answer seems to be that a virtual identity of aims existed between the officer corps and Milošević and broad agreement on the strategy of territorial linkup. Both parties had the same attitude toward the Yugoslav crisis, the same sense of Serb superiority and of Serb solidarity. As for military tactics and methods at the front, the army command appears to have done more or less as it liked. This approach was convenient for Milošević because it gave him room for international maneuver and scope for "deniability." But as the war developed in both Croatia and Bosnia-Hercegovina, the army was not the only force operating on the Serb side. By far the most fearsome were the local Serb militias and irregulars who set new post-World War II standards in savagery. It was they who mainly took over the fighting in Bosnia-Hercegovina after federal units had been officially withdrawn. Milošević could not fully control these units either, but, in the main, they were doing his dirty work for him. Moreover, his initially good relations with the ferocious Šešelj only gave the impression of connivance in the barbarities at the front. In Serbia he primed the propaganda pumps, as did Tudjman in Croatia. In fact, the misuse of the media, especially television, has been a characteristic of the Yugoslav civil war. Both Belgrade and Zagreb used television, newspapers, and journals to paint the most hideous possible picture of the other side.[41] In addition, Milošević used his media in attempts to refute the multiplying charges of Serbian atrocities, seeking, with considerable effect, to portray his compatriots as victims of a world conspiracy of denigration. True, the odd Serbian sinner may exist, but the Serbian nation was much more sinned against than sinning. The self-pity gushed.

Spreading to Kosovo?

In Tito's time there consistently had been more unrest in Kosovo than in any other part of Yugoslavia. The rioting in 1968 has been mentioned, and throughout the 1970s a whole series of incidents, isolated and connected, occurred, usually unreported, even in the local press. Sporadic violence between the proliferating Albanians and the dwindling Serbians became part of a Kosovo way of life that climaxed with the riots in 1981. Throughout the 1980s the violence escalated and began to be reported, if often inaccurately, in different sections of the Yugoslav press; it also was picked up in the Western media.

The sharpening of ethnic tensions reflected the shifting moods of the nations concerned. The Muslim Albanian Kosovars, backward and subservient, historically had presented little problem to Serbian rule, although some Serbs always had seen them as a potential threat. Like the Bosnian and Sanjak Muslims (and the Christian Macedonians), the Kosovars generally were dismissed throughout the Balkans as backward and submissive. But occasionally they did punctuate their passivity with fits of bloodcurdling fury. Besides, the creation of Greater Albania during World War II—the union of Kosovo with Albania proper—had been historically uplifting for all Albanians. Never mind it being Axis-sponsored! Albania's enemies were not Germans and Italians but Serbs and Montenegrins, on many of whom they wreaked terrible vengeance during the war. But after World War II, with the dream of Greater Albania shattered and the historic Balkan seesaw swinging once again, it was the Kosovars' turn to taste Serb revenge.

The Serbs' response to the growing Albanian assertiveness in the 1960s was one of outrage, plus the hardening suspicion that it was part of the Yugoslav anti-Serb conspiracy. In addition, the famous Serb heroic slogan, "Only Solidarity Saves the Serb," with all its ominous implications, again acquired meaning. Kosovo was indeed the Serbs' Jerusalem, and they never would give it up. But this determination was now being met, not only by the Kosovars' growing self-confidence, but by the beginnings of a rudimentary Kosovar structure of resistance. The real authority in the province lay not with the Serbs' Albanian collaborators, but with "true Kosovars," intellectuals, schoolteachers, professional men, and Muslim clergy. These leaders commanded an ever-wider loyalty, especially among the young, and steadily among Kosovar workers and peasants, too. The lines of confrontation were being drawn, as history was turning against the Serbs. And in the Serbs' anger it was Milošević to whom they turned.[42] He first tried repression in 1989, and failed; then he resorted to "legal" means — basic changes in the constitutional status of Kosovo.

It was becoming necessary for the Kosovars to act quickly. On July 2, 1990, a historic decision was made by the Albanian ethnic majority in the Kosovo provincial assembly, the province's constitutional legislative body. It may go down in history as one of the great days in the entire history of Albanian nationhood. The members declared Kosovo "an independent unit" in the Yugoslav community, equal to the other republics. The demand of republican status for Kosovo had now been met by the Kosovars themselves. Kosovo declared its sovereignty according to the principle of self-determination. In the future this decision may become known as Kosovo's own "declaration of independence." It came on the same day that the Slovenian assembly in Ljubljana declared Slovenia's sovereignty, a move that concluded a long period of political and national reawakening. Whether the timing of the moves in Ljubljana and Priština, the capital of Kosovo, was orchestrated is not particularly important, but the Albanian action was of decisive importance in Yugoslav politics, attracting much sympathy throughout the federation as well as in the West.[43]

The Serb response was indeed swift. A new Serbian constitution was approved in September 1990. It did pay lip service to democracy by legalizing the multiparty system, free elections with opposition participation, the separation of powers, and the market economy. But its leitmotiv was nationalism and its thrust anti-Albanian. It made Serbia a unitary, sovereign republic. Neither the province of Kosovo nor Vojvodina disappeared as such, but their former constitutions were abrogated. They lost the large degree of autonomy that they had enjoyed since 1974. The new Serb constitution also reflected Belgrade's determination not to give the Albanians in Kosovo any specific minority rights. It guaranteed *all* citizens of Serbia the same rights whatever their nationality. Thus, while the Kosovars were demanding a sovereign republic, the Serbs were refusing to recognize their collective legal existence.

The mass of Kosovars did not physically resist; rather, they indulged in militant noncooperation, and it was then that Serbia began to treat Kosovo as an occupied territory. Some Albanian legislators already had been imprisoned; others had taken refuge in Croatia and Slovenia. Some members of the Kosovo government also had been arrested, and in the many factories in which a Serbian administration was installed, thousands of Albanian workers were dismissed. Many Albanian doctors, lawyers, teachers, and other professional people also lost their jobs in 1991. It was estimated that, in all, more than 100,000 people were affected up to July 1992.[44] Albanian schools were shut down, and the University of Priština, a center of Kosovar nationalism, was closed. The Serbian authorities in Belgrade also refused to register legally the Kosovo Democratic Union that had been established in the summer, considering it a subversive, national organization, although the Union had been accepted and registered at the federal level. The vast majority of Albanians responded by boycotting the presidential and parliamentary elections held throughout Serbia in December 1991.

The boycott was an impressive demonstration of Albanian power, and a sign of just how far the Albanian Kosovars had come. Their boldness was a factor, too, in the mobilization of the anticommunist forces in Albania itself in the course of 1991. Indeed, as the border with Albania became more porous, despite Serbian attempts to seal it, the "subversive" traffic across it increased in both directions. Kosovar resistance became all the broader, tougher, and more articulate. In September 1991 a referendum on Kosovar independence was held, despite strenuous Serb efforts to prevent it. The result was a foregone conclusion: an overwhelming majority for it. There was no going back.

But, as the Croatian situation drifted into war, and then war broke out in Bosnia-Hercegovina, too, something of a lull descended on Kosovo, although Serbian repression continued. After March 1992, however, with the big democratic victory in Albania itself and the increasingly open concern being expressed there about Kosovo, developments in the two parts of the Albanian-speaking world began to interact even more strongly; obviously, the chaos in other parts of the former Yugoslav federation had its influence. Kosovar confidence increased along with Serbian nervousness. At the end of May 1992 the Kosovars held an "illegal" election for a secret, independent parliament. Ibrahim Rugova, the quiet intellectual who had led the historic rebellion, was elected president of the independently proclaimed Kosovar republic.[45] His party, the Kosovo Democratic Union, won a clear majority of votes.

Serbia did not react massively, as some had expected. But for the bloody imbroglio in Bosnia-Hercegovina and the extent of world reaction, it almost certainly would have done so. The breaking point, though, seemed near. Serbia's position might be unsustainable, but that did not mean the Serbs would accept this situation quietly. If ever they used force, they would face a Kosovo Albanian population that, while not exactly defenseless, had practically no military organization. And the Kosovars then would look for support to Albania where some prominent figures had indicated that in such a contingency Albanians would have to intervene. Kosovo could be the spark for a general Balkan conflagration; and with the Muslim factor added, an even broader outbreak could occur. In addition, the United States as well as members of the European Community had specifically warned Serbia against massive repression in Kosovo.

Albania and Kosovo

In an interview with a West European newspaper in August 1992, Ibrahim Rugova emphatically ruled out any further constitutional association with Serbia or with any present or future Yugoslavia. Kosovo's aim was an independent, neutral republic. That, said Rugova, would be the best solution for both Serbia and Albania. But then came the inevitable rider. "Over the longer term, it is the declared aim of the Kosovo Democratic Union to seek union with the Motherland."[46] Rugova, however, urged the need for realism: the CSCE rules unmistakably laid down that borders could be changed only by consent and peaceful means. He sensed a general international understanding for the plight of the Kosovars, but they still lacked effective partners. Such statements were those of a moderate, criticized by many younger Kosovar radicals as being "Gandhi-ite." The question was how long patience like Rugova's could contain a major violent outbreak.

For many years after World War II neither Kosovars nor Albanians had been much interested in reunion. No public support whatsoever under Hoxha was shown for such a move, and the communist ruling elite always had been highly circumspect about claims to Kosovo. This hesitance on the issue was partly because Albania was more or less in a continual state of siege as well as because, as many suspected, Albanians were indulging in their own variation of historical tribalism. The communist elite was overwhelmingly Tosk, the dominant tribe of southern Albania. But the Tosks made up only about 35 percent of the entire population, with the northern Albanian Ghegs numbering 63 percent. The Kosovars are overwhelmingly Gheg. Their incorporation into Albania, therefore, would have meant that it would become that much more difficult for the Tosks to retain control.

On the other side of the border, once the post-World War II Serb "pacification" of Kosovo had been completed, and especially after the fall of Ranković, the lot of the Kosovars noticeably improved. Although Kosovo remained the most backward part of Yugoslavia, it still was much better off than Albania. Life under Tito was a paradise compared with life under Hoxha, and, however great their grievances, the Kosovars were not interested in changing. Yet the awareness of belonging to the same nation lingered. In *Surge to Freedom* I quoted a poignant example:

> A friend of mine knew one of the few senior Yugoslav civil servants of Albanian nationality. This man—sophisticated, cosmopolitan, Yugoslav—made an official visit to Tirana in 1986. When asked his impression of what is unquestionably the most retarded metropolis in the whole of Europe, he replied that he had never in his life felt more at home—and less Albanian.[47]

And the Kosovars' penchant for flying the Albanian flag whenever they could get away with it—the famous black double-headed eagle on the dark red field—obviously meant something. They knew what it meant; so did the Albanians. So did the Serbs.

Macedonia: Freedom's Fragility

Macedonia and Albania were the last two big remnants of the Ottoman empire. As the empire collapsed, both of them were prey to successor states that refused to recognize for others the same rights of national expression that they themselves had wanted and got. Both of them suffered as a consequence, the Macedonians more than the Albanians in one crucial respect. Whereas the Albanians at least were recognized as a distinct nation, however despised, the Macedonians were not—and their own sense of nationality was dim and undeveloped, anyway. While Albanians, whatever their religion—Muslim, Catholic, or Orthodox—generally had been regarded as Albanians, Macedonians were not accorded a separate nationality at all. Most of them were considered Greek or Bulgarian, depending on which national branch of the Eastern Orthodox Church they belonged to. Inhabitants of the same village often had been thus divided.[48]

In 1893 the Internal Macedonian Revolutionary Organization (IMRO) was established, designed to rekindle the ancient idea of nationhood and fight for an independent Macedonia. It suffered a serious defeat in 1903, split into two, one part still insisting on Macedonian independence, the other for incorporation into Bulgaria; eventually, IMRO became a byword for gangsterism and international terrorism. After operating freely in Bulgaria for many years, it was fully suppressed in 1936. But the ideal of the original IMRO—for a free, independent Macedonia—was never lost sight of.[49]

After their oppressive treatment by Serbia in prewar Yugoslavia, Macedonians blossomed in the dignity that Tito offered them. But Macedonia continued to be the object rather than the subject of Balkan relations. Its existence was accepted, but Greeks, Bulgarians, and most Serbians viewed it as artificial. And many Macedonians seemed content with a status that was tolerated rather than fully recognized.

This Macedonian passivity lasted about forty years. But as Yugoslav unity began to crumble in the late 1980s, a more positive, assertive, and politicized Macedonian nationalism began to develop. Several factors inspired it: the Slovene and Croat examples; the growing threat of Serbian nationalism; the realization that, not only Yugoslavia, but the whole international order was changing and that Macedonia faced both dangers and opportunities. But there was another reason, within Macedonia itself: the proliferation of the Albanian minority and the dangers, as seen by Slav Macedonians, of its interacting with developments in Kosovo and Albania (see chapter 6). The whole situation was changing, and particularly many young Macedonians were eager to board the Balkan nationalist carousel that was already quickly spinning. Alexander the Great and IMRO were their sources of inspiration.[50]

Majority opinion in Macedonia, though (as far as it could be judged), was very late in abandoning the Yugoslav idea and aspiring to total independence. Along with the Bosnian government, the authorities in Skopje at first favored the continuation of a looser form of federation and then a "confederation." While Bosnian hesitation stemmed mainly from its ethnic divisiveness, Macedonia was concerned mainly with its economic and international vulnerability.

This persisting sympathy with the Yugoslav idea — practical, rather than emotional and ideological — found its principal political expression in the reformed and renamed communist party (now the Party of Democratic Transformation). It was headed by Titoist veteran Kiro Gligorov (see chapter 6). His background dogged him, but Gligorov, like the former communist Milan Kučan in Slovenia, emerged as a responsible leader. His reform communists had been expected to win Macedonia's first-ever democratic elections in November 1990, as their counterparts had done in Serbia and Montenegro, thus ensuring the survival of at least a Yugoslav triangle of states. But what happened showed the complexity of Macedonian ethnic politics in general and an ominous similarity with those of Bosnia-Hercegovina. The Macedonian nationalist parties were expected to make a respectable showing — nothing more. The Movement for All-Macedonian Action (MAAK), which included some prominent intellectuals, called for the unity of all Macedonians but remained vague about Yugoslavia's future and Macedonia's place in it. The second nationalist grouping was the reincarnated IMRO, legalized in the summer of 1990 and already a focal point of rising nationalist sentiment. It was drawing support away from MAAK because it was more radical.

In the first round of elections, general expectations were fulfilled; the former communists did appreciably better than the nationalists. But the party unofficially representing the Albanians in the republic did surprisingly well. What followed in the second round reflected the power of nationalism and national prejudice. On the strength of anti-Albanian feeling, IMRO now topped the poll and finished with the most seats in the new assembly. It was far from having a majority, but it was back.[51] Back, though not quite with the bang that many expected. Gligorov used his tactical skills to deny it the political influence its numbers seemed to warrant. He was much more than a match for the IMRO leader, Lupčo Georgievski, a political sheep in his nationalist wolf's clothing.[52]

But with the collapse of Yugoslavia and its own declaration of independence, Macedonia moved out of the protective shelter it had enjoyed for four decades and into the center of a Balkan imbroglio that seemed to take history back, not to the end of World War II, but to the years before World War I. As is pointed out in chapter 6, the historical "Macedonian Question" was back. Its context now was somewhat different but its crux remained constant: Macedonia's crucial geopolitical importance.

Bosnia, Serbia, and the West

Western attempts to mediate and settle the conflicts that had arisen in what soon became known as the "former Yugoslavia" remain to be discussed. An outline for a settlement of the Bosnian-Hercegovinan conflict was presented in January 1993 in Geneva by Cyrus Vance, chief UN negotiator, and Lord (David) Owen, his European Community counterpart. It was accepted with alacrity by the Croats and reluctantly by the Muslims, but appeared in danger of permanently stalling through Serb intransigence. Although the outline proposed the preservation of the sovereignty of Bosnia and Hercegovina, it also suggested the massive dilution of the powers of the surviving organs of central government. Much power then would devolve to the governing authorities of the ten autonomous provinces into which the republic would be divided. Of these ten provinces, there were three each in which Serbs, Muslims, and Croats would predominate, with Sarajevo remaining the nominal capital. The central power, such as it remained, would be shared among the three constituent nationalities. The Vance-Owen proposal came after a number of critical developments relating to the former Yugoslavia during the previous six months.

The *first* of these developments involved events inside Serbia. In elections in December 1992 Milošević had emerged victorious in the presidential election, and his Socialist Party, together with Šešelj's Radicals, which polled ominously well, won a clear victory in the parliamentary elections.[53] The event was marked by extensive and palpable fraud, but honest elections would not have materially changed the outcome in spite of the early optimism of the democratic opposition and the predictions of many Western journalists.

If not fairly and squarely, Milošević won clearly. His victory occurred in spite of a sharp reduction in his popularity during the course of 1992, mainly because of the growing destitution caused by the UN embargo imposed in May of that year. But destitution had not yet become disaffection. Milošević still could manipulate the Serb fighting spirit and sense of grievance. However perverse this variation of *Serbia contra mundum* was, it continued to have drawing power. The election also marked the end of the influence of Milan Panić, the Serb-American businessman who had jetted in from Los Angeles earlier in the year to become prime minister of rump Yugoslavia (Serbia and Montenegro). Many first suspected him of being Milošević's stooge, brought over specially to disarm an increasingly exasperated West. Others saw him as a Serbian Ross Perot, full of well intentioned vim and folksiness. But, whatever Panić began as, he became a strong enemy of Milošević, patriotically Serb but still opposed to the Bosnian war and the spiritual as well as material effect it was having on Serbia. Panić stood against Milošević for the presidency in December, but his late-starting, amateurish campaign had no chance. At the end of 1992 he was voted out of the premiership of Yugoslavia by his vindictively victorious opponents, and thus he seemed to move irrevocably out of Serbian history. But while he lasted he had been a breath of fresh air in an increasingly fetid atmosphere.

Serbia's main hope now seemed to lay with Dobrica Ćosić, president of the rump Yugoslavia. Many also had considered him to be Milošević's stooge. But Ćosić was nobody's stooge. His earlier support for Milošević changed when he saw the disgrace and eventual ruin the latter embodied. He seemed more likely than any opposition politician to end the war and restore sense to Serbia. But already he had fallen foul of Šešelj and the extreme nationalists. First, they threatened to impeach him, but he seemed too strong and sure of Milošević's support. Then, in a surprise move at the beginning of June 1993, he was toppled by a vote in the Yugoslav parliament. Although the move may have been initiated by Šešelj, it could not have succeeded without Milošević's support. The latter's motives remained obscure. Was Ćosić becoming too "big" a figure, and too conciliatory to Serbia's "enemies," both within and without, thereby threatening both Milošević's preeminence and his policies? Or was his removal not just on Šešelj's initiative but at his insistence? Whatever the answer, it was becoming clear that Šešelj was emerging as an independent political factor. He showed this the following October when he openly turned against Milošević. For men like Šešelj, there were definitely "blank spots" in Milošević's conduct of the war—his temporary peace settlement with Croatia in early 1992, for example, and his pressure on Radovan Karadžić, the Bosnian Serb leader, into acceptance of the Vance-Owen plan for Bosnia-Hercegovina, an acceptance that was subsequently repudiated by the Bosnian-Serb "parliament."[54] No doubt for some extreme Serbs Milošević was becoming too much the diplomat, the peacemaker, the appeaser rather than the patriot-redeemer he once seemed to be.

The *second* critical development was the increasing Western concern, particularly American, and the increased discussion about whether and how to protect the Bosnian Muslims and to punish the Serbs. This concern reflected not so much a hardening of Western resolve but a pricking of the Western conscience over Serbian conduct in Bosnia-Hercegovina as well as the realization that international sanctions were not working fast enough. But apparently no strategic concept was clear of how the war there should be brought to an end or how the postwar situation in the region should look.[55] And for all its concern, the West's credibility also was weakened by recurring statements, both in the United States and in Western Europe, about the difficulties and risks of military involvement.[56] Many Western public figures, particularly in the United States, seemed content to bask in the self-indulgent rays of moral outrage, rather than coolly devise a policy and define aims that weighed possible gains against the evident risks.

The *third* critical development was the increasing concern in the Muslim world about the fate of the Bosnian Muslims and the talk of intervention by Islamic international organizations and by individual Muslim countries. By the end of 1992, however, probably only about a thousand mujaheddin were fighting in Bosnia and the prospects of the early arrival of large contingents of Muslim troops seemed remote.[57] But the fear could not be entirely discounted. The likelihood of large supplies of weapons from Muslim countries to beat the international arms embargo that affected not just the Serbs but the Muslims was much more imminent. And eventually, as mentioned, there was the fear of the war spreading into other Muslim parts of the Balkans and this larger conflict then becoming a Slavic-Muslim or Christian-Islamic confrontation. The role of Turkey in such a context—a possible Turkish return to the Balkans—was becoming the subject of increased speculation (see chapters 6 and 8). Some of these fears about a larger war and Muslim involvement may have been overdrawn, but they served to quicken Western concern and enliven the agitation for preventive action.

Western Illusions and Confusions

The Western powers, particularly the United States, France, and Britain, for too long had hoped that Yugoslavia in some form could be maintained. (All three countries also began with a considerable pro-Serb bias, which steadily was eroded as Serbian atrocities began to mount.) Slovenia's successful resistance in June–July 1991 against the Yugoslav federal army was the beginning of the end of such hopes. The hope then was that if Yugoslavia had to fall apart, it would do so peacefully. The federal army's subsequent intervention in Croatia scuttled that hope. The civil war then began in earnest, and, not until after some debate as to whether the Balkans were worth any effort at all, the West tried to stop it. But the feeble attempts showed, not the West's influence, but its impotence.[58]

The Yugoslav situation seemed to be mainly the European Community's responsibility. This war was, after all, becoming the biggest threat to European peace since 1945 and, as such, fell, at least implicitly, within the Community's terms of reference. But in its first big test as international arbiter and domestic European peacekeeper, the Community's performance was little short of pitiable. The peace conference on Croatia that the Community organized at The Hague in 1991 had sponsored fourteen cease-fires already by the end of that year, all of which were broken; the conflict in Croatia simply escalated. The Community appeared totally ineffectual, and Lord Carrington, a former British foreign secretary, had to bear the brunt of the criticism. The real explanation for failure, though, was the Community's lack of both experience and unity. It had neither adequate institutions nor mechanisms, and it lacked credibility because it still had no effective military component.

The Community's indecision soon was demonstrated over the question of recognizing Croatia. (About recognizing Slovenia, no real problem arose; it became almost automatic.) The German government, especially its foreign minister, Hans-Dietrich Genscher, began to press in late 1991 for the unconditional recognition of Croatia and threatened to do so unilaterally. His move was backed by an aggressive right-wing German press campaign that only deepened Serb paranoia about a revival of Germany's World War II aggressive intentions and its historical sympathy with "fascist" Croatia.[59] The case for delay, as presented mainly in the United States, Britain, and, for a time, France, rested on four arguments. (1) The Croatian government was not in total command of its territory (because of Serb insurrections), and its policy on minorities—despite concessions recently made—was internationally unacceptable. (2) Unilateral German recognition would damage efforts to form a common Western foreign policy. (3) Premature recognition of Croatia could set a dangerous precedent, especially in what was still the Soviet Union. (4) In Yugoslavia itself, premature recognition could spread the war (initially into Bosnia-Hercegovina) because it would provoke Serbs throughout Yugoslavia to defend themselves and prompt the Serbian government to support them. The German government's case for early recognition sprang not so much from any historical sympathies with Croatia (not, at any rate, with Ante Pavelić's wartime regime) or from any hankering after influence as the Serbs and others claimed. It rested mainly on an acceptance that Yugoslavia was a thing of the past and that the European Community had to be jolted into recognizing this.

In early 1992 Germany had its way and the European Community recognized Croatia and Slovenia. At the same time, Cyrus Vance, former U.S. secretary of state, who had been made special UN negotiator in October 1991 when that body belatedly came onto the scene, succeeded in arranging a cease-fire in Croatia that was, at last, to prove effective. Advocates of early recognition of Croatia were quick to connect the two. The fact of recognition had been a sharp lesson to both Serbia and to the Serb minority in Croatia, they argued, and the successful cease-fire was the result. Involved in the cease-fire was an arrangement whereby UN peacekeeping forces were generally deployed on the boundaries between the three main Serb enclaves and the rest of Croatia, with the enclaves put under UN protection and enjoying virtual home rule. The arrangement was meant to be temporary; it originally was scheduled to last till only March 1993.[60] What would happen then was left vague, but the principle of Croatian sovereignty over the whole of its territory was maintained. This principle was later accepted, even by the Serbian government, though reluctantly, in August 1992, but whether the Serbs in the localities concerned ever would accept it became one of the big, uncertain questions in the entire Yugoslav equation. More to the point was the question of how long the Tudjman government would tolerate the local Serb determination to achieve independence.

With a relative peace descending on Croatia in early 1992, two questions became paramount: (1) When would the United States recognize Croatia? (2) Would a new conflagration start in Bosnia? Both questions were soon to be answered. Washington recognized Slovenia and Croatia in April 1992. Not only that: obviously deciding that it was time to replace inactivity with vigor, the United States recognized Bosnia-Hercegovina at the same time, as did the European Community. Washington also initiated its much tougher stand against Serbia in general. In the light of the events that soon follow three new questions soon arose: (1) Did the recognition of Bosnia-Hercegovina precipitate the outbreak of war there? (2) Had full international recognition of Bosnia-Hercegovina come earlier—say immediately after the recognition of Croatia—could it have prevented the outbreak of war because the Serbs would have been effectively warned? (3) In view of the outbreak of war in Bosnia-Hercegovina, was the recognition of Croatia at the beginning of the year such a good idea after all?

In the perspective of the Bosnian catastrophe the following answers to these three questions can be hazarded: (1) Yes, largely. (2) No. (3) No.[61] In short, Western policy turned out to be disastrous in Yugoslavia. Everybody deserved blame. Britain's role was particularly undistinguished. Its reversal from no intervention at all to one of ruminating about the possibility of it was so tepidly and conditionally expressed that, instead of frightening Milošević and company, it probably convinced them that they had little to worry about. The Americans not only were too slow in realizing that Yugoslavia had no future, but they also were preoccupied with the Soviet breakup and its consequences. French policy gave the impression of inconsistency and an unusual amateurishness. The German insistence on Croatian recognition, whatever its logic at the time, subsequently appeared obstinate and premature. To the East, still in the background, was Russia. Yeltsin firmly supported the West's anti-Serb position, but many prominent Russian conservatives did not, citing the traditional Russian-Serb alliance. If they succeeded in getting Yeltsin to modify his position, then a serious, new East-West diplomatic rift over the former Yugoslavia could be expected.

Edward Mortimer in the London *Financial Times,* whose analyses have been among the coolest in the huge Western coverage of the Yugoslav tragedy, took a retrospective look at Western policy as the war in Croatia merged into the Bosnian catastrophe and suggested what should—and should not—have been done. He is worth quoting at some length:[62]

> –June–July 1991. When the Yugoslav People's Army (JNA) began military operations against Slovenia, the EC could have responded by according immediate diplomatic recognition to that republic, while warning the Croatian government it could only expect the same support if it reached a power-sharing agreement with the Serb minority.
> –Autumn 1991. The EC and the international community as a whole should have responded much more firmly to JNA and Serb attacks on Croatia, notably by imposing an oil embargo and using naval power to stop the bombardment of Dubrovnik and other coastal towns.
> –January 1992. The Twelve should have withheld recognition of Croatia until the conditions set the previous month on constitutional freedoms and minority rights were fully satisfied. They should . . . have made it clear that they would recognize Bosnia-Hercegovina only when it had a constitution agreed between the elected leaders of all three communities. . . .
> –Spring–summer 1992. Having, [however,] recognised Bosnia-Hercegovina as an independent state and admitted it to the UN, other states should have come to its assistance. They were not obliged to intervene directly in the Bosnian civil war, but the UN Security Council could have ordered Serbia, Montenegro, and Croatia to stay out of it. Those three republics could have been told to take effective steps, under UN supervision, to prevent armed men, weapons or strategic supplies from going into Bosnia; and if they refused could have been subjected to serious economic sanctions, enforced strictly from the start, on land, sea, and river. More should have been done, and sooner, to help Mr. Milan Panić and other pro-peace politicians get their message across to the Serbian electorate. . . .
> –Summer–autumn 1992. Having recognised Bosnia-Hercegovina but failed to defend it, and having helped thereby to bring about the civil war and determine its course, western powers must be considered morally responsible for the appalling fate that befell the Moslem population. They were therefore, and in my judgment are still, under a moral obligation to intervene directly to save that population, securing it in a "safe haven" as they had done the Kurds of northern Iraq the previous year. . . .

Mortimer certainly would recognize that retrospective journalism is easier than actual diplomacy, but his exercise was useful in that it helps chart a path through some of the quicksands of former Yugoslavia and might help those confronted in the future by situations not entirely dissimilar.

Mortimer's thoughts were published during the Geneva conference in January 1993 on the peace plan (see p. 262) presented by Vance and Lord Owen, who had taken Carrington's place as chief European Community negotiator. The basic problem Vance and Owen had wrestled with was simple. Bosnia-Hercegovina had been both the microcosm and the linchpin of Yugoslavia. Now that there was no longer any excuse for Yugoslavia, was there still any excuse for Bosnia-Hercegovina? However, for moral and political reasons no international mediators could accept the ruthless logic of this question. If the old Bosnia-Hercegovina no longer had any logical right to exist, a new and artificial one would have to be diplomatically invented. And the peace plan, presented at Geneva, was what Vance and Owen invented.

It was described at the time as "both a considerable diplomatic achievement and an unhappy compromise."[63] The plan denied the Serbs what they had wanted most: a wholly autonomous or independent Bosnian state that could, at some time in the future, merge with Serbia proper. Still, the Serbs would have gained a percentage of Bosnian-Hercegovinan territory much in excess of their some 33 percent of the total population of the republic, although the package would have involved them giving up some of the territory they had grabbed, or "cleansed," in the war.

As for the Croats, they could feel satisfied. They had got as much as they could have expected and were considered to be the "victors" of the whole deal. The plan confirmed their grip on most of western Hercegovina, which was heavily Croat-populated. The Zagreb government's real concern, though, was with the Serb enclaves on Croatian territory. How long could they tolerate their virtual independence?

The Muslims were the ones to lose under the Vance-Owen plan. After several hundred thousand of them had lost or left their homes,[64] some 50,000 of them had been killed, and many of those who survived had been subjected to cruelty, suffering, and indignity, Muslim control was essentially reduced to a rump territory mainly in central Bosnia. Their leader, Alija Izetbegović, could justly complain that they, the victims, had been penalized, and the Serbs, the aggressors, had been rewarded.[65]

Judging from the widespread condemnation of the Geneva package proposals in many parts of the world, many international observers agreed with the Muslim assessment. In the event, agreement on the package, which had once looked likely, became indefinitely delayed because of Bosnian Serb intransigence; the fighting dragged on, with the Muslims suffering more casualties and losing more territory. Eventually, in the spring of 1993 the package was, in effect, abandoned. The West was having to face the fact that it was not only the Bosnian state that had disintegrated but Bosnian society, too. The three communities — Muslim, Serb, and Croat — could never live together again. This was, indeed, implicit in a new United Nations — European Community plan put forward in the summer of 1993. It meant that some of the "ethnic cleansing" would have to be accepted.

The international community's task now — dictated by both morality and realism — was to ensure a viable Muslim state. For this, force — or the *credible* threat of it — might be necessary. If so, it would be primarily directed against Serbia. Despite their appalling economic situation, most Serbs still supported Milošević's policy, as they showed in the parliamentary elections in December 1993, in which all the main candidates toed the nationalist line, including Drašković, who abandoned his recent moderation. But Tudjman's Croatia might also have to be forcibly persuaded. Though not the main problem to peace, it was also an intractable one. And it cannot be forgotten that, enemies though Serbia and Croatia are, they are united on one thing: a desire to partition Bosnia-Hercegovina. (They began secretly negotiating this in 1991.) Could the West let them do what Germany and Soviet Russia did to Poland in 1939? Make no mistake: they would do it if they thought they could get away with it.

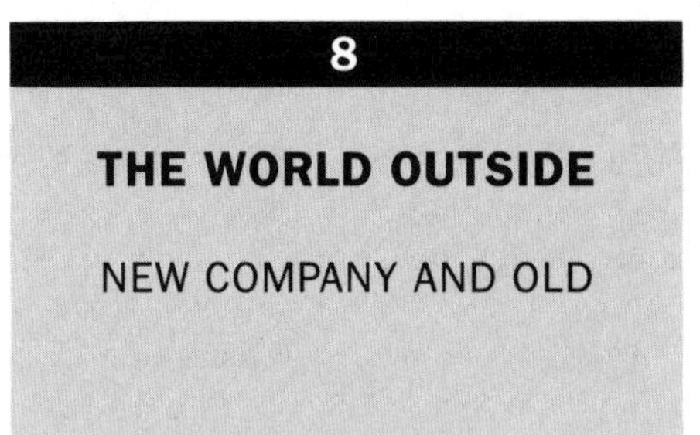

8

THE WORLD OUTSIDE

NEW COMPANY AND OLD

After 1989 the hoops that bound the East European countries to the Soviet Union, and to each other, in unwilling alliance, quickly weakened and then broke. The drive now, stronger in some countries than in others, was to join, or rejoin, the West. During the course of 1990 it seemed almost impossible to read an article, especially in the East-Central European press, without seeing some reference to the "European mainstream" and the need to join it. By early 1993 the intensity had somewhat abated, although this point remained one of the most discussed — sometimes one of the most belabored — topics in public life throughout the region.

In this context, it is worth examining the motives and the opportunities of those countries that have played, or could in the future play, the most important external role in the future of Eastern Europe. These countries are the United States, Germany, Italy, Austria, Turkey, the former Soviet Union, and the new Russia. Neither France nor Great Britain is included in the list. French influence, paramount in the 1920s, has rapidly diminished and continues to do so — even in the cultural sphere, where it was once unassailable. The occasional ostentatious gesture or rhetoric coming from Paris ("La France prendra sa part," etc.) cannot conceal this greatly reduced influence. As Pierre Hassner has written: "From Napoleon III to Mitterrand via de Gaulle, French policy can be interpreted as an attempt to resurrect past grandeur in the absence of means that had once made it possible."[1] For well over a century these attempts had been remarkably successful. But now, in Eastern Europe at least, they were failing. As for Britain, it has had little influence in Eastern Europe since World War II; now it has virtually none. The irony is that many people in the Balkans still see Britain as having a major role and pursuing its old balance of power policy, by allegedly supporting Serbia in order to guard against further German "encroachments." Some German and

Austrian commentators, in their cobwebbed paranoia, say more or less the same.

When most East Europeans after 1989 talked about the "European mainstream," they tended to mean either something culturally nebulous or, more specifically, a Europe represented by its multilateral, unifying, institutions, most notably the European Community. The prime international ambition of most, if not all, the East European states (as well as some European successor states of the Soviet Union) is to join the Community. Poland, Czechoslovakia, and Hungary gained economic associate status in 1991, and Romania and Bulgaria in 1992. How long it would be before any of the East European countries became full members was still far from clear. Some optimists in Brussels among the "wideners," rather than the "deepeners," in the Community were forecasting entry for Poland, the Czech Republic, and Hungary as early as the mid-1990s. Others, and not only the French-led "deepeners," were looking to the twenty-first century at the earliest.[2] Membership still would be keenly sought after, although with fewer illusions, regardless of when it might be granted. But the Community's lack of purpose in the early 1990s, the inability of its putative military arm, the West European Union (WEU), to materialize effectively, has not gone unnoticed by many East Europeans. The Community's impotence in the Yugoslav conflict caused many to look more hopefully than ever to NATO for their future security needs.

Widening NATO?

At NATO headquarters considerable differences arose over what the nature of its association with Eastern Europe should be and what kind of military commitment should be promised. The East Central European states — Poland, the Czech Republic, and Hungary — wanted full membership, especially as the instability on their Eastern borders and beyond, in Russia itself, became more nerve-racking. At first, the thinking in NATO, both European and North American, was that formal, institutional membership was out of the question but that a wide range of semi-official contacts, designed to give psychological reassurance to the East Central Europeans, could be arranged. Such contacts, it was hoped, were all that the East Central Europeans would need. Later, though, by about the second half of 1992, voices were being raised urging full inclusion of these states.[3] (Albania, too, in late

1992 made a *formal* application for admission to NATO, obviously in view of the danger from Serbia—see chapter 4.) The discussion in NATO, therefore, paralleled the more intensive, widening or deepening, discussions in the European Community—specifically if and when to offer full membership to some East European states. In 1993 NATO opinion seemed to be swinging in favor of seriously considering Poland, the Czech Republic, and Hungary for full membership. At the same time pressure from these three countries for membership greatly increased.

This question is worth examining in some depth; it became a hotly debated issue in the diplomatic and defense communities of the United States and both parts of Europe.[4]

The Poles, Czechs, and Hungarians wanted membership for the following interacting reasons: (1) It would enhance their security in the face of the unstable situation developing in the successor states of the Soviet Union and in the face of a possible future threat to their independence from Russia itself. (2) It would enhance their security in other aspects, too. For example, some Poles saw it as protection against a possible future German threat, while some Hungarians saw NATO membership as strengthening their case in the disputes with neighboring countries over Hungarian minorities. (3) It would assure an American military presence or at least influence in the region. Many East Europeans considered this especially important in view of the European debacle over Yugoslavia. (4) It would be an important factor generally in bringing Poland, the Czech Republic, and Hungary more into the European, or Western, "mainstream." It would also, it was argued, ensure the development of democracy and a market economy. NATO membership would, therefore, be complementary to European Community membership.

Transcending these four reasons was the *psychological* assurance this membership would give, an assurance that might also have a calming impact on the domestic as well as foreign affairs of the countries concerned. In short, NATO membership would be Eastern Europe's multipurpose stabilizer.

The pressure coming from influential circles in the United States for widening NATO arose largely from a genuinely international desire to maintain an American role in foreign affairs at a time when that role was being questioned domestically, and, more specifically, to maintain the United States' links with its European allies. This was the best way, it was argued, to avoid another dismal showing like the one in

Yugoslavia. Some advocates were mainly concerned, of course, with keeping NATO alive, but the self-serving motives of these were obvious and should not have prejudiced consideration of the serious arguments being put forward. (The self-servers—military and civilian—were found in Western Europe, too.)

In the reunited Germany the NATO issue was caught up in the great national debate about a wider, fuller, more responsible German role in the world as a whole. Those urging such a role favored expansion to include Poland, the Czech Republic, and Hungary. Those opposing, or nervous about, such a role tended to oppose it. But some advocates of widening were also convinced that being together in the same military and political alliance as Germany—an alliance that would also include the United States—would finally rid Poland of its traditional fear of Germany.

The NATO-widening debate was dramatized by the alarming success of the extremist nationalist demagogue, Vladimir Zhirinovsky, in the Russian parliamentary elections of December 1993. Zhirinovsky tapped many sources of actual and potential discontent, but the biggest was probably the Russian national humiliation, the wounding sense of lost greatness. And what specifically worried the successor-states of the former Soviet Union and East European countries like Poland was his remarks about Russia recovering not just the former Soviet, but former tsarist, possessions as well.

The new Zhirinovsky factor certainly sharpened the ongoing NATO debate, without altering its basic course or character. Advocates of NATO widening saw it as an extra string to their bow. Zhirinovsky, they maintained, had borne them out. Some went further: to deny NATO membership to Poland, the Czech Republic, and Hungary (and probably Slovakia, too) would be tantamount to the British and French appeasement of Hitler before World War II. Such a lack of resolution would not only leave Eastern Europe to its fate but would also lead to destabilization in Western Europe and, probably, to the breakup of the Western alliance. Sometimes the case was powerfully and rationally argued, but sometimes it was raucously declaimed by Russophobes for whom Russia was the eternal center of damnation and Zhirinovsky was but Yeltsin writ large.

But Western opponents of early NATO widening, however much shaken by the Zhirinovsky surge, drew quite different conclusions from it. Appeasement was certainly to be avoided, they argued, but so was needless provocation. Russia was a big, important power and had to be treated as such. As Michael Howard said already in 1989: "The

Cold War may be over but international politics will go on."[5] More to the point, however dangerous the forces of darkness in Russia had shown themselves to be, they were still not in power and there was at least two years to try to head them off and strengthen the fledgling democracy. Appearing to throw a *cordon sanitaire* around Russia would not only hurt Russian democrats but might endanger precisely those East European countries it was designed to protect by making Russia more, not less, aggressive. Writing off the Russian democrats could easily become a self-fulfilling prophecy. Better, therefore, wait! And, in the meantime, help Russia! Avoid branding it as an outcast!

This, then, was the core of the debate. But there were also crucial, down-to-earth factors impinging on it. They were:

(1) The sheer difficulty in getting unanimity in NATO on practical action.

(2) The danger that NATO in Eastern Europe would not only find itself protecting states against a possible Russian threat but also be expected to adjudicate, or intervene if necessary, in the dispute some of these countries had with each other over, say, territories or minorities. Some argued that NATO membership would at least dull the edge of the historical intraregional disputes. But there was absolutely no guarantee of this — another argument for those urging caution over widening.

(3) Expansion to include just Poland, the Czech Republic, Hungary, and possibly Slovakia was very much taking the soft option. Despite the existing instability among the European successor states of the former Soviet Union and the prospect of even more, possibly resulting in greater Russian influence, none of the East European NATO applicants had reason to feel *militarily* threatened by Russia, even by a more nationalist Russian government than exists at present. The Baltic states — Lithuania and especially Estonia and Latvia — had greater cause for worry, as, of course, did Ukraine and Belarus. These countries might need the long arm of NATO to prevent the kind of "Yugoslav" chaos that the proponents of widening believe it is capable of managing. Turning to the Balkans, Albania, Macedonia, and Romania would seem to be candidates for this kind of protection — again, much more so than any East Central European country. In East Central Europe it would seem to be Slovakia that could be the most likely scene of the instability against which NATO might be a deterrent. But would Western countries have the stomach to get involved in Slovakia — or anywhere else — especially in a situation too complex to be reduced to the black and white issues of aggression and the defense against it?

(4) The "ideological compatibility" factor. Some in the West argued that "commitment to democracy" (and the market) was as important a condition for NATO entrance as exposure to a potential Russian threat. It was this that made Mečiár's Slovakia, one of the most exposed of all the East European countries, such a difficult proposition. But the elections in Poland in September 1993 had thrown up a government (see chapter 3) which, though democratic enough, offended many ideological purists, especially in the United States. What, too, if the Hungarian socialists did well in the forthcoming elections in 1994 and, looking further ahead, what if the Bulgarian socialists were voted back to power? In short, what were the real criteria of club membership?

Eventually, in January 1994, the Clinton administration came up with "Partnership for Peace," offering closer military and security cooperation to *all* the East European countries and to the European successor states of the Soviet Union, *including* Russia, with Poland, the Czech Republic, Hungary, *and* Slovakia being put on tenure track (of indefinite length) for NATO membership. A solution worthy of Solomon, or a make-shift worthy of Chamberlain? Opinion in the West continued to be divided along predictable lines. As for the East Europeans, they took their disappointment with generally good grace (even the Poles, who had pressed particularly hard for early NATO membership) and resolved to make the best of it. As for the Russians, Zhirinovsky railed against it, a few hailed it, and many quietly admitted that it was an astute and not unfriendly piece of diplomacy. These latter were probably right. "Partnership for Peace" made the best of a difficult situation.

In retrospect, and after allowing for the genuine fright caused by Zhirinovsky, it can be argued that Eastern Europe's scramble for NATO was misplaced, or at least premature. The concept of "security" can no longer be confined to military security. The main immediate security threats to Poland, the Czech Republic, Slovakia, and Hungary are not military but those having to do with migration, refugees, crime, nuclear reactors (possibly another Chernobyl), and above all with the dangers of failure in economic reconstruction. And the institution, with all its falterings and weaknesses, that is best suited to meet such security threats is the European Community—certainly not NATO. Most countries in the Community also share the same kind of threats to *their* own security, an important factor that might influence closer association. Therefore, membership in the Community would seem to demand priority. And the Russians could have no legitimate objection against membership in this organization.

Finally, in this context, a word on CSCE (or the Helsinki Process). This movement had played a role in undermining communist rule in Eastern Europe and, hence, in winning the Cold War. It was now beginning to be totally discredited. Enlarged to more than fifty members so as to accommodate *all* of the successor states of the Soviet Union, and becoming submerged under increasing layers of bureaucracy, the CSCE was starting to look like one organization too many. Hopes that it might serve as a peacekeeping or local crisis management body seemed increasingly unrealistic. Unless it reexamined and reorganized itself, the only realistic future for CSCE lay in its demise.[6]

The United States: Distant, and How Determining?

Nowhere in the world was American prestige higher at the end of 1989 than in Eastern Europe. Although the East European countries, against a background of Soviet permissiveness, had largely freed themselves from communist rule, they realized that the role of the United States, as the leader of the Western alliance throughout the Cold War and as the Western power that generally had been more uncompromising in opposing communist rule than any other, had been indispensable to their deliverance. Finally, the United States had won the Cold War against the Soviet Union. It won, therefore, not just gratitude and prestige but admiration and respect—even awe.

Even more: the United States always had exercised a strong popular and cultural fascination for many East Europeans, especially among the young. The attraction went back to the last decades of the nineteenth century when large-scale emigration from Eastern Europe to the United States began. The United States then acquired the aura of promise, prosperity, opportunity, and democracy that it never lost, despite communist efforts to denigrate the myth.[7]

When the revolutions of 1989 were over and the euphoria had subsided, this general admiration, however gratifying it was for Americans, presented the United States with problems, too. Admiration carried expectations: of reward, special treatment (especially economic), and American involvement, particularly as a security guarantor. All of these expectations could not be fulfilled, despite the intense goodwill that existed in the United States and the persuasive, well-organized activity of some East European ethnic lobbies there, most notably the Polish.

The United States had to base its long-term policy toward the region, not on emotion, but on an assessment of its own interests and possibilities. The basic question was how far Washington felt it could go in converting the moral and cultural influence it had into a strategic, political, and economic role. How much commitment was Eastern Europe worth in view of other U.S. global commitments and the relative advantage and responsibilities that Western Europe, particularly Germany, would have in the region? The fate of the Soviet Union also was important. At the end of 1989, although Soviet political influence in Eastern Europe was seriously declining, Red Army troops still were stationed in Poland, Hungary, and Czechoslovakia, and the crucial Soviet economic role in the entire region still continued. Within two years this situation had changed completely. The Soviet Union no longer existed. Eastern Europe had become a vacuum into which Western countries were moving. A now united Germany was the prime mover, and its economic penetration began to be evident. But no single West European country, nor the European Community itself, was showing the *degree* of interest and solicitude that East Europeans had expected. The vacuum left by the Soviet withdrawal and collapse was not being filled. The West had been equipped to deal with the Soviet presence in Eastern Europe but not with its sudden disappearance.

By this time, however, it already was evident that the United States was not prepared to become the major player in the region. Some talk apparently took place in Washington about seeking to offset the development of German influence in Poland, or to "get between" Germany and Russia, something the Poles would very much like to have seen. The Czechoslovaks (the Czechs in this particular case) also would have liked to have felt more of an American presence or impact. The historical German domination of Czechs, the World War II experience, the fear of possible German demands rising out of the mass expulsions after World War II, all contributed to a nervousness in Prague about the new international situation.

The American reluctance to assume a major security role in Eastern Europe was understandable, not only in light of its other commitments, but in view of increasing pressure for more attention to be paid to domestic issues. This shift to domestic problems now was deemed possible in view of the American victory in the Cold War. In the case of Eastern Europe, the disintegration and final demise of the Soviet

Union at the end of 1991 appeared to lend additional justification for avoiding any heavy security commitment in the region. Eastern Europe was considered the responsibility mainly of the West Europeans. The West Europeans obviously were prosperous and could make themselves militarily capable. Whether they had the will was another matter, but hardly an American concern. The United States had its own problems, and they were mounting.

But the decision apparently was to *limit* the American commitment, not to deny it altogether. Despite the decisions on retrenchment in Western Europe, involving major troop withdrawals, the United States remained committed to the security of its longtime allies there. And these allies, including France despite its posturings, wanted that multilateral commitment, mainly through NATO, to continue. This meant at least a partial U.S. interest in the security and even stability of Eastern Europe, too. Western European security obviously would be affected by developments in the other half of the continent, and, even before the euphoria of East European liberation had worn off, some developments there already were giving cause for concern. The rapid reemergence of national conflicts (see chapter 6) was giving the most concern. But mass migration, the drugs and arms traffic, and terrorism could also affect the stability of the whole continent. These dangers had to add to American anxiety.

The Economic Relationship

But there was more to the American relationship with Eastern Europe than military or strategic security. There was at first a strong feeling in the United States that it was not only in the American *interest* to help promote democracy and a market economy in Eastern Europe, but it also was its *moral obligation* to do so. The Cold War had had, after all, a strong moral and ideological content, and it would not be finally won until the Eastern European states had undergone the transformation from communism to liberal democracy. The United States could best help assure this transformation by a strong economic commitment to postcommunist reconstruction. It also was realized that economic reconstruction was an important element in the overall security of Europe.

Robert D. Hormats has usefully listed the principles necessary for the United States to observe in its policy of economic assistance to Eastern Europe:[8]

(1) Economic change in Eastern Europe is a *long-term* process requiring a *long-term* American commitment of advice, resources, and patience.
(2) Although the East European will and commitment to change is the prime essential, the United States must join with other Western countries in helping them to mobilize their own human and financial resources and in supplementing these with outside technical and economic assistance.
(3) American aid should be both bilateral and as part of an international, multilateral effort. The United States would have to work as closely as possible with the European Community. As much coordination as possible was necessary in the financial, commercial, and technical spheres.
(4) American business needed to be encouraged by the U.S. government in order to get a foothold in East European markets. "The more constructive and successful the U.S. government's role in fostering the transition to market systems and stable growth in the area, the greater the likelihood that U.S. companies will feel comfortable investing there and will be able to take advantage of growing commercial opportunities."

Some of the more detailed aspects of this question are discussed in chapter 5. But Hormats's principles fully cover the motivations and the imperatives of the American economic presence in Eastern Europe.

The Cultural Connection

If it weighed its options realistically, the most lasting and effective way in which the United States could influence Eastern Europe was neither militarily nor economically; it would have to do so culturally, in the broad sense of that word. The most promising American target was the young people. The United States needed a policy of penetration and initiation. It had to take its cultural message into Eastern Europe itself—penetration—and to bring as many promising young people to American universities and schools as possible—initiation. America Houses could be a potent instrument in penetration, as could radio broadcasts by a revamped Radio Free Europe and an enlivened Voice of America, not to mention the right sort of individual Americans, young and old. But the real rewards would come from the initiation of young East Europeans into American education and the American way of life in general—warts and all. Specifically, university graduate schools and public schools were the best instruments. Products of the former would be returning to their countries and most likely would form an influential section of the next governing cadre, a basically pro-American freemasonry at the center of power. As for public school graduates, they could form a larger pool of pro-Americanism among the broader public. What was needed was as many stipends as possible, both from government and from private sources. Successful candidates would be chosen jointly by the concerned East European governments and by American representatives in Eastern Europe. (Successful candidates obviously would need to sign an agreement that they return to their country at the end of their studies: initiation, in this case, hardly meant immigration.)

Some efforts were being made to do these things, but more was needed. Pessimists could argue, of course, that ultimately it would be German cultural as well as economic influence that would win out (except in Poland where resistance to the side effects of German economic penetration always would remain strong) because the latter would inexorably carry the former along with it. These pessimists could point to the increasing number of young East Europeans wanting to learn German rather than English (see below, p. 283), obviously the result, not only of the early German economic penetration that had begun well before 1989, but of a more general resignation to the fact that Germany would set the pace throughout the entire region. But for the United States to give up on this account would be unworthy of it. If it made the effort, the United States could, despite the enormous advantages enjoyed by Germany, carve out a unique place for itself in Eastern Europe. *And it could do it at relatively little financial cost.*

The long-term mutual advantages of this policy would be considerably greater than the bucket loads of "assistance" proffered immediately after 1989 in the form of American advisors, consultants, and the like, usually in the economic sphere. Some of these people were both genuine and capable, and they did good work. But some had neither quality, and their work was bad. In it for the quick profit and then the quick exit—and instantly recognizable—these opportunists swarmed over Eastern Europe in the three years after 1989. Many would defend themselves with the argument that they personified just the kind of entrepreneurial mentality and skills (and lack of "sentiment") that Eastern Europe needed. After all, the United States itself had been built by such as they. Their claim was extravagant, to put it mildly. Besides, one only could hope—piously perhaps—that the new Eastern Europe could be spared some of the uglier features of American, British, and West European capitalist growth and remain unresponsive to some of its crasser values.

Former East European exiles — mostly from the United States but also from Western Europe — launched their own kind of invasion after 1989. Some of them were as much on the make as the Western marauders, but others were moved by a mixture of motives: patriotism and civic spirit; affection; the opportunity for a constructive, fulfilling adventure; or the "returning conqueror" complex. Some of them did excellent work. Others, however, were less effective, lacking tact, modesty, and the ability or willingness to recognize how much had changed, including themselves. Least successful of all have been the "politicals," either active or advisory. They would, with few exceptions, have been doing their native country a favor by staying in their adopted one. Too many exiles, in fact, remind one of the remark of the Canadian novelist Robertson Davies: "The world is full of people whose notion of a satisfactory future is . . . a return to an idealized past." All in all, the returning natives have been a mixed blessing. Their compatriots who had stayed and suffered the privations of communist rule needed very careful handling by those returning, especially those soon retreating again to Western comforts. The general attitude was that the returning exiles were neither heroes nor deserters (and certainly not miracle men), but countrymen who may have much to teach but also much to learn.

Germany: A Reluctant and Nervous Supremacy

The Economist put it well in early 1992:

> When Germany turns East, others are not sure whether to cheer or to tremble. So it was when Willy Brandt launched West Germany on its *Ostpolitik* just over two decades ago; so it is now that newly united Germany, its clout further increased by the collapse of the Soviet Union, is forging ahead with *Ostpolitik* mark-two.[9]

But, as *The Economist* admitted, it was bound to happen. Historically, Germany has looked more East than West, constructively as well as destructively, and now, after 1989, a growing vacuum in the East has presented an opportunity, a challenge — a serious threat, too, if the situation were not stabilized. And Germany was the Western country that could best fill the vacuum. Some East European nations, most notably the Poles, were and have remained uneasy about this.[10] But there was no real alternative. Even with the unexpected magnitude of the task of digesting the former GDR, a task likely to go on into the next century, German interests in Eastern Europe would steadily outstrip those of other Western countries.

German penetration was becoming cultural and educational as well; here, it was challenging the Americans on a field that should have been theirs. Although the Goethe Institutes (the German counterpart of the America Houses) had been rather slow getting off the mark in the 1980s, they subsequently began making up for lost ground. In early 1992, out of 18 million people estimated to be studying German throughout the world, 12 million were in the old East bloc as a whole (including the former Soviet Union). In Czechoslovak schools in the summer of 1991, when pupils could choose their foreign languages for the first time instead of, as in the past, having Russian dumped on them, about half chose German as against 30 percent who chose English. Even in Poland, German accounted for 30 percent of all foreign language instruction.[11] And, except for the Serbs, the Poles and the Czechs had been the most anti-German nations in the whole region. German business executives were quick to see the connection between language study and economics, quicker than any of their international competitors.

German Political Leadership?

Would this economic and partly cultural leadership become converted into political leadership or eventual political domination? One perceptive observer was fatalistic about it:

> Germany is the only big power that remains in these parts, economically, politically, and eventually in security terms. Foreign economic domination of central Europe cannot be avoided. The question is whether German domination will be disguised as that of the EC. If the EC can close ranks and present a common front, it would look better politically. If it fails, we will have overt German domination.[12]

It was too early to say if this outcome would occur. Resigned as they might be to economic domination, the Poles certainly would strongly resist other forms of domination. They were, for example, still dragging their feet over an imaginative German scheme for the development of large stretches of territory on both sides of their common border. Many Poles, although aware of the economic benefits involved, shrank from the specter of German "colonization."[13] And one of the misgivings that some Czechs had about the breakup of Czechoslovakia was that it would tend to increase German political dominance (see chapter 3).

How much political leadership or authority would the Germans want to assert, anyway? Here, the evolving, reunited Germany must be distinguished from the old West Germany. The latter started establishing its economic presence in Eastern Europe in the early 1960s. But there was little serious talk then about West German political leadership. The international environment, of course, was different. The Soviet Union not only existed but was a superpower. The German Democratic Republic also existed and was deemed to be a strong, medium-sized economic power. The Warsaw Pact and Comecon were still in place. But most important of all was the fact that no West German will for leadership existed. Technically, West Germany was not a fully sovereign state, was under the military and the partial political tutelage of the United States, and had no real international responsibilities or worries. "Economic giant, political dwarf" was an expression Willy Brandt apparently first coined. His statement was true, and the West Germans liked it that way.

How far has this attitude changed with the new, reunited Germany? A new German decisiveness certainly was shown with the process of reunification itself, Chancellor Kohl grasping the nettle in a manner that few had thought him capable of. The decisiveness continued with the recognition of Croatia in late 1991, a matter in which Bonn forced the hand of its reluctant West European allies (see chapter 7). Subsequently, the combination of Serb aggression and Serb atrocities in Bosnia-Hercegovina raised political pressure for a revision of the German constitution (*Grundgesetz*), enabling Germany to join its allies in military action outside the area prescribed by its membership in NATO.

Despite the continuing reservations about this more activist posture among certain sections of the population, the official conception of Germany's role — at least in Europe — was changing. It was bound to. Economic weight now meant at least some political assertiveness. The Kohl government at first was not ready to sign a treaty with

Poland that finally would abandon any German claim to a revision of the Oder-Neisse frontier without Polish concessions on the status of the German minority (see chapter 6). Eventually, world opinion, together with Polish resistance, forced Bonn to back down.[14] Similarly, although the Kohl government officially never made such claims, its Bavarian political ally, the Christian Social Union (CSU), wanted Czechoslovak agreement on compensation for the German expellees after World War II before the bilateral treaty between the two countries was signed in 1991.[15] In 1993 after Czechoslovakia had split apart, CSU politicians brought the subject up again with the Czech government.

But Kohl, despite his new essays in power diplomacy, belonged to the old West German generation that had come to maturity in a world where basic decisions were made for it, not by it. (The great exception was Willy Brandt's Ostpolitik in the late sixties and early seventies, but that was an exercise not in power but in reconciliation.) By the beginning of the 1990s, however, a new political generation, moving into power, wanted a more active Germany, one that would initiate and not just acquiesce. The members of this generation were by no means sinister nationalists, but they wanted a role for Germany and were ready to see the country assume international responsibilities consistent with its strength. They saw themselves more as internationalists rather than nationalists, working within the United Nations, NATO, and the European Community. But they saw Germany's role—certainly in the European Community—as inescapably increasing, and they were ready for it. Not, perhaps, at present, with the German economy faltering (by its own high standards), the new *Bundesländer* a millstone, and the whole nation in one of its periodic hours of self-doubt. But, later, by the end of the century, if German resilience showed, they would want Germany to think and act positively. Those fearful of this prospect should consider what Eastern, and Western, Europe would be like if Germany did not recover from its nervousness in the nineties but rather lapsed into self-questioning introspection. The stability of the entire continent would suffer.

The Specter of Migration

The greatest threat to German resilience lay neither in economics nor in the former GDR. It was the "migration specter": exposure to the new "threats" from migrants, refugees, asylum seekers—threats for which most Germans were unprepared. Germany was again on the front line; for many Germans it seemed more dangerous than the old Cold War one.[16] *And the greater part of this human influx came from, or through, Eastern Europe.* In 1991 the number of asylum seekers was more than 250,000. In 1992 it was nearly 440,000.[17] (These figures do not count the ethnic Germans pouring in from the East—about 220,000 in 1991 alone.) The prospect of famine and anarchy hitting the former parts of the Soviet Union was becoming a new German nightmare.

The last great westward migration of peoples in Europe had taken place fifty years earlier, when millions of Germans, settled in the Soviet Union, Romania, Hungary, Yugoslavia, Poland, and Czechoslovakia—often for centuries—moved in the wake of the retreating Wehrmacht toward the end of World War II, or after the war were forcibly expelled from their homelands. They presented serious problems of absorption to both parts of Germany that emerged from the war. *But they were German.* Now, the new migrants were mostly Gypsies, Slavs, Romanians, Africans, or Asians, and absorbing them was not just a matter of economics but one of attitudes, prejudices, and outlook. It could mark just the beginning of the biggest problem Germany, and Europe, has had since 1945.

A large number of asylum seekers and migrants who were simply slipping illegally into Germany—many of them Gypsies—were coming from South-Eastern Europe, not counting the refugees from the Yugoslav civil war to whom the Germans, unlike most other European nations, were generously opening their doors: well above 200,000 in 1992. But the Bosnian Muslim refugees were a different kind of problem, relatively minor and temporary. The asylum seekers in a way also were taking advantage of German generosity, this time as laid down in the *Grundgesetz,* which contained the most liberal clauses in the world regarding asylum. The whole question of migration into Germany became highly complex during 1992, and none of the ongoing attempts to solve it had been successful. What is relevant here is the impact, direct and indirect, that it had on the East European countries. Already during 1992 the German and Romanian governments had signed an agreement providing for the repatriation (in fact, deportation) of an unspecified number—but tens of thousands—of "Romanian citizens" (actually Gypsies in their vast majority, although, of course, this was not specified) who had entered Germany as asylum seekers or illegally. The German government would make cash grants to Bucharest for their resettlement.[18] Now a new asylum law approved in 1993, in effect, would virtually block entry to Germany from any part of Eastern Europe. But this law would, in itself, not stop the westward migration flows from many parts of war-torn, war-threatened, or simply destitute parts of South-Eastern Europe, or from the former Soviet Union. They still would come and now would either illegally enter Germany or would back up mainly in neighboring Poland and the Czech Republic.[19] Thus, whether Germany had solved its own problem or not, it certainly had exported a good part of it to these two countries, both of which were much less capable of dealing with it. By the middle of 1993, problems relating to east-west migration already had become a contentious issue in German relations with Eastern Europe and, despite the temporary success of some negotiations, would remain so.

Austria: Not As a Stranger

There was an incompleteness about Vienna throughout the Cold War. Austria, though resuming its Western association toward the end of the 1950s, seemed to have lost forever the Central European and Eastern orientation that, historically, had given it its power and sense of purpose. Large, visible reminders of this old orientation still survived—from the *Prunk* monuments, to the restaurants, to the number of Navratils in the Vienna telephone book. But they were traces, parts of the past clinging to the present, with little hope for a future. Vienna was virtually cut off from its *hinterland*—some would say its heartland. The course of empire had been eastward, and now the rollback was complete.

This isolation actually had begun with the collapse of the Habsburg empire in 1918. In the interim, however, between the two world wars, commercial relations with the successor states of its old empire—Hungary, Poland, Czechoslovakia, and Yugoslavia—continued at a brisk rate, accounting for about half of Austria's total trade. After 1945, when eastern and southeastern Europe became part of another empire, most of these links were broken, and it seemed they never would be restored. But after 1989, Austrian industrialists, bankers, and traders rushed to revive old connections and forge new ones.

Hungary, with which the historic links had been closest, and with which considerable contacts already had developed before the collapse of communism, was the prime target (see chapter 5). But it was not the sole one. Exports to Czechoslovakia rose more than 70 percent in 1990 and later increased substantially to Poland. Regarding Czechoslovakia, Austrian exporters were convinced that when the Czech-Slovak divorce did come about, investments to the two new countries would continue at a quick rate.[20]

The collapse of Yugoslavia and the emergence of Slovenia and Croatia as two of its successor states were leading to speculation in early 1993 about the degree of Austrian economic involvement in those two countries, especially after Austrian diplomacy had worked so hard for their independence and international recognition. Slovenia, compact, trouble-free, and Germanically dominated for a millennium, would likely get priority treatment. Croatia, though, would receive scant attention until its situation was clarified and stability restored.

Austria's early showing in postcommunist Eastern Europe had, therefore, been promising. Its performance was small, of course, compared with that of Germany, but, because of Germany's unexpected domestic preoccupations and its obligations to the successor states of the Soviet Union, Austria was playing a relatively bigger role than had been expected. The country was compact and relatively wealthy, a success story—something of a model for the East European states. It also benefited from Habsburg memories. Experience of other empires had made many East Europeans rightfully wistful about the good old "*k. und k.*"

But Austria was not without serious problems of its own that soon were likely to get worse. The flood of immigrants and refugees was becoming administratively unbearable and politically explosive. "*Wien ist kein Chicago*" was the slogan to be found on many walls in the less fashionable districts of the Austrian capital. Such displays could portend a turn to the right, revisiting a past that Austria, unlike Germany, had made little attempt to come to terms with,[21] and they also could threaten Austria's reputation and its role in the new Europe. It was not a likely outcome, but it had to be vigorously guarded against.

Italy: Drawn Despite Itself

The dramatic attempted flight to Bari in southeastern Italy of more than 20,000 Albanian "boat people" in August 1991, carried by television throughout the world, had three different kinds of impact. (1) It brought home the wretched conditions in Albania itself. (2) It dramatized the distinct possibility of vast numbers of East European refugees swarming into Western Europe. (3) It raised urgent questions about Italy's present and future role in Eastern Europe, questions going much further than the furious dispute that erupted in Italian public life about the way in which authorities had handled the Albanian invasion.

Since the end of the fifteenth century, a large Albanian community had resided in southern Italy. But in the twentieth century it had been Italian acquisitive designs on Albania that had dominated relations between the two nations. Italy had supported Albanian independence before World War I, largely to gain influence on the other side of the Adriatic. In the secret Treaty of London (1915), designed to get it into the war on the allied side, Italy was offered the strategic island of Sazan (Saseno) and the area around Vlorë (Valona) at the entrance to the Adriatic. Under the same treaty, what was left of an independent Albania would have been placed under Italian protection. After World War I, Italy, though technically one of the victors, felt dissatisfied with the peace settlement. It began looking for fields to conquer and started where it had left off before the war—across the Adriatic, with the two new states of Yugoslavia and Albania. After 1925, Albania progressively became a virtual colony of fascist Italy. It received significant Italian economic and technical assistance, but the cost in political independence was great. After 1936, Italy practically took over the running of the country, and some Italian colonists even settled there. The whole process ended in 1939 with the Italian invasion and conquest of Albania.

After World War II, much Italian penitential goodwill was displayed toward Albania, but with the onset of the Cold War and the particular churlishness of the Hoxha regime in Tirana, very few opportunities for expiation arose. Now, however, more than forty years later, the chance seemed to have returned. But the Albanian "invasion" of August 1991 presented more of a dilemma than an opportunity which the Italian government chose to solve in a decisive way. It sent the Albanians back, firmly and unceremoniously.

Italy received a bad world press for its action, but it would be difficult to imagine any other country behaving differently. At the same time, too, the Italian government quietly proceeded to help Albania on a bigger scale than any other Western country. It was not altruism, of course; Italy simply did not want the unwelcome arrivals to show up again. But the assistance was effective, and welcome.

Across the Adriatic

The aid began in a dramatic enough fashion. Italian troops were seen in Albania in early September 1991 for the first time for nearly a half-century, this time in a totally different capacity and context. Seven hundred of them patrolled the port cities of Durrës and Vlorë to supervise the distribution of emergency food aid over a period of three months. An agreement already had been signed between the two countries on police cooperation, with Italians training some members of the Albanian police force. A special agreement provided for joint Albanian and Italian naval patrols in the Gulf of Otranto. Allegedly, this move was not just to prevent another exodus of Albanians across the Gulf, but to stop drug trafficking to Albania, which officials feared could become a problem. Italian help also was made available in education, the Albanian system having more or less broken down.

A three-year plan for economic cooperation involving some $800 million worth of Italian aid also was agreed on. But of more immediate value were the large amounts of food sent promptly from Italy to avert starvation. At the same time, about $200 million a year in economic aid was promised. In effect, Albania once again became something like an Italian protectorate. Italians were back in the Balkans, and this time the natives were glad.[22]

The new Italian involvement in Albania signaled that Italy was moving out from under the inhibiting shadow that prewar fascist imperialism had thrown over its relation to Eastern Europe. Italy had not been totally passive during the Cold War; still, there was a certain hesitance, almost reluctance, about its initiatives. A more active policy for the Balkans would have been appropriate for geopolitical reasons alone, and Italy could have been influential. But successful Italian governments were content to sit back. Relations with Yugoslavia, apart from settling a vexed border question with Slovenia, seemed on a day-to-day basis to have been left largely to the Italian Communist Party (PCI), which maintained particularly good relations with the Tito regime in Belgrade.

This diffidence may partly explain the slowness of Italy's response to the Yugoslav situation. In the autumn of 1991 Italy was one of the strongest opponents of the recognition of Croatia and Slovenia, refusing to be persuaded by growing German and Austrian demands for this decision. With France, Britain, most other European Community members, and the United States, Italy took its stand on the continued survival of Yugoslavia in one form or another—including, it was hoped, Croatia and Slovenia.[23]

An Eye on Germany

Actually, the Italian government may have realized better than most that the final disintegration of Yugoslavia had begun. It seems to have hesitated to accept the consequences of this fact, partly because of its wish to act in conjunction with the rest of its European allies, and partly because it did not wish to be seen as "obediently" following the German initiative. Whatever the reason, Italy suffered one of its most serious diplomatic defeats since World War II. By its delay in recognizing the two breakaway Yugoslav states, it simply surrendered the initiative to Germany. Instead of reducing German influence, it increased it. Germany, not neighboring Italy, now was the most influential state in the western Balkans and had the economic power to consolidate its advantage. The sudden reversal of Italy's position on Slovenia and Croatia toward the end of 1991 may be explained by its realization of what it was losing. But by this time it was too late. In January 1992 President Francesco Cossiga paid an official visit to both Ljubljana and Zagreb, becoming the first foreign head of state to visit the two states since independence. The intention clearly was to recover lost ground—and everybody knew it.

That Italy was neither unaware of the new opportunities in Eastern Europe, nor of the danger that Germany might collar most of them, was shown by its "*Pentagonale*" initiative. In November 1989 Italy took the lead in establishing an informal international association involving itself, Austria, Hungary, and the then Yugoslavia—the *Quadrangolare.*[24] With the adhesion of Czechoslovakia in May 1990, the association became known for a considerable period as the *Pentagonale.* Then, in July 1991, Poland adhered, and, during 1992, after considerable Italian hesitation, so did Slovenia and Croatia as new states, while Yugoslavia as such dropped out. This association then became the *Hexagonale* and, finally, the Central European Initiative. (The *Central,* not *Middle,* European Initiative, it should be noted.

Middle would have sounded too much like *Mittel,* with all of its historical Germanic connotations!) Apart from being a useful example, or symbol, of East-West cooperation, the *Hexagonale* obviously was an instrument of Italian influence not confined to South-Eastern Europe but, through the membership of Czechoslovakia, Poland, and Hungary, extending to East-Central Europe.[25] The attempt to counter German influence was clear. Countries like Poland and perhaps both the Czech Republic and Slovakia would be happy to see Italy in this role. But the probabilities were that German economic strengths would mean more than Italian diplomatic skills.

What of the future? Is there an Italian role in Eastern Europe? Clearly not until Italy climbs out of the morass it was in during the early 1990s. But assuming that resilience can overcome the current domestic malaise, Italy could play a major role, not in Eastern Europe as a whole, but in the Balkans. And not just in Albania, but in the vast and volatile hinterland beyond it. It is precisely there, in the south and east Balkans, that Italian influence might be needed the most. Kosovo and Macedonia were two of the most neuralgic points in Eastern Europe. This vulnerability only points up the dire need of active leadership. Italy would be (could have been?) a suitable country to provide it. The alternative might be Turkey, whose influential presence would be much more controversial than Italy's. A distant alternative might be Russia, perhaps even more controversial than Turkey.

Turkey: The Reluctant Return?

The upheavals in what was once Yugoslavia and the threat of more in the Balkan peninsula inevitably raised the question of Turkish reaction—not so much whether Turkey would react, as in what form.[26]

Between the end of the fourteenth century and the beginning of the eighteenth, the Ottoman empire dominated the Balkan peninsula. For the next two centuries it was steadily pushed back until, with its final collapse after World War I, Turkish territory in Europe was restricted to a small area in Thrace, centered on Istanbul, the historic capital. Istanbul, straddling two continents, became unique, with its downtown in Europe and its growing suburbs, across the Bosporus, in Asia. The new Republic of Turkey, founded by Mustafa Kemal Atatürk, with its new capital in the Anatolian city of Ankara, jettisoned all Balkan ambitions along with many other pieces of the Ottoman impedimenta. Turkish attention abroad now became riveted on Western Europe with the aim of education and emulation. After World War II, in the context of the Cold War, this Turkish preoccupation with the West now broadened, evolving into a close alliance with the United States, membership of NATO, association with the European Community, and subsequent application for full membership of it.

Not that Turkey turned its back totally on the Balkans. After the successful war with Greece from 1919 until 1922 and the massive population transfers following it, Turkey actively sought reconciliation with Athens, which was achieved, largely through the statesmanship of Atatürk and the dominant Greek politician of the first part of the twentieth century, Eleftherios Venizelos. With the other Balkan countries, those that were to become communist after 1945—Albania, Bulgaria, Romania, and Yugoslavia—Ankara's bilateral relations were correct but far from close. It was at the multilateral level, however, that relations broke new ground. Turkey took part in four Balkan conferences from 1930 through 1933 and signed the Pact of Balkan Entente, or Balkan Pact, in February 1934, the other signatories being Greece, Romania, and Yugoslavia. A newly founded Balkan Chamber of Commerce actually had its headquarters in Istanbul. But these prewar attempts at Balkan cooperation came to nothing. Albania and Bulgaria never joined, and, in any case, German and Italian encroachments in South-Eastern Europe soon exposed their frailty.[27]

Turkey's neutrality during World War II enabled it to escape the devastation and dislocation that some other Balkan nations suffered. But it now found itself on the front line of the incipient Cold War, with Stalin pressing Ankara for territorial concessions, for a revision of the 1936 Montreux Convention regulating navigation through the Straits, and even for a naval base on the Bosporus. It was this pressure that led Turkey into alliance with the United States and membership in NATO in 1952. Greece, too, torn by civil war, and with its neighbors, Albania, Yugoslavia, and Bulgaria, now hostile Soviet satellites, also needed American protection. Protection was provided to both countries under the terms of the Truman Doctrine of 1947. Turkey and Greece, therefore, became allies—or, more correctly, Cold War associates.

They soon were to be joined by Yugoslavia. Tito broke with Stalin in 1948, and for several years Yugoslavia faced every form of pressure, except military, from Moscow and its allies. Yugoslavia also became dependent on the West, particularly American military support, for survival. As a communist state, however, it hardly could join NATO or be eligible for assistance under the Truman Doctrine. No obstacles appeared, however, first to a rapprochement, and then to active cooperation, between Yugoslavia, Greece, and Turkey. Thus, in sharply different circumstances, these three countries reassumed the cooperation that had begun in the 1930s. This time, however, the emphasis was on defense against the Soviet-directed threat. In 1953 the three countries concluded in Ankara a Treaty of Friendship and Cooperation, the Balkan Pact, and a year later they signed a treaty containing a formal pledge of mutual military assistance in case of attack.

The Balkan Pact, however, fell into desuetude largely because of the revival of enmity between Turkey and Greece, this time over Cyprus. Yugoslavia, too, quickly lost interest in the pact when its relations with the Soviet Union improved after Khrushchev's visit of reconciliation to Belgrade in 1955. From the middle of the 1950s, therefore, Turkey ceased active diplomacy in the Balkans. With the four communist countries it maintained correct relations, and it managed to conclude an agreement with Bulgaria in 1968 on the further repatriation of a small number of ethnic Turks.[28] But Turkey's foreign policy concerns were elsewhere — with Greece, primarily, over Cyprus, with the Soviet Union, the United States, the European Community, and the Middle East Arab states.

The Balkan Muslim Factor

It has been the collapse of Yugoslavia — more specifically, the Muslim factor involved — that has drawn Turkey's attention back to the Balkans. As the discussion of nationalism in chapter 6 indicates, Muslims are involved in several actual or potential conflict situations throughout the region. To repeat: in Bosnia they were being subjected to something close to genocide; in Kosovo and the Sanjak they were in increasing danger; in Macedonia the Muslim Albanian minority's relations with the Slav majority were increasingly strained. Ethnic Turks in Macedonia, numbering up to 100,000, also could face a precarious future. Albania, with its nearly 70 percent Muslim population, was in danger of becoming involved in a conflict with Serbia and Montenegro — perhaps Macedonia and Greece, also. The large Turkish minority in Bulgaria, much better treated now than in the communist era, lived in strained relations with at least part of the Bulgarian majority, precisely because its situation was better. And the Turkish minority in Greek Thrace, although by no means the biggest bone of contention between Athens and Ankara, was an element of tension, easily aggravated if the political skies darkened.

This agenda was, indeed, potentially action-packed. But as late as the first half of 1992, Turkey had other seemingly more pressing concerns. It was preoccupied with the war between Azerbaijan and Armenia and the Kurdish revolt within its own territory. In the former, it strongly supported the Azeris, and saber-rattling from President Özal downward caused serious uneasiness in the West and a sharp response from Russia. In their suppression of renewed Kurdish disturbances at home, the Turks also drew unwelcome attention, and this episode at first caused a near-rupture in their relations with Germany. More positively, Turkey was laying the basis for a growing, influential relationship with the Turkic-Muslim successor states of the Soviet Union (although by 1993 there were doubts whether Turkey could sustain this relationship). It was also preparing its plans to launch its Black Sea economic cooperation zone project (see below pp. 298–300), which it did in June 1992.

But as the fighting in Bosnia-Hercegovina intensified, it was inevitable that Turkish concern would be directed toward it. In June 1992 Turkey hosted a meeting of the foreign ministers of the Islamic Conference that promised to support outside military intervention if United Nations sanctions failed to deter the Serbs. Later, at the UN, Turkey joined with Iran to form a committee that would work with the secretary-general to try to get action on the situation.[29] Still, the Turkish response was relatively muted. There was hope in Ankara that the sanctions might work and that UN and/or European Community efforts to end the fighting would succeed. It also was not clear to many what course the fighting in Bosnia-Hercegovina would take — how far the Serbs were prepared to go in carving out for themselves large parts of the republic, and to what extent Serbs and Croats would agree on dismembering it at the Muslims' expense.

Very soon, however, with the growing numbers of valid reports about "ethnic cleansing" and its attendant Serb atrocities, Turkish expressions of concern mounted. The extent of the Serbs' land-grab in Bosnia, and their future intentions, also were becoming clear. So was Serb-Croat collusion in dividing up parts of Bosnia-Hercegovina, despite their ever-growing mutual hatred. Any excuses for Turkish inaction were becoming more untenable.

Pressures on Turkey to Act

The Bosnian war was taking on new dimensions, and the reasons for a more active Turkish role were mounting to include:

(1) The strength of public opinion in Turkey itself. Although it was wrong to speak of the "re-Islamization" of Turkey, there had been enough movement away from Kemalist secularization since the end of World War II to make large sections of the Turkish public responsive to demands (usually from more fully "Islamisized" compatriots) that something be done in Bosnia.[30] The Kemalist elites in Istanbul and Ankara were still reluctant to see Turkey involved again in the Balkans, and in a "religious war" at that, as one of their number privately put it to me in conversation. But the political power of these elites had been considerably weakened over the past quarter century, while that of moderate Muslims had increased, a fact reflected in the strength of the True Path and Motherland parties and personified by leading politicians like Turgut Özal and Suleyman Demirel. And, religion aside, Turks and the Bosnian Muslims generally felt ethnically and historically close to one another. After Austria took control of Bosnia-Hercegovina in 1878, many Bosnian Muslims moved to Turkey, and several hundred thousand Turks today are believed to have Bosnian ancestry.[31] Also, Bosnian and many Turkish Muslims have generally shared an easygoing attitude to their religious faith.

(2) The lack of a firm Western response to the situation. The disunity and indecision shown mainly by the European Community, the United Nations, and the United States in their response to Bosnia-Hercegovina seemed only to be shifting responsibility increasingly toward Turkey.

(3) Western impotence regarding Bosnia was lending credibility to suspicions throughout Islam that the "West" was ready, or even anxious, to see this Muslim "outpost" in Europe liquidated. The West was seen as leaving the Bosnian Muslims to the mercy of their more powerful enemies. (The Serbs, for their part, were only too glad to pose as the defenders of European civilization against what they claimed to be this new historic threat from Islam.) These suspicions of Western intentions were gathering strength, even among some liberals

in Turkey. Mehmet Ali Birand, for example, a distinguished, generally pro-Western journalist, said that his whole Weltanschauung had been shattered by the recent Balkan developments. "The events in Bosnia-Hercegovina show," he is quoted as saying, "that the West does not want a Muslim country in Europe. Their non-intervention shows this. They are letting the Serbs do their dirty work."[32]

Inevitably, the contrast with Western firmness over Iraq's invasion of Kuwait in 1991 was drawn by many commentators. It was not just a question of Bosnia-Hercegovina having no oil. It was also, the argument went, because it had too many Muslims. An educated Turk put the question to me with piercing truth in another way in the summer of 1993: "What if the Bosnians had not been Muslims but Jews? Would the West, particularly the Americans, have done nothing then?"

(4) Charges of Western complicity in Serbian genocide were being heard throughout Islam, but they were obviously the loudest in the militant Islamic states, as were the calls for united Muslim action against the Serbs. A jihad was being called for with increasing frequency.[33] Iran was taking the lead in this agitation, some pronouncements by its prominent clerics recalling the uncompromising ferocity of Ayatollah Khomeini's heyday. Just as in the internal Iranian domestic context those who were more moderate had to try to keep pace with the extremists, so in the international Muslim context moderate Turkey could not afford to be demonstrably less concerned than extremist Iran.

(5) The growth of Turkish influence in the Muslim-Turkic republics of the old Soviet Union since the beginning of 1991, however temporary it might prove to be, had been an important consequence of the Soviet Union's collapse. If this influence could be maintained, Turkey could become a major regional power—perhaps a major world power. These new republics tended to look to Turkey rather than Iran because their populations were of a similar ethnic background (except in the case of Tadjikistan) and because Turkey represented a more modern Muslim outlook bent on technical and economic progress. But both their governments and their political elites would be watching Turkey's response to the Bosnian crisis. Therefore, if Turkey could not, itself, deliver the Muslims in Bosnia-Hercegovina, it at least must take the lead in organizing measures that might.

The result of all these pressures was feverish Turkish diplomatic activity beginning in the summer of 1992 to try to strengthen Western resolve against Serbia. Turkey also offered to place at least a thousand troops at the disposal of a combined expeditionary force and urged the bombing of Serbian targets from a number of directions.[34] But the real test of Turkey's commitment to the Bosnian Muslims, at least in the eyes of Islam generally, would be its reaction to any Western peace or cease-fire agreement that was severely damaging to the Muslims. And, in the event, Turkey did strongly oppose the Vance-Owen plan in 1993 (see chapter 7) and continued its strong opposition to subsequent Western sponsored peace moves.

In sum, the situation in Bosnia-Hercegovina appeared to put Turkey on notice. It wanted to concentrate on other things, but it was being forced back to the Balkans. In February 1993 Özal visited Sofia, Skopje, and Tirana in a tour that dramatized Turkey's renewed regional interest. Turkey and Albania were developing relations in an almost spectacular way.[35] And if the Yugoslav conflict did spread to Kosovo and then spilled over into Albania and Macedonia, Turkey could be in the thick of a conflict it did not want, in a region to which it would have preferred not to return. The death of Özal in April 1993 was not likely to change the Turkish position or relieve the dilemma.

Muslims apart, none of the Balkan nations wanted the Turks back in any capacity. The prospect of new waves of "Mehmetçiks" roving the peninsula was not one in which they reveled. Once the Turks got there, would they ever leave?[36] In Bulgaria, especially, with its large Turkish minority and its recent memory of persecution, the prospect could be particularly unsettling. It certainly would put an end to the promising improvement in relations between Ankara and Sofia, which began in 1991. Finally, taking the region as a whole, Turkish reentry in any kind of military capacity would both hasten and broaden the Slav-Muslim confrontation (see chapters 6 and 7). Some of the early speculation about such a confrontation had centered on whether Turkey would be able to stay aloof from it. The question might have to be answered earlier than expected.

A Peaceful Initiative

One cannot leave the subject of Turkey's role in the Balkans without mentioning the Black Sea Cooperation Region Project (BECR). It might seem indecorous to mention an initiative predicated on peaceful cooperation at a time when the Balkans were in such turmoil, and when the Balkan countries were, in any case, only peripheral to this initiative, but it serves to illustrate a new Turkish constructive interest in the region, and it certainly reflects Turkey's increasing international stature.

The BECR was the brainchild of Turgut Özal, prime minister and later president of Turkey. Its main objective was to "create favorable conditions and establish institutional arrangements among the Black Sea countries for the development and diversification of their economic relations by making efficient use of advantages arising from geographical proximity and the complementary nature of their economies."[37] A multinational constituent conference was held in Ankara in December 1990, that is, one year before the final collapse of the Soviet Union. Romania and Bulgaria took part; the Soviet delegation also included deputy foreign ministers from Azerbaijan, Georgia, Moldavia, and Armenia. In the first half of 1991, meetings to discuss the initial stages of the project also were held in Bucharest, Sofia, and Moscow. These sessions were designed to create favorable conditions for both intergovernmental and nongovernmental cooperation.

Hardly surprising for an Özal initiative, great stress was laid on private enterprise in international cooperation. Such an emphasis, the Turks argued, would assist the transition to the free market economy that the successor states of the Soviet Union, Bulgaria, and Romania were undergoing. The eventual, broader ambition of the project was for the Black Sea region to become an "integral part of the world economy." The BECR, it was claimed, followed on from the end of the Cold War and the breaking down of hostile world blocs, a process that it would help to accelerate.

It was an imaginative project, typical of Özal's resourcefulness. But the main economic aim for Turkey was to get into the old Soviet market and gain access to its raw materials. The emphasis given to cooperation, not only with the then-Soviet center, but also with the individual republics, was a move to reinsure against the eventual breakup of the USSR, which was to occur much sooner than expected. The specifically Balkan aspect of the project, however, at first looked meager. Although neither Bulgaria nor Romania could be optimistic about early acceptance by "Europe," this goal was given higher priority than any southern and eastern gravitation implicit in the BECR proposal.

The immediate aftermath of the Soviet collapse delayed progress in developing the Turkish initiative. During a period of breakup and then of revived antagonisms and conflicts in parts of the old Soviet empire, any proposals for regional cooperation were seen by many as premature, if not illusory.[38] But the Turks persisted, and in June 1992 eleven heads of government met in Istanbul to officially launch the Black Sea economic cooperation project. Greece and Albania, not Black Sea countries and not initially envisaged as members, were represented, along with Romania and Bulgaria. From the former Soviet Union, so were Azerbaijan, Armenia, Georgia, Ukraine, Moldova, and Russia.

The Black Sea project has become a symptom of Turkey's confidence and a reflection of its extraordinary good luck in the early 1990s. The project was conceived at a time when its international stature actually seemed to be shrinking rather than expanding. Rejected by Europe and apparently marginalized by the end of the Cold War, the project at first had a *faute de mieux,* fallback look about it. Then came the Soviet collapse, and the project was infused with new meaning and took on a new importance. Far from becoming peripheral, as it had seemed doomed to be only a few months earlier, Turkey now became pivotal, expanding its economic, political, and cultural influence, penetrating into some regions, and, as with the Balkans, perhaps being sucked in by others.

The Old and the New Russia: Reduced but Relevant

Who lost Eastern Europe? No sooner had the last revolution ended in their former satellites than the debate in Moscow started. It was all part of the larger domestic dispute involving conservatives, reformers, and radicals, with the conservative anger directed against Mikhail Gorbachev, the man whose reform had turned into rout. And the loss of Eastern Europe was the first big, tangible disaster that the conservatives could point to. But it was not just that. The East European revolutions of 1989 exploded the myth of Soviet Russian acceptability in Eastern Europe, of the "togetherness" that had been preached so assiduously and believed so gullibly by many because they wanted to believe it. This myth was also part of the Great Liberation War mystique, a war in which the Soviet Union had suffered so grievously — not just for its own salvation, the official teaching went, but for that of the East Europeans, who now were turning their backs on it. And with the downfall of the German Democratic Republic and the subsequent reunification of Germany, the worries about Eastern Europe became part of the bigger bewilderment and disillusion.

But these external disasters, however huge, were only a small part of these worries when weighed against the collapse of socialism at home and the impending disintegration of the Soviet Union itself. The indescribable sufferings under Stalin and then the wartime sacrifices — they all had turned out to be in vain. The struggle had, indeed, been unavailing.

This landscape of disintegration and uncertainty was a fertile field for Gorbachev's enemies, and they plowed it thoroughly, nowhere more so than at the 28th Soviet Party Congress in June 1990. As Gorbachev moved steadily away from reform and toward the conservative camp, it was left mainly to foreign minister Eduard Shevardnadze to defend the new policy of abjuring the Brezhnev Doctrine and letting Eastern Europe go the way it chose. The best counter to the conservative attacks, however, came not from Shevardnadze but from the liberal commentator, Alexander Bovin, in *Izvestia:*

> Spears should not be thrown at our international policies. . . . The fact that we were not able to create a truly developed society that would be on a par with the modern world in terms of economy and democracy — this is the reason for everything that has taken place in Europe. . . . We lost [Eastern] Europe because we lost ourselves. We failed, in every respect, to create a modern developed society.[39]

The "Who Lost Eastern Europe?" debate soon petered out, however. It always had been irrelevant to the East Europeans, anyway (as long, of course, as the Moscow conservatives did not recover power). What was relevant to the East Europeans were (1) the practicalities of consummating their disentanglement from Soviet control; (2) what new policy the Soviets now might devise in relation to them.

The Disentanglement

Comecon and the Warsaw Pact expired, in effect, in 1990. The Soviets, and probably some weaker East European states like Bulgaria, would have liked some kind of economic association to replace Comecon, but none of the East Europeans wanted anything implying Soviet control. In any case, the Soviets' insistence at the beginning of

1991 that their trade with Eastern Europe be put on a hard currency basis (see chapter 5) effectively killed the hopes of any such association. As for the Warsaw Pact, Moscow would have liked it to evolve into a political association; Gorbachev himself was keen on the idea. At first, there was some interest in this idea, especially on the part of Czechoslovakia, which saw the survival of the alliance in a political form as a stabilizing element in a European situation that would continue to be highly volatile.[40] Poland, too, because of the perceived German "threat," was not pressing for the alliance's demise (see chapter 6). But Hungary had made clear its determination to leave the pact, and this step, combined with indecision and division in Moscow, plus the end-of-epoch mood in the region as a whole, gave even an emasculated Warsaw Pact no future.

The pact might be as good as dead, but Soviet troop concentrations in Poland, Czechoslovakia, and Hungary were very much alive, although obviously at a loose end now that the Cold War had melted away. Czechoslovakia, Hungary, and eventually Poland wanted the troops out. But withdrawal of Soviet military forces was no simple matter. First, the Soviet military was reluctant to withdraw from any territory. Second, the Soviets wanted compensation for the military property they would abandon, while the Poles, Czechoslovaks, and Hungarians wanted compensation for the unholy mess their "guests" would be leaving behind.

In spite of such disputes, the withdrawals from Czechoslovakia and Hungary went surprisingly smoothly. The last Soviet troops left both countries in May and June of 1991. With Poland, the situation was more difficult. The Soviets were not nearly as amenable to departing as they had been in the case of Czechoslovakia and Hungary. The mood was hardening in Moscow, with the military and the conservatives increasing their power and their influence on Gorbachev. Besides, genuine difficulties arose concerning the agreed-upon presence of Soviet troops in the former GDR till 1994 and the Soviets' insistence that they needed transit facilities in Poland. The negotiations were tough, bitter, and frequently interrupted. They also reflected the dislike that the Poles and Russians harbored for each other, and the pride, arrogance, and sense of humiliation felt by the Russian side, forcefully expressed in the vivid outbursts of their commanding general.[41]

Had the Soviet Union survived, negotiations could have been protracted indefinitely. Had the August 1991 coup in Moscow succeeded, the talks almost certainly would have been broken off, leading to serious tension between the two countries. But with the disintegration of the Soviet Union after the failure of the coup, and with Boris Yeltsin determined to settle the issue quickly, negotiations began to proceed more smoothly. In the fall of 1992 the last Soviet troops left Poland, too. An important obstacle to the mending of Polish-Russian relations had been removed, but an even bigger one also was demolished in the fall of 1992. Moscow finally and formally admitted that the Soviets, not the Germans, were responsible for the Katyn murders of Polish officers during World War II.[42] Everybody already knew this to be true, but, in the Polish-Russian context, the Russian admission was imperative.

Reluctantly Relinquishing

The demise of the Warsaw Pact and Comecon and the withdrawal of Soviet troops from East-Central Europe were all formal acts closing the lid on forty years of Soviet domination. But in the last two years of its existence, the Soviet Union was not prepared to let Eastern Europe go entirely. It regarded its security interests and, above all, its standing as a great power as resting on the recognition of its regional sphere of influence. The relationship may have changed, but if Moscow had lost its *droit de seigneur,* it wanted to keep a *droit de regard.*

All the power players in Moscow were agreed on that point, albeit with different motives, emphases, and views about the gradations of influence. The military, reluctant about troop withdrawals and still fighting the Cold War if only as a means of fighting off the liberals at home, wanted as little recognition as possible of the new regional reality. What made them particularly nervous was the reunification of Germany and the prospect of countries like Czechoslovakia and Poland joining NATO. The attitude of the Communist Party of the Soviet Union (CPSU) was much the same, but it was expressed more covertly and usually with more finesse. A memorandum circulated by the Central Committee's international department in early 1991 emphasized the need to develop bilateral ties with the East European countries, to prevent them joining NATO, to keep them within the Soviet Union's economic orbit, and to "discourage" anti-Soviet tendencies in the politics of those nations.[43] Moreover, neither the military nor the party liked the East Europeans ganging up together—if not *against* the

Soviet Union then certainly *without* it—as the Poles, Czechoslovaks, and Hungarians seemed to be doing with their Visegrád association (see chapter 6).

The official foreign ministry line was different in that it accepted the sovereignty of the Eastern European countries (which the military and the party, at least by implication, did not) and downplayed both the likelihood of Western machinations in the region and of the East Europeans wanting to join NATO. This line was made clear when Shevardnadze was at the foreign ministry, much less clear, though, after he resigned in December 1990. His resignation had been a striking demonstration of the conservatives' gains in Moscow, and it set the stage for a considerably tougher governmental line on Eastern Europe as well, including that of the foreign ministry. This hardening was best expressed by deputy foreign minister Yuli Kvitsinski, former ambassador to Bonn and of the "walk in the woods" (Geneva) fame. While ruling out any return to past domination, Kvitsinski claimed that the Soviet Union had "legitimate interests" in Eastern Europe that had "historical and geopolitical roots" and that "had to be taken into account."[44] The government continued voicing this line right up to the end of the Soviet Union itself.

But how much *real* difference existed between the Shevardnadze and Kvitsinski lines is difficult to tell. Although Shevardnadze is not on record as expatiating on the subject, several like-minded liberals, while protesting that their sovereignty was fixed, total, and inviolable, still saw the East European countries as something special. Oleg T. Bogomolov, for example, one of the most sincere liberals, was no exception: "Like others, I'm concerned about our loss of interest in the group of countries seen until recently as a Soviet foreign policy priority. We used to assign them a special place in our policy but everything changed almost overnight. We are beginning to forget that we will have to live with them in the years ahead."[45] What practically everyone in Moscow wanted was a sphere of influence in Eastern Europe. For conservatives and middle-of-the-roaders, this was clear. But, however much many liberals would have wanted to avoid the expression, they did regard Eastern Europe as special to Soviet concerns in the way that, say, Central America was to American interests. Complete internal freedom they were prepared to concede, but they would have liked a foreign policy ultimately circumscribed by the Soviet interest. Few Russians would have regarded this status as being inconsistent with East European freedoms or as anything that reasonable East Europeans should find demeaning. This view persisted because few of them — even the best and the brightest in terms of liberalization and westernization — could shake off the last traces of the Russian imperialist mind-set. Nor was this complex unique to Russia; the citizens of the old Western imperialist powers had believed much the same. The mind-set simply comes with the status and does not evaporate when the status is lost. The Russians, though, were to become particular victims; it was not only losing Eastern Europe that disturbed them, but the other parts of the Soviet Union as well, parts they considered their own blood and limbs.

The mechanism to which Moscow resorted in trying to shore up its special status in Eastern Europe was the bilateral treaty. This mechanism also had been the organizational key to the Soviet system in Eastern Europe. Moscow had bilateral treaties with all of its satellites and they, in turn, had bilateral treaties with each other. These treaties formed the systemic bedrock on which the multilateral organizations like Comecon and the Warsaw Pact were superimposed. Now, of course, the new situation demanded new treaties. None of the new postcommunist East European states were averse to them, for they wanted to regularize their relations with the Soviet Union by agreements reflecting their new status. But for most of them, the first of these treaties, signed by the Soviets with Romania in April 1991, smacked more of the old relationship than the kind of new one that they wanted.

The new Soviet-Romanian treaty contained clauses forbidding either side to join an alliance directed against the other and prohibited the stationing of foreign troops on either's territory. It also contained general provisions about military cooperation and about consultations in case of military threat.[46] The treaty obviously reflected the Soviet fear of the East Europeans being tempted into NATO. (Whether the new Romanian treaty disbarred Bucharest from joining the European Community as well was questionable.) The agreement obviously was meant as a model for the other East European countries. It would have meant virtual "Finlandization" in the classic sense. But the East-Central Europeans, much as they would have welcomed this option just a few years earlier, were in no mood for it now. They saw themselves as part of the West in every category that the West was prepared to open up to them. Anyway, with the end of the Cold War, neutrality was surely passé — if not for Romania, then certainly for them. They rejected the model, as, after some hesitation, did the Bulgarians, whom the Soviets had hoped would have few doubts about subscribing to it.

Why, therefore, had Romania gone out on a limb? It seemed all the more ironical that a country that, for a quarter-century under communism, had shown much skill and nerve in keeping the Soviets at arm's length, now should be so ready to assist them in their East European salvage operation. It is too simple to explain it on the grounds that Iliescu, the Romanian president, was a "Gorbachev clone," ready to throw in his lot with a reformed Soviet Union rather than with the capitalist West. (The Romanian opposition simply saw it as Iliescu showing his true colors.) Nor is the realpolitik explanation wholly convincing: that Moldova and the volatile situation there necessitated a respectful policy toward the Soviet Union. The main explanation probably is to be found in the Romanian leadership's calculation that the Soviet Union, whatever its current tribulations, was there to stay as a world power with dominant interests in Eastern Europe, these interests at the very least encompassing Romania, its immediate neighbor. As for the West, its interest in Romania was likely to be minimal, its willingness to protect Romania even less. In this light, the treaty made sense at the time.

But to the East-Central Europeans a new status of neutrality would imply subservience. In any case, they were much more hopeful of the West's protective and benevolent embrace than were the Romanians. The eventual Bulgarian decision to reject the Romanian precedent probably required considerable nerve because Bulgaria's prospects of Western acceptance seemed nearly as dim as those of Romania. Bulgaria's economy also was more closely tied to that of the Soviets than was any other East European economy, giving Moscow real chances to apply pressure. But Bulgaria's former communist reputation as the most subservient satellite now made it imperative to seek a new image. In any case, the danger soon passed. After the failure of the August 1991 coup, Moscow dropped its insistence on the objectionable security clauses that characterized the Romanian treaty and concluded agreements between equals with Bulgaria, Poland, Hungary, and Czechoslovakia.

And after January 1, 1992, none of it mattered anyway. The Soviet Union became the Commonwealth of Independent States (CIS) and the East Europeans now had different eastern problems on their hands: the new struggling successor states. They had shed one huge problem and acquired several smaller ones. As indicated in chapter 6, these problems could well be serious and lasting. But, comparing their new neighbors with their old one, all of the East Europeans were breathing an audible sigh of relief.

What now of Russia? Its own domestic preoccupations—psychological, political, economic, and ethnic—have dominated since it emerged from the demise of the Soviet Union at the beginning of 1992. Externally, apart from its global diplomacy, it had been mainly concerned with relations with the Ukraine, the most important part of the "near abroad," the significant and far from reassuring description many important Russians gave to former parts of the Soviet Union. But Eastern Europe had not been entirely neglected. By the end of 1993 President Yeltsin had visited all the East European states except Romania. His aim was to placate and please, to present a benevolent image of the new Russia. He partly succeeded. But the East Europeans knew that it was much too early to tell what Russia's future intentions toward them might be. Those more realistic and historically minded knew that Russia would eventually seek a special relationship. The question was: how special?

The East Europeans would be especially watching Russia's relations with the "near abroad." If a man like Zhirinovsky ever came to power, then Russia would have become, not a partner in international relations, but a rogue elephant bent on trampling them. The West's "Partnership for Peace" was predicated on the assumption that he must not and would not come to power. But the West, and the East Europeans, had to be aware that a well-governed, civilized Russia—temporarily poor but powerful and proud—would still have national interests it would defend and exert. Anybody not prepared for this would be living in cloud-cuckoo land; anybody rejecting it would be threatening the peace more than the Russians he was accusing. The question was *how* Russia pursued its interests and what the response was. It was not impossible for its interests to be both satisfied and contained within an international system that avoided both appeasement and provocation. History had returned to Europe; so must diplomacy.

9

THE OUTLOOK

PRECARIOUS BUT NOT PRE-DOOMED

> A good democratic government not only considers the demands of its citizenry (that is, is responsive), but also acts efficaciously upon these demands (that is, is effective).—Robert D. Putnam

> Democracy is not fancy shop-windows. . . . It's back-breaking work.—Ewa Letowska, former Polish ombudsman

> In a way it is a race to build the new Europe before the old one takes over.—R. C. Longworth, *Chicago Tribune*

In 1994 most of the East European states moved into the fifth year of their revolution. And, as this book has emphasized more than once, the only way is forward—forward, at least, to somewhere. Not that the models before them are uncompromisingly rigid. In politics, such models take in strong presidencies or strong parliaments; in economics, they can encompass virtual laissez-faire, social liberalism, and social democracy. But they do demand, in public and private life, as much freedom as mutually agreed constraints permit.

In the West the models have been evolving for generations—centuries even. And they are still evolving. Perhaps they will always be an aspiration rather than an attainment; the standards that they set are breached almost as often as they are observed. But the models work, however faultily. Now East Europeans are trying to do in one or two decades what has taken so much longer in the West. Some Western observers and—more depressing—a growing number of East Europeans are concluding that the task is impossible. Eastern Europe has bitten off too much; going for both liberal democracy and the market will mean ending up getting neither.

The danger inherent in the attempt certainly is there. The increasing social hardship that the economic reform is inflicting threatens both the economic reform itself and the fledgling political democracy. Hardly surprising, therefore, that there are increasing calls for a slower pace of reform that would ease the burden on those millions of East Europeans materially worse off now than under communism. But therein lies one of the great dilemmas now facing Eastern Europe: the longer it takes for living standards to improve, new jobs to be created, and inflation to abate, the greater the risk of political disarray. Political institutions already are in place, and competitive politics are in operation, however creakily in some places and frenetically in others. Democratic politics, or at least the political process, are more vigorous than market economics. But if the economy fails, politics will, too.

The opposite is not necessarily the case. There are enough current East Asian examples, not to mention General Pinochet's Chile for a while, of flourishing capitalist-type economies cohabiting with partly or profoundly undemocratic political systems. But, as argued in chapter 1, such a recourse might be fatal for the East European countries. Whether some might be forced into authoritarianism is too early to say, but the longer the market economy takes to deliver the goods under democracy, the more attractive the authoritarian alternative could become. It need not happen. In Poland, the Czech Republic, and Hungary, real signs of economic promise were apparent in early 1994. Much would depend on how judicious the admixture was between stick and carrot, shock and therapy. In economic policy people will endure much present privation if there is hope of future improvement. But, as they had already shown in Poland, they were getting impatient. The short term is proving too long, and the long term might stretch on indefinitely. Poland was not relapsing into authoritarianism; in fact, democracy might ultimately be strengthened by the left-wing victory. But the contradiction between economic and social imperatives had been dramatized in Poland. Could they ever become compatible?

Not surprisingly, there was much impatience with economists per se. Adapting Clemenceau, many East Europeans would maintain that the economy was too important to be left to the economists. These were seen as never fully in control of the forces they unleash, many of them little more than sorcerer's apprentices. But not only individual economists must bear the burden of decision. International institutions like the IMF are crucially caught up in Eastern Europe's future. Understandably, they are worried about the easy come, easy go propensities of many of their borrowers. But they perhaps could do with a bit less dogmatism in their own lending, a bit more understanding, too, of the history that their borrowers are up against.

Many observers were seeing 1993 and 1994 as the crucible years—

the make-or-break years — for several East European countries. These countries, therefore, still were given a chance. Other observers, however, had given them practically no chance — right from the start. The "fundamentalists" argued that the very task — democracy and the market together — is simply too herculean. Others adduced sociological and cultural arguments to discount the East Europeans' chances. Some pointed to the almost total lack in the region of a middle class — both the motor and the anchor of modern democracies. For the past and the immediate present, this argument might be well taken. A native East European middle class always has been in short supply. Except for the emergence of a Czech middle class early in this century, historically the bourgeoisie was largely German or Jewish in several countries. World War II, its aftermath, and the Holocaust virtually removed this bourgeoisie. Then came communism, notoriously unsympathetic to the notion of a middle class.

But this argument may be too pessimistic. Many entrepreneurs are springing up in Eastern Europe on the heels of the burgeoning new private sector. True, many of them are not the solid burghers that one traditionally has had in mind when picturing the middle class — law-abiding and dependable, securing the state and forwarding the economy, something from Rembrandt, for example, or out of Thomas Mann. They are more reminiscent of post-World War II London barrow boys, dodging the law rather than deferring to it, here today gone tomorrow, a moving target for the tax man. For them, postcommunist economics is not so much a free market as a flea market. It would be wrong, though, to give up on them entirely. Historically, the ancestors of many doughty burghers started off in this way. Respectability comes later.

"Nomenklatura-privatization," however hard to stomach, also will help create a middle class of sorts. Many Sauls are indeed becoming Pauls (with a little financial inducement); the traffic jam on the road to Damascus is getting bigger by the day. Few would have the breathtaking insouciance of a Gaidar Aliev, Brezhnev's resilient old buddy now back in power in Baku: "I was always a democrat," he assured bemused reporters. "You just never noticed." But many are showing a surprising talent for adjustment. And — who knows? — many may be as successful in coping with the mysteries of capitalism as they were in getting round the idiocies of socialism. Galling, certainly, but nothing new: every revolution casts parts of its flotsam and jetsam unharmed onto the farther shore. Eastern Europe's revolution is the rule, therefore, not the exception.

There also is a new middle class emerging from vastly different origins — through the restitution to former owners and their descendants of businesses and properties confiscated by the communists. This process is moving faster in some countries than in others, and, like all restitution procedures, it often is a matter of arcane complexity. The whole principle, too, of restitution is controversial. Still, provided that the new owners are more active than absentee, that they discover or rediscover entrepreneurial talents, and that they *turn their clocks forward rather than back,* they could become the most solid element — the burghers — of the evolving East European middle class.

The economic and political need of a strong middle class — to motivate economic life, to keep political extremes apart and secure the state — is almost universally accepted. But in postcommunist Eastern Europe, as well as in the successor states of the Soviet Union, it is only a vigorous middle class that also can realize the concept of "civicness," or "civic-mindedness," "public spirit," which is essential for all-round political development. "Civic-ness" is needed to break the "them" and "us" syndrome, to temper and steer the development of liberal institutions and the liberal habit of mind. It is an adjunct of liberalism, and it certainly is not incompatible with it. In former Ottoman Eastern Europe there was no tradition of this kind whatsoever, and precious little of it developed after liberation. In some of the Habsburg lands, though, such a tradition did become established — in Bohemia and Moravia, for example, in Hungary, to some extent, and in some parts of Poland. It needs to be revived because no functioning democracy is complete without it. Whether, of course, the flea-market privateers or the nomenklatura capitalists are ideally suited to this task is another matter. But, again, if "civic-ness" were to become accepted at least as an *aspiration,* it might be surprising how many of these apparent sociopaths might adapt. Here, the "former people," those returning from exile, could set the pace, provided they are interested in more than material restitution. George Soros, although firmly resident in New York, is a towering example of what can be done. More of the Soros spirit is needed. If he remains the exception, the very idea of "civic-mindedness" is defeated.

A middle class, therefore, might not be too hard to conjure up. But what about the cultural argument advanced by the doomsayers? Basically, this argument holds that the communist system has turned most East Europeans into vegetables. No matter how good the new democratic institutions might look, they cannot operate in a cultural vacuum that vitiates competitive politics, civil society, and economic individualism. The communist heritage on the individual level is selfishness, jealousy, and distrust. Its debilitating legacy makes any notion of government of the people, by the people, and for the people either a pious hope or a sick joke. The corollary, of course, is authoritarianism—the stronger the better—because it is the only thing that will head off the kind of chaos that leads to something worse: autocracy.

This argument has substance. But, although Eastern Europe since 1989 has indeed displayed symptoms of a malevolent shiftlessness, it also has been the scene of strenuous activity that belies the image of one vast cabbage patch. As mentioned, economic activity sometimes amounts to frenzy, and in most countries there is real political liveliness—proportionally more than in most Western countries. That some of this liveliness has been to little avail is more the institutions' fault than the people's. And the political apathy that has been growing in countries like Hungary and Poland derives less from popular sloth as from a feeling of exclusion from the political games that the new establishment is seen as playing. Historically, too, there has been a resilience about the different East European nations that has enabled them to overcome longer and more enervating deprivations than communism. Five hundred years of Ottoman rule certainly has left its impression on the Bulgarians, for example. But not overwhelmingly so—despite the excuses often made. (History in Eastern Europe often is used for excuses rather than instruction.) How much, then, is forty-odd years of communism eventually going to mean? The best guess is that all of the East European nations will shake off the enfeebling legacy of communism sooner than many fear. Therefore, the colonels, the priests, and the policemen, seen by some pessimists as filling the vacuum of power and responsibility as the new lords of the East European cabbage patch, have not yet appeared. They may be waiting in the wings, but they are nowhere near center stage. With a bit of luck, they may get nothing but bit parts.

No cause exists for complacency, though. Crime and corruption, organized and spontaneous, is surging to such a degree that it could become undermining—morally, psychologically, politically, and economically. The Mafia (the real Sicilian original), as well as scores of homegrown mafias, are operating with seeming impunity, often in collaboration with parts of the business nomenklatura, the police, almost all of which is a carryover from the old regime, as well as politicians. The security of ordinary citizens, too, on the streets and sometimes in their homes, is seriously threatened. These kinds of crime, on such a scale, could become enveloping. But as big a danger could lie in the impact on the democratic political process that might result from any ruthless efforts to fight crime. It is a subject obviously made for demagogy, but the real threat in any offensive against crime could be in the suspension of individual and institutional freedoms. These freedoms are simply too fragile to withstand serious battering, however well-intentioned.

Nor can the new East European institutions, or the spirit of liberal tolerance needed by them, *survive* the obsession with issues that distract and divide, issues dominated by the past rather than directed to the future. "Decommunization," and its offspring "lustration," have been the most retarding of these. Much already has been written in this book on the subject. Still, no concluding chapter can fail to return to it. Briefly, two camps face each other. One, although insisting that communist criminals be brought to book, considers the fight against communism to be essentially over; the other camp rejects this approach and sees the decisive phase of the struggle only just beginning. Indeed, for many in this second camp, especially those who played a conspicuously passive role before 1989, the postrevolutionary struggle is imperative, and their combative zeal is in inverse ratio to their lack of it before and during the revolution. Then, there are those Savonarolas who did fight the red devil, and suffered for it, but whose vengeful self-righteousness is unrelenting.

Decommunization temporarily unites these two implacable elements, and there have been spectacular examples of their excesses. For example, the labyrinthine case of Jan Kavan in Prague, also with anti-Semitic undertones — "From Kafka to Dreyfus," as one American headline put it; the squalid fiasco in the Polish Sejm over the security files; István Csurka's atavistic rantings in Hungary. Certainly, more will appear in the future. Such cases are not just politically crippling, but morally blighting and internationally damaging. There are those, of course, who would cringe as much as anybody else at the three examples just cited but would defend lustration on the grounds that Eastern Europe needs a "catharsis." Maybe. The problem, though, with some of these people is that, once this catharsis was over, they would start looking for another. And what is involved here is not a relatively quick purgation, but a never-ending, tortuous undermining of public life. Lustration and what it symbolizes mean not catharsis but corrosion.

The decisive political struggle in most East European countries today is not between "democrats" and "communists" but between the "liberals" and "radicals" in the anticommunist camp—between the Girondists and the Jacobins. On the issue of "decommunization," the Girondists advocate moderation and seek conciliation, the Jacobins demand retribution (or revenge) and seek confrontation, with anticommunism become virtually an end in itself. "Decommunization" also is symptomatic, not only of the many other specific issues dividing "liberals" and "radicals" in postcommunist Eastern Europe, but of the gulf between them in values—in fact, in the whole Weltanschauung that inspires the politics of each side.

What Eastern Europe needed was liberal institutions and procedures, which it largely had, pervaded by the liberal spirit, which needed both deepening and widening. Liberal institutions are easy to define and recognize: parliamentary government, democratic constitutions, independent courts administering the rule of law, a market economy, and the freedoms of speech, association, and religion. The liberal spirit, though, is much less easy to define and its absence is often easier to detect than its presence. But Peter Pulzer, in discussing German nineteenth-century liberalism, has useful pointers: "Liberalism . . . was a set of moral qualities, those of rationalism, humanism, and—to give it its German context—Aufklärung." Pulzer continues: "To be 'Liberal' means, in German even more than in English, to be just, broad-minded, and generous."[1]

Obviously, this is the liberal *ideal,* often more honored in the breach than the observance. But at least this ideal sets a standard by which political life in Eastern Europe must be judged. Above all, liberal institutions and procedures must be honored not only when they work to the citizen's advantage but also when they work to his perceived disadvantage. The attitude "when we win, it's democracy; when we lose, it's cheating" was persisting in Eastern Europe long after the conduct of elections gave any justification for it. And often it had not been the elections themselves that gave rise to this attitude but the entrenched inability of many people to understand what democratic elections are all about. It was well worth noting, too, that many vociferous anticommunists were just as much the victims of this attitude as many former communists. The heirs to Eastern Europe's widespread antidemocratic tradition are alive and kicking today. They are depressingly numerous and they cover the entire political spectrum.

The liberal concept, on which any new democratic order must be based, is still fragile. It could be damaged not just by entrenched attitudes but also by social damage inflicted by economic policy. A comparison with the late nineteenth century in most of Western and Central Europe is illustrative. Nineteenth-century liberalism, in its dedication to laissez-faire and its lack of concern for social consequences, brought on massive opposition from peasants, from the proliferating working class, skilled and unskilled, and from artisans and small shopkeepers. These were the groups that divided their opposition between left and right. Today, nothing like the social callousness of that time remains; attitudes are different, and a welfare net of sorts exists in all of the East European countries. But "shock therapy," dogmatically applied, coming after the coddling of the communist era, carries with it social and eventually political dangers similar in principle to the laissez-faire indifference of a century ago. So do the conspicuous consumption and the tasteless flaunting of wealth found throughout the region. True, the money being made now in Eastern Europe is peanuts compared with the earnings possible in Western and Central Europe then, but its impact is the same, and there is the same distaste for many of the people who are spending it.

The antiliberal forces in Eastern Europe today, still more potential than actual in terms of danger, also would divide, as their Central European predecessors did, between left and right. Serious social hardship could not just consolidate but strengthen the *unreformed* communist elements that exist, open or lurking, throughout Eastern Europe—and make them more unreformed than ever. (A roaring red comeback in Russia, though, however much it might hearten these elements, would neutralize their electoral prospects.) But for several years, anyway, the main danger could come from the conservative, clerical, nationalist, in some cases neofascist right. Partly through its own fault, liberalism could find itself caught again and crushed, as it was in the early twentieth century, by the antiliberal forces closing in from all directions.

What is needed to avoid this possibility? First, more genuine liberals! And here the *immediate* prospects are hardly promising. "Liberals" have steadily lost their grip on the power and influence that they held in the immediate postcommunist phase. Hailed as the victors in 1989, especially in Poland, Czechoslovakia, and, to some extent, in Hungary and Bulgaria, they are either in eclipse, on the fringe, or in a state of siege. The liberal Solidarity intellectuals in Poland were shattered in the September 1993 elections. Even Václav Havel was being politically marginalized along with most of his like-minded supporters who led the velvet revolution. In Hungary the situation is more complicated because the philosophical liberals, who made up most of the dissidents under communism, lost the free election in 1990 and went into opposition. The decisive day for them will be the parliamentary elections in 1994. In Bulgaria, Zhelyu Zhelev, a liberal par excellence in a country seldom distinguished for its moderation, acts as one increasingly beleaguered in his own presidential palace.

How is this reversal of fortunes to be explained? *First:* Many of the liberals had been dissidents. Hence, (a) except partly in the Polish case, they are part of an era most people now prefer to forget; (b) they are also part of the bad conscience of those who did not resist. (The fact that some of them were disillusioned communists enables this bad conscience to be dimmed in the vapors of self-righteousness.) *Second:* Their liberalism with regard to decommunization, lustration, the rule of law, societal reconciliation does not sit well with many of their vociferous compatriots. With regard to Havel, for example, it is partly his moral standing that has become his political liability. *Third:* The sprinkling of Jews in liberal ranks recharges old prejudices and makes all liberals fair game for demagogues. *Fourth:* Some liberals, once resourceful in resistance, subsequently revealed a political ineptitude that made their eclipse as deserved as it was unavoidable.

Some famous dissidents may disappear politically forever. But other, mostly lesser names probably will emerge from the present doldrums. They will need allies, however, and if enough allies come from the ranks of mainly younger reform communists, unburdened by the old communist mind-set, and from some of the relative moderates still hovering around the center of the political spectrum, then the liberal ranks can be maintained and reinforced. Just as important, though, for the liberal cause will be the conduct of economic and social policy. Here, there is a crucial difference between liberalism at the end of this century and at the end of the last. Then, liberals ("Manchester men"), if they had a social conscience—as many did—conceived of it in terms of private charity rather than public policy. Now, an active *public* social conscience has been added to the arsenal of modern liberalism. Hence, the dangers of "shock therapy," today's equivalent of laissez-faire, are smaller. Still, the balance always must be watched and often may need adjusting. Too much Milton Friedman can set back the prospects for liberal democracy. And as if such considerations are not enough, increased crime, corruption, and immigration have become threats. There always will be enough problems to test liberal convictions and the liberal stamina in postcommunist Eastern Europe.

But, as will have emerged from this book, in most East European countries nationalism is also a mortal threat to liberalism. Here, the distinction between nationalism and patriotism needs to be made. Patriotism implies self-fulfillment (often self-satisfaction). Nationalism springs from unfulfillment, sometimes even self-debasement. It is antagonistic and needs an enemy. Patriotism is narcissistic and likes a mirror. Far more nationalism than patriotism exists in Eastern Europe. Only when patriotism starts to catch up will the prospects brighten for overcoming this threat. But, as we have seen, prospects in the Balkans could hardly be dimmer. Nor is East Central Europe immune from the nationalist virus.

The situation, therefore, is serious everywhere. And without outside help it could become hopeless in some countries. This book must conclude by returning to the issue of the Western role in the region, its responsibilities, possibilities, and opportunities. As of early 1994, after making every allowance, that role continued to be a moral and political self-indictment. Indeed, the Yugoslav situation and the attempts to defuse it brought to mind one of the axioms of the incomparable Sir Charles Eliot, enunciated at the beginning of this century: "What they [the Great Powers of Europe] shy at one day, what they denounce with diminishing invective as impossible, revolutionary, *saugrenu,* or crude, they accept a few years later as a matter of course, provided that it is presented to them with decent formalities."[2] However much truth there was, and still may be, in what Eliot says, it would be disastrous if this feebleness were the hallmark of Western policy over the next few years. Obviously, gradations of seriousness in situations call for gradations of response, and these must be gauged by the Western authorities concerned. Similarly, there are mechanisms of response, and these must be effectively devised by the Western powers. So must a policy framework and an underpinning philosophy. Without these, Eastern instability only will grow and could have an increasingly destabilizing, debilitating, and demoralizing effect on the West itself. Nor must effective Western attention be limited or diverted by a concentration on Russia and other Soviet successor states. There can be no stability east of Eastern Europe if there is none within it.

If Europe is to be worthy of the aspirations that the East Europeans have toward it, then it is *West Europeans* who must eventually assume the main external responsibility—political and economic and eventually in terms of security—for the region. Western Europe must help Eastern Europe help itself. What the United States was for Western Europe after 1945, Western Europe must largely become for Eastern Europe. The United States will always have a role, but not a primary one. Once this is understood, and once the West Europeans assume their responsibilities, then American–West European relations will be placed on a sounder footing and will mature. Western Europe must, therefore, rebound from the dreadful years of 1992 and 1993. The European Community can lead the way by thinking big instead of little, in historical rather than parochial terms, and offer *early* admission to full membership to the Czech Republic, Poland, and Hungary, with closer association, on a calibrated basis, to Slovakia and the South-East European states. Western Europe could best respond to its own crisis of confidence and aspiration by a *fuite en avant.* Embracing Eastern Europe, for example! In Vienna in February 1993 Hanna Suchocka, at that time prime minister of Poland, made a plea, both passionate and logical, for greater Western involvement. She ended her address by saying:

> The situation forces all Europeans to a renewed examination of the European order, to answer the question how the vision of freedom, democracy, and prosperity that brought unity to Western Europe can serve as a yardstick for uniting the whole of the continent. Only in this way can we tackle the current problems and the potential dangers, and exploit the opportunities offered to Europe since the fall of communism.[3]

Only in this way can the revolution in which the East Europeans are engaged have a real chance of succeeding and the postcommunist expectations be eventually fulfilled. Hope is in order, but it is still touch and go. And the stakes could hardly be higher.

NOTES

1 Introduction

1. J. F. Brown, *Surge to Freedom: The End of Communist Rule in Eastern Europe* (Durham, N.C.: Duke University Press, 1991), pp. 247–69.

2. Ralf Dahrendorf, *Reflections on the Revolutions in Europe* (London: Chatto and Windus, 1990), p. 104.

3. J. F. Brown, "The East European Agenda," in Ivo John Lederer (ed.), *Western Approaches to Eastern Europe* (New York: Council on Foreign Relations, 1992), p. 23.

4. Dahrendorf, *Reflections,* pp. 36–37.

5. Quoted by Carl-Gustaf Ströhm, *Die Welt* (Hamburg), November 23, 1990.

6. Prague Československý rozhlas, October 13, 1991; FBIS-EEU-91-199, October 15, 1991, p. 12.

2 Regional Politics: No Promised Land

1. The best book on this transition remains, Zbigniew Brzezinski, *The Communist Bloc: Unity and Discord* (Cambridge, Mass.: Harvard University Press, 1960).

2. This theme is explored at some length in J. F. Brown, *Eastern Europe and Communist Rule* (Durham, N.C.: Duke University Press, 1988), passim, and in Brown, *Surge to Freedom.* On the national factor in communism, see the pioneering work by R. V. Burks, *The Dynamics of Communism in Eastern Europe* (Princeton, N.J.: Princeton University Press, 1961).

3. For a stimulating argument, see Giuseppe di Palma, "Democratic Transitions: Puzzles and Surprises from West to East," paper presented at the Conference of Europeanists, Washington, D.C., March 1990. This paper is updated, with some emphasis on Eastern Europe, in di Palma's *To Craft Democracies: An Essay on Democratic Transitions* (Berkeley: University of California Press, 1990). The most voluminous collection of works on the subject of transitions is, Guillermo O'Donnell, Philippe Schmitter, and Law-

rence Whitehead (eds.), *Transitions from Authoritarian Rule,* 4 vols. (Baltimore: Johns Hopkins University Press, 1986). For the undoubted East European interest, especially in the Spanish example, see Volker Mauersberger, "Ein Modell für die Reformer im Osten," *Die Zeit* (Hamburg), December 22, 1989. For a realistic and perceptive appraisal of the difficulties and necessities of the East European transition, see Ellen Comisso, "Property Rights, Liberalism, and the Transition from 'Actually Existing Socialism,' " *East European Politics and Societies,* Winter 1991.

4. On progress toward the rule of law in Eastern Europe generally and in parts of the former Soviet Union, see the special issue, "Toward the Rule of Law," *RFE/RL Research Report,* no. 27, July 3, 1992. The magazine *East European Constitutional Review,* which began publication in 1992, has given excellent coverage of legal and constitutional questions throughout the region. On the constitutional courts, see Herman Schwartz, "The New East European Constitutional Courts," *Michigan Journal of International Law,* Summer 1992.

5. By the beginning of 1992 considerable pressure was being brought especially from Hungary, for minority rights to become a security issue as well as a legal issue. This proposal was offered by the Hungarian delegation to the follow-up CSCE meeting in Helsinki in March 1992. RFE/RL Special Report—Helsinki, April 1, 1992. See also Hungarian foreign minister Géza Jeszenszky's speech at that meeting, in Ministry of Foreign Affairs, Hungary, "Report on Current Policy," no. 4, 1992.

6. See John Keane, *Democracy and Civil Society: On the Predicaments of European Socialism, the Prospects for Democracy, and the Problems of Controlling Social and Political Power* (London: Verso, 1988); Conor Cruise O'Brien, "Democracy Is Not Enough: Eastern Europe Now Has the Vote, But It Has Yet to Learn Tolerance," *Times* (London), November 18, 1991. See also Kathleen E. Smith, "Civil Society in Eastern Europe," unpublished paper, department of political science, University of California, Berkeley, May 22, 1989.

7. George Schöpflin, "Post-Communism: Constructing New Democracies in Central Europe," *International Affairs,* April, 1991. Schöpflin's is an excellent analysis for Poland, Czechoslovakia, and Hungary. For an earlier, more optimistic appraisal of the East Central European situation, see Charles Gati, "East-Central Europe: The Morning After," *Foreign Affairs,* Winter 1990–91. Another prudent assessment is by Paul Lendvai, "Osteuropa zwischen Liberalismus und Nationalismus," *Neue Zürcher Zeitung,* April 1/2, 1992.

8. The best book on Solidarity remains Timothy Garton Ash, *The Polish Revolution: Solidarity* (New York: Scribners, 1984). On the role of the intellectuals in Solidarity, see his review article, "Poland After Solidarity," *New York Review of Books,* June 13, 1991.

9. Smith, "Civil Society in Eastern Europe."

10. See Richard Crampton, "The Intelligentsia, the Ecology, and the Opposition in Bulgaria," *World Today* (London), February 1990.

11. See J. F. Brown, *Nationalism, Democracy, and Security in the Balkans* (Aldershot, U.K.: Dartmouth, for RAND, 1992), pp. 61–80.

12. *Profil* (Vienna), March 6, 1992.

13. *Financial Times* (London), August 17, 1991.

14. Western aid substantially increased after this episode, obviously aimed at blunting the desire to leave. See Louis Zanga, "Albania: Aid Stepped Up from Italy and Elsewhere," *RFE/RL Report on Eastern Europe,* no. 37, September 13, 1991.

15. Ulrich Schmidla, "Den Polen droht die Jugend davonzulaufen," *Die Welt* (Hamburg), April 22, 1992.

16. On emigration generally, see Bernd Knabe, "Faktoren und Perspektiven der Ost-West-Wanderungen in Europa," *Berichte des Bundesinstituts für ostwissenschaftliche und internationale Studien,* no. 43, 1992; Alasdair Stewart, "Migrants, Minorities, and Security in Europe," *Conflict Studies,* no. 252, June 1992.

17. In the first round of the presidential elections it was about the same. Polish Press Agency (PAP), November 26, 1990.

18. Louisa Vinton, "Wałęsa Elected President," *RFE/RL Report on Eastern Europe,* no. 51, December 21, 1990.

19. David McQaid, "Poland: The Parliamentary Elections: A Postmortem," *RFE/RL Report on Eastern Europe,* no. 45, November 8, 1991.

20. Zoltan D. Barany, "The Hungarian Democratic Forum Wins National Elections Decisively," *RFE/RL Report on Eastern Europe,* no. 17, April 27, 1990.

21. Béla Weyer, "Klein Interesse an der neuen Politik," *Süddeutsche Zeitung* (Munich), January 24, 1992.

22. See Jan Obrman, "The Czechoslovak Elections," *RFE/RL Research Report,* no. 26, June 26, 1992.

23. See Michael Shafir, "Romania's Elections: Why the Democratic Convention Lost," *RFE/RL Research Report,* no. 43, October 30, 1992.

24. *Demokratsiya* (Sofia), June 6, 1990.

25. *Otechestven Vestnik* (Sofia), October 15, 1991.

26. The 98.6 percentage was reported by *Zëri i Populit* (Tirana), April 18, 1991; the 90.35 percentage in March 1992 by *Rílindja* (Priština).

27. See Mária M. Kovács's article in "Reports from Central Europe: Hungary," *Partisan Review* (Boston), no. 4, 1991, pp. 665–69.

28. *Express* (Bucharest), May 21, 1992.

29. See Paul Lendvai, "A New Crop of Dictators," *Washington Post,* February 5, 1993.

30. See Anna Sabbat-Swidlicka, "The Wałęsa Factor," *RFE/RL Report*

on Eastern Europe, no. 17, April 27, 1990; Louisa Vinton, "Solidarity's Rival Offspring: Center Alliance and Democratic Action," *RFE/RL Report on Eastern Europe,* no. 38, September 21, 1990.

31. See Schöpflin, "Post-Communism."

32. On Antall, see "Das Undenkbare nicht nur geträumt," *Frankfurter Allgemeine Zeitung,* April 8, 1992.

33. For a revealing interview, see Ion Iliescu, "Views Cannot Be Changed Overnight," *New Times* (Moscow), June 15, 1991.

34. Zhelev's integrity is perhaps best demonstrated in a public letter he wrote on the role of the presidency to the Coordinating Council of the Union of Democratic Forces, Sofia Radio Khorizont Network, November 27, 1991, FBIS-EEU-91-230, November 30, 1991, p. 1.

35. On Berisha, see Dirk Kurbjuweit, "Albaniens neuer Präsident—Arzt und Wunderheiler?", *Die Zeit* (Hamburg), April 24, 1992.

36. Göncz is a personality in his own right, more outgoing, warmer, and more liberal than Antall; see interview with him in *Süddeutsche Zeitung,* April 24, 1992.

37. On Alia, see, for example, *Current Biography,* January 1991. See also Henry Kamm, "Albania's Alia Is the Great Survivor of Communism in Eastern Europe," *New York Times,* March 16, 1992.

38. For an article that captures Mečiár, see "Ich werde kandidieren und gewinnen," *Die Presse* (Vienna), April 7, 1992.

39. The publicity-conscious, multilingual Roman was widely covered in the Western press; see his interview with Anneli Ute Gabanyi, *Süddeutsche Zeitung,* May 6, 1992.

40. On Torgyán, see, for example, Edith Oltay, "Hungary: The Coalition Government," *RFE/RL Report on Eastern Europe,* no. 48, November 29, 1991.

41. On Stănculescu and the role of the Romanian army as a whole, see Gilles Schiller, "L'Armée roumaine dans le jeu politique," *Libération,* November 19, 1990.

42. On military discontent in late 1992, see defense minister Aleksandûr Staliski's comments in *Demokratsia,* October 2, 1992. For background on the Bulgarian military, see Daniel L. Nelson, "Political Dynamics and the Bulgarian Military," *Berichte des Bundesinstituts für ostwissenschaftliche und internationale Studien,* Cologne, 43-1990.

43. Sylvie Kauffmann, "M. Wałęsa et le gouvernement s'affrontent sur le contrôle de l'armée," *Le Monde,* April 16, 1992. Parys was to become one of Wałęsa's bitterest enemies.

44. See Thomas S. Szayna, "The Military in Postcommunist Czechoslovakia" (Santa Monica, Calif.: RAND, 1992).

45. Ken Jowitt, *New World Disorder: The Leninist Extinction* (Berkeley: University of California Press, 1992), pp. 249–305.

46. The decommunization issue generated much coverage and comment in the West. Four noteworthy discussions were Flora Lewis, "Retribution Now Could Only Hurt," *International Herald Tribune,* December 20, 1991; A.O., "Der Ruf nach Sühne—Osteuropas Dilemma," *Neue Zürcher Zeitung,* January 13, 1992; Véronique Soulé, "L'est à l'heure de la revanche anticommuniste," *Libération,* December 19, 1991; "The Complexities of Justice," *The Economist,* March 21, 1992.

47. I am grateful to Jiri Pehe and Jan Obrman for drawing my attention to these facts. Their information specifically referred to Czechoslovakia, but it has general application.

48. No case aroused more interest or caused more general concern than that of Jan Kavan, a former active Czechoslovak dissident based for twenty years in London, who returned home and became a member of the federal parliament. He was accused on the basis of security files of having collaborated with the secret police. He earnestly denied any wrongdoing and received strong, widespread support. Kavan also was the victim of considerable chicanery by political opponents within the Czechoslovak government. See Jeri Laber, "Witch Hunt in Prague," *New York Review of Books,* April 23, 1992. For critical responses to Laber's article, see the *New York Review of Books,* May 28 and June 11, 1992. For a magisterial article on the whole issue of Kavan and lustration in general, see Lawrence Weschler, "The Velvet Purge: The Trials of Jan Kavan," *New Yorker,* October 19, 1992. See also his follow-up article, "From Kafka to Dreyfus," *New Yorker,* November 5, 1992.

49. See Dan Ionescu, "Romania's Public War Over Secret Police Files," *RFE/RL Research Report,* no. 29, July 17, 1992.

50. See Louisa Vinton, "Wałęsa and the Collaboration Issue," *RFE/RL Research Report,* no. 6, February 5, 1993.

3 Country Politics: East Central Europe

1. For an excellent review and analysis of the Czech-Slovak relationship, see Carol Skalnik Leff, *National Conflict in Czechoslovakia: The Making and Remaking of a State, 1918–1987* (Princeton, N.J.: Princeton University Press, 1988).

2. See Stanley Riveles, "Slovakia: Catalyst of Crisis," *Problems of Communism,* May 1968; Robert W. Dean, *Nationalism and Political Change in Eastern Europe: The Slovak Question and the Czechoslovak Reform Movement,* University of Denver Monograph Series in World Affairs, 10 (Denver: University of Denver, 1972–73).

3. J. F. Brown, *Eastern Europe and Communist Rule* (Durham, N.C.: Duke University Press, 1988), pp. 300–301.

4. Leff, *National Conflict in Czechoslovakia,* p. 225.

5. See Brown, *Eastern Europe and Communist Rule,* p. 313.

6. On the Slovak nationalists, see Harry Schleicher, "Erst die Staatssprache und dann das ganze Land," *Frankfurter Rundschau,* October 22, 1991.

7. On the basic Czech-Slovak misunderstandings, see Berthold Kohler, "Aus der Vernunftheirat ist keine Liebesehe geworden," *Frankfurter Allgemeine Zeitung,* October 19, 1990. Havel, for his part, was well aware of the dangers to the federation of many Czechs' attitude: "the Czechs' main task is to rid themselves of the arrogant, cold shoulder, and patronizing, self-centered attitude toward Slovaks." Interview with Radio Bratislava, May 21, 1990 FBIS-EEU-90-099, May 22, 1990, p. 11.

8. See C. Sr., "Umbenennung der CSSR in CSFR," *Neue Zürcher Zeitung,* April 1–2, 1990 (Fernausgabe Nr. 76).

9. See, for example, the bitter exchange between the Czech writer, Ludvík Vaculík, and his Slovak counterpart, Vladimír Mináč. (This is the same Mináč quoted in chapter 6 as inveighing against the Hungarians.) Each concentrated on the national faults and the historical failures of the other nation. Peter Martin, "Relations Between the Czechs and the Slovaks," *RFE/RL Report on Eastern Europe,* no. 36, September 7, 1990.

10. Harry Schleicher, "Slowakische Nationalisten ehren einen rechten Führer," *Frankfurter Rundschau,* October 31, 1990. Havel himself strongly criticized these tendencies, referring, for example, to "the totalitarian, fascist methods" of certain Slovak groups, which, he said, were an expression of "a sort of nostalgia for the Slovak state (1939–1945), i.e., for a fascist regime." Interview with CTK (Prague), June 10, 1990, FBIS-EEU-90-112, June 11, 1990, p. 37.

11. For a good example of Czech exasperation with the Slovak style of negotiation, together with more than a touch of Czech arrogance, see Czech premier Petr Pithart's outburst on Radio Prague in August 1991; referring to the then Slovak premier, Ján Čarnogurský, he said: "Please say all that you really want to say, do not abuse our patience, do not protract the state of uncertainty by constantly coming up with new demands. After all, you want to be perceived by the world as grownups, please, behave accordingly." Prague Československý rozhlas, August 6, 1991, FBIS-EEU-91-152, August 7, 1991, p. 12.

12. For example, CTK (Prague) reported in June 11, 1991, that 55 percent of 1,290 respondents in the Slovak Republic, in a poll conducted by the Slovak Statistical Office in May, wanted the federation to continue on the basis of the constitutions of two sovereign, equal republics. FBIS-EEU-91-117, June 18, 1991, p. 11.

13. For a perspicacious view of Czech and Slovak motives and concerns,

see Edward Mortimer, "East of Maastricht," *Financial Times* (London), October 7, 1992.

14. CTK, July 23, 1992; see Jiri Pehe, "Majority of Czechs and Slovaks Opposed to Split of Czechoslovakia," RFE/RL Research Institute Program Brief, July 24, 1992. For a retrospective debate on the value of a referendum, see the exchange between Rita Klimová and Theodore Draper, *New York Review of Books,* April 8, 1993. Klimová was responding to Draper's criticism of Klaus's attitude in his original article in ibid., "The End of Czechoslovakia" (January 28, 1993), a follow-up to his article "A New History of the Velvet Revolution," ibid. (January 14, 1993).

15. See Michael Frank, "Slowakei: Besichtigung eines Landes, das sich entscheiden muss," *Süddeutsche Zeitung,* July 4, 1992.

16. See, for example, Henry Kamm, "A Czech Leader Regrets The Coming Split With Slovakia," *New York Times,* September 29, 1992. Klaus was married to a Slovak, a fact, he contended, that ruled out his being anti-Slovak.

17. On the splits in Mečiár's Movement for a Democratic Slovakia, see Reuters (Bratislava), February 9, 1993; for his attempts to control the media, see Jan Obrman, "The Slovak Government versus the Media," *RFE/RL Research Report,* no. 6, February 5, 1993; for his moves against the new university at Trnava, see Adele Kalniczky, "Academic Freedom in Slovakia: The Case of Trnava University," *RFE/RL Research Report,* no. 11, March 12, 1993.

18. See Alfred Reisch, "Mečiár and Slovakia's Hungarian Minority," *RFE/RL Research Report,* no. 43, October 30, 1992.

19. See J. F. Brown, *Surge to Freedom: The End of Communist Rule in Eastern Europe* (Durham, N.C.: Duke University Press, 1991), pp. 90–98.

20. On "them" and "us," see Hans-Henning Hahn, "Zur Dichotomie von Gesellschaft und Staat in Polen," *Berichte des Bundesinstituts für ostwissenschaftliche und internationale Studien,* Cologne, 20-1989.

21. For a good discussion of anti-Semitism in Poland, and in Eastern Europe generally, see Henryk M. Broder, "Kehrt mit der Freiheit im östlichen Mitteleuropa auch der Antisemitismus zurück?" *Die Zeit* (Hamburg), May 18, 1990. Regarding Wałęsa's alleged anti-Semitism, see Thomas Urban, "Allzusimple Worte über ein gefährliches Thema," *Süddeutsche Zeitung,* May 18, 1991.

22. *Surge to Freedom,* p. 97.

23. For a perceptive portrait of Mazowiecki, see *Le Monde,* August 20–21, 1989.

24. George Schöpflin, "Post-Communism: Constructing New Democracies in Central Europe," *International Affairs,* 67-2-1991.

25. See Helga Hirsch, "Polen braucht den klärenden Disput," *Die Zeit* (Hamburg), June 15, 1990; Barry Newman, "Wałęsa Is Working Hard to

Consolidate His Political Position," *Wall Street Journal Europe,* April 17, 1990.

26. Roger Boyes, "Lech Wałęsa, Child of Communism," *Los Angeles Times,* September 30, 1992. This is a review of Wałęsa's autobiography, *The Struggle and the Triumph: An Autobiography of Lech Wałęsa,* written with Arkadiusz Rybicki, trans. Franklin Philip and Helen Mahaut (Berkeley, Calif.: Arcade, 1992). (Boyes himself is the author of a biography of Wałęsa.) For a revealing interview, see "Wałęsa's Poisoned Chalice," interview with Nicholas Bethell, *Observer* (London), August 16, 1992.

27. For an excellent analysis of the dispute between Wałęsa and the intellectuals in Solidarity, see Stefan Dietrich, "Die Splitter der Solidarność reagieren wie Eisenteilchen auf einen Magneten," *Frankfurter Allgemeine Zeitung,* November 5, 1990. The article was written shortly before the presidential elections of December 1991. Dietrich echoed the opinion of many observers when he supported Wałęsa against the Solidarity intellectuals. "The presidential election in Poland involves a choice between those who fear democracy and those who do not consider themselves smarter than the people."

28. Antony Polonsky, *The Little Dictators: A History of Eastern Europe since 1918* (London: Routledge, Kegan Paul, 1975), pp. 32–33.

29. On the Kaczyński twins, see Thomas Urban, "Doppeltes Spiel im Präsidentenpalast—In Polen gelten die Zwillingsbrüder Kaczyński, die schon im Untergrund für die Solidarität gearbeitet haben, als wichtigste Berater Lech Wałęsas," *Süddeutsche Zeitung,* June 26, 1991.

30. The best treatment of the Polish presidential campaign is by Lawrence Weschler, "A Reporter at Large: Shock," *New Yorker,* December 10, 1990.

31. Louisa Vinton, "Poland: The Anguish of Transition," *RFE/RL Research Report,* no. 1, January 3, 1992.

32. On Bielecki's views on economic reform, see his article, "Problems of the Polish Transformation," *Communist Economics and Economic Transformation,* vol. 4, no. 3, 1992.

33. See Thomas Urban, "Prellbock für den Präsidenten," *Süddeutsche Zeitung,* July 11, 1991.

34. See David McQuaid, "Poland: The Olszewski Cabinet," *RFE/RL Research Report,* no. 3, January 17, 1992.

35. See Louisa Vinton, "The Polish Government in Search of a Program," *RFE/RL Research Report,* no. 13, March 27, 1992; Anna Sabbat-Swidlicka, "Poland: Weak Government, Fractious Sejm, Isolated President," ibid., no. 15, April 10, 1992.

36. See Sylvie Kauffmann, "Le ministre de la défense a été contraint à la démission," *Le Monde,* May 20, 1992.

37. Probably the best blow-by-blow account of this episode is by Mary Battiata, "Polish Police Files Provoke Political Mudslinging," *Washington Post,* July 9, 1992.

38. Parys used the expressions "crypto-communist" and "pro-Russian," PAP (Polish Press Agency), September 20, 1992.

39. See the biography of Suchocka in Louisa Vinton, "Poland's Government Crisis: An End in Sight?" *RFE/RL Research Report,* no. 30, July 24, 1992.

40. See Louisa Vinton, "Poland's 'Little Constitution' Clarifies Wałęsa's Powers," *RFE/RL Research Report,* no. 35, September 4, 1992.

41. For a glimpse into Suchocka's personality and politics, see her interview in *Le Monde,* September 17, 1992.

42. See Louisa Vinton, "Poland Goes Left," *RFE/RL Research Report,* no. 40, October 8, 1993.

43. See J. F. Brown, *Eastern Europe and Communist Rule* (Durham, N.C.: Duke University Press, 1988), pp. 208–23.

44. See Zoltan Barany, "The State of the Parties as the Election Approaches," *RFE/RL Report on Eastern Europe,* no. 11, March 16, 1990.

45. For an excellent analysis of the elections and their significance in Hungary's democratic development, see A.O., "Ende und Aufbruch in Ungarn," *Neue Zürcher Zeitung,* April 11, 1990 (Fernausgabe Nr. 84). The article points to the danger of the low voter turnout. See also Zoltan Barany, "The Hungarian Democratic Forum Wins National Elections Decisively," *RFE/RL Report on Eastern Europe,* no. 17, April 27, 1990.

46. For biographical details on Antall, see MTI (Hungarian News Agency), in English, May 23, 1990. The best guide to his philosophy and policy is contained in his opening speech to parliament as prime minister, carried live by Radio Budapest Domestic Service on May 22, 1990, FBIS-EEU-90-101, May 24, 1990, pp. 45–57.

47. For an excellent review of the HDF government's first year, see A.O., "Ein Jahr Regierung Antall in Ungarn," *Neue Zürcher Zeitung,* May 17, 1991.

48. On the strike, see Tibor Fényi and Peter Martos, "Bald werden Fahrräder doppelt so teuer," *Die Presse* (Vienna), October 30, 1990; Alfred Reisch, "The Gasoline War: Order or Chaos?" *RFE/RL Report on Eastern Europe,* no. 45, November 9, 1990.

49. Mária M. Kovács, "Report from Central Europe: Hungary," *Partisan Review* (Boston), no. 4, 1991.

50. The constituency was in Komárom-Esztergom county. Several votes were necessary before the required minimum percentage needed to validate a by-election could be obtained.

51. President Göncz refused to agree to Antall's demands for the dismissals of the heads of state radio and television. There was wide coverage of this issue in the Western press. For a balanced assessment, see A.O., "Zuspitzung im ungarischen Medienkrieg," *Neue Zürcher Zeitung,* July 8, 1992.

52. See Judith Pataki, "Role of Smallholders' Party in Hungary's Coalition Government," *RFE/RL Research Report,* no. 14, April 3, 1992.

53. Csurka's article, published in the August 20, 1992 edition of *Magyar Fórum,* received extensive coverage in the West. For a comprehensive treatment, see Judith Pataki, "István Csurka's Tract: Summary and Reactions"; J. F. Brown, "A Challenge to Political Values"; and Edith Oltay, "A Profile of István Csurka," all three articles in *RFE/RL Research Report,* no. 40, October 9, 1992.

54. *Magyar Fórum,* August 20, 1992.

55. *Manchester Guardian Weekly,* January 16, 1991.

56. The best foreign comment of the conference and its implications was by Hansjakob Stehle, "Heiliger Schwachsinn," *Die Zeit* (Hamburg), January 29, 1993; see also, "Hungary—Steady Does It," *The Economist,* January 30, 1993.

57. Agence France Presse, June 22, 1993.

58. For a good commentary on the Horthy burial, see Hansjakob Stehle, "Ein Trauriger Held," *Die Zeit* (Hamburg), September 3, 1993.

4 Country Politics: South-Eastern Europe

1. On the elections, see Michael Shafir's "Romania's Election Campaign: The Main Issues," *RFE/RL Research Report,* no. 36, September 11, 1992; "Romania's Elections: Why the Democratic Convention Lost," ibid., no. 43, October 30, 1992; and "Romania's Elections: More Change Than Meets the Eye," ibid., no. 44, November 6, 1992.

2. See C. Sr., "Wahlsieg der Opposition in Bukarest," *Neue Zürcher Zeitung,* February 26, 1992 (Fernausgabe Nr. 46).

3. For a stimulating study of Romanian political culture in a contemporary setting, see Michael Shafir, "Political Culture and the Romanian Revolution of December 1989: Who Failed Whom?," unpublished manuscript, RFE/RL Research Institute, Munich, 1991.

4. See Viktor Meier, "Iliescu Sieger der Präsidentenwahl in Rumänien," *Frankfurter Allgemeine Zeitung,* September 29, 1992.

5. See Viktor Meier, "Der Graben zwischen Stadt und Land," *Frankfurter Allgemeine Zeitung,* October 10, 1992; Sylvie Kauffmann, "Les Intellectuels d'Opposition Sous Le Choc," *Le Monde,* May 29, 1990. Meier's article was written after the second presidential and parliamentary elections in 1992, Kauffmann's after the first in 1990.

6. Jonathan Eyal, "Hungary and Romania Meet Over Ethnic Tension," *Guardian,* February 14, 1990. See also A.O., "Ceauşescus Erbe in der Minderheitenpolitik," *Neue Zürcher Zeitung,* February 25–26, 1990; Viktor Meier, "In Bukarest wächst der Druck der Nationalisten auf die Regierung," *Frankfurter Allgemeine Zeitung,* March 10, 1990. Meier gives the reactions of Romanians to some of the "extreme" Hungarian demands.

7. See J. F. Brown, *Nationalism, Democracy, and Security in the Balkans* (Aldershot, UK: Dartmouth for RAND, 1992), pp. 170–72.

8. For a considered view of this incident, see the editorial by A.O., "Rumänische Teufelskreise der Gewalt," *Neue Zürcher Zeitung,* June 17/18, 1990. See also Harry Schleicher, "Die Rettungsfront sah sich vom Putsch bedroht," *Frankfurter Rundschau,* June 27, 1990. For a minority view at the time, see Conor Cruise O'Brien, "Mobs of Both Persuasion Menace Romanian Liberty," *Times* (London), June 26, 1990. For an excellent review of the Romanian situation three months after the riots, see José-Alain Fralon, "La Roumanie Entre Fantasmes et Contradictions," *Le Monde,* October 4, 1990.

9. See Dan Ionescu, "Riots Topple Petre Roman's Cabinet," *RFE/RL Report on Eastern Europe,* no. 42, October 18, 1991.

10. See C. Sr., "Rumänische Rettungsfront vor der Spaltung," *Neue Zürcher Zeitung,* December 13, 1991; Joachim Sonnenberg, "Zerbricht Rumäniens Rettungsfront am Wochenende? Tiefe Graben zwischen Petre Roman und Ion Iliescu," *Die Presse,* March 2, 1992. Later in 1992, Roman wrote a book — in French — "Le devoir de liberté," part autobiographical and part contemporary political history (Paris: Éditions Payot, 1992); see his interview in *Le Figaro* (Paris), December 31, 1992.

11. See Jean-Baptiste Naudet, "La police roumaine reconnaît avoir mis sous surveillance des opposants et des étrangers," *Le Monde,* December 23, 1992. For a graphic description of the tenacity of the old nomenklatura, see Richard Wagner, "Auch im Fernsehen arbeiten die gleichen Leute wie unter Ceauşescu — Angst vor der Demokratie in Rumänien — Alte Zustände von der Securitate bis zu den Kirchen," *Frankfurter Rundschau,* April 5, 1992.

12. Robert Bishop and E. S. Crayfield, *Russia Astride the Balkans* (New York: Robert M. McBride, 1948), p. 34.

13. The most sensible review of the plot theories remains Michael Shafir, "Preparing for the Future by Revising the Past," *RFE/RL Report on Eastern Europe,* no. 41, October 12, 1990.

14. See Michael Shafir, "National Liberal Party Quits Democratic Convention," *RFE/RL Research Report,* no. 24, June 12, 1992.

15. On the temporary burst of enthusiasm for the restoration of the monarchy see André Cornea, "Délire monarchiste en Roumanie," *Libération,* June 25, 1992.

16. See Michael Shafir, "The Movement for Romania: A Party of 'Radical Return,' " *RFE/RL Research Report,* no. 29, July 17, 1992.

17. See Dan Ionescu, "The Communist Party Re-emerges Under Another Name," *RFE/RL Report on Eastern Europe,* no. 51, December 21, 1990.

18. See Kjell Engelbrekt, "Bulgaria" in "Toward the Rule of Law," a special issue of *RFE/RL Research Report,* no. 27, July 3, 1992.

19. See Rada Nikolaev, "President Mladenov Resigns," *RFE/RL Report*

on Eastern Europe, no. 31, August 3, 1990. For a perceptive comment, see the editorial "Fièvre dans les Balkans," *Le Monde,* July 7, 1990.

20. At the time there was some speculation as to whether the fire had actually been started by the communists to discredit the opposition—a Reichstag Fire kind of tactic. See Antonia Dimitrova, "Bulgarien: Feuer und Flamme für dieses System?," *Der Standard* (Vienna), September 5, 1990.

21. On the preelection mood, see Berthold Kohler, "Über Sofia leuchtet noch immer der Rote Stern des Sozialismus," *Frankfurter Allgemeine Zeitung,* May 15, 1990. On the Socialist victory, see Judy Dempsey, "The Anatomy of a Rare Communist Victory," *Financial Times* (London), June 15, 1990.

22. See Duncan Perry, "Lukanov's Government Resigns; New Prime Minister Nominated," *RFE/RL Report on Eastern Europe,* no. 51, December 21, 1990.

23. For revealing glimpses of Zhelev, see his interviews in *Die Welt* (Hamburg), November 20, 1990, and the *Frankfurter Allgemeine Zeitung,* March 15, 1991.

24. On Simeon and the royalist issue in Bulgaria, see Dimitûr Statkov, "Die monarchistische Propaganda in Bulgarien," *Neue Zürcher Zeitung,* May 31, 1991; Berthold Kohler, "Blick zurück in Hoffnung—wird Bulgarien wieder Monarchie?", *Frankfurter Allgemeine Zeitung,* April 23, 1992.

25. On Dimitrov, see his interview with the *Süddeutsche Zeitung,* January 11, 1992.

26. See C. Sr., "Krisenstimmung bei den Sozialisten Bulgariens," *Neue Zürcher Zeitung,* September 25, 1990 (Fernausgabe Nr. 221).

27. See Brown, *Nationalism, Democracy, and Security in the Balkans,* pp. 117–21.

28. On Doğan and the early days of the Movement of Rights and Freedoms, see Mike Power and Denise Searle, "Bulgaria's Turks Nervously United Against Oppression," *Guardian,* May 25, 1990.

29. See Duncan Perry, "Ethnic Turks Face Bulgarian Nationalism," *RFE/RL Report on Eastern Europe,* no. 11, March 15, 1991, and, on the language dispute, Associated Press (AP) from Sofia, February 4, 1992.

30. See Rada Nikolaev, "The Bulgarian Presidential Elections," *RFE/RL Research Report,* no. 6, February 7, 1992.

31. See C. Sr., "Die Last der Vergangenheit in Bulgarien: Umstrittene Pläne zur 'Entkommunisierung,'" *Neue Zürcher Zeitung,* May 9, 1992.

32. On the beginning of the Zhivkov trial, see Carl E. Buchalla, "Untaten, die nicht im Gesetzbuch stehen," *Süddeutsche Zeitung,* February 22, 1991. On the end, see Kjell Engelbrekt and Duncan M. Perry, "The Conviction of Bulgaria's Former Leader," *RFE/RL Research Report,* no. 42, October 23, 1992.

33. See C. Sr., "Schwere Regierungskrise in Bulgarien," *Neue Zürcher Zeitung,* November 24, 1992 (Fernausgabe Nr. 273).

34. See Kjell Engelbrekt, "Technocrats Dominate New Bulgarian Government," *RFE/RL Research Report,* no. 4, January 22, 1993.

35. C. Sr., "Politische Wirren in Bulgarien," *Neue Zürcher Zeitung,* February 19, 1993.

36. See Berthold Kohler, "Bulgarien will sich nicht in einen Krieg mit Serbien verwickeln lassen," *Frankfurter Allgemeine Zeitung,* February 20, 1993.

37. Misha Glenny, *The Fall of Yugoslavia: The Third Balkan War* (Harmondsworth, UK: Penguin, 1992), p. 69.

38. See Liam McDowall, "Death and Revenge Turn to Small Town Albania," *Guardian* (London), June 26, 1992.

39. J. F. Brown, *Eastern Europe and Communist Rule* (Durham, N.C.: Duke University Press, 1988), pp. 374–77.

40. See Peter Humphrey, "Albania Opts for Reforms with a Socialist Face," *Independent* (London), February 24, 1990.

41. Kadare returned home in May 1992; see Louis Zanga, "Albania's Leading Writer Returns Home," *RFE/RL Research Report,* no. 28, July 10, 1992.

42. See C. Sr., "Wahlsieg für Albaniens Opposition," *Neue Zürcher Zeitung,* March 24, 1992.

43. For the Nexhmije Hoxha case, as well as some thoughtful remarks about Albania generally, see Jeri Laber, "Slouching Toward Democracy," *New York Review of Books,* January 14, 1993.

44. On Berisha, see Dirk Kurbjuwelt, "Albaniens neuer Präsident—Arzt oder Wunderheiler," *Die Zeit,* April 24, 1992.

45. See "Too Broke to Mend," *The Economist,* July 4, 1992.

46. See Louis Zanga, "Albania's Local Elections," *RFE/RL Research Report,* no. 37, September 18, 1992.

47. See Louis Zanga, "Albania Moves Closer to the Islamic World," *RFE/RL Research Report,* no. 7, February 12, 1993; also, C. Sr., "Albaniens aussenpolitischer Balanceakt," *Neue Zürcher Zeitung,* April 25/26, 1993.

5 The Economy: The Painful Ascent

1. Paul Marer, "Central and Eastern Europe: An Economic Perspective," in Dick Clark (ed.), "United States Relations with Central and Eastern Europe," proceedings of Eleventh Aspen Institute Conference, Vienna, August 23–27, 1992.

2. *Neue Zürcher Zeitung,* April 19, 1990 (Fernausgabe No. 87).

3. Ibid., April 5, 1991.

4. For discussions on the subject, see János Kornai, *The Road to a Free Economy* (New York: W. W. Norton, 1990); Keith Bush (ed.), *From the Command Economy to the Market* (Aldershot, U.K.: Dartmouth for the RFE/RL Research Institute, 1991).

5. I am indebted to Ben Slay of Bates College for helpful conversations on this and many other economic topics.

6. Marer, "Central and Eastern Europe." Balcerowicz, though, in his article referred to in note 71 of this chapter, places considerable importance on the speed factor.

7. See J. F. Brown, *Eastern Europe and Communist Rule* (Durham, N.C.: Duke University Press, 1988), pp. 119–20.

8. See Ben Slay, "The Economy: Perceptions and Reality," *Report on Eastern Europe,* no. 40, October 4, 1991; also, "Poland: The Rise and Fall of the Balcerowicz Plan," *RFE/RL Research Report,* no. 5, January 31, 1992.

9. See Stephen Engelberg, "Poland, An Economic Success Story," *New York Times,* December 17, 1992.

10. Slay, "The Economy: Perceptions and Reality."

11. Anthony Robinson and Christopher Bobinski, "Polish Economy Declines Despite Private Growth," *Financial Times* (London), February 3, 1992.

12. Slay, "The Economy: Perceptions and Reality."

13. Ibid.

14. Ht., "Polens Kater nach dem 'Big Bang,' " *Neue Zürcher Zeitung,* October 18, 1991; Slay, "Poland: The Rise and Fall of the Balcerowicz Plan."

15. Slay, "Poland: The Rise and Fall of the Balcerowicz Plan."

16. Julian Borger, "Poland Unveils Reflation Plan," *Guardian* (London), February 17, 1992; Anthony Robinson, "Up Against the Limits," *Financial Times* (London), February 18, 1992.

17. *The Economist,* January 9, 1993; see also the article on Poland's economic reforms, *The Economist,* January 23, 1993.

18. *Agence France Presse* (AFP), November 27, 1992, quoting planning minister Jerzy Kropiwnicki.

19. See finance minister Václav Klaus on the schools of thought among Czechoslovak economists in *Narodná obroda* (Bratislava), July 12, 1991, FBIS-EEU-91-138, July 18, 1991, p. 13. Klaus, of course, made no bones about who was right and who was wrong.

20. Havel's preferences were widely reported. A CIA report about them caused some embarrassment in Prague. See federal minister of economics Vladimír Dlouhý's qualified denial of this report in *Rudé právo* (Prague), May 20, 1991.

21. Among the many analyses of the economic effects of Czech-Slovak relations, one of the fullest and most perceptive is Patrick Michel, "La Tchéchoslovaquie gagnée par la tempête," *Le Monde Diplomatique* (Paris), January 1991. For an OECD view one year later, see *Financial Times* (Lon-

don), January 8, 1992; also Karl-Peter Schwarz, "Wie weit ist Pressburg von Prag entfernt?: Gravierende Differenzen auf dem Weg zum Markt," *Die Presse* (Vienna), February 17, 1992.

22. See profile of Klaus, "Populist Slayer of Dreams," *Financial Times* (London), November 19, 1990.

23. Anthony Robinson, "Czech Minister Says Perestroika Bans Radical Reforms," *Financial Times* (London), March 26, 1991.

24. See Peter Martin, "Scenario for Economic Reform Adopted," *RFE/RL Report on Eastern Europe,* no. 42, October 19, 1990.

25. Reuters (Prague), February 17, 1991.

26. See Peter Martin, "An Economic Strategy for 1991–1992," *RFE/RL Report on Eastern Europe,* no. 20, May 17, 1991. This essay gives a full analysis of the government document.

27. "No student of economics at any U.S. university would survive his freshman year if he displayed a similar level of knowledge," Milan Zelený, Czech-American economist, *Rudé právo,* March 5, 1991, FBIS-EEU-91-049, March 13, 1991, p. 28. For a more balanced though critical view, see Erich Hoorn, "In der CSFR ist eine Belebung noch nicht in Sicht," *Die Presse* (Vienna), October 14, 1991.

28. Reported in the *Neue Zürcher Zeitung,* January 9, 1992.

29. This issue drew worldwide attention. See, for example, Ariane Genillard, "Slovak MPs Fight to Keep Weapon Industry in the Face of Federal Efforts to Curb Output," *Financial Times* (London), March 11, 1992; Klaus-Peter Schwarz, "Slowakische Waffen-Lobby unterläuft Havel," *Die Welt* (Hamburg), July 13, 1991. Czechoslovak federal Premier Marián Čalfa defended arms production thus: "To us, tanks are goods like any other that we sell, and this way we obtain the money we need to stop arms production." Interview in *Lidové noviny* (Prague), May 10, 1991, FBIS-EEU-90-093, May 14, 1991, p. 17.

30. Interview with *Narodná obroda* (Bratislava), January 14, 1991, FBIS-EEU-91-016, January 24, 1991, p. 27.

31. Federal foreign minister Jiří Dienstbier, interview with *Narodná obroda* (Bratislava), March 18, 1991, FBIS-EEU-91-044.

32. Petr Pithardt, Czech prime minister, in interview with *Mlada Fronta Dnes* (Prague), February 23, 1991, FBIS-EEU-91-044, March 6, 1991, p. 25.

33. Tyler Marshall and Carl J. Williams, "Optimism Eases Eastern European Economic Gloom, *Los Angeles Times,* January 26, 1993.

34. Interview in *Die Presse* (Vienna), January 12, 1993.

35. Ian Traynor, "Big Bang Should Learn from Cautious Hungary," *Guardian* (London), January 22, 1992.

36. Ibid.

37. See Will Hutton, "Stable Economy Wins Investors," *Guardian,* January 22, 1992.

38. "Im wirtschaftlichen Umwälzungsprozess hat Ungarn grosse Fortschritte erzielt," *Handelsblatt* (Düsseldorf), January 30, 1992.

39. Nicholas Denton, "Hungary Sees End to 3-Year Economic Slide," *Financial Times* (London), January 9, 1993.

40. Keno Versack, "Das Leben wird immer schwerer," *Die Tageszeitung* (Berlin), January 25, 1992.

41. "Für die ungarische Wirtschaft dürfte der erhoffte Aufschwung erst 1994 kommen," *Handelsblatt,* September 15, 1991. See also Blaine Harden, "Post-Communist Hungary Enjoying Economic Rebirth," *Washington Post,* December 16, 1991.

42. Harry Schleicher, "Auch Ungarn sieht das berühmte Licht am Ende des Tunnels," *Frankfurter Rundschau,* January 22, 1992.

43. These and the following statistics are taken from a Plan Econ report discussed by Michael S. Lelyveld, *Journal of Commerce,* January 5, 1993.

44. Schleicher, "Auch Ungarn."

45. In October 1991 he announced publicly that he was considering food rationing for the following winter. AP (Bucharest), October 17, 1991.

46. Ibid., November 6, 1991.

47. Reuters (Bucharest), December 1, 1991.

48. Ibid., December 3, 1992.

49. Radio Bucharest, March 9, 1992.

50. For a well-informed article advocating caution in the progress of reform, see Viktor Meier, "Rumänien kann sich im Interesse seiner Stabilität nur ein behutsames Reformtempo erlauben," *Frankfurter Allgemeine Zeitung,* February 20, 1992.

51. See, for example, Rodica Seward, Steven Glick, and Jean-Yves Martin, "Romania Pursues Its Own Road to the Market Economy," *Financial Times* (London), November 17, 1991.

52. See Jean-Baptiste Naudet, "Le gouvernement veut renforcer le rôle de l'État dans la transition économique," *Le Monde* (Paris), January 7, 1993.

53. Brown, *Eastern Europe and Communist Rule,* pp. 325–26.

54. J. F. Brown, *Surge to Freedom: The End of Communist Rule in Eastern Europe* (Durham, N.C.: Duke University Press, 1991), pp. 181–97.

55. See Kjell Engelbrekt, "Bulgaria's Foreign Debt Predicament," *RFE/RL Research Report,* no. 8, February 21, 1992.

56. See Ht., "Bulgarien setzt zur Aufholjagd an—Eine Wirtschaftsreform 'zehn nach zwölf'," *Neue Zürcher Zeitung,* June 30/July 1, 1991; also, Marvin Jackson, "The Dangers of Procrastination in the Transition from Socialism to Capitalism," *RFE/RL Report on Eastern Europe,* no. 15, April 12, 1991.

57. "Verspätete Reformen in Bulgarien," *Die Presse* (Vienna), June 29, 1991.

58. Reuters (Sofia), December 1, 1991.

59. Theodore Troev, "Bulgaria Resumes Talks with Banks Over Foreign Debt," *Times* (London), January 27, 1992.

60. MS, "Bulgarien braucht Auslandskapital," *Süddeutsche Zeitung* (Munich), March 5, 1992.

61. Ht., "Düstere Wirtschaftslage in Bulgarien," *Neue Zürcher Zeitung,* December 18, 1991.

62. Andreas Oplatka, "Disorder and Early Troubles in Bulgaria," *Swiss Review of World Affairs* (Zurich), June 1991.

63. Dimitrov's visit to Washington, D.C., in March 1992 made a good impression. See Blaine Harden "US Official's Speech Seen in Bulgaria as Act of Deliverance," *Washington Post,* March 6, 1992 (the official was then Under-Secretary of State Lawrence Eagleburger); see also *Washington Post* editorial, "Eastern Europe's Surprise," March 9, 1992.

64. *Der Standard* (Vienna), December 3, 1991.

65. Valtr Komárek, "Economic Therapy Endangers the Patients," *International Herald Tribune,* January 7, 1992; see also his interview in *Newsweek,* March 9, 1992.

66. *International Herald Tribune,* January 22, 1992. See also Jenny Corbett and Colin Mayer, "Financial Reform in Eastern Europe: Progress with the Wrong Model," *Oxford Review of Economic Policy,* vol. 7, no. 4, Winter 1991.

67. See Viktor Meier, "Weisheit und Realismus," *Frankfurter Allgemeine Zeitung,* October 17, 1991.

68. RFE/RL, *Report from Washington,* January 28, 1992.

69. Ibid., January 24, 1992.

70. Zbigniew Brzezinski, "The West Adrift: Vision in Search of a Strategy," *Washington Post,* March 2, 1992.

71. See his article, "Der Erfolg einer radikalen, aber nicht dogmatischen Transformation," *Neue Zürcher Zeitung,* April 25–26, 1993. For a less enthusiastic view, see Konstanty Gebert, " 'Shock' Crock: Poland's Overrated Reforms," *Washington Post,* May 2, 1993. Gebert is one of Poland's most prominent journalists.

72. RFE/RL, *Report from Frankfurt,* November 22, 1991.

73. Ivan Major, "Why Eastern Europe Is Going Nowhere," *New York Times,* January 21, 1992.

74. *The Economist,* "A Survey of Business in Eastern Europe," September 29, 1991. On privatization as a whole, see the special issue of *RFE/RL Research Report,* no. 17, April 24, 1992.

75. Ibid.

76. AP (Washington), June 22, 1993, quoting World Bank and IMF sources.

77. In Czechoslovakia the Bată family reclaimed the headquarters of its shoe empire. As to Budweis beer, Anheuser-Busch, makers of the American brew with the similar name, tried to take control of it, but beer lovers the

world over were resisting; see, for example, Ulrich Glauber, "Böhmen lassen sich nicht ins Bier spucken," *Frankfurter Rundschau,* April 9, 1992.

78. On Poland, see Ht., "Umstrittene polnische Massenprivatisierung," *Neue Zürcher Zeitung,* October 22, 1991; on Romania, see Dan Ionescu, "Romania: Testing Large-scale Privatization," *RFE/RL Research Report,* no. 2, January 10, 1992.

79. See Paul Gafton, "The Privatization Law," *RFE/RL Report on Eastern Europe,* no. 40, October 4, 1991. Reuters (Bucharest), April 20, 1993, reported that the government was stepping up its campaign to sell privatization voucher packages. Reuters also reported the resistance to the scheme by "bureaucrats in various economic ministries concerned they might lose control of state enterprises."

80. The Czechoslovak scheme drew worldwide coverage. See, for example, John Tagliabue, "Czechoslovakia's Daring Leap into Capitalism," *New York Times,* November 19, 1991; Michael Frank, "Schlange stehen um Kapitalist zu werden," *Süddeutsche Zeitung* (Munich), January 24, 1992; Natalie Nougayrede, "Prague spécule sur les privatisations," *Libération* (Paris), January 23, 1992; Burton Bollag, "Czechs by Millions Invest $35 in Big State Sale," *New York Times,* January 21, 1992.

81. "Poland's Economic Reforms: If It Works, You've Fixed It," *The Economist,* January 23, 1993.

82. See Karoly Okolicsanyi, "Hungary: Modest Growth of Private Companies," *RFE/RL Research Report,* no. 2, January 10, 1992.

83. See Yves-Michel Riols, "Le gouvernement lance un programme de privatisations pour jeter les bases d'un capitalisme populaire," *Le Monde,* April 18/19, 1993.

84. Judy Dempsey, "Wayward Bulgaria Returns to Path of Reform," *Financial Times* (London), April 9, 1992.

85. Most of the following information is taken from Elizabeth Teague (ed.), "Unemployment Provisions in the USSR and Eastern Europe," *RFE/RL Research Report,* no. 2, January 10, 1992. The Bulgarian information is from *Zname* (Sofia), no. 3, January 15–21, 1992, the Albanian from AP (Tirana), April 14, 1992.

86. "Better Sorry Than Safe," *The Economist,* May 4, 1991.

87. See John M. Kramer, *The Energy Gap in Eastern Europe* (Lexington, Mass., Lexington Books, 1990); also Brown, *Eastern Europe and Communist Rule,* pp. 137–57.

88. John M. Kramer, "Eastern Europe and the Energy Shock of 1990–91," *Problems of Communism,* May–June 1991.

89. Ibid.

90. Ibid.

91. See Judy Dempsey, "Eastern Europe Struggles to Fill Energy Gap," *Financial Times* (London), February 1, 1991; also Franz-Josef Schmitt, "Die

Lage der Energieversorgung in Osteuropa," *Neue Zürcher Zeitung,* January 9, 1991.

92. Blaine Harden, "Energy Crunch in Poland," *Washington Post,* January 25, 1992.

93. An official announcement in Moscow put the figure for 1992 exports of oil to non-former Soviet Union countries at 66.2 million tons as compared with 54.1 million in 1991. It did not itemize importing countries but there would seem no reason why Eastern European countries should not have benefited from the increase. Reuters (Moscow), January 11, 1993.

94. Victor Keegan, "Fiddling While the Soviet Union and Eastern Europe Burn," *Guardian* (London), June 2, 1991.

95. See Patrice Dabrowski, "East European Trade, (Part I): The Loss of the Soviet Market," *RFE/RL Report on Eastern Europe,* no. 40, October 4, 1991.

96. The Romanian request was reported by Reuters (New York) on December 12, 1991, the Bulgarian by RFE/RL, *Report from New York,* February 4, 1991. Both requests were, in effect, stalled.

97. See Howard LaFranchi, "East Europeans Lay Plans to Scale the Walls of Fortress Europe," *Christian Science Monitor,* December 30, 1992. East European steel exports were greeted in Western Europe with charges of dumping. See, for example, Tom Redburn, "Pillar of European Unity, Steel Now Divides East and West," *International Herald Tribune,* January 28, 1993.

98. *Wirtschaftswoche* (Düsseldorf), October 2, 1992.

99. Two experts, J. M. C. Rollo and Alastair Smith, writing in the April 1993 issue of *Economic Policy* (published by Cambridge University Press), estimated that between 40 and 50 percent of the exports of Central and East European countries could fall in the European Community's "sensitive" category. See Samuel Brittan, "Iron Curtain in the Way of Trade," *Financial Times* (London), April 29, 1993.

100. For an excellent review of the opposing arguments, see Slay, "The Economy: Perceptions and Reality." For a vigorous article oriented to "shock therapy," see Jan Winiecki, "The Inevitability of a Fall in Output in the Early Stages of Transition to the Market: Theoretical Underpinnings," *Soviet Studies,* vol. 43, no. 4, 1991.

101. For this kind of argument as applied to the Soviet Union, see Charles Wolf, Jr., "Reasons for Economic Optimism in the Ex-USSR," *Wall Street Journal,* January 8, 1992.

102. See Brown, *Eastern Europe and Communist Rule,* pp. 130–37.

103. Most of the points made in this section are taken from Timothy N. Ash, "East European Agriculture at a Crossroads," *RFE/RL Research Report,* no. 4, January 24, 1992.

104. For examples of the practical difficulties in two widely differing

countries, see Ulrich Glauber, "Bei den Bauern keimt Unsicherheit," *Frankfurter Rundschau,* April 18, 1991 (for Czechoslovakia); and C. Sr., "Chaos in Rumäniens Dörfer," *Neue Zürcher Zeitung,* December 20, 1991.

105. *Statistická rocenka* 1991 (Prague: Czech and Slovak Statistical Office, 1991), p. 188.

106. *Duma* (Sofia), February 1, 1991.

107. Ash, "East European Agriculture at a Crossroads." The details for other East European countries are taken from this source.

108. The Romanian situation regarding restitution was particularly disorderly; see C. Sr., "Chaos in Rumäniens Dörfer"; "Romanians Can't Afford Land That Is Theirs," unsigned article, *New York Times,* February 12, 1992.

109. *The Economist,* June 5, 1993.

110. F. N. Nevendorff-Falk, "Bei der Versorgung der Landwirtschaft in Osteuropa droht eine Katastrophe," *Handelsblatt* (Düsseldorf), December 20, 1991.

111. Ash, "East European Agriculture at a Crossroads."

112. The drop in domestic demand for agricultural produce was leading to large surpluses of grain in most countries; "Steigende Getreideüberschüsse in Mittel- und Osteuropa," *Neue Zürcher Zeitung,* December 5, 1991.

113. See Wałęsa's interview with Roger Boyes, *Times* (London), March 17, 1992. For the West's unresponsive attitude, see the excellent article by R. C. Longworth, "East Europe's Friendless Road to Capitalism," *Chicago Tribune,* November 2, 1991.

114. Ash, "East European Agriculture at a Crossroads."

115. Ibid. See also Patrice Dabrowski, "East European Trade (Part II): Creative Solutions by the Former East Bloc," *RFE/RL Report on Eastern Europe,* no. 41, October 11, 1991.

116. See Josef C. Brada, "The European Community and Czechoslovakia, Hungary, and Poland," *RFE/RL Report on Eastern Europe,* no. 49, December 6, 1991. For earlier negotiations, see David Buchan, "Brussels Opens Its Doors to Trade with Eastern Europe," *Financial Times* (London), April 19, 1991.

117. Tom Redburn, "EC Opens Door to East European Nations," *International Herald Tribune,* June 23, 1993.

118. I have been helped greatly in this subject and on East European economics generally by Steven Popper of RAND; see his essay, "Aid from Western Governments: The First Steps," in Charles Wolf, Jr., *Promoting Democracy and Free Markets in Eastern Europe* (San Francisco: Institute for Contemporary Studies Press, 1992), pp. 169–93.

119. This survey is taken largely from Judy Dempsey, "Time To Sort Out Who Owns What," *Financial Times* (London), April 16, 1991, and "A Survey of Business in Eastern Europe," *The Economist,* September 21, 1991.

120. Rodica Seward, Steven Glick, and Martin, "Romania Pursues Its Own Road."

121. Ht., "Bulgarische Restitutions- und Investitionsgesetze," *Neue Zürcher Zeitung,* February 1, 1992; Reuters (Sofia), January 17, 1992. The prohibition on farming was mainly designed to prevent "land grabbing" by Turks from Turkey.

122. See "Einstieg des VW-Konzerns bei Škoda," *Neue Zürcher Zeitung,* February 12, 1992; him., "Deutsche Investoren in der Tschechoslowakei führend," *Frankfurter Allgemeine Zeitung,* January 16, 1992; Karl-Peter Schwarz, "Sorge ums Familiensilber," *Die Presse* (Vienna), February 3, 1992; Blaine Harden, "In Poland, Particular Fear of German Investors," *Washington Post,* February 5, 1992.

123. The memorandum was originally published in *Lidové noviny,* December 31, 1991, FBIS-EEU-92-006, January 9, 1992, pp. 17–18.

124. See the statement by a senior commercial official in *Handelsblatt* (Düsseldorf), April 1, 1992.

125. "A Survey of Business in Eastern Europe," *The Economist,* September 21, 1991.

126. Stephen Engelberg, "With Some Misgivings, East Europe Snaps Up German Money," *New York Times,* January 23, 1992. See also Guy Halverson, "Western Firms Get a Foot in the Door in Eastern Europe," *Christian Science Monitor,* February 10, 1992.

127. Czech Premier Pithardt was reported by AP (Prague) on January 27, 1992, as saying he would like more U.S. and Far East investment to balance the inflow of German capital. Mary Battiata, "In Czechoslovakia, German Investors Outpace Americans," *Washington Post,* February 10, 1992, reported that Germany and Austria accounted for 60 percent of the deals made and 80 percent of all foreign investment in Czechoslovakia.

128. "In the Middle of Mittel-Europa," *The Economist,* January 25, 1992.

129. *East European Investment Magazine,* December 29, 1992. For a less optimistic view, see "Eastern Promise Fails to Deliver for West," *The European,* January 7–10, 1993.

130. I am grateful to Patricia Hudson and Robert L. Hutchings for their help in this section on foreign investment.

131. See Hiroko Yamane and Paul Blamire, "Japan and Eastern Europe—the Case for Patience," *World Today* (London), April 1991.

132. Agence France Presse (Budapest), December 19, 1991. The difficulties apparently continued; see Timothy Aeppel, "Suzuki Plant Discovers Japanese Style Doesn't Play Well in Hungary," *Wall Street Journal Europe,* May 7, 1993.

133. Erik Ipsen, "Bleak Picture Painted of Eastern Europe," *International Herald Tribune,* December 20, 1991; Peter Norman, "Brighter Outlook For Eastern Europe," *Financial Times* (London), December 20, 1991.

134. GS, "Wann greifen in Osteuropa die Reformen?", *Neue Zürcher Zeitung,* February 9, 1991.

135. Ibid.

136. *Financial Times* (London), December 20, 1991.

137. See Steven Greenhouse, "UN Group Warns of Economic Collapse in Europe," *New York Times,* December 3, 1991.

138. Wolfgang Münchau, "Pleading Patience in Eastern Europe to Fight Reform Fatigue," *Times* (London), January 8, 1992. See also René Höltschi, "Verlorene Illusionen in Mittel- und Osteuropa," *Neue Zürcher Zeitung,* January 26–27, 1992; and Ww., "Harziger Reformprozess in Mittel- und Osteuropa," *Neue Zürcher Zeitung,* April 7, 1992.

139. Münchau, "Pleading Patience in Eastern Europe."

140. Stephen Engelberg, "Eastern Europe Struggles to Develop a Post-Communist Mindset," *New York Times,* April 8, 1992.

141. Michael Shields, Reuters (Budapest), October 21, 1992.

142. Brown, *Surge to Freedom,* pp. 258–59.

143. World Bank report, quoted by René Höltschi, " 'Dreckschleudern' und Zeitbomben," *Neue Zürcher Zeitung,* July 12–13, 1992 (Fernausgabe Nr. 159). See also "Socialism's Trash," *Time,* June 1, 1992.

144. Höltschi, " 'Dreckschleudern' und Zeitbomben."

145. Gordon Hughes, "Are the Costs of Cleaning Up Eastern Europe Exaggerated? Economic Reform and the Environment," *Oxford Review of Economic Policy,* vol. 7, no. 4. This essay was extensively reviewed in *The Economist,* February 1, 1992.

146. For an excellent report of this and other problems, see Dan Stets and Mark Jaffe, "Poland's Heavy Industry Assaults the Atmosphere," *Philadelphia Inquirer,* May 18, 1992.

147. Höltschi, " 'Dreckschleudern' und Zeitbomben."

148. See Berthold Kohler, "Prag ein schwefelgelb-graues 'explodiertes Chemiedepot,' " *Frankfurter Allgemeine Zeitung,* February 6, 1993.

149. See Marlise Simmons, "Investors Back Off from Polluted Eastern Europe," *New York Times,* May 13, 1992.

150. Höltschi, " 'Dreckschleudern' und Zeitbomben."

151. *The Economist,* August 15, 1992. See also Christoph Bertram, "Ach, so schlimm wird's schon nicht werden!", *Die Zeit* (Hamburg), January 29, 1993. As the title of Bertram's article implies, he contrasts the universal nervousness about what might happen with the lethargy when it comes to doing something about it.

152. Kozloduy continued to be the object of world attention and the various minor hush-ups at the station were extensively reported. See, for example, Malcolm W. Browne, "Bulgarians Strive to Update Nuclear Power Plant," *New York Times,* December 8, 1992.

153. " 'Temelín wird gebaut': Protest aus Österreich," *Die Presse* (Vienna), January 9, 1993.

6 Nationalism: The Imprisoning Past

1. Interview with Nathan Gardels, "Two Concepts of Nationalism: An Interview with Isaiah Berlin," *New York Review of Books,* November 21, 1991. I quoted the passage in *Nationalism, Democracy, and Security in the Balkans* (Aldershot, U.K.: Dartmouth for RAND, 1992), p. 173. See also Pierre Hassner, "L'Europe et le spectre des nationalismes," *L'Esprit* (Paris), October 1991.

2. Thomas S. Szayna, "Polish Foreign Policy under a Non-Communist Government" (Santa Monica, Calif.: RAND note, April 1990), p. 27.

3. Joseph Rothschild, *Ethnopolitics: A Conceptual Framework* (New York: Columbia University Press, 1981), p. 14.

4. Ibid., p. 29.

5. See Dennison Rusinow, *The Yugoslav Experiment, 1948–1974* (London: C. Hurst, 1977), passim.

6. Ernest Gellner, *Nations and Nationalism* (Ithaca, N.Y., Cornell University Press, 1983), p. 1. I quoted this passage in *Nationalism, Democracy, and Security in the Balkans,* p. 173.

7. Ibid. Also quoted in *Nationalism, Democracy, and Security in the Balkans,* p. 173.

8. These points constitute an amplification of the points in J. F. Brown, "Crisis and Conflict in Eastern Europe," *RFE/RL Research Report,* no. 22, May 29, 1992. On Balkan crises, see F. Stephen Larrabee, "Long Memories and Short Fuses: Change and Instability in the Balkans," *International Security,* Winter 1990–91.

9. See Louis Zanga's two essays: "The Question of Kosovar Sovereignty," *RFE/RL Research Report,* no. 43, October 30, 1992, and "Albania Afraid of War over Kosovo," ibid., no. 46. November 20, 1992. For a cautionary view on the prospects of an early pan-Albanian reunion, see Viktor Meier, "Die Albaner im früheren Jugoslawien wollen eigene Lösungen," *Frankfurter Allgemeine Zeitung,* March 17, 1992.

10. In early 1993, there were Western press reports about ethnic cleansing; see, for example, Rm., "Vertreibungspolitik im Kosovo," *Frankfurter Allgemeine Zeitung,* February 22, 1993. In "Keeping Kosovo's Fragile Peace," *Wall Street Journal Europe,* February 23, 1993, Alexandra Tuttle described the situation as having slightly eased in some respects. On June 5, 1993, the former Priština-based Albanian language journal, *Rilíndja,* now

published in Zurich, reported that 120,000 Albanians in Kosovo had been fired from their jobs "in these past few months."

11. On the basic dangers in Kosovo, see Flora Lewis, "Foreboding in Kosovo: This War Isn't Going to Prevent Itself," *International Herald Tribune,* January 29, 1993. On "Arkan," see Blaine Harden, "Serbia's Treacherous Gang of Three," *Washington Post,* February 7, 1993.

12. They were revived toward the end of 1990 in Montenegro's parliamentary election campaign; for example, by Novak Kilibarda, of the People's Party, Tanjug (Yugoslav News Agency), November 23, 1990.

13. See Duncan M. Perry, "Macedonia: A Balkan Problem and a European Dilemma," *RFE/RL Research Report,* no. 25, June 19, 1992; Patrick Moore, "The 'Albanian Question' in the Former Yugoslavia," ibid., no. 14, April 3, 1992.

14. Louis Zanga, "Albanian-Greek Relations Reach a Low Point," ibid., no. 15, April 10, 1992; Gabriel Partos, "Albania and Greece at Daggers Drawn," BBC Central Talks and Features Current Affairs Unit, CARIS Talk, No. 58/92; Frederick Kempe, "Greek-Albanian Border Holds Latest Tensions In Balkan Powder Keg," *Wall Street Journal Europe,* March 4, 1993.

15. In early February 1993 Greece began the process of forcibly repatriating Albanian refugees; AP (Tirana), February 4, 1993.

16. The appointment, by the Constantinople Patriarchate, of a Greek citizen to be the new archbishop of the Albanian Autocephalous Orthodox Church only increased the fears of some Albanians of Greek "penetration"; see Reuters (Tirana), February 17, 1993.

17. See J. F. Brown, *Eastern Europe and Communist Rule* (Durham, N.C.: Duke University Press, 1988), pp. 331–32.

18. See Perry, "Macedonia: A Balkan Problem and a European Dilemma."

19. See C. Sr., "Mazedoniens labiles inneres Gleichgewicht," *Neue Zürcher Zeitung,* November 18, 1992 (Fernausgabe Nr. 268).

20. See Paul Shoup, *Communism and the Yugoslav National Question* (New York, Columbia University Press, 1968), pp. 144–83. For a thoughtful explanation of the Greek position, see Thanos Lipowatz, "Die Griechen fühlen sich zwischen zwei Feuern," *Frankfurter Rundschau,* May 14, 1993.

21. Greece's refusal to recognize Macedonia became the subject of an enormous Western press coverage, the vast majority of it critical of Greece. For a pungent exchange, giving each side, see the two articles in the *Spectator* (London): Noel Malcolm, "The New Bully of the Balkans," August 15, 1992, arguing the Macedonian case; and Patrick Leigh Fermor, "A Clean Sheet for Paeonia," September 12, 1992, arguing the Greek case. ("Paeonia" was the name Leigh Fermor suggested for Macedonia.)

22. See ps. "Athen, Skopje und die EG," *Neue Zürcher Zeitung,* June 26, 1992 (Fernausgabe Nr. 145).

23. On the Bulgarian attitude, see Sylvie Kauffmann, "Macedoine, le rêve perdu des Bulgares," *Le Monde,* December 12, 1992.

24. See Robert Kaplan, "The Next Balkan War," *Guardian* (London) December 22, 1992.

25. For a general picture of the increasing pressure on the Hungarian minority, see A.O., "Die Vojvodina—Jugoslawiens vergessene Provinz," *Neue Zürcher Zeitung,* February 23–24, 1992 (Fernausgabe Nr. 44).

26. See Hugh Poulton, "Rising Ethnic Tension in Vojvodina," *RFE/RL Research Report,* no. 50, December 18, 1992.

27. Ibid.

28. Ibid.

29. Interview with *Die Presse* (Vienna), October 16, 1992.

30. Viktor Meier, "Sorge wegen Sowjetrepublik Moldav," *Frankfurter Allgemeine Zeitung,* November 6, 1990.

31. See Vladimir Socor, "Moldavia Builds a New State,"*RFE/RL Research Report,* no. 1, January 3, 1992.

32. Mihai Carp, "Cultural Ties Between Romania and Moldavia," *Report on Eastern Europe,* no. 30, July 27, 1990.

33. See Vladimir Socor, "Creeping Putsch in Eastern Moldova," *RFE/RL Research Report,* no. 3, January 17, 1992. For the broader implications of Trans-Dniester-Moldovan clash, see John Rettie, "Slav Tiger Straining at the Leash," *Guardian* (London), June 27, 1992.

34. On the danger of war in Moldova, see "Russia and Moldova—The Next Bosnia?" *The Economist,* June 6, 1992.

35. See Socor's article, "Why Moldova Does Not Seek Reunification with Romania," *RFE/RL Research Report,* no. 5, January 31, 1992.

36. Reuters (Bucharest) on August 7, 1992, reported a poll of about two thousand people, of which 55 percent wanted immediate union with Moldova. On overall Romanian opinion, see Viktor Meier, "Die Wiedervereinigung mit Moldova ist ein nationaler Wunsch," *Frankfurter Allgemeine Zeitung,* October 6, 1992.

37. See, for example, Reuters (Bucharest), March 11, 1992, and July 1, 1992.

38. Rompress (Romanian News Agency), in English, January 23, 1991.

39. *Magyar Nemzet* (Budapest), June 4, 1990.

40. In an interview with *Le Monde* (Paris) on January 16, 1993, the Romanian foreign minister, Teodor Meleşcanu, said the treaty had been negotiated to 85 percent. It was the questions of the frontiers and the minorities that had still to be settled. (Obviously a very big remaining 15 percent!) Meleşcanu referred to these two questions as the "Gordian knot."

41. See Dennis Deletant, "The Role of *Vatra Românească* in Transylvania," *RFE/RL Report on Eastern Europe,* no. 5, February 1, 1991.

42. This interview was originally given to the Romanian journal, *Ba-*

ricada, and was then carried with some gusto by *Népszabadság* (Budapest) on January 21, 1991. FBIS-EEU-91-024, February 5, 1991, p. 42. I am grateful to Michael Shafir for drawing my attention to this reference.

43. For Roman's role in this incident, see Michael Shafir, "Schöpflinian Realism and Romanian Reality," *RFE/RL Report on Eastern Europe,* no. 7, February 15, 1991.

44. See Tom Gallagher, "Ultranationalists Take Charge of Transylvania's Capital," *RFE/RL Research Report,* no. 13, March 27, 1992.

45. AP (Bucharest), August 6, 1992. For an excellent overall view of Funar, see A.O., " 'Ceauşescu war ein guter Rumäne': Ansichten und Wirken des Bürgermeisters der Stadt Cluj," *Neue Zürcher Zeitung,* July 18, 1992.

46. On the statue of Mathias Corvinus, see Andreas Oplatka, "Die Kraft nationaler Symbole in Osteuropa," *Neue Zürcher Zeitung,* April 30, 1993.

47. A.O., *Neue Zürcher Zeitung,* July 18, 1992.

48. See his "The Movement for Romania: A Party of Radical Return," *RFE/RL Research Report,* no. 29, July 17, 1992.

49. A.O., " 'Ceauşescu war ein guter Rumäne.' "

50. J. F. Brown, *Eastern Europe and Communist Rule* (Durham, N.C.: Duke University Press, 1988), p. 433. On the Slovak consciousness, see Peter Brock, *The Slovak National Awakening* (Toronto: University of Toronto Press, 1976).

51. On "arrogant" minorities, see Brown, *Eastern Europe and Communist Rule,* p. 421.

52. See Jan Obrman, "Language Law Stirs Controversy in Slovakia," *RFE/RL Report on Eastern Europe,* no. 46, November 16, 1990.

53. DPA (Bratislava), January 14, 1993. On Mečiár's general attitude to the Hungarian minority, see Alfred A. Reisch, "Mečiár and Slovakia's Hungarian Minority," *RFE/RL Research Report,* no. 43, October 30, 1992.

54. See Michael Frank, "Kaum Sehnsucht nach der Rückkehr," *Süddeutsche Zeitung* (Munich), February 19, 1993.

55. See Karoly Okolicsanyi, "Hungary Cancels Treaty on Danube Dam Construction," *RFE/RL Research Report,* no. 26, June 26, 1992.

56. Karoly Okolicsanyi, "Slovak-Hungarian Tension: Bratislava Diverts the Danube," *RFE/RL Research Report,* no. 49, December 11, 1992.

57. *Rzeczpospolita* (Warsaw), September 3, 1992. I am grateful to Anna Swidlicka for unearthing these figures.

58. See Jan B. de Weydenthal, "The Polish-Lithuanian Dispute," *RFE/RL Report on Eastern Europe,* no. 41, October 11, 1991; and Stephen R. Burant, "Polish-Lithuanian Relations: Past, Present, and Future," *Problems of Communism,* May–June 1991.

59. See the excellent, balanced article on the overall situation by M. Sc., "Vorbelastete Minoritätenpolitik in Litauen," *Neue Zürcher Zeitung,* March 12, 1992.

60. Roman Korab-Żebryk, quoted by Klaus Bachmann, "Wem gehört die litauische Hauptstadt Wilna?" *Stuttgarter Zeitung,* June 12, 1992.

61. Private conversation, July 1992.

62. Hannes Gamillsche, "Die polnische Minderheit bangt um ihre Rechte," *Frankfurter Rundschau,* February 17, 1992.

63. See Thomas Urban, "Erste Botschaft Weissrusslands in Polen," *Süddeutsche Zeitung* (Munich), June 26, 1992.

64. M. L., "Erfolg polnischer Aussenpolitik," *Frankfurter Allgemeine Zeitung,* June 25, 1992.

65. For essays on the historical background to Polish-Ukrainian relations, see Peter J. Potichnyj (ed.), *Poland and Ukraine: Past and Present* (Edmonton/Toronto: Canadian Institute of Ukrainian Studies, 1980).

66. For the historical background, see Andrew Sorokowski, "Ukrainian Catholics and Orthodox in Poland Since 1945," *Religion in Communist Lands* (Kent, Eng.: Keston House, Winter 1986).

67. See the excellent roundup in *Le Monde* (Paris), March 8/9, 1992; also Michael Ludwig, "Skubiszewski entwickelte die 'zweigleisige Ostpolitik' Polens," *Frankfurter Allgemeine Zeitung,* May 19, 1992. But despite this huge improvement of relations at the official level, there still was much suspicion, especially on the Polish side. A Polish opinion poll showed that 38 percent of those asked feared an independent Ukraine, against 28 percent who feared Germany; Klaus Bachmann, "Umfrage: Viele Polen fürchten die Ukraine," *Stuttgarter Zeitung,* March 4, 1992.

68. fy., "Was wird aus Königsberg? Polen dementiert territoriales Interesse," *Frankfurter Allgemeine Zeitung,* February 17, 1992. For a brilliant, depressingly evocative picture of Kaliningrad, past and present, together with the continuing German interest in it, mainly, though by no means solely, nostalgic, see Amos Elon, "The Nowhere City," *New York Review of Books,* May 13, 1993.

69. See Mark Rybakow, "Wohin blickt Königsberg?", *Stuttgarter Zeitung,* February 22, 1992; and DPA (Königsberg), December 4, 1992.

70. David McQuaid, "The Growing Assertiveness of Minorities," *Report on Eastern Europe,* no. 50, December 13, 1991.

71. Ibid.

72. *Rzeczpospolita* (Warsaw), September 27, 1993, quoted in Louisa Vinton, "Poland Goes Left," *RFE/RL Research Report,* no. 40, October 8, 1993.

73. See Phillip Sherwell, "Poles Angered as Ethnic Germans Honour War Dead," *Daily Telegraph* (London), November 4, 1992.

74. *Polytika* (Warsaw), February 13, 1993.

75. *Ekonom* (Prague), no. 19, 1992.

76. See Rudolf L. Tökes, "From Visegrád to Kraków: Cooperation, Competition, and Coexistence in Central Europe," *Problems of Communism,* November–December, 1991.

77. See J. F. Brown, *Surge to Freedom: The End of Communist Rule in Eastern Europe,* (Durham, N.C.: Duke University Press, 1991), pp. 265–66.

78. Interview with *Le Figaro* (Paris), January 8, 1993. In an interview with the Czech Service of Radio Free Europe on January 11, Klaus attempted to modify his remarks by saying that Visegrád cooperation was still of "key importance." See also Susan Greenberg, "Klaus Snubs His Billionaire Santa," *Guardian* (London), January 12, 1993. The "Santa" is George Soros, who founded the university.

79. Z. A. B. Zeman, *The Making and Breaking of Communist Europe* (Oxford: Basil Blackwell, 1991), p. 193.

80. *Népszabadság* (Budapest), December 17, 1992.

81. *Time* (European edition), January 20, 1992. (It is a depressing reflection on the Tudjman regime in Zagreb that Drakulić and several other like-minded ladies were being officially denounced as antipatriotic "witches" in early 1993.)

82. Ibid.

83. Lord Acton, "Essay on Nationality," 1862, reproduced in Peter Pulzer, *The Rise of Political Anti-Semitism in Germany and Austria,* rev. ed. (Cambridge, Mass.: Harvard University Press, 1988), pp. 67–68.

84. Paul Lendvai, *Anti-Semitism Without Jews* (Garden City, N.Y.: Doubleday, 1971).

85. Ernst Nolte, *Martin Heidegger: Politik und Geschichte im Leben und Denken* (Berlin, Propyläen-Verlag, 1992), pp. 29–30, quoted by Thomas Sheehan, "A Normal Nazi" (a review article on Heidegger), *New York Review of Books,* January 14, 1993.

86. Zoltan Barany, "Democratic Changes Bring Mixed Blessings for Gypsies," *RFE/RL Research Report,* no. 20, May 15, 1992. See also David Crowe and John Koltsi (eds.), *Gypsies in Eastern Europe* (Armonk, N.Y.: M. E. Sharpe, 1991).

87. Ibid.

88. CTK (Czech News Agency), September 3, 1993. Evidently aware of the international damage his remarks caused, Mečiár blusteringly denied he had made them. But further inquiry left no doubt that he did make them.

89. C. L. Sulzberger, *A Long Row of Candles* (Toronto: Macmillan, 1969), p. 61.

7. The Yugoslav Tragedy

1. Joseph Rothschild, *East Central Europe Between the Wars* (Seattle: University of Washington Press, 1974), p. 201. See also Barbara Jelavich,

History of the Balkans (2 vols.), (Cambridge: Cambridge University Press, 1983), esp. vol. 2, *Twentieth Century.*

2. Rothschild, *East Central Europe Between the Wars,* p. 202.

3. See, for example, Nora Beloff, *Tito's Flawed Legacy: Yugoslavia and the West Since 1939* (Boulder, Colo.: Westview, 1986); Michael Lees, *The Rape of Serbia: The British Role in Tito's Grab for Power* (San Diego: Harcourt Brace Jovanovich, 1990).

4. I have discussed these points at some length in *Surge to Freedom: The End to Communist Rule in Eastern Europe* (Durham, N.C.: Duke University Press, 1991), pp. 221–23, and in *Nationalism, Democracy and Security in the Balkans* (Aldershot, U.K.: Dartmouth for RAND, 1992), pp. 62–63.

5. The best biography of Tito is still that by Milovan Djilas, *Tito: Eine kritische Biographie* (Vienna: Molden, 1980).

6. Paul Lendvai is excellent on the "Club of 41" in his *Eagles in Cobwebs: Nationalism and Communism in the Balkans* (Garden City, N.Y.: Doubleday, 1969), pp. 61–65.

7. Brown, *Nationalism, Democracy, and Security in the Balkans,* p. 63.

8. Duncan Wilson, *Tito's Yugoslavia* (Cambridge: Cambridge University Press, 1979), p. 141.

9. On the rotation system, see Slobodan Stanković, *The End of the Tito Era: Yugoslavia's Dilemmas* (Stanford, Calif.: Hoover Institution Press, 1981).

10. On Yugoslavia's attempts to tackle its economic problems during the 1980s, see Brown, *Surge to Freedom,* pp. 234–36.

11. See Brown, *Nationalism, Democracy, and Security in the Balkans,* pp. 66–70.

12. Ibid., p. 67.

13. Veselin Djuretić, *The Allies and the Yugoslav War Drama.*

14. On Ćosić, see the short biography by Milan Andrejevich in "What Future for Serbia," *RFE/RL Research Report,* no. 50, December 18, 1992.

15. Brown, *Surge to Freedom,* p. 228. See also Aleksa Djilas, "A Profile of Slobodan Milošević," *Foreign Affairs,* Summer 1993.

16. Christopher Cviic, "The Background and Implications of the Domestic Scene in Yugoslavia," in Paul Shoup (ed.) and George W. Hoffman (project director), *Problems of Balkan Security: Southeastern Europe in the 1990s* (Washington, D.C.: Wilson Center, 1990), p. 92.

17. Brown, *Surge to Freedom,* pp. 229–30.

18. For an excellent brief review of the Slovene struggle toward independence, see Milton Viorst, "A Reporter at Large: The Yugoslav Idea," *New Yorker,* March 18, 1991. On Slovenia's difficulties immediately after independence had been achieved, see Viktor Meier, "Schwieriger Beginn in Ljubljana," *Frankfurter Allgemeine Zeitung,* August 1, 1991, and Viktor Meier, "Die Slowenen wollen sich selber helfen," *Frankfurter Allgemeine Zeitung,* August 24, 1991.

19. On Tudjman, see Michael Schwelien, "Der Kroate, der die Krise will," *Die Zeit* (Hamburg), May 10, 1991. For Tudjman's earlier relative caution, see his interview in the Slovenian *Delo,* May 4, 1991, JPRS-EER-91-085, June 17, 1991, p. 37.

20. See, for example, "The Serbs Start to Play It Rough," *The Economist,* August 25, 1990. For a good later article that gives details on the Serb-majority districts in Croatia, see "Im Hintergrund: Serben in Kroatien," *Frankfurter Rundschau,* July 30, 1991.

21. See Sabrina P. Ramet, "Primordial Ethnicity or Modern Nationalism? The Case of Yugoslavia's Muslims Reconsidered," *South Slav Journal,* Spring–Summer 1990.

22. On Milošević's ideas about the future of Yugoslavia as a "democratic federation . . . not a confederation," see his speech in Belgrade, May 30, 1991, carried by Radio Belgrade on the same day; FBIS-EEU-91-105, May 31, 1991, p. 24. For a caustic commentary on Milošević's earlier propagation of such ideas, see Hansjakob Stehle, "Unruhen in Belgrad: der Zauberlehrling des Marschalls," *Die Zeit* (Hamburg), March 15, 1991.

23. On the Serb superiority complex, see, for example, C. Sr., "Serbiens Traum von der alten Grösse," *Neue Zürcher Zeitung,* March 20, 1989 (Fernausgabe, Nr. 72); Marie-Pierre Subtil, "Le Rêve de la Grande Serbie," *Le Monde* (Paris), August 13, 1991. No Western observer has shown more understanding of Serbia and of the Yugoslav tragedy as a whole than Misha Glenny. See his two books, *The Rebirth of History: Eastern Europe in the Age of Democracy* (1990), and *The Fall of Yugoslavia: The Third Balkan War* (1992), both published by Penguin in London. See also his articles in the *New York Review of Books:* "The Massacre of Yugoslavia," January 30, 1992; "Yugoslavia: The Revenger's Tragedy," August 13, 1992; and "Bosnia: The Last Chance," January 28, 1993.

24. *Neue Zürcher Zeitung,* December 8, 1990 (Fernausgabe Nr. 285). See also his interview with the Sarajevo *Oslobodjenje,* February 27, 1991, FBIS-EEU-91-046, March 8, 1991, p. 53.

25. See, for example, Šešelj's interview with *Der Spiegel* (Hamburg), August 5, 1991.

26. Interview with Thomas Ross, *Frankfurter Allgemeine Zeitung,* November 6, 1990.

27. NIN (Belgrade), March 20, 1992, quoted by Gordon N. Bardos, "The Serbian Church Against Milošević," *RFE/RL Research Report,* no. 31, July 31, 1992.

28. This information is based on conversations I had in Zagreb in March 1991.

29. It was estimated that they numbered 30 percent of Croatian party members and about 60 percent of the police. See Viktor Meier, "In Jugoslawien nichts mehr verloren," *Frankfurter Allgemeine Zeitung,* October 5,

1990; Carl-Gustaf Ströhm's interview with Tudjman, *Die Welt* (Hamburg), September 1, 1990.

30. Brown, *Nationalism, Democracy, and Security in the Balkans,* p. 151.

31. The figure of 20,000 was given by a European Community team. See William Drozdiak, "Serb Forces Rape 20,000 in Bosnia, EC Team Finds," *Washington Post,* January 9, 1993. The higher figures were given mainly by Bosnian or other Muslim sources.

32. See C. Sr., "Wachsender Nationalismus in Zagreb," *Neue Zürcher Zeitung,* March 24, 1990 (Fernausgabe Nr. 69).

33. Originally quoted by Ivo Banac, *The National Question in Yugoslavia: Origins, History, Politics* (Ithaca, N.Y.: Cornell University Press, 1984), p. 107.

34. I am grateful to Patrick Moore for recalling this story.

35. See Viktor Meier, "Das Serbien Milošević's schafft im Sandzak ein zweites Kosovo," *Frankfurter Allgemeine Zeitung,* June 25, 1991; Milan Andrejevich, "The Sandzak: The Next Balkan Theater of War?" *RFE/RL Research Report,* no. 50, December 18, 1992.

36. See David Rieff, "Letter from Bosnia: Original Virtue, Original Sin," *New Yorker,* November 23, 1992.

37. For brief discussions of the military's role throughout the 1980s, see J. F. Brown, *Eastern Europe and Communist Rule* (Durham, N.C.: Duke University Press, 1988), pp. 361–62, and *Surge to Freedom,* pp. 237–38.

38. See Viktor Meier, "Yugoslavia: Worsening Economic and Nationalist Crisis," in William E. Griffith (ed.), *Central and Eastern Europe: The Opening Curtain* (Boulder, Colo.: Westview Press, 1989), pp. 271–72.

39. For a review of this incident, and other incidents, in which the military were involved, see Milan Andrejevich, "The Military's Role in the Current Constitutional Crisis," *RFE/RL Report on Eastern Europe,* no. 45, November 9, 1990.

40. See Viktor Meier, "Weshalb der Armee Jugoslawiens das Putschen schwerfällt: Serben beherrschen das Offizierkorps, die anderen Nationalitäten stellen die Mannschaften," *Frankfurter Allgemeine Zeitung,* October 17, 1990. See also Maren Köster-Hetzendorf, "Höllische Spiele verrückter Politiker; der Widerstand innerhalb der jugoslawischen Bundesarmee wächst," *Die Presse* (Vienna), September 24, 1991. For a fascinating article on the Red Army in November 1991, in a situation not dissimilar from that of the Yugoslav army, see U.Sd., "Neugestaltung des sowjetischen Unionsvertrags," *Neue Zürcher Zeitung,* November 17–18, 1991 (Fernausgabe Nr. 267).

41. For comments on this media misuse by the founding editor of *Vreme,* which in mid-1993 was the only remaining independent magazine in Belgrade, see "Quiet Voices from the Balkans," *New Yorker,* March 15, 1993.

42. See Brown, *Surge to Freedom,* pp. 228–29. For an excellent historical

review of the Kosovo crisis, see Arshi Pipa and Sami Repishti, "Reflections on the Kosovo Crisis," *Across Frontiers,* Winter–Spring 1989.

43. Milan Andrejevich, "Kosovo and Slovenia Declare Their Sovereignty," *RFE/RL Report on Eastern Europe,* no. 30, July 27, 1990.

44. *Zëri,* January 9, 1993 (*Zëri* is a Kosovo journal, which, because of Serb restrictions, was being published in Zurich).

45. For a conversation with Rugova, see Viorst, "A Reporter at Large."

46. A.O., "Wir Kosovo-Albaner sind keine Minderheit," *Neue Zürcher Zeitung,* August 11, 1992. See also Henri Guirchoun's interview with Rugova in *Le Nouvel Observateur* (Paris), September 3–9, 1992.

47. Pp. 227–28.

48. For excellent background to the Macedonian Question, see Robert D. Kaplan, "History's Cauldron," *Atlantic Monthly,* June 1991, and Duncan M. Perry, "Macedonia: A Balkan Problem and a European Dilemma," *RFE/RL Research Report,* no. 25, June 19, 1992.

49. See Duncan M. Perry, *The Politics of Terror: The Macedonian Revolutionary Movements, 1893–1903* (Durham, N.C.: Duke University Press, 1988).

50. See Yves Heller, "Skopje avide de reconnaissance," *Le Monde* (Paris), April 15, 1992.

51. See Milan Andrejevich, "The Election Scorecard for Serbia, Montenegro, and Macedonia," *RFE/RL Report on Eastern Europe,* no. 51, December 21, 1990.

52. On Georgievski, see his interview with Carl-Gustaf Ströhm, *Die Welt* (Hamburg), January 4, 1991.

53. The election attracted worldwide press coverage. For a good report, see Blaine Harden, "Defiant Serbs Reelect Milošević," *Washington Post,* December 22, 1992; for a good, balanced editorial, see "Serbia's Vote," *Financial Times* (London), December 23, 1992.

54. On Karadžić, see "Dr. Radovan Karadžić: Just What The Doctor Ordered," *Financial Times* (London), January 16, 1993.

55. One of the most perceptive commentaries on this growing possibility was by Tony Barber, "West Fears of Balkan War Coming True," *Independent* (London), December 20, 1992.

56. See, for example, Douglas Hurd's article in the *Daily Express* (London), December 30, 1992.

57. Reports on numbers varied between two hundred and about two thousand. The Serbs exaggerated the numbers so as to give the impression of a developing Muslim-Christian war. For a good color piece, see Chuck Sudetic, "Islamic Nations Come to Aid of Bosnian Muslims," *New York Times,* November 14, 1992.

58. For an excellent review of Western diplomacy on Yugoslavia, see John Newhouse, "The Diplomatic Round: Dodging the Problem," *New*

Yorker, August 24, 1992. See also Brown, *Nationalism, Democracy, and Security in the Balkans,* pp. 182–87.

59. The campaign was led by the *Frankfurter Allgemeine Zeitung* and *Die Welt.* The former is the most influential paper in Germany and its campaign for the early recognition of Croatia was believed to have had considerable influence in Bonn. In Germany and Austria there was much rhetoric about Catholic Croatia, the Habsburg link, Central European civilization, etc. For Otto Habsburg's views, see "Die Kroaten sind ja unsere Landsleute," *Die Presse* (Vienna), October 8, 1991.

60. See Paul Shoup, "The UN Force: A New Actor in the Croatian-Serbian Crisis," *RFE/RL Research Report,* no. 13, March 27, 1992.

61. Strong evidence suggests that the Yugoslav People's Army in Bosnia was already on a war footing by the summer of 1991. But to construe this capability as being proof that the JNA intended hostilities there, regardless of the diplomatic situation, is one-dimensional and unconvincing. See James Gow, "One Year of War in Bosnia and Herzegovina," *RFE/RL Research Report,* no. 23, June 4, 1993.

62. "What We Should Have Done," *Financial Times* (London), January 6, 1993.

63. Martin Woollacott, "Bosnia's Crippling Three-Way Stretch," *Guardian* (London), January 16, 1993.

64. By the end of 1992, even the approximate number was still not known. For an excellent account of the overall refugee situation toward the end of 1992, see Iva Dominis and Ivo Bićanić, "Refugees and Displaced Persons in the Former Yugoslavia," *RFE/RL Research Report,* no. 3, January 15, 1993.

65. On Izetbegović, see the interview with Carl-Gustaf Ströhm, *Die Welt* (Hamburg), November 23, 1990.

8 The World Outside: New Company and Old

1. Pierre Hassner, "The View from Paris," in Lincoln Gordon, *Eroding Empire: Western Relations with Eastern Europe* (Washington, D.C., The Brookings Institution, 1987), p. 191.

2. For rather a somber view, see Jan B. de Weydenthal, "EC Keeps Central Europe at Arm's Length," *RFE/RL Research Report,* no. 5, January 29, 1993. For a forceful criticism of the Community's attitude, see Richard Davy, "You Can Have Our Aid, But Don't Ask For Trade," *Independent* (London), May 26, 1992.

3. Dick Cheney, U.S. defense secretary in the Bush administration, was one of the senior Western officials in favor of inclusion. For his comments shortly before leaving office, see AP (Brussels), December 11, 1992. See also

Howard E. Frost, "Eastern Europe's Search for Security," and Jeffrey Simon, "Does Eastern Europe Belong in NATO?" *Orbis,* Winter 1992. For a powerful argument in favor of widening NATO, see Ronald D. Asmus, Richard L. Kugler, and F. Stephen Larrabee, "Building a New NATO," *Foreign Affairs,* September–October 1993.

4. I am grateful to Arnold Horelick for a helpful conversation on this subject in June 1993.

5. Michael Howard, *Times* (London), July 21, 1989.

6. For a perceptive comment, see Doe, "KSZE—weniger Substanz und grössere Löcher," *Neue Zürcher Zeitung,* December 18, 1992.

7. For a development of this theme, see J. F. Brown, "Eastern Europe's Western Connection," in Gordon, *Eroding Empire,* pp. 41–42.

8. Robert D. Hormats, "An Economic Policy for the United States and the West," in Lederer (ed.), *Western Approaches to Eastern Europe,* esp. pp. 45–47.

9. "Germany's Eastern Question," *The Economist,* February 29, 1992.

10. Ian Traynor, "German Giant Awakens Ghosts as It Steps into the Vacuum of Eastern Europe," *Guardian* (London), February 1, 1992.

11. Marc Fisher, "Eastern Europe Swept by German Influence," *Washington Post,* February 16, 1992.

12. Quoted by Traynor, *Guardian* (London), February 1, 1992.

13. See Jan B. de Weydenthal, "German Plan for Border Region Stirs Interest in Poland," *RFE/RL Research Report,* no. 7, February 14, 1992.

14. See Jan B. de Weydenthal, "Settling the Oder-Neisse Issue," *RFE/RL Report on Eastern Europe,* no. 31, August 3, 1990.

15. For Prague's attitude on this question, see Ladislav Valek, "Prag lehnt Entschädigung ab," *Süddeutsche Zeitung,* April 27, 1991.

16. See the overall view by Pierre Hassner, "L'émigration, problème révolutionaire," *Esprit* (Paris), July 1992; also F. Stephen Larrabee, "Down and Out in Warsaw and Budapest: Eastern Europe and East-West Migration," *International Security,* Spring 1992.

17. Deutsche Presse-Agentur (DPA) (Bonn), January 5, 1993.

18. Ferdinand Protzman, "Germany to Deport Thousands of Romanians," *New York Times,* September 19, 1992.

19. The reaction in Poland was particularly strong. See M. Sc., "Furcht Polens vor einer Asylantenflut," *Neue Zürcher Zeitung,* February 11, 1993.

20. See Erich Hoorn, "Österreich greift Slowaken unter die Arme," *Die Presse* (Vienna), September 12, 1992.

21. See dk., "Verhärtete Fronten in Wiens Ausländerpolitik," *Neue Zürcher Zeitung,* November 6, 1992 (Fernausgabe Nr. 258).

22. See Louis Zanga, "Aid Stepped Up from Italy and Elsewhere," *RFE/RL Report on Eastern Europe,* no. 37, September 13, 1991.

23. See R. St., "Italienischer Katzenjammer wegen Jugoslawien," *Neue Zürcher Zeitung,* January 21, 1992 (Fernausgabe Nr. 15).

24. For the *Quadrangolare,* see the remarks of the Italian foreign minister at that time, Gianni de Michelis, in "Reaching Out to the East," *Foreign Policy,* Summer 1990.

25. Viktor Meier, "Neue Nachbarn für Triest: Zentraleuropäische Initiative gegründet," *Frankfurter Allgemeine Zeitung,* December 3, 1991.

26. Much of this section is based on my chapter, "Turkey: Back to the Balkans?" in Graham Fuller, Ian O. Lesser, with Paul B. Henze and J. F. Brown, *Turkey's New Geopolitics: From the Balkans to Western China* (Boulder, Colo.: Westview Press, 1993).

27. Aurel Braun, *Small-State Security in the Balkans* (London: Macmillan, 1983), pp. 40–44.

28. J. F. Brown, *Communist Rule in Bulgaria* (New York: Praeger, 1970), p. 296.

29. Fred Halliday described this move as "the first time in modern history that these countries have taken an active stance on a conflict within Europe." See his "Bosnia and the Sword of Islam," *Guardian* (London), August 10, 1992.

30. See "Turkey—Islam Returns to Politics," *The Economist,* February 27, 1993.

31. Michael Binyon, in his article, "Iran Urges Islamic States to Intervene," *Times* (London), August 6, 1992, put the figure at about a million. In his article, written from Istanbul, "Turks Tread Tightrope Over Bosnia," *Independent* (London), January 9, 1993, Hugh Pope writes: "At least 10 million of Turkey's 60 million population descend from Balkan Turks and Muslims, who fled here as Ottoman rule in Europe collapsed. Immigrant groups claim up to 4 million are of Bosnian parentage, but nobody really knows."

32. As reported in Ömer Erzeren, "Türkei: Bomben auf serbische Stellungen," *Tageszeitung* (Berlin), August 11, 1992.

33. Halliday, "Bosnia and the Sword of Islam"; Amir Taheri, "Die islamische Welt ruft zu Dschihad gegen Serbien auf," *Die Welt* (Hamburg), August 10, 1992.

34. Jonathan Rugman, "Turkey Offers 1,000 troops for UN Force," *Guardian* (London), August 17, 1992.

35. See Louis Zanga, "Albania and Turkey Forge Closer Ties," *RFE/RL Research Report,* no. 11, March 12, 1993.

36. See Wolfgang Günter Lerch, "Und wenn die Türken kämen," *Frankfurter Allgemeine Zeitung,* August 12, 1992.

37. Quotations taken from the paper by Sükrü Elekdağ, Turkish foreign ministry, "Black Sea Economic Cooperation Region Project," draft paper for

Turkish Economy and Dialogue, May 1991. See also Ian O. Lesser, *Bridge or Barrier? Turkey and the West After the Cold War* (Santa Monica, Calif.: RAND, 1992), pp. 6–7. Lesser's work, generally, is an excellent analysis of Turkey's relations with the West.

38. "Black Sea Zone—Black Hole, *The Economist,* June 27, 1992.

39. Radio Moscow, March 24, 1991. I am grateful to F. Stephen Larrabee for his help in this section of the chapter.

40. Michael Dobbs, "Warsaw Pact Summit Transformation Urged," *Washington Post,* June 8, 1990.

41. The general in question was General Viktor Dubynin. On the overall problem, see Douglas Clarke, "Poland and the Soviet Troops in Germany," *RFE/RL Report on Eastern Europe,* January 25, 1991.

42. See Vera Tolz, "The Katyn Documents and the CPSU Hearings," *RFE/RL Research Report,* no. 44, November 6, 1992.

43. The document was first reported in the West by the *Frankfurter Allgemeine Zeitung,* June 7, 1991.

44. See Kvitsinski's interview in *Pravda* on Eastern European relations, March 18, 1991, FBIS-SOV-91-055, March 21, 1991, p. 16.

45. Oleg T. Bogomolov, "From Eastern Europe into a United Europe," *International Affairs* (Moscow), October 1991.

46. See Vladimir Socor, "The Romanian-Soviet Friendship Treaty and Its Regional Implications," *RFE/RL Report on Eastern Europe,* no. 18, May 3, 1991.

9 The Outlook: Precarious But Not Pre-Doomed

1. *The Rise of Political Anti-Semitism in Germany and Austria,* rev. ed. (Cambridge, Mass.: Harvard University Press, 1988), p. 29.

2. *Turkey in Europe* (London: Frank Cass, 1965), p. 440.

3. *Süddeutsche Zeitung* (Munich), February 26, 1993.

BIBLIOGRAPHY

Apart from conversations and observations in Eastern Europe, this book is based on secondary sources, although the FBIS (Foreign Broadcast Information Service) daily reports have been invaluable. So have the research reports of the RFE/RL Research Institute.

I have used various articles in the Western scholarly press. Western newspapers and journals have been the most helpful source—the German-language press above all: *Neue Zürcher Zeitung, Die Zeit, Frankfurter Allgemeine Zeitung, Frankfurter Rundschau, Süddeutsche Zeitung, Die Presse, Die Welt,* and *Tageszeitung*. In France, *Le Monde* often has been excellent, as has *Libération.* Of the English-language press I have found the following most helpful: *Financial Times, Guardian, The Economist, New York Review of Books, New Yorker, New York Times, Washington Post, Wall Street Journal,* and *Los Angeles Times.* The BBC World Service and External Service programs maintain their very high standard.

The following books have been helpful in enabling me to write my own book:

Axt, Heinz-Jürgen. *Griechenlands Aussenpolitik und Europa: Verpasste Chancen und neue Herausforderungen.* Baden-Baden: Nomos Verlagsgesellschaft, 1992.

Anderson, Benedict. *Imagined Communities: Reflections on the Origin and Spread of Nationalism.* Rev. ed. London: Verso, 1991.

Banac, Ivo (ed.). *Eastern Europe in the 1990s.* Ithaca, N.Y.: Cornell University Press, 1991.

Barnes, Julian. *The Porcupines.* London: Jonathan Cape, 1992.

Bishop, Robert, and Crayfield, E. S. *Russia Astride the Balkans.* New York: Robert M. McBride, 1948.

Braun, Aurel. *Small-State Security in the Balkans.* London: Macmillan, 1983.

Brock, Peter. *The Slovak National Awakening.* Toronto: University of Toronto Press, 1976.

Brown, J. F. *Eastern Europe and Communist Rule.* Durham, N.C.: Duke University Press, 1988.

——. *Surge to Freedom: The End of Communist Rule in Eastern Europe.* Durham, N.C.: Duke University Press, 1991.

——. *Nationalism, Democracy, and Security in the Balkans,* Aldershot, U.K.: Dartmouth, 1992.

Bush, Keith (ed.). *From the Command Economy to the Market.* Aldershot, U.K.: Dartmouth for the RFE/RL Research Institute, 1991.

Chirot, Daniel (ed.). *The Origins of Backwardness in Eastern Europe: Economics and Politics from the Middle Ages Until the Early Twentieth Century.* Berkeley: University of California Press, 1989.

—— (ed.). *The Crisis of Leninism,* Seattle: University of Washington Press, 1991.

Crowe, David, and Koltsi, John (eds.). *Gypsies in Eastern Europe.* Armonk, N.Y.: M. E. Sharpe, 1991.

Cviic, Christopher. *Remaking the Balkans.* London: Pinter Publishers for the Royal Institute of International Affairs, 1991.

Dahrendorf, Ralf. *Reflections on the Revolutions in Europe.* London: Chatto and Windus, 1990.

De Bardleben, John (ed.). *To Breathe Free: Eastern Europe's Environmental Crisis.* Baltimore: Johns Hopkins University Press, 1991.

Di Palma, Giuseppe. *To Craft Democracies: An Essay on Democratic Transitions.* Berkeley: University of California Press, 1990.

Feffer, John. *Shock Waves: Eastern Europe After the Revolution.* Boston: South End Press, 1992.

Fuller, Graham E., Leffer, Jan O., with Paul B. Henze and J. F. Brown. *Turkey's New Geopolitics: From the Balkans to Western China.* Boulder, Colo.: Westview Press, 1993.

Gabanyi, Anneli Ute. *Die unvollendete Revolution: Rumänien zwischen Diktatur und Demokratie.* Munich: Piper, 1990.

Gellner, Ernest. *Nations and Nationalism.* Ithaca, N.Y.: Cornell University Press, 1983.

Geremek, Bronislaw. *La rupture: La Pologne du communisme à la démocratie.* Paris: Seuil, 1990.

Glenny, Misha. *The Rebirth of History: Eastern Europe in the Age of Democracy.* Harmondsworth: Penguin, 1990.

——. *The Fall of Yugoslavia: The Third Balkan War.* Harmondsworth: Penguin, 1992.

Gordon, Lincoln. *Eroding Empire: Western Relations with Eastern Europe.* Washington, D.C.: Brookings Institution, 1987.

Greenfeld, Liah. *Nationalism: Five Roads to Modernity.* Cambridge, Mass.: Harvard University Press, 1992.

Havel, Václav. *Disturbing the Peace: A Conversation with Karel Hvízdala.* New York: Knopf, 1990.

——. *Summer Meditations.* New York: Knopf, 1992.

Howard, Michael. *The Lessons of History.* New Haven, Conn.: Yale University Press, 1991.

Jowitt, Ken. *New World Disorder: The Leninist Extinction.* Berkeley: University of California Press, 1992.

Keane, John. *Democracy and Civil Society: On the Predicaments of European Socialism, the Prospects for Democracy, and the Problems of Controlling Social and Political Power.* London: Verso, 1988.

King, Robert R. *Minorities Under Communism: Nationalities as a Source of Tension Among Balkan Communist States.* Cambridge, Mass.: Harvard University Press, 1973.

Kohn, Hans. *Nationalism: Its Meaning and History.* New York: D. Van Nostrand, 1971.

Lederer, Ivo John (ed.). *Western Approaches to Eastern Europe.* New York: Council on Foreign Relations Press, 1992.

Leff, Carol Skalnik. *National Conflict in Czechoslovakia: The Making and Remaking of a State, 1918–1987.* Princeton, N.J.: Princeton University Press, 1988.

Lendvai, Paul. *Eagles in Cobwebs: Nationalism and Communism in the Balkans.* Garden City, N.Y.: Doubleday, 1969.

——. *Anti-Semitism Without Jews: Communist Eastern Europe.* Garden City, N.Y.: Doubleday, 1971.

Lukacs, John. *The End of the Twentieth Century and the End of the Modern Age.* New York: Ticknor and Fields, 1992.

Nelson, Daniel N. *Balkan Imbroglio: Politics and Security in Southeastern Europe.* Boulder, Colo.: Westview Press, 1991.

O'Donnell, Guillermo. Schmitter, Philippe, and Whitehead, Lawrence (eds.). *Transitions from Authoritarian Rule.* 4 vols. Baltimore: Johns Hopkins University Press, 1986.

Oplatka, Andreas. *Der Eiserne Vorhang reisst: Ungarn als Wegbereiter.* Zurich: Neue Zürcher Zeitung Press, 1991.

Polonsky, Antony. *The Little Dictators: A History of Eastern Europe Since 1918.* London: Routledge and Kegan Paul, 1975.

Potichnyj, Peter J. (ed.). *Poland and Ukraine: Past and Present.* Edmonton/Toronto: Canadian Institute of Ukrainian Studies, 1980.

Poulton, Hugh. *Minorities in the Balkans.* London: Minority Rights Group, 1990.

——. *The Balkans: Minorities and States in Conflict.* London: Minority Rights Publications, 1991.

Przeworski, Adam. *Democracy and the Market.* Cambridge: Cambridge University Press, 1992.

Pulzer, Peter. *The Rise of Political Anti-Semitism in Germany and Austria.* Rev. ed. Cambridge, Mass.: Harvard University Press, 1988.

Putnam, Robert D. *Making Democracy Work: Civic Traditions in Modern Italy.* Princeton, N.J.: Princeton University Press, 1993.

Ramet, Sabrina P. *Social Currents in Eastern Europe: The Sources and Meaning of the Great Transformation.* Durham, N.C.: Duke University Press, 1991.

Rates, Nestor. *Romania: The Entangled Revolution.* New York: Praeger and the Center for Strategic and International Studies, 1991.

Rothschild, Joseph. *Ethnopolitics: A Conceptual Framework.* New York: Columbia University Press, 1981.

——. *East Central Europe Between the Two World Wars.* Seattle: University of Washington Press, 1977.

——. *Return to Diversity: A Political History of East Central Europe Since World War II.* New York: Oxford University Press, 1989.

Rusinow, Dennison. *The Yugoslav Experiment, 1948–1974.* London: C. Hurst for the Royal Institute of International Affairs, 1977.

Seton-Watson, Hugh. *Eastern Europe Between the Wars.* Hamden, Conn.: Archon Books, 1962.

Shoup, Paul. *Communism and the Yugoslav National Question.* New York: Columbia University Press, 1968.

Soros, George. *Underwriting Democracy.* New York: Free Press, 1991.

Sulzberger, C. L. *A Long Row of Candles.* Toronto: Macmillan, 1969.

Szoboszlai, György (ed.). *Democracy and Political Transformation: Theories and East Central European Realities.* Budapest: Hungarian Political Science Association, 1991.

Zeman, Z. A. B. *The Making and Breaking of Communist Europe.* Oxford: Basil Blackwell, 1991.

INDEX

About the Author

J. F. (Jim) Brown was a Senior Analyst at RAND between 1989 and 1991. He is a former head of Radio Free Europe (RFE) Research and between 1978 and 1983 was Director of Radio Free Europe. He has taught at the University of California at Berkeley and at the University of California at Los Angeles and has been a visiting research associate at Columbia University and St. Antony's College, Oxford. He is the author, inter alia, of *Eastern Europe and Communist Rule* and *Surge to Freedom: The End of Communist Rule in Eastern Europe,* both published by Duke University Press, as well as of *Nationalism, Democracy and Security in the Balkans.* Between 1991 and 1993 he was Distinguished Scholar in Residence at the Radio Free Europe–Radio Liberty Research Institute in Munich. He lives in Oxford.